Identity in Applied Linguistics Research

LISA MCENTEE-ATALIANIS

BLOOMSBURY ACADEMIC

LONDON • NEW YORK • OXFORD • NEW DELHI • SYDNEY

BLOOMSBURY ACADEMIC
Bloomsbury Publishing Plc
50 Bedford Square, London, WC1B 3DP, UK
1385 Broadway, New York, NY 10018, USA

BLOOMSBURY, BLOOMSBURY ACADEMIC and the Diana logo are trademarks of
Bloomsbury Publishing Plc

First published in Great Britain 2019
Reprinted 2019

Cover design by Olivia D'Cruz
Cover image © Getty Images/Jolie Clifford

A catalogue record for this book is available from the British Library.

Library of Congress Cataloging-in-Publication Data
Names: McEntee-Atalianis, Lisa, author
Title: Identity in applied linguistics research / Lisa McEntee-Atalianis.
Description: London: Bloomsbury Academic, [2019] |
Includes bibliographical references and index. |
Identifiers: LCCN 2018019112 (print) | LCCN 2018026680 (ebook) |
ISBN 9781623565688 (ePDF) | ISBN 9781623564070 (ePUB) |
ISBN 9781623564728 (hardback) | ISBN 9781623564667 (pbk.) |
ISBN 9781623564070 (eBook)
Subjects: LCSH: Applied linguistics–Research–Methodology. |
Language and culture. | Identity (Psychology) | Sociolinguistics. Classification:
LCC P53.755 (ebook) | LCC P53.755 .M33 2019 (print) | DDC 418.0072–dc23
LC record available at https://lccn.loc.gov/2018019112

ISBN: HB: 978-1-6235-6472-8
PB: 978-1-6235-6466-7
ePDF: 978-1-6235-6568-8
eBook: 978-1-6235-6407-0

Typeset by Newgen KnowledgeWorks Pvt. Ltd., Chennai, India
Printed and bound in Great Britain

To find out more about our authors and books, visit www.bloomsbury.com
and sign up for our newsletters.

Dedicated to the memory of my beloved mother

&

to Christos, Theano and Andreas

CONTENTS

FIGURES

TABLES

ACKNOWLEDGEMENTS

I am indebted to many people who have contributed in various ways to the writing of this book. I'm grateful to colleagues and students who I have had the great pleasure and privilege to work with over many years, particularly my colleagues (past and present) within the Department of Applied Linguistics and Communication, Birkbeck, University of London, my former and current doctoral students and many of my postgraduate and undergraduate students who have received lectures and contributed to rich discussions on many of the issues discussed here. They have given generously of their time and experience. In some cases, our mutual interests evolved into joint projects and publications, slowing the progress of this book, but nonetheless, I hope, enriching it. Thanks too to colleagues who I have met at many international and national conferences who have provided feedback on my work and valuable insight into their own.

Thank you especially to colleagues and friends who have provided moral support, good humour and debate over the years of the book's gestation. I'm especially grateful to those who were closely involved in its planning and those who have read and provided insightful feedback on various chapters, especially Colleen Cotter, Malcolm Edwards, Penelope Gardner-Chloros, Tim Grant, Jim Kyle, Erez Levon, Li Wei, Lia Litosseliti, Marjorie Lorch and Leigh Oakes. I apologize to those colleagues whose publications I have not included … but space would not permit!

Many thanks to all at Bloomsbury Press who have been patient and responsive to requests for information. The usual disclaimer applies: the responsibility for all errors and misinterpretations is mine alone.

As with any extended project, those closest to us offer the most support, patience and (constructive) criticism. I owe immense gratitude to Christos, Theano and Andreas, who forgave me on many occasions for scurrying away to write and carry out research on 'the book', excused me from many duties and family activities and became a willing audience when discussing its content … even on holiday. Most importantly, they did not ask too often, 'When will it be finished?' This book is dedicated to them and to the memory of my beloved mother, who sadly passed away before its completion.

CHAPTER ONE

Historical and Theoretical Overview

Introduction

On 8 April 2013, Baroness Margaret Thatcher died and within hours of her passing a barrage of divisive media and public analysis of her life and legacy ensued. Throughout the debate she was variously described as an academically successful daughter of a humble shopkeeper and the product of a working-class Methodist upbringing; a devoted/distant wife and mother; a short-lived chemist and barrister; a reviled/respected politician; the longest-serving British prime minister in the twentieth century; the *first* female prime minister; 'an iron lady' with an uncompromising will; a war hero/villain; an anti-Unionist; a victim of failing ill health … and so the characterizations and descriptions went on. In some accounts, selective aspects of her identity, for example, the familial, were emphasized; in others, they were silenced. In her working life, she, like many politicians, had taken steps to fashion her public image through dress, rhetorical style and voice training, as well as the appropriation and manipulation of externally constructed epithets – imagery and tropes – most famously the image of the 'iron lady' and the metaphor of JOURNEY, as expressed via the much-quoted entailment of 'the lady's not for turning'. The days leading up to her funeral were consumed with much debate about who she had been, what and who she identified with, who identified or distanced themselves from her, and the enduring positive and negative consequences of her existence and ideology – 'Thatcherism'. The debate continues, for in July 2017, attempts to construct a public memorial, a 10-foot bronze statue, were met with derision by some, and fear by her more sympathetic admirers who believed the threat of vandalism to be too great to allow it to be erected in Parliament Square in London.

In death, as in life, it would seem that issues relating to identity are inconsistent, neither predetermined nor self-determined, mutable and immutable, ever ubiquitous, open to revision and apparently never clear-cut or final. They appear challenged by self and others across contexts and time. But what is 'identity' and how might we define it? This question has existed since at least the time of Plato and remains not only a 'philosophical aporia' (Riley 2008: 70) but also one that challenges many in the social sciences. While some question the usefulness of the term as a concept and analytic category (Brubaker & Cooper 2000), few can deny that it is prevalent in public discourse and has become central to many studies in the social sciences, including applied linguistics, with some scholars even suggesting that it is a separate 'field of inquiry' (De Fina 2010: 263).

In his philosophical account of modern Western[1] identity, Taylor (1989/2006) asserts that we cannot understand subjectivity (and by extension define it) without examining the 'sources' of its transformation within and across different sociocultural, epistemological and philosophical traditions over at least three to four centuries. Although such a comprehensive undertaking cannot be achieved here, nor attention be given to the differences and complexities within and across different intellectual traditions, inspired by, and drawing upon such historical accounts as Benwell and Stokoe (2006), we briefly examine the influence of major schools of thought and selective 'thinkers' on historical and contemporary treatments of 'identity'[2] of relevance to applied linguistics research. We initially review major paradigmatic shifts, particularly emerging within the fields of philosophy, psychology, anthropology and sociology, revealing how new ways of conceptualizing identity, in synergy with changing sociocultural and political conditions and intellectual endeavours, served to destabilize old perspectives and fashion new theoretical trajectories. As the discussion progresses, we see how different conceptualizations from diverse fields of enquiry continue to influence contemporary research. In the second part of the chapter, different theoretical perspectives of identity are discussed. While these are far from the only theoretical frameworks of identity appropriated in applied linguistics research, these illustrate how different conceptualizations and representations of identity, arising from different disciplinary bases, can influence theoretical, methodological and analytic frameworks and trends in particular subfields of applied linguistics. We discuss how these and other frameworks have informed contemporary research later in the book.

We begin with early accounts of identity (or 'self-hood') followed by a consideration of modernist, postmodernist and post-structuralist considerations.

Historical overview

Philosophical musings on identity can be traced as far back as the Ancients: Plato, Aristotle, Aquinas and Pericles to name but four. For centuries, philosophers and orators have debated the temporal continuity of self-hood and the relationship of mind and body. In *Republic*, Plato asserts a belief in the individual possession of a metaphysical, true identity. His dialogues are concerned with how individuals accomplish self-knowledge. Aristotle, in contrast, mused over the multiplicity of individual identity, while Pericles' funeral oration alluded to Athenian collective identity.

Early influential theorizations in the West emerged throughout the Renaissance during which time notions of 'identity' focused on the individual project of self-determination emerging from the principles of humanism. The self was no longer conceived as unquestionably beholden and subject to political or religious ideology and social mores, but as autonomous and free thinking. Medieval society had previously restricted social and intellectual mobility and provided limited opportunities for self-reflection or criticism. Rather, truth was 'revealed' and power and control held mainly in the hands of the Church and in monarchical rule. Self and societal determination gained ground over the centuries fuelled by rationalism, increasing secularization and democracy, in addition to scientific innovation in the eighteenth century (Benwell & Stokoe 2006).

In the seventeenth century, the philosophical doctrine of René Descartes (1596–1650), known as Cartesianism, became established in parts of Europe and marked a shift in thinking about the sources of reasoning and morality, 'reason [came] to be understood as rational control, the power to objectify body, world and passions ... the sources of moral strength [could] no longer be seen as outside us ... certainly not in the way they were for Plato' (Taylor 2006: 151). In Cartesian dualism, the mind was conceived as functioning independently of its corporeal body and the material world. The shift to an intrapsychic, first-person viewpoint emphasized the importance of 'cogito' – thought and reasoning – in ordering ideas, gaining knowledge and developing insight into God. The 'self' was positioned as innately and methodically cognizant, rational agent, capable of 'radical reflexivity' (Taylor 2006: 130) and deduction, and of developing a system of knowledge by reflecting on its own awareness and experiences. Irrational desires did not intrude on the understanding of the self. In this frame the subject was viewed as in control, as 'disengaged' from God, sensations and perceptions of the physical, corporeal body and from habitual practices or traditions. Instead the subject was capable of objectification, of transcending physical/sensual experience and 'first-person stance' to theorize about how things exist or work (Taylor 2006: 163). Descarte's philosophy was revolutionary; instead of conceiving of 'truth' as an external reality, or as given by God, he conceived of it as under the control of the subject, the human agent, the 'sovereign self'. The 'I' (in echoes of the Ancient philosophers) was therefore self-determining, not determined by nature or God. 'Cogito Ergo Sum', first written in French by Descartes in 1637, until appearing in his later work in 1644, has become a symbol of this doctrine. This Latin phrase, often translated as 'I think, therefore I am', served to underpin Western philosophy and laid the foundation for modernist thinking, that is, should one question one's existence, proof can be found in one's ability to 'think'. Thought provides the material for the self and also constructs the product of a unified, essential identity.[3]

Like Descartes, John Locke (1632–1704), a British philosopher, subsequently appropriated the dualism of disengagement and reflexivity in his writing; however, for him, knowledge did not arise from 'innate ideas' (Taylor 2006: 164) but through lived experience and social engagement, and crucially through the setting down of memories. Unlike previous philosophers, Locke drew on psychological criteria in defining personal identity as 'knowledge'. He proposed that it could be formed and reformed instrumentally through disciplined scrutiny and reflection. Agency in Locke's doctrine was recognized as contingent on experience, consciousness and self-control – distinct however from tradition and authority. Echoes of his work continue to resonate in some recent theories and writings of identity which conceive of it as under the control of the individual and as seated in memory, although its contingency on social forces is recognized (Giddens 1991).[4] Riley (2008: 71) observes how shared memories are often cited as fundamental to the construction of minority collective identity and 'movements' of identity politics, in addition to the maintenance of personal relationships. The condition of disrupted or lost memory/ies (e.g. following trauma or dementia) is often cited as an experience of identity/personal loss on the part of the individual experiencing the memory loss or those close to them (see Chapter Three for further discussion).

Towards the end of the eighteenth century and into the first half of the nineteenth, Romanticism emerged as a rebellion against neoclassical formal strictures and traditions imposed on such cultural forms as art, literature and music, and the social and political conditions of the time, including the impact of the Industrial Revolution. '[T]he Romantics affirmed the rights of the individual, of the imagination, and of feeling' (Taylor 2006: 368ff), defining identity in terms of rational choice and self-expression. In contrast to the scientific empiricism of the Enlightenment, Romantics viewed the 'self' and 'truth' as emerging in response to feelings, sentiments and impulses, stressing the importance of nature as the source and 'locus' of life and goodness (Taylor 2006: 349). They theorized the importance of the individual in achieving self-fulfilment and self-determination. For example, reinforcement of Cartesian dualism continued in the work of the German philosopher Immanuel Kant (1724–1804), who defined the self in similar terms to Descartes: as unified, consistent, self-determining and autonomous. For Kant, self-autonomy depended on a rational, conscious self-governing will, which was guided by universal principles independent and unencumbered by social influences.

A political and moral thrust of collective identity also appeared at this time and had a long-term effect on the development of nationalism. Rousseau (1712–1778) and Herder (1744–1803) both argued for the 'sovereignty' and self-definition of a people defined 'by a common purpose or identity'.

A consequence of 'Romantic expressivism' was the constructed nature of national identity through narrative, which is resonant even today (Taylor 2006: 415–416; also see Chapter Eleven).

By the end of the nineteenth century and early twentieth century, scholars, from different disciplines, began to destabilize modernist notions of the rational, centred, self-determining whole subject, unencumbered by the influences of the social. Among these the 'Masters of Suspicion' (Ricoeur 1970), Marx, Freud and Nietzsche,[5] questioned what was deemed to be given and 'natural', viewing individuals as embedded in social and cultural systems which influenced the nature of their agency (beliefs/moral/practical agency). Self-knowledge, it was argued, was not achieved simply through introspection but rather through the mediating actions of therapy (in the case of Freud) and political and social parties/movements. Their work and that of others throughout the twentieth century (Adorno 1981; Adorno & Horkheimer 2002) led to a deconstruction, a questioning, of the foundations of Western psychology, culture and civilization laid down historically in religions, philosophies, social, political and economic structures. Structural social theories began to undermine the former modernist accounts of self, as individuals were recognized as part of cultural and social systems.

Marx (1818–1883) argued that one's sense of self arose from one's social and politico-economic situation and 'consciousness', even 'false consciousness' brought about through the dominant ideologies of the ruling classes in society which served to naturalize the subordination of the working classes. One's sense of self in his view was not self-determining, not a centred consciousness, that is, a psychic state unified by universal principles of truth, as argued by Descartes or Locke, but rather determined by one's position within the social order: '[i]t is not the consciousness of men that determines their being, but, on the contrary, their social being determines their consciousness' (Marx 1859/1971: 3). His work influenced later philosophical writing, such as Gramsci (1891–1937) and Althusser (1918–1990). Althusser (1972, 2012) introduced the concept of 'interpellation' which he defined as subjects' recognition of themselves and their own complicity in their domination through ideology. Both ideology and interpellation, he argued, were fundamental to the construction of individuals by such state institutions as education, media, law and the family. Indeed, the notion that identities can be interpellated (tacitly or otherwise) has subsequently been debated by many researchers who investigate the positioning[6] of subjects through various media.

The idea that one is shaped by external influences was also expressed in psychoanalytic theory developed initially through the influential work of Freud (1856–1939) (1920/2015, 1923/2010) and later Lacan (1977). Freud rejected the notion that the self is centred by a single self-conscious, self-defining identity. For him, identity was not rational, unitary or stable but rather dislocated (outside of the self) and conflicted. Through his structural model of the human psyche, he decentred the subject by illustrating a tension and division between the instinctive impulses of the 'id', the moral and critical 'superego' and the mediating 'ego'. Freud argued that our sense of self is not transparent to us but rather complex, developed from forces and experiences which may not even be in our consciousness or remembering, for example, early childhood experiences, desires, even an instinct for death. Freud's depiction of the 'self' emphasizes the influence of the unconscious on the conscious and the role of early socialization on one's sense of self. His account of the impulsive, compulsive, conflicted individual is arguably a somewhat bleaker characterization than that depicted by earlier Renaissance or Romantic writers.

The foundations of Western philosophical thinking were further radically shaken by the work of Friedrich Nietzsche (1844–1900). He questioned the value and objectivity of 'truth', arguing that truth could not be gained through rational or objective means but was rather subject to construction and interpretation. Identity was derived from a project of agentive self-realization and self-mastery influenced by a 'will to power' and circulating social values, not from 'truth' or reliance on a higher being. Through critical engagement with history, using a method termed 'genealogy', he demonstrated how the ethical self is constructed from values which are socially constituted and which therefore become contested and reconstituted over time. His philosophy engaged with the meaning and importance of values to human existence and their significance in fulfilling man's desire for power.

Clear echoes and influences of the philosophy of Nietzsche and the writings of the other 'Masters' can be found in later critical and cultural writing. Reflexivity and the continued questioning of an immutable, stable identity was taken up later in a 'linguistic turn' towards the self as a multiple and fragmented construction of language (and other semiotic resources) through action and thought. This linguistic orientation towards an understanding of the formation of social and cultural groups and their norms and practices, in addition to the construction of identity through the process of language mediation, rejected previous philosophical staples of 'universal truths', 'essential' or 'natural' states and replaced them with an argument for the social construction of situated identity (in time and space). Derrida (1930–2004), Foucault (1926–1984), Lacan (1901–1981) and Ricoeur (1913–2005) are just four influential figures, who, in contrast to earlier theorists, such as Saussure (1857–1913)[7] or Lévi-Strauss (1908–2009), viewed language as a fluid meaning-making system. The latter notwithstanding, Saussure's work served as a necessary and important precursor to subsequent (post-structural) accounts.

For Saussure, linguistics was a branch of 'semiology'. He distinguished between *langue* (language) and *parole* (speech) – the former referring to a system of rules or conventions which pre-exist and are independent of language users and the latter referring to their use in particular contexts. Saussure focused on *langue*; for him, understanding the underlying structures and rules of a semiotic system was more important than actual performance or linguistic practices and he approached the study of language from a synchronic rather than diachronic perspective. Meanings, he argued, were constructed and interpreted psychologically through signs which consisted of two interdependent components, the 'signifier' (the 'sound pattern') and the 'signified' (the 'concept'). The relationship between the signifier and signified was referred to as 'signification':

> A linguistic sign is not a link between a thing and a name but between a concept [*signified*] and a sound pattern [*signifier*]. The sound pattern is not actually a sound; for a sound is something physical. A sound pattern is the hearer's psychological impression of a sound, as given to him by the evidence of his senses. (Saussure 1916/1983: 66)

This dyadic model of a sign challenged the seemingly self-evident association between object and concept or signifier and signified and pointed to the importance of understanding the relational nature of signs within a system and the importance of convention in meaning-making. Saussure pointed out the importance of contrast and distinction in meaning-making, noting that 'concepts ... are defined not positively, in terms of their content, but negatively by contrast with other items in the system. What characterises each most exactly is being whatever the others are not' (Saussure 1916/1988: 115).

Subsequent post-structural accounts argued against universal deep structures (in society, language, the human psyche), undermining the foundationalism of self and the social structures tied to group identity and social position; structures were rather considered as highly fluid, complex and unstable, subject to both diachronic and synchronic change. As such, social identities/structures (e.g. social class) were not considered as stable or fixed. Derrida's philosophical writing employed a form of textual analysis referred to as 'deconstruction'. Although variously debated, Derrida's (1976) statement that 'there is nothing outside the text' has been interpreted as asserting the discursive construction of reality and identity formation (e.g. see Benwell & Stokoe's 2006 interpretation). In this frame, the self is constantly under negotiation and construction through the practices and processes of (Saussaurian) signification across a range of texts and contexts. Derrida's work challenged the notion of a self-defining, stable, unitary self, arguing instead for its fluid construction through a process of recontextualization across space and time.

In Foucault's philosophy, subjectivity and reality were determined through the mutually constitutive components of power knowledge. Power produces its own 'truth' and fields of knowledge; while knowledge assumes and constructs power relations in establishing and reproducing hierarchies of authority, 'power produces knowledge ... power and knowledge directly imply one another: that there is no power relation without the correlative constitution of a field of knowledge nor knowledge that does not presuppose and constitute at the same time power relations' (Foucault 1995: 27). For Foucault, humanism did not lead to emancipation from power and control exercised by the Church during medieval times; rather, power and control shifted to the state and elite. Power was not considered by him as a stable central or sovereign state but as contextually and relationally contingent and determining – as a fluid local phenomenon. In medieval times, power was justified through 'revealed truths', contingent upon the doctrine of the Church; in postmodern times, Foucault argued, it was brought about through humanism and reasoning (Riley 2008). Through this lens, one can account for how the power and influence of particular state structures (education, media, police, law, government) or powerful agents serve to generate and propagate dominant discourses (often perceived as unquestioned 'truths') which in turn serve to construct representations of particular identities. For example, the power and status of the politician in contemporary society who may produce a discourse about immigration in which immigrants are depicted as threatening agents, for example, as 'leeches' or 'terrorists'. This discourse produces a knowledge/'truth' that empowers the politician (the powerful) and delegitimates the immigrant (the disempowered). As an immigrant, finding oneself outside of the 'régime of truth', one is likely to be judged negatively and marginalized from the mainstream. Foucault argued that every society has its own system of 'truth/s' built upon discourses which regulate and govern the distribution and production of new forms; these discourses, in turn, serve to (re)produce 'knowledge'/'truth'. In Foucault's terms, our identities are therefore constructed by and in the discourses and cultures that we are subjected to (our subjectivity) – discourses that serve the interests of power and support social control. An examination of context, he argues, leads not only to an understanding of self but also the contexts themselves, in which selves are created. They are formed in the power/ knowledge nexus.

No less influential is the work of the French psychoanalyst Jacque Lacan (1977, 1989/2012), who, building on the work of Freud, also questioned the role of the unconscious and conscious in the formation of a split, multiple and 'decentred' ego. Lacan's work emphasized the influence of the social on subjectivity; for example, he stressed the importance of the shared 'symbolic order' on early child socialization. In his early writings, he observed that in infancy (from six months onwards), children become fascinated by reflections of themselves, for example in mirrors, or in the gaze of their caretakers, and through this process are able to objectify themselves, perceiving and mistaking themselves to be unified, coherent and in control, while also experiencing separation. Prior to this stage, he contended, they are unable to consider themselves as separate beings or to consider themselves in the second or third person. He called this developmental phase the 'mirror stage' and suggested in later work that this process of identification is not necessarily marked by a moment in infancy but continues throughout life as we search for imaginary states of coherent subjectivity through fragmented images. The 'ego' for Lacan was a false object of artificial unified subjectivity which served as a barrier against reality. Fragmentation and multiplicity of subjectivity means that we never really come to terms with who we are. We experience a desire to achieve wholeness through partial identification with the other. Lacan's theory implies that, however fragmented and incomplete, identity does not arise from an innate or essential state, but through social engagement and influence. His theory has been taken up by a number of writers as witnessed later in this book, for example, those investigating language and gender and language and sexuality (see Chapter Nine). For example, Weedon (1987/1997), working in the tradition of feminist post-structuralism asserted that subjectivity (i.e. 'the conscious and unconscious thoughts and emotions of the individual, her sense of herself, and her ways of understanding her relation to the world', p. 28) is achieved via language and social relationships – the individual both subject *to* and positioned *by* power. Rejecting a philosophical or ethical humanist stance of identity as stable and essential, Weedon aligns with a poststructuralist view of subjectivity as fluid, dynamic, discursively built and influenced by time and space.

Lacan's contemporary, Paul Ricoeur, offered a philosophical anthropology of identity encouraging an understanding of the 'self' based on a narrative exploration. He disagreed with the Cartesian proposition of 'cogito' and the anti-Cartesian perspective of the self as an outcome of a politico-economic structure, a 'will to power' or as subject to the unconscious. Rather, personal identity he claimed to be embodied, consisting of the *idem-* and *ipse* – the former responsible for a sense of constancy and the latter responsible for the agentive ability to alter and change over time and contexts. Idem- and ipse-identity always imply a narrative identity: 'The narrative constructs the identity of the character, what can be called his or her narrative identity, in constructing that of the story told. It is the identity of the story that makes the identity of the character' (*Oneself as Another*, 147–148). He proposed that we come to understand our personal identities through narrative and interaction with others, both as characters and as narrators. This identity is not necessarily stable or unitary but rather dynamic; nor is it necessarily autonomous but intertwined with other identities which enable us to construct 'second-person identities' such as national identity. Through the narrative frame, we have the power to maintain persistent character traits, change our roles/traits and influence others to do so as well, although this may be constrained by biological and psychological factors.

Some contemporary accounts

Towards the end of the twentieth century and into the twenty-first, a period often referred to as 'high/late/post'-modernity, other prominent academics – philosophers and sociologists – such as Giddens (1991) and Bauman (2000) pointed to the fragmentation and insecurity of the late modern subject and the need for 'ontological security'. The latter brought about, in part, by the impact of globalization and changes to Western thinking and behaviour in different spheres (e.g. cultural, economic, political, social and technological). A tension arises in postmodern writing, however, between notions of fluidity and fixity – between conceptualizations of identity which favour essentialized/stable/'pre-discursive' and 'constructed'/non-essentialized/ discursive perspectives or descriptions of identity.

An essentialist viewpoint conceives of identity in terms of stability, as a bounded and consistent category or product – even a 'true self' (Barker & Galasiński 2001: 30), an essence or a persistent identity, understood by oneself and others. Identity (categories) can be determined *a priori* by the researcher or *brought to* an interactional event by the language user. Within such theorizations, it is recognized that individuals may be influenced by social forces and may take on the behaviour of groups to which they identify; nevertheless, it is considered that the identity of the individual or group is delimited, homogeneous and bounded, for example, in descriptions of the shared behaviour of ethnic, gender or national groups. A useful definition of essentialism (in reference to groups) is provided by Bucholtz (2003: 400) who asserts that it is

> the position that the attributes and behaviour of socially defined groups can be determined and explained by reference to cultural and/ or biological characteristics believed to be inherent to the group. As an ideology, essentialism rests on two assumptions: (1) that groups can be clearly delimited; and (2) that group members are more or less alike.

However, some rile against an essentialist perspective of identity, for example:

> Much writing about identity treats it as some*thing* that simply *is*. Careless reification of this kind pays insufficient attention to how identification[8] works or is done, to process and reflexivity, to the social construction of identity in interaction and institutionally. Identity can only be understood as a process of 'being' or 'becoming'. One's identity – one's identities, indeed who we are is always multi-dimensional, singular *and* plural – is never a final and settled matter. (Jenkins 2008: 17)

This contrasting non-essentialist perspective has gained ground in recent times and conceives of identity as a never-ending project of 'becoming'. The focus is less on product and more on process. The identity 'project' is never considered to be complete or finite; rather, it is an ongoing construction, executed and embodied through different semiotic (linguistic and non-linguistic) means. This perspective holds that individuals may enact multiple and intersecting identities which may be inflected and influenced by changes in location, context, time, motivation and so on. Further, groups are not considered as bounded, fixed, homogeneous entities but are complex and heterogeneous.

Despite the neat dichotomy detailed here between essentialist and non-essentialist accounts of identity, as illustrated in the case of Tracy's framework of identity below, even social constructionist accounts of identity draw on essentialized or 'fixed' category labels in their theorizations and analyses. This is discussed in greater detail below as we consider some contemporary accounts in more depth. Contemporary research on identity in the social sciences reflects great diversity in its definition and operationalization. For example, some studies focus on the individual, while others on groups. Some see it as seated within the mind, as an individual psychological and/ or cognitive phenomenon, while others argue for its social and relational emergence and dependence (Antaki & Widdicombe 1998; Edwards 1995; Giddens 1991). Some consider the relationship and mediation between the cognitive and the social (Van Dijk 2010). Moreover, the ontological status of the 'self'/identity is differently theorized, even within different approaches to the analysis of discourse (see below). Different perspectives and conceptualizations of identity have motivated different research questions, methods and approaches.

We have seen how the concept of identity as a phenomenon emerging through social practice and interaction developed in postmodern writing in the social sciences,[9] in synergy with the deconstruction and critique of the 'self' as a unified, self-determining subject (Hall 1996/2012). The role of intersubjectivity, social engagement and, crucially, language in the formation and representation of identity has now become accepted by many. The post-structuralist turn has questioned essentialist conceptions of identity, and this shift in thinking can be seen over time in the burgeoning field of applied linguistics and more particularly in the emerging field of sociolinguistics in the 1960s. In this subfield, issues of group identity became prevalent and the relationship between language and society an important area of study, particularly following the seminal work of William Labov. Within variationist sociolinguistics, we have witnessed changes to the treatment of identity, from its operation as a static bounded analytic construct, predetermined and imposed by the researcher, to one which is considered fluid and emergent within language practice. 'The principle move in the [most recent] third wave ... was from a view of variation as a reflection of social identities and categories to the linguistic practice in which speakers place themselves in the social landscape through stylistic practice' (Eckert 2012: 93). Variation in language use is therefore not considered to reflect social categories or identities but rather speaker/writer stances and styles constitute identity categories/personae in locally managed contexts. Speakers are considered able to productively appropriate and adapt linguistic styles/meaningful variables in encounters. They are not determined by their position within the social structure but rather have the potential to be active agents in their own production (see further discussion in Chapters Two, Five and Nine).

The seminal work of Le Page and Tabouret-Keller (1985) entitled 'Acts of Identity' also brought issues of personal and group identity centre stage in sociolinguistic research (see Chapter Two). Their fieldwork in Creole-speaking Caribbean and West Indian communities led them to conclude that speakers' language use involves speech acts of 'identity' which reflect ethnic and social group affiliation/difference. Language use is defined as 'a series of *acts of identity* in which people reveal both their personal identity and their search for social roles' (p. 14).

In social-psychological theorizations, Mead (1934) has been credited with emphasizing the role of social interaction and collective processes of meaning-making in the formation and maintenance of one's sense of self (also later emphasized by Goffman [1959] and Erikson [1980], among others), proposing that the mind is dependent on language and social meaning for its existence. Barth and others, focusing on group identity, argue that identity formation is contingent on the reaction and response of interactional 'others' (Jenkins 2008: 44). This perspective appears in writing post-dating the 1960s which emphasizes the role of language, interaction and intersubjectivity in mediating the psychological (intrapersonal) and social (interpersonal) in the construction of identity. Contemporary cultural and postcolonial theorists such as Butler, Bhabha and Hall, influenced by the work of, for example, Althusser, Lacan and Foucault, combine a consideration of the intra- and interpersonal (including power dynamics) in their treatments of identity, or more specifically 'identification'. Their approach to identity is also seen as an ongoing 'process' rather than a product or prior accomplishment – one in which discourse and other semiotic representations (e.g. film) are seen as the crucial site of identity construction through their regulatory and reiterative power. Hall (1990: 226) asserts that identity is 'not an essence but a positioning'. They acknowledge the political implications of identity and the invocation of strategic essentialism in identity politics; however, they argue for transitory realizations or 'attachments' rather than an 'essential/stable "core" of self' (Benwell & Stokoe 2006: 29). However, unlike Foucault, who concentrated on the discourses underpinning the construction of subjectivity, Hall, Bhabha and Butler (among others) have attempted to account for the process of identification by suggesting that it is an active and agentive undertaking; the subject is not passively 'hailed' or interpellated by circulating discourses as suggested by Althusser, nor an 'effect' of discourse.

For Hall, identities/identifications are formed through difference (or 'différance'[10]) and dislocation, that is, by the external, which may be emancipatory and/or restrictive or denying, and 'interpellated' or 'sutured' to the identities circulating in discourse via unconscious processes (du Gay et al. 2012: 2). Through a joint consideration of psychoanalytic and cultural perspectives:

> [t]he concept of identity … is [seen] not [as] an essentialist, but a strategic and positional one … identities are never unified … [they are] increasingly

fragmented and fractured; never singular but multiply constructed across different, often intersecting and antagonistic, discourses, practices and positions. They are subject to a radical historicization, and are constantly in the process of change and transformation … Identities are thus points of temporary attachment to the subject positions which discursive practices construct for us. (Hall 2012: 17, 19)

They are therefore conceived as provisional, as a product of their time and location (including circulating power relations), and emerge from patterns of difference and exclusion from others rather than, or necessarily due to, patterns of similarity or inclusion.[11] Hall, as Butler (see below), recognizes the political importance of the theorization of identity and emphasizes the role of ideology and powerful discourses in representing and constituting particular subjectivities (e.g. gender, race, immigrant, youth) and in the establishment of personal meaning.

Judith Butler's (1990) appropriation and adaptation of the term 'performativity' from the philosophy of language (Austin 1962) into post-structuralist feminism and queer theory has taken on widespread currency in discursive accounts of identity construction. Butler has argued that gender is a 'performance' involving the enactment of social action. Rather than 'being' a particular identity, one is perceived as 'doing' identity. Her account dispels with notions of stability, rationalism and essentialism. Gender performances, she argues, are subject to cultural regulation and norms of appropriateness (which extend to sexual norms also). It is the repetition and reiteration of 'gender-appropriate' performances that serve to reinforce normative practices and perceptions. Taking on the structure/agency debate ('[t]he issue here is to do with whether people are free to construct their identity in any way they wish … or whether identity construction is constrained by forces of various kinds, from the unconscious psyche to institutional power structures'; Benwell & Stokoe 2006: 10), Butler argues that subjects are not fully constrained by circulating norms, for these can be subverted and violated through agentive acts. Her account challenges the notion of the 'natural' and a fixity of core identity characteristics, arguing instead that both gender and sexual identity take on social meaning within culturally, historically, and contextually situated systems/sites of power, and as such identity is constantly in flux and subject to redefinition and negotiation (see Chapter Nine for further discussion).[12]

Qualitative analyses of discursive 'performance' and practice have therefore become prominent over recent decades. An emphasis on the role of interaction, discourse and power on individual and group identity construction and negotiation has developed from theories and approaches arising from different disciplinary perspectives (De Fina 2010), including symbolic interactionism (Mead 1934; Blumer 1969), ethnomethodology (Garfinkel 1967), social constructionism (Berger and Luckmann 1967), cultural and social theory (Giddens 1991; Goffman 1967/2004, 1981; Hall

1990) and as evident from the above, post-structural feminism and queer theory (Butler 1990; Weedon 1987/1997). Different approaches, methods and analyses have been adopted.[13] Benwell and Stokoe (2006: 34) note how a

> discursive paradigm has now spread across the disciplinary spectrum, evidenced in the Foucauldian-inspired *critical discourse analysis*, the constructionist, anti-cognitivist approach of *discursive psychology*, the studies by *narrative analysts* and the work of *conversation analysts* and *ethnomethodologists*. These different approaches share a focus on the central work of language and interaction as the site of identity *work*, although they vary in the extent to which 'identity' is actually theorised or treated as an analytic priority.

Indeed, the differences and tensions between these macro- and micro-level discursive approaches are discussed below in order to foreground studies which will be reviewed later in the book.

Critical discourse analysts (CDAs) often begin their studies by assuming the significance of identity categories (e.g. race, gender), as well as the impact of historical processes and asymmetric power relations on identity. CDA is often seen and sometimes criticized for being ideologically and politically motivated – researchers interested in identifying powerful agents and discourses that serve to regulate and control social ideology and the construction and positioning of certain identities, particularly subaltern, less powerful, identities. Analysts work 'top down' to uncover the linguistic and discursive representations of particular individuals or groups and the attitudes and ideologies underlying these. Although there are many different approaches to CDA (Chouliaraki & Fairclough 1999; Fairclough 1995 and the Discourse Historical Approach, e.g., see Reisigl 2017, they adhere to the principle that the meaning of a text, whether spoken, written or signed, cannot be derived exclusively from the text itself and therefore investigate intertextual and interdiscursive patterns of sociocultural and historical influence. They consider that language use is never neutral or necessarily transparent, but rather mediates a subjective positioning of experiences, opinions and identities. Analysts are often criticized by adherents of other approaches (e.g. conversation analysis), for looking beyond the data for interpretative resources, working with an agenda and seeing individuals as an effect of discourse, thereby granting them limited agency.

In contrast, ethnomethodologists and conversation analysts view 'identity' as not something that can be determined *a priori* but as something which is emergent in talk and connected to the accomplishment of social action (Antaki & Widdicome 1998). They investigate how speakers cast/index/occasion or make identity relevant with regard to orientations to social category membership(s) and the implications of this for interactional labour. For example, investigating how identity categories or indices may be used to categorize or label speakers or others; to present speakers/others in a particular light, or how speakers draw on, or challenge, normative features and categorizations in the casting or alter-casting of identity/ies through interaction. Researchers do not begin their analyses with a particular agenda or viewpoint on identity, or with regard to its ontological standing; rather, their analyses develop 'bottom up' via a detailed turn-by-turn examination of talk. Ethnomethodological and conversation analytic approaches have revealed the fluid and sometimes contradictory orientations of speakers to identity categories and memberships. Conversation analysis therefore takes an emic approach to speakers' orientations and concerns in moments of interaction avoiding reference to cognitive processes, discourses or speaker intention. They, in turn, have been criticized for taking a narrow and decontextualized focus on short extracts of talk without attending to broader cultural, social or political issues.

The methods of conversation analysis are applied by discursive psychologists in their examination of individuals' accounts; however, this approach combines both, micro and macro approaches, undertaking fine-grained analyses of conversational texts but linking their content to culturally recognized master narratives/discourses or shared repertoires. The latter are interpreted as discursive resources in the local construction of identity (see Chapter Eight, for a more extensive discussion of this approach).

While there are many approaches to narrative analysis, some analysts (Bamberg et al. 2007; Bamberg & Georgakopoulou 2008), as critical discourse analysts, also look beyond the data and discourse context in their examination of the discursive construction of identity (for which they are sometimes criticized). For these researchers, stories, whether 'big' or 'small', provide the material for the construction of the self, albeit in edited form. They also provide a means to construct the 'other' through positioning and evaluation. Within this framework, '[t]he emphasis is on identity as performed rather than as prior to language, as dynamic rather than fixed, as culturally and historically located, as constructed in interaction with other people and institutional structures, as continuously remade, and as contradictory and situational' (Benwell & Stokoe 2006: 138). Narratives are understood as providing a sense of identity continuity and temporality, connecting different events in coherent renderings. Narrative theorists often connect the content of individuals' stories with larger master narratives or interpretative repertoires[14] which circulate within defined cultural contexts or communities/places and explore the manner by which subjects display, counter or assume positions for themselves and others (Bamberg 1997, 2011a, 2011b).

Investigations of the interactional processes and mechanisms of identity performance and construction in discourse have coined and adopted different, sometimes interconnecting, concepts and frameworks such as 'crossing' (Rampton 1995/2014/2018), 'footing' (Goffman 1981), 'indexicality' (Ochs 1992; Silverstein 2003), 'membership categorizat ion'/'categorization' (Sacks 1995), 'positioning' (Davies & Harré 1990), 'stance' (Jaffe 2009) and style and stylization (Auer 2007). Many of these will be discussed in greater depth in later chapters. Goffman (1981), for example, addressing the presentation of self in interaction, introduced the concept of 'footing' to describe the enactment of situated identity in order to illustrate the different roles and changes of alignment that speakers take towards themselves, others and the subject of their discourse. These roles may combine or be differentiated and consist of 'animator' (the person who produces the physical form of the message), 'author' (the person who composes the message), 'principle' (the person 'whose position is established by the words that are spoken, someone whose beliefs have been told, someone who is committed to what the words say' p. 144) and 'figure' (the image constructed by the audience via the utterance spoken). Changes in footing may align with shifts in perspective in narrative retellings and/or involve the 'voicing' of story characters or institutional/social discourses. Goffman suggested that speakers can 'animate' different selves within an interaction through the strategic enactment of voices which are socially recognizable. Audiences will construct images of the social types, although these may differ to those intended by the speaker. As such 'voice' is not necessarily a personal attribute but dependent upon shared understandings of social types. The layering of multiple voices, referred to by him as lamination, reveals the self as multiple.

Emerging from much of this contemporary research is an interest in examining the relationship between structure and agency and their influence on identity, the complexity and plurality of identities and how these are invoked in discourse and become communicatively meaningful and, related to the latter, how issues of consistency and/or fluidity are established in the accomplishment of the 'self' and the 'other'. An issue of debate in critiques of the post-structuralist and postmodern work is whether stability exists even within instability.

One way in which we might conceive of this apparent paradox is to consider Tracy's (2002) sociocultural and rhetorical model of identity. This model encapsulates four identity categories: 'master', 'personal', 'interactional' and 'relational' which can be reconfigured to represent two dichotomies: stable versus dynamic identities and social versus personal identities. 'Master' and 'personal identities' encapsulate 'stable pre-existing' (p. 20) features: 'Master' refers to aspects of our identity which remain continuous and persistent, for example, our place of origin. These aspects of identity reflect an anchoring and embeddedness within larger biological and/or social categories. 'Personal identity' characterizes the individual by reference to other's perceptions, based on persistent behaviour or conduct (e.g. kind, intelligent, honest), or references to associations between the individual and other (social) categories, for example, using a sign language will index an association with Deaf culture and the Deaf community; speaking with a particular accent may indicate our place of origin or our social standing. Personal identities are therefore defined as being unique to the individual and constructed both by the individual and others.

In contrast to these comparatively stable or persistent aspects of identity, other aspects are more dynamic and may be realized differently in different contexts. For example, 'interactional identities' depend on the context and the people we are conversing with. These may be influenced by, for example, familial, professional and social relationships. Interactional identity may influence language use, for example, the medium through which we communicate (e.g. email, telephone, face-to-face), the subject matter, the expression of politeness and control over the interactional encounter, although one's role does not necessarily prefigure or determine the nature or content of the interaction itself or indeed how it will unfold. The projection of identity/ies in conversation is what Tracy (2002) refers to as 'relational identity', which is illustrated in the following extract. Here we see how a doctor repositions her identity, from that of a medical professional (as determined by the institutional context), to that of a parent when breaking difficult news to the parents of one of her patients (Maynard 1989: 64, in Arminen 2005: 103):

Dr. D:	I think-you know I'm sure you're anxious about today and I know this has been a really hard year for you. And I think you've really done an extraordinary job in dealing with some thing that's very hard for any human being or any parent- and you know Mrs. Roberts and I can talk as parents as well as
Mrs. R:	True
Dr. D:	uh my being a professional. Its HARD when there's something not all right with a child, very hard.

This repositioning performs an important interactional function; it enables the doctor to align herself with the parents of her patient and through this common 'parental' identity she conveys a shared understanding and empathy which serves to foreground and mitigate the force of her subsequent diagnosis.

Tracy's (2002) model provides one frame through which to picture 'identity' and consider the role of language in its development and projection. It separates *personal/unique* ('personal' and 'relational') and *social* ('master' and 'interactional') categories, while reconfiguring these to illustrate the comparatively *stable* ('master' and 'personal') versus *dynamic* ('interactional' and 'relational') aspects of identity construction.

In the discussion so far, we have considered how conceptualizations of the 'self', as a cognizant and physiological entity, have evolved in Western thinking and theoretical traditions over centuries and decades across a range of disciplines, from descriptions of a unified, self-determining consciousness, to accounts of the socially effected, self-defined and centred subject, to the psychological subject contending with unconscious experiences and forces, to theories of the socially and discursively constructed subject as decentred, multiple and fluid, in which manifestations of personal and social identity may become context-dependent and context-creating. In this school of thought, there is not one central, 'true', fixed or *a priori* identity; rather, the 'self' emerges through the processes of socialization, networks of contact and momentary encounters and 'becomings'. In the following section, we flesh out, in a little more detail, two contrasting theories and frameworks of identity which have been influential in applied linguistics research and which arise from different ontological and epistemological bases. This account is far from exhaustive or inclusive but it is hoped that through an examination of just two perspectives we can illustrate how different treatments of identity can lead to different research orientations, questions, assumptions and methodological and analytic foci. We begin with 'Social Identity Theory' (SIT), a social-psychological theory developed towards the end of the twentieth century by Tajfel and Turner (1979) and still applied in contemporary research of group membership in applied linguistics, before considering a more recent sociocultural, interactional treatment of identity, as outlined in the work of Bucholtz and Hall (2005).

Two contrasting perspectives

A social-psychological perspective: Social Identity Theory

Towards the latter decades of the twentieth century and into the twenty-first, psychological and sociological theories of group identity influenced applied linguistics research. Among these, SIT, developed by the social psychologists Tajfel and Turner (Tajfel 1982; Tajfel & Turner 1979) proposed that individuals categorize themselves and their social world in relation to social groupings. Self-categorization in this theory gives rise to a repertoire of memberships (e.g. national, political, sporting, role memberships, such as swimmer, grandfather) and a sense of belonging and self-definition which becomes part of one's self-concept and self-image, one's 'social identity'. Social identity both describes and prescribes member characteristics – determining affective, cognitive and physical behaviour. Through the psychological processes of evaluation, comparison and identification, we may assess our memberships positively or negatively in comparison and in contrast to out-group members. A positive evaluation of group membership, made through an assessment of oneself on measures of significance to the in-group, leads to high self-esteem and pride in one's social identity. Through the processes of identification and comparison, we may take on and/or practice the behaviour (including linguistic) of the in-group. This becomes normative, stereotypical and self-regulatory. While cultivating a positive self-image, we may simultaneously recognize and construct boundaries between ourselves and the out-group by adopting behaviours which denote our belonging to an alternative group (e.g. speaking in a different language or accent to members of the out-group). This behaviour, depending on the nature of intergroup relations, may in some situations become competitive and discriminatory. In contrast to positive social identity, however, the preferential adoption of out-group behaviour and identity may result from a negative evaluation of one's social identity leading to negative self-concept as a consequence of reduced self-esteem and/or desire for distinctive recognition. Negative social identity may therefore give rise to social mobility towards another group.

SIT assumes the activation of two socio-cognitive operations: categorization[15] and self-enhancement. In context, through categorization, normative and stereotypical perceptions and actions establish intergroup borders and category membership for subjects. The process of categorization depersonalizes the individual through a process of self-identification and evaluation of contextually relevant (prototypical) in-group norms. The individual, via group membership, adopts group behaviour (both cognitive and performative) and through self-enhancement, positively values in-group norms and stereotypes. It is assumed that subjects have a basic desire and need for a positive self-concept: to evaluate themselves more positively in comparison to specific others and therefore compare themselves with others on dimensions that favour the in-group. Context is important, as in each context the subject evaluates the salient characteristics of the group which will endow him/her with the most positive self-concept.

With its socio-cognitive emphasis, SIT represents identity as an internalized, pre-discursive product/property of actors and collectives, which serves to construct and reflect both psychological and social reality. The individual and social structures/categories are conceived as independent; however, individuals internalize social influences through the process of socialization. Through the conceptual frame of categorization, emphasis is placed on demographic/identity labels which are deemed to represent pre-existing and delimited biological and social structures, such as age, sex, gender, ethnicity, social class and political groupings. These categories, and more besides, have been used by social-psychologists and sociolinguists as explanatory variables to investigate and predict linguistic behaviour by speakers of different biological and social status via such analyses as statistical correlation, for example, in studies of ethnolinguistic vitality. In many instances, questionnaires have been used to gather data to determine the status of the ethnolinguistic vitality of minority groups. (See Chapter Eight for further discussion.)

An interactional and sociocultural perspective

Other research invoking theories and principles of intergroup relations[16] has suggested that a focus on establishing broad linguistic norms, based on fixed identity categories, for any individual or speech community may ignore the complexity and heterogeneity of language use within and across social groupings. Moreover, identity, they argue, is constructed interactionally.

In discursive and sociocultural approaches, as discussed above (Benwell & Stokoe 2006; Bucholtz & Hall 2005; Tracy 2002), identity is seen as something which is situated and temporary, something which may be *brought about* in social interaction intersubjectively rather than *brought to* the conversation/text as a predetermined individual or social reality or state. Such a perspective foregrounds local understandings and context in understanding identity. This view is taken up in Bucholtz and Hall's (2005 framework, in which identity is viewed as a sociocultural and relational process, as *the social positioning of the self and others* (2005: 586). Basing their framework on a consideration of research in multiple fields, ranging from the social-psychological to the linguistic-anthropological, the authors propose five principles underlying and informing the investigation of identity and available for analytic interrogation: 'emergence', 'positionality', 'indexicality', 'relationality' and 'partiality'. These principles, they argue, do not inhere in subjects or in social ideology or practice but offer important analytic foci.

The first principle of 'emergence' conceives of identity as realized in and through social action rather than as pre-discursive or pre-existent phenomena in the mind of the individual. This is seen as a dialogical process in which semiotic resources for performing identity may be drawn from elements of prior discourses/structures (including ideological and linguistic structures). This principle has been developed from research in linguistic anthropology, including Mannheim and Tedlock's (1995) perspective of 'culture as emergent through dialogical processes … produced as speakers draw on multiple voices and texts in every utterance' (cited in Bucholtz & Hall 2005: 587) and research in interactional and sociocultural linguistics.

The second principle of 'positionality' encapsulates a nested and complex view of identity as 'encompass[ing] (a) macro-level demographic categories; (b) local, ethnographically specific cultural positions; and (c) temporary and interactionally specific stances and participant roles' (2005: 592). For example, in an investigation of language choice and use among multilingual teenagers in a London school, we might learn something about how these individuals and groups subjectively and intersubjectively position themselves and others by taking into account the possibility of shared or distinct social identities as encapsulated in such demographic categories as age cohorts or ethnic groups. Through an ethnographic investigation of local, cultural parameters, we might tap into emergent and divergent styles among and between different cohorts and through a close analysis of conversation we might be able to investigate how particular positive or negative stances and evaluations are displayed towards in- and out-group members through language choice. This more nuanced perspective attempts to account for the local and momentary realization of identity in interaction, which may or may not reference broader social identity categories (e.g. age, gender and ethnicity). This principle accounts for the shifting and multiple nature of identity performance in the construction of 'self' and 'other' in and through discourse. The authors argue that the temporary and alternating positions occupied by social actors in discourse 'may accumulate ideological associations with both large-scale and local categories of identities ... these ideological associations ... may shape who does what and how in interaction' (2005: 591).

The third principle of 'indexicality' draws on vast literature in semiotics, sociolinguistics and sociocultural studies to explain the manner by which identity positions are constructed within the context of the interaction. Indexicality is dependent on larger ideological frameworks, cultural beliefs and values, which serve to associate performance at different linguistic levels with language users. Bucholtz and Hall (2005: 594) note that 'identity relations' are indexed via multiple processes, including reference to identity labels and categorizations, pragmatic 'implicature and presuppositions' about subjective and intersubjective positions, 'displayed evaluative and epistemic orientations to ongoing talk, as well as interactional footings and participant roles' and the use of linguistic forms associated with individuals or groups/communities. A consideration of all of these levels provides for a comprehensive understanding of 'subjectivity and intersubjectivity' (p. 598).

The fourth principle of 'relationality' (also referred to as 'tactics of intersubjectivity') highlights the importance of considering the intersubjective dimension of identity formation and the influence of 'culture, power and agency' (Bucholtz & Hall 2006). It highlights the reasons for 'doing' identity. This principle encapsulates two main arguments: that 'identities are never autonomous or independent but always acquire social meaning in relation to other available identity positions and other social actors' and that an investigation of identity relations involves more than a consideration of similarity or difference, but must include factors such as 'genuineness/artifice and authority/delegitimacy' (2005: 598). They list three pairs of complementary identity relations, or 'tactics', that are invoked by interlocutors in their enactment of goals, although are at pains to emphasize that these are not an exhaustive rendering of all possible relations, nor are the relations mutually exclusive. Their differentiation is based on the way in which identity may be used interactionally and each in turn relate to the concepts of 'markedness', 'essentialism' and structural/'institutional power'.

The first pairing is referred to as 'adequation and distinction'. These terms are adopted as a deliberate contrast to the more traditional labelling of 'similarity' or 'difference'. The term 'adequation' combines the words 'adequate' and equate', drawing on their meaning to describe instances of intersubjective or intergroup relations, in which individuals or groups emphasize aspects of similarity in order to service interactional goals, while at the same time, silencing difference. The effects of this social accomplishment may be transient or more permanent. The authors note that adequation is strategically exploited for political ends, often in the pursuit of political alliances, and this may lead to 'politically motivated strategic essentialism' (2006: 383). In contrast, in marking a 'distinction' between an individual or grouping, actors emphasize areas of difference, while downplaying areas of similarity. 'Distinction' is therefore the flip-side of 'adequation' and is often expressed by the construction of binary or dichotomous representations in opposition or in contrast to one another. In the case of both adequation and distinction, similarities or differences may be marked along one or multiple axes.

The second set of intersubjective relations/tactics is 'authentication and denaturalization ... processes by which speakers make claims to realness and artifice respectively' (Bucholtz & Hall 2005: 601). This pairing is primarily concerned with the interactional performance of authenticity; however, these are subtly differentiated. 'Authentication' is concerned with the manner by which agents make claims discursively to genuine/'real' identities. It 'refers to how speakers activate [their] essentialist readings in the articulation of identity' (Bucholtz & Hall 2006: 386), for example, language contributes to national identity formation by engendering a sense of unity and belonging for its members. In turn, language choice may index a nationalist stance. Authentication may be activated through 'essentialist readings' (p. 385) and correlations of identities and language choice. 'Denaturalization' refers to the destabilization or rupture of essentialized ideologies/naturalized identities which may lead, for example, to the performance of an identity which is different to the expected. For example, Bailey (2001; also see Chapter Five) reports on the language use of Dominican American youths who switch between different varieties of Spanish and English – standard and vernacular, African American Vernacular English and hybrid forms – exploiting these in their construction of and resistance to ethnic and racial boundaries. Through this performance, they disrupt essentialized ideologies of African American identity.

The third and final pairing – 'authorization and illegitimation' makes reference to the role of institutions and social structures in the legitimization/illegitimization of identity. 'Authorization' refers to the power of institutional structures to impose or pronounce on an identity/ies. 'Illegitimation' is the manner by which identities may be disregarded, excluded and delegitimized by social structures and institutions. Of course, even without an identifiable authority, ideology/ies about identity can permeate and be reproduced in interaction through the process of hegemony (Bucholtz & Hall 2005: 604). Illegitimation may also be enacted in opposition to larger social structures, such as the nation or state, or other powerful authorities (Bucholtz & Hall 2006).

Finally, Bucholtz and Hall's (2005) fifth principle of 'partialness' outlines the influence and constraints imposed by macro and micro structures on identity realization – influences such as the social structure, the situation and local setting (including e.g. interlocutors, subject matter, physical setting, interactional goals) and how these lead to the performance and interpretation of shifting and fragmentary identities. Crucial to this principle is the influence of the relational, contextual and ideological. '[I]dentity', the authors assert 'is inherently relational, it will always be partial, produced through contextually situated and ideologically informed configurations of the self and other' (p. 605).

Bucholtz and Hall's framework offers a broad approach to a sociocultural and interactional consideration of identity, aspects of which will be explored later in the book.

Conclusion

'Late modern identity is bound up with both *challenge* and *conformity* to essentialism, and throughout its texture we can also trace lines left by the earlier movements' (Benwell & Stokoe 2006: 21). The postmodern self in Western society is often referred to as fragmented, partial, unstable or dislocated while striving for coherence and meaning; exposed to and engaged with the influences of late-Capitalist society and the impact of globalization, regional coalitions, transnational migration and movement and advanced technological innovation; influences such as commodification, lifestyle choices, mobility and the global media. These are said to infiltrate consciousness and provide material opportunities for agency, mutability and creativity. However, they also impose constraints on how agency is performed and interpreted. As such, identity is contingent and something that can be shaped, tried on, manipulated, maintained and even disposed of. The postmodern subject, many argue, questions authority and claims to truth, engages and seeks fulfilment through commodification and the 'hyper-real' (Baudrillard 1998[17]; Eco 1990) and understands itself as having multiple and mobile identities.

The effect of post/high modernity for identity is differently viewed and critiqued by theorists[18] – some envisioning it as leading to crises, uncertainty and instability (Bauman 2000), others as providing productive and liberatory capacities, for example, permitting individuals to 'cross' (Cutler 1999; Rampton 1995) or move between identities for instrumental or other benefits. The latter perspective acknowledges the creative power of identity performance and that while identity may be fluid and constantly under negotiation, particular momentary or interactional constructions may facilitate temporary attachments and formations. Some still view the self as decentred, while others, acknowledging the role of discursive mediation, view the socially constructed subject as self-centred and self-defining – whether through narrative, a moral compass or via other means.

So far, we have reviewed selective historical and contemporary treatments of identity from different disciplinary perspectives. Some of these are compatible, others not and yet many have influenced work in applied linguistics that we are about to review in the following chapters.

CHAPTER TWO

Linguistic Idiosyncrasy

All talk displays its speaker's individual voice. This is necessary because self-expression is necessary: no matter how much a society may value conformity or define people in relationship to others, individuals must on some level express individuated selves.

In order to do this, speakers must do things with language that other speakers do not do. Each speaker must, quite literally, be idiosyncratic.

BARBARA JOHNSTONE (1996: 187)

Introduction

An enduring debate in sociolinguistics is the relationship between the individual and society. Scholars have questioned how individual patterns of language use relate to community-wide ideologies, language practice and change, with recent studies increasingly attempting to account for the fluidity and variability of language use within and across individuals as aspects of personal and social identity are signalled.

The development of variationist sociolinguistics and linguistic anthropology in the 1960s and 1970s, most notably through the quantitative urban dialectological research of William Labov and the development of an approach known as 'ethnography of speaking' by anthropologists Dell Hymes and John Gumperz, made variation in linguistic performance within speech communities an important object of study. Since the early identification of stratified patterns of language use in social groups on the east coast of the United States (Labov) and language variation in the multilingual nations of India and Norway (Gumperz and Hymes), variationist research has developed significantly and with it interest in idiosyncratic language use and identity.

In this chapter, we focus on selective studies that have taken the individual and idiosyncratic language use as their primary object of study. We begin with a review of the historical treatment of identity within traditional variationist sociolinguistics and end with a consideration and description of selective contemporary studies of individual variation and style which adopt a phenomenological approach with nuanced analytical specificity. We begin with the work of Le Page and Tabouret-Keller (1985), who in their investigation of postcolonial multilingual communities took idiosyncratic language use as their analytic foci in an investigation of variation, observing how a community or social group is constructed through individual linguistic 'acts of identity'. We next consider how linguistic personae accrete (Rauniomaa 2003) via the particularities of individual language style and stance drawing on the concepts of individual 'voice' and 'lingual biographies' (Johnstone 1996). We finally review concepts such as language repertoires, rational choice/strategy and extend our discussion of style, focusing on more recent work which draws on the models of indexicality and enregisterment. First, however, we situate our discussion within the field of variationist sociolinguistics.

Variationist sociolinguistics and identity

As noted in Chapter One, three phases, or 'waves' (Eckert 2012)/'types' (Mendoza-Denton, 2011), of variationist research have developed since the mid-twentieth century with an increasing emphasis on making the 'voice' of the individual an object of analytic foci. The first phase statistically correlated predetermined socio-demographic categories (e.g. socio-economic class, age and sex of informants) with linguistic variables employing a survey methodology, often in tightly knit speech communities, to determine quantitative patterns of language use. Data were gathered from individuals, but results were amalgamated and statistically analysed to determine group patterns. Linguistic variables, known as dependent variables (e.g. the realization of postvocalic (r) versus non-realization of postvocalic (r)), were correlated with independent variables, such as socio-economic class, while other non-linguistic variables, for example, sex and ethnicity, were determined as emerging from within these socio-economic categories and also correlated – speakers seen as orienting towards their status within the social hierarchy. Individuals (and speaker identity) were therefore operationalized as stable packages of demographic variables, with linguistic behaviour considered to be determined by social status. Speakers were not perceived as active agents but products of their social position which they in turn reinforced through their language use.

The second wave, influenced by anthropological and sociological research, introduced an ethnographic, emic-centred approach to the construction of analytic categories, introducing local meanings, rather than etic, researcher-defined categories, into the analysis. The work of Gumperz and Hymes is notable here, as is an approach which, similar to Labov's (1963) initial study on Martha's Vineyard, viewed language variation as an expression of identity and language change a consequence of this. In an innovative twist in sociolinguistic studies, the strength of an individual's social network, calculated via the density and complexity of relationships in the local community (Milroy 1980), was determined as influencing language use. Geographic and social mobility were identified as important, and studies recognized agents responsible for language change ('innovators'/'adopters'). Synchronic and diachronic fluidity in linguistic performance was recognized in social groups across time and context.

In synergy with the postmodern 'turn' to the construction of 'reality' through language, the third phase/'wave' has witnessed a change in perspective from seeing variation as arising from (or being reflective of) social structures/meanings,[1] to defining individual's language use as constitutive of social reality. Variation is not seen as correlating with pre-established a priori (pregiven or distinct) categories but rather language users are considered to construct (intersecting) social categories through their language use enabling the marking of in- and out-group boundaries and multiple, complex identities. Some sociolinguists, critical of descriptive correlational studies, have become interested in how language variation is used as a semiotic tool in identity performance. Just like other forms of semiotic expression – such as dress and appearance – variation in language use is conceived as fundamental to a complex social system and the presentation of multiple identities. Language is recognized as stylistically mutable, permitting speakers to adapt to different contexts or circumstances. Unlike previous phases of variationist research therefore, linguistic variables are not considered to carry or reflect fixed, stable categories or meanings (e.g. denoting a working class identity or status) but are fluid, potentially marking alterations in speaker stance and style. Stance and style act as a means of building contextually situated personae. Speakers are therefore perceived as active agents (whether consciously or unconsciously) in the construction of reality – not predetermined by their position within the social order.

Studies of individual language use have gained in prominence in recent decades (Bell 1999; Bucholtz 1999a, b; Rampton 1995, 1999; Schiffrin 1996; Schilling-Estes 2004 and others below). 'A return to individualism in linguistics is in some ways a return to the pre-Saussurean nineteenth-century Romantic view of humanity. The individual voice is valued because it represents autonomous, creative choice in the expression of individual spirit or genius' (Johnstone 1996: 20). Where previously, the individual was defined according to (researcher-determined) membership within a hierarchical system, and speaker agency related to the ability to self-correct from the vernacular to more standard forms of language use, and (relatedly) language style was a term used to refer to variant language use according to the degree of formality or the amount of attention a speaker paid to his or her speech, studies in the third 'wave' offer a more nuanced consideration of speaker choice and language performance through in-depth case study analyses in a range of genres, speech events and mono and multilingual contexts. The vernacular is no longer considered the favoured object of study, and linguistic features/phenomenon beyond the phonological or morphosyntactic (e.g. discourse features, code-switching, translanguaging) have become a staple in the research literature. Recent studies investigating style (Bucholtz 2004; Davies 2007; Johnstone 2009; Reyes 2007) have illustrated how individuals employ different linguistic resources in a process referred to as 'bricolage' when building their identities. Fluidity in linguistic performance is seen as the expression of a complex semiotic system whereby a range of social indexicalities are afforded by the same or different linguistic features in different contexts and speech events. Also, in attempting to resolve the apparent contradiction in treatments of communities as bounded groups (e.g. research on 'national', 'ethnic', 'professional', 'religious groupings'), a focus on the individual has enabled researchers to investigate the breadth and fluidity of linguistic resources within group and individual repertoires (Benor 2010), while also accounting for mobility (virtually and physically) and the linguistic and cultural heterogeneity of many in a networked and globalized world.

'Acts of identity'

In an early sociolinguistic account of language and identity, Le Page and Tabouret-Keller (1985) reported on an investigation of multilingual language practice in conversations and narratives, as well as informant reports of language use and ethnic and social difference, in Caribbean communities in Belize, St. Vincent and London. They questioned why speakers used particular language varieties rather than assuming a direct correlation with demographic status within a community. They noted that interlocutors frequently switched between different language varieties and determined that this was a consequence of their desire to variably project the ethnic and national identity/identities of the group/s to which they wished to identify. It is through these acts, the authors argued, that individuals 'reveal both their personal identity and their search for social roles' (p. 14), arguing that:

> Each individual creates the systems for his verbal behaviour so that they shall resemble those of the group or groups with which from time to time he may wish to be identified, to the extent that

a. he can identify the groups,

b. he has both opportunity and ability to observe and analyse their behavioural systems,

c. his motivation is sufficiently strong to impel him to choose, and to adapt his behaviour accordingly,

d. he is still able to adapt his behaviour.

Their work represented a shift of analytic focus in sociolinguistics away from linguistic varieties to the study of repertoires of linguistic resources employed by individuals in communities. Agency and fluidity became paramount in their work with speakers recognized as actively manipulating available linguistic resources in order to project different personal and social identities and achieve communicative success.

In their account of the development of pidgin languages through contact between creoles and more standard codes, they employ the metaphor of a GAME to illustrate how individuals adapt innovatively and idiosyncratically to difficult communicative barriers via code-mixing and switching:

> language is … a game, in which the players invent the rules and, we would add, also act as umpires.… . In our data from the West Indies we can see that, even though there may be several fairly highly focussed broad creole vernaculars with fairly regular rules, Creole speakers coming into contact with speakers of more standard varieties of English will nevertheless try a variety of code-switching or code-mixing or modifying devices adjusting their Creole to meet the needs of the situation. In fact, any community we find that language use ranges from the highly inventive and idiosyncratic to the highly conventional and regular. (Le Page & Tabouret-Keller 1985: 11–12)

While recognizing idiosyncrasy, LePage and Tabouret-Keller also recognized constraints on individual language use and the need for speaker accommodation (in a similar vein to Giles's 'Communication Accommodation Theory', see Giles et al. 1991 and Giles & Ogay 2007) observing that speech may coalesce into a regular linguistic pattern.

Although illustrative texts are provided, their work lacks in-depth contextual analyses of individual stylistic acts of identity performance and therefore as noted by Coupland (2007: 111):

> the rubric of creating styles 'to resemble those of the group or groups with which from time to time [a person] wishes to be identified' doesn't shed sufficient light on how styling acts are subjectively designed or affectively motivated. 'Resembling' can imply different sorts of indexical relationships and different stances, such as projections made playfully, or some degree of identity fictionalising or qualification, versus projections

designed to show a speaker to 'pass as' a member of a particular social group.

In order to get at how speakers construct/project/'leak' (Coupland 2007: 111) their identities in discourse, one needs to attend to focused rigorous analyses of discursive acts. It is to these that we now turn in the following sections.

The idiosyncratic voice and the 'lingual biography'

Also recognizing the determinism inherent in the first and second waves of variationist sociolinguistic research, and a need to shift analytic foci away from language as a shared code, Barbara Johnstone (1996) called attention to individual agency in mediating social phenomena and a need to explain as well as describe generalized patterns of language use by analysing the individualized operation of linguistic resources in different genres and registers in monolingual discourse.[2] Her work has placed the individual centrally within discussions of identity and language variation and change. She emphasizes the importance of studying the individual 'voice' recognizing the need and desire by all to express themselves distinctively even within and alongside the constraints of conventional patterns of language use. She has long argued for a theory of language that is informed by the study of creative idiosyncrasy.

In her 1996 book, 'The Linguistic Individual' and other publications (1995, 1997, 1999, 2000, 2009), she explores the personal narratives and public discourse of well-known and less well-known individuals in the United States, concluding that variation in language use arises from idiosyncratic language choice – individuals drawing on conventional, codified forms (e.g. standard varieties and/or in/out-group styles) and/or features previously gleaned from specific contexts or speakers. Her point is that not all speakers have access to or indeed employ the same range of linguistic resources. She demonstrates how the expression of individuated personalities is crucial for successful communication and uncovers consistency in the stylistic expression of individual persona across speech events. For example, in a comparative analysis of the personal narratives of a dying African American lady and a middle-aged white man, Johnstone (1996) concludes that differences in self-expression cannot be defined solely along sociolinguistic (e.g. differences in race, gender or social class) or indeed rhetorical lines (audience and purpose of the exchange); rather, variation in language use arises from psychological motivation – the desire on the part of the speaker to narrate him or herself into being in a particular way. Through their varied use of linguistic resources, they create a 'voice' that is uniquely theirs. Indeed, even in contexts in which one might imagine self-expression to be stifled or constrained, for example, as a consequence of professional modes of communication, such as scripted text to be used by an interviewer in telephone surveys, or persuasive academic discourse in a conference, Johnstone reveals marked patterns of idiosyncratic variation that demonstrate interviewer/academic agency and preferred interviewee/academic expectations with respect to this (also see Hyland 2010). Successful interaction is revealed to be dependent on individuated language style. In the case of the telephone survey, callers are found to respond negatively to what may appear as automated or scripted, 'personality-less' discourse. Personal 'voice' is revealed as both self-motivated (a desire on the part of the speaker to present a particular 'self') and dependent on speaker expectations with respect to their interlocutor. It is at the same time individually/cognitively and socially/culturally contingent. Individual language choice and innovation, Johnstone argues, is crucial for language change and social relatedness; despite social influences and constraints, no two speakers/language users will ever express themselves in the same way and language change (as previously demonstrated by Milroy 1980, for example) cannot arise except through the innovations of the individual:

> The ways individuals talk indubitably have something to do with how they are identified by others with social groups and how they identify themselves, or refuse to identify themselves, with social groups. Individuals' speech equally indubitably has something to do with shared linguistic and pragmatic conventions about how to create and interpret sentences and discourses. We would not be able to understand each other if this were not the case. But intervening between the social fact and the linguistic output is individual choice, in the service of self-expression. (Johnstone 1996: 186)

In examining the rich texture of individual style through a close analysis of discourse features, phonology, morphology and syntax, Johnstone coined the term 'Lingual Biography' (1999). In a case study of Molly Ivins, a professional journalist and resident of Texas, she demonstrates how Molly establishes her personal identity through the manipulation of Texan and standard American English speech variables. Despite not originating from Texas, Ivins employs Texan features to affect humour, irony and to construct a Texan identity, switching from these to the standard to index a cosmopolitan and intellectual persona. Johnstone identifies four features of Ivins's discourse which are strategically used to mark her particular brand of Texan: 'a highly performed narrative involving marked non-standard forms and comedy; speech play ...; figurative language; and directness, including swearing and earthiness of diction' (p. 317). These index traits of toughness and humour; however, this style is easily traded with standard American English in a display of verbal and written creativity. The linguistic resources employed are highly idiosyncratic establishing associations with

Texas, masculinity and education, thereby expressing characteristics of 'conviction', 'toughness' (p. 319) and intellectual acumen.

In a similar application of her biographical analysis, Johnstone (2009) examines the individual speaker style of a well-known US politician, Barbara Jordan, who consistently enacts a rhetorical style seated with 'moral and epistemological authority' (p. 29) – a persuasive strategy referred to as the 'ethos of self' (p. 30). Through the repeated performance of moral certainty and epistemic stance through narratives of life experience, Jordon displays a style which accretes to display a unique consistent identity. Johnstone illustrates how this style develops from multiple sources of influence – people and situations from within Jordon's sociolinguistic milieu – further supporting her claim that individuals draw on their uniquely constructed lingual repertoires.

Johnstone argues for a sociolinguistics that begins with a close examination of individual speakers and interactional phenomenon which may permit generalizations about individual patterns of language use across genres and speakers. She also concludes that speaker stance and style may not just index social identities but individual identities too (also see Johnstone & Bean 1997; Johnstone & Baumgardt 2004).

Ideology, indexicality and style

One outcome of Johnstone's work and that of other contemporary sociolinguists (see below) is that the distinction between social and stylistic variation becomes opaque (see Johnstone 2000 for further discussion). Whereas previously social variation was considered the outcome of a speaker's social situation, and stylistic variation a strategic response to the demands of the situational context in which the individual found themselves, social variation is now seen as arising, at least in some instances, from individual strategic choice evident in stylized performance. The traditional social categories of age, gender, ethnicity etc. are now invoked more critically in sociolinguistic analyses (and discussed further in the chapters to follow).

Sociolinguists have re-theorized style as a fluid, multifaceted phenomenon semiotically linked to individual as well as social identities and local contexts. Linguistic features are recognized as being potentially bi/multivalent. Through an examination of individual patterns of use, we can also see how actors relate to, or challenge, group/community practices and/or ideologies, and also understand how linguistic variables become associated with varieties (regional/social) or speakers – also how the articulation or presentation of particular styles of speaking/signing or writing is linked to particular ideologies/identities/situations/genres/activities or communicative aims (see discussion of indexicality below).

Ethnographic methods, interviews, discourse analyses (sometimes in synergy with quantitative analyses) have provided tools to investigate shifting identity performance, revealing how interactants manage the situational exigencies of their social settings and how they manipulate and shape language via the variable exploitation of a fluid set of linguistic features (e.g. see Benor's 2010 account of the 'ethnolinguistic repertoire', see Chapter Eight; Eckert & Rickford 2001; Eckert 2005; studies in Coupland 2007). Analysts have drawn on such theoretical constructs and models as 'crossing' (Rampton 1995, see below), 'enregisterment'[3] (Agha 2003, 2006), 'framing' (Goffman 1974), 'heteroglossia' (Bakhtin 1981, e.g. see Tagg 2016), 'indexicality' (Silverstein 2003, see below) and 'stance' (to name but a few) to explain the complexity of their observed phenomena. Speakers are revealed to construct and experience identity and social reality in multifarious ways, employing linguistic resources for different purposes. Moreover, alternations in personal language choice are associated with language change.[4]

An emphasis on strategic[5] language use has become prominent in accounts of identity. Speakers are considered to make 'rational choices' about how they present themselves and 'others' and how they may align, resist or alter normative or stereotypical practices and ideologies about particular identities and power structures.[6] For example, Rampton (1995) reports on language 'crossing' among teenagers in the north of England who invoke a Caribbean Creole speech style in order to perform a 'cool' adolescent identity and in so doing garner covert prestige and break down interethnic borders. He also investigates the way in which individuals 'style the other' (1999), that is, use particular linguistic forms to mark group affiliation in contexts in which such performances may not be considered appropriate or legitimate (see Chapter Five for further discussion). Natalie Schilling-Estes (1998) reports on the exaggerated use of phrases by Okracoke Islanders when in contact with tourists and other out-group interactants. Bucholtz (1999b), in a study that we will explore in greater depth in Chapter Five, illustrates how a community of high school girls constructs a 'nerd' identity strategically through agentive language choices. While other case studies (as shown in the examples below) explore the variable exploitation of code choice or linguistic features in the construction of 'self' by children, adolescents and adults demonstrating that behaviour may not necessarily pattern in the same fashion within or across a group, with individuals demonstrating idiosyncratic linguistic performances and practices at any one time and even across their lifespan as they adapt to local demands.

For example, Bolonyai (2005) analyses the strategic use of Hungarian and English by two English-dominant preadolescent girls (Emma and Linda) as they engage in the pretend enactment of a 'Hungarian school' in the home of one of the girls (Emma) in the United States. The study examines how differences in linguistic resources can limit, or alternatively afford, advantage to even young speakers as they construct different identities and negotiate structural and interactional relations of power – in this instance as they compete for the prized status of 'cat expert'. Hungarian is the expected code choice in a 'real' Hungarian school and also the preferred language of the home for both children; however, frequent code-switching is evident. The results of both quantitative and qualitative analyses of code choice (Hungarian, English and code-switching) as the girls alternate between school/home frames and discourse roles reveal different patterns of language use by both speakers, leading Bolonyai to conclude (as Johnstone, previously) that 'the ways in which these girls created and shifted between various aspects of their identities, forms of power, and linguistic codes are better seen as a product of socio-cognitively motivated, purposeful, and meaningful selectivity, rather than pre-specified or invariant response to pre-determined constraints' (Labov 1989; Lakoff 1975, p. 23). Her study supports the claim that language can be used to alternate between and invoke different identities and thereby strategically build hierarchical relationships and negotiate power. It reveals marked idiosyncrasy and variability across and within subject's language use.

In another account, Zilles and King (2005) examine the interview discourse of two adults of German origin in southern Brazil (Alice and Lina), both of different ages and social backgrounds. Through an examination of the historical and social context, the speaker's language ideologies, 'their idealized identities' (p. 75) and patterns of language use, the authors explore the manner in which the informants employ multiple codes and features to express their individual identities. A quantitative analysis of three German-associated phonological features, '(a) [the] replacement of stressed, word-final /ãw/ with /on/; (b) retention of alveolar /l/ in word-final position; and (c) devoicing of consonants' (p. 79), complemented by a detailed discourse analysis reveals how the informants employ multiple codes and features to express their individual identities. The quantitative analysis reveals differences in the realization of /ãw/, while similar patterns of use are found in the case of the other two features. A qualitative content analysis offers a nuanced exploration of differences in the informant's identity positioning and self-presentations. Alice positions herself happily within her place of residence but she is also deeply proud of her German roots; Lina, in contrast, projects a strong association with modernity and the national context of Brazil rather than her local setting. Their multifaceted and individual identities are also evident in the way in which they employ linguistic variables, for example, 'Lina tending to engage in thematic vowel alternation in first person plural verb forms, employing /e/ instead of /a/, and Alice favouring /on/ instead of /ãw/ in stressed, word-final positions, during their discussions of local, community, and in many instances, ethnically German practices' (p. 91). Overall, German-associated features are used as markers of in-group allegiance; Brazilian forms are used to index regional Brazilian and local German identities. The fluidity of the employment of linguistics variants throughout their interviews is concluded to enable the expression of varied and apparently contradictory aspects of their identity as they position and reposition themselves throughout their accounts. Differences in identity performance are explained both with respect to the exigencies of the discourse event and in relation to broader historical, social, cultural and personal parameters.

With an emphasis on 'ethnic styling', Cutler (1999) describes how a privileged white adolescent, 'Mike', style-shifts over time to present black and white personal identities: appropriating African American Vernacular English (AAVE) in his early to mid-teens in the performance of a cool 'hip hop' urban youth identity; later shifting to more standard American in his late teens. Despite limited contact with AAVE speakers or gang culture, Mike regularly used AAVE phonological features such as [d] for [ð], lexical forms such as 'phat' for 'great' and grammatical markers, for example, copula deletion (p. 431). Coupland (2007: 128) presents a reanalysis of an extract of talk between Mike and two of his friends who ridicule the 'inauthentic' styling of gang speech by their peers. Coupland argues that crossing into AAVE is not simply a process of 'ethnic styling' but also indexical of the speakers' current attitudes to place, class and 'cool' versus 'uncool' in/out-group identity: 'Mike and his friends were drawing on specific historical and linguistic relationships as resources against which they could design their own personal identity projects and their relationships with their peers'. In other words, AAVE had taken on higher-order indexicality in the speech repertoires of these adolescent speakers (see below).

In a similar investigation of the appropriation of AAVE by a white youth ('Brand One') in the United States, Bucholtz (1999a) describes how AAVE – or 'CRAAVE' ('Cross-racial African American Vernacular English' as she refers to it – 'an emblematic use of AAVE' in which speakers appropriate some, but not all AAVE features, p. 446) – is similarly employed not only to present 'an urban youth identity' but also to project a particular gender identity. CRAAVE is appropriated by Brand One (in addition to other discourse strategies) in a narrative of interracial conflict to build his and others' identities. Bucholtz notes how the combination of CRAAVE with the mechanisms of, for example, 'lamination' (the layering of voices), 'double-voicing' and 'framing'[7] in dialogic sequences allows him to reformulate and contest his antagonist's construction of his gender identity to project a hegemonic, strong 'masculine' persona.

These studies (as copious others; see further accounts later in this book) illustrate how language varieties and linguistic features are not fixed, socially determined indices of identities, as suggested in the first wave of variationist research, but rather can be used to project and negotiate fluid, shifting aspects of personal presentation. This is not to deny that consistent use of particular features in different performative styles by individuals or social groups can carry social meaning such that the styles enacted can relate to a particular way of living or acting. This can be explained using the theoretical model of 'indexicality', as previously alluded to in the account of Mike above – a model devised by Silverstein (1992, 1993, 2003) that asserts that associations between linguistic features and social meaning can occur in 'orders of indexicality'.

An nth-order indexical (or 'first-order' indexical) refers to a linguistic feature that can be correlated with a socio-demographic set (e.g. class, ethnicity); however, this feature may not vary stylistically and speakers may be unaware of the association between the form and the independent variable. The second-order indexical (or n + 1th order) relates to a linguistic feature that has taken on stylistic and social significance ('it has become enregistered'[8]), and speakers may use different forms in different contexts. For example, in British English, the pronunciation of [a] or [æ] carries regional and class status – [a] indicative of southern or upper-middle-class speech and [æ] of northern or lower-class speech. A speaker sensitive to this difference and also using this form variably may alternate his or her use according to the context or interactional aims, for example, if wishing to sound more affluent or educated a greater realization of [a] may be heard; in contrast, if returning home to the north of England, a greater percentage of [æ] may be articulated. A further, third-order indexical – (n + 1) + 1th order – relates to a shift in the ideological association n + 1 features, which may become commodified or the focus of social discussion or parody.[9]

We can see more explicitly how a linguistic feature takes on indexical characteristics within cultural schemata using Podesva (2007) as an example. Podesva describes how a medical student, Heath, projects different persona through the act of style shifting in two different contexts: a workplace and social setting. At work, he adopts a professional, serious stance, while with friends at an informal barbecue he enacts the role of fun 'diva'. These shifting enactments of persona are marked phonologically through the variant realization of intervocalic /t/: a greater percentage of /t/ release is found in the medical context; however, those released in conversation at the barbecue have lengthier, exaggerated stretches of aspiration which evoke a more 'prissy' hyperarticulation – an articulation noted to be suggestive of an enregistered school teacher style. Podesva claims this contributes to the construction of his 'diva' identity. Eckert (2012) notes how intervocalic /t/ has also become an enregistered style in the speech of other social groups, notably '"geek girls" (Bucholtz 1996) [and] ... Orthodox Jews (Benor 2001) ... [who similarly] exploit the indexical value associated with hyperarticulation, no doubt mediated by enregistered sources as divergent as British English, Yiddish and schoolteacher talk' (p. 96).

While such studies offer important insights into the role of indexicality, sociolinguists are increasingly aware that they must take care not to 'impose' or 'read-off' (Johnstone & Kiesling 2008) identities without careful consideration of the historical and sociocultural context, the interpretations of individual speakers and listeners and a self-reflection of their own personal and sociocultural frames of reference which they, in turn, may apply to an interpretation of their data. Johnstone and Kiesling (2008) argue that some linguistic features may only carry first-order indexicality and 'that different indexical links between linguistic form and social meaning may become relevant at different moments in interaction or across different discourse genres, and that different people may draw on different, even sometimes idiosyncratic, senses of what choices among variable forms mean, or about whether they mean anything at all' (p. 12). Indexical associations in performance and perception may therefore be momentary, mutable and highly individual.

Through an investigation of the Pittsburgh feature of /aw/ monophthongization (Johnstone & Kiesling 2008) and 'Pittsburgh dialect enregisterment in radio comedy sketches' (Johnstone 2011), we see how the indexical value of linguistic variables may vary significantly within a speech community and the potential error in assuming that speakers and listeners assign the same value to linguistic features. In an interpretation reminiscent of Johnstone's earlier work (see section above), Johnstone and Kiesling (2008) and Johnstone (2011) acknowledge that although recurrent links between linguistic features and social meanings may pattern in a speech community and be linked with socio-demographic categories and shared ideological structures, individual interpretations of these forms may be idiosyncratic at the local interactional level due to differences in sociolinguistic experience and the manner in which they are used as a resource: 'people … may draw on more personal experiences to interpret form-meaning links, or they may not create such links at all, so it is highly unlikely that a linguistic form will have the same indexical meaning across a socially stratified geographical community... Indexical relations are forged in individuals' phenomenal experience of their particular sociolinguistic worlds' (Johnstone & Kiesling 2008: 7, 29). In discussing 'Jim Krenn's radio show', they conclude that people who listen to the show

> may come to think of the stereotypical Pittsburgher as Polish, since Krenn's stereotypical-Pittsburgher character has a Polish name. Another person may associate /aw/-monophthongization with Polishness because he has a Polish aunt who used this form a lot when he was a child. What is necessary, in order for indexical meaning to arise, is that there be a correlation available in an individual's environment to which second-order indexical meaning can be attached: a correlation between the name 'Stanley P. Kachowski' and a local sounding accent, or between the presence of a particular aunt and the presence of particular linguistic forms. There need be no correlation in the speech community at large between being Polish and monophthongizing, nor need the indexical meaning be discussed or shared with others. (p. 29)

This perspective offers new methodological and theoretical insights into the study of variation and change, accounting for apparent similarities in group data and idiosyncrasies in language use and perception. It also offers new insights into how linguistic forms may come to carry group meanings as they gain in metapragmatic currency so that indexical meanings become established, stable forms.

Conclusion

In this chapter, we reviewed selective studies exploring idiosyncratic language use and identity. We saw how research in sociolinguistics has evolved since the mid-twentieth century – with an increasing emphasis placed on the linguistic practices of the language user and how individuals construct their identity and that of others through the manipulation of variable linguistic forms and idiosyncratic style. An increasing emphasis in sociolinguistics has been placed on researching speaker/writer stances and styles (see further accounts in ensuing chapters, e.g., Chapters Five and Nine). We also discussed the development of theoretical and analytical models which have informed our understanding of the particularities of individual language performance and identity construction, which may differ to larger group patterns. We acknowledged the importance of researcher reflexivity – understanding the historical, sociocultural context and the local occasioning of individual identity construction.

CHAPTER THREE

Clinical Studies

[t]he human world is unimaginable without some means of knowing who others are and some sense of who we are … Equally familiar is the theme of lost or confused identity: people who can't prove who they are, who appear to not know 'who they are'; who are one thing one moment and something else the next, who are in the throes of identity crises … Situations such as these provide occasional cause to reflect upon identity.

JENKINS (2008: 26)

Introduction

A state of identity loss or confusion frequently ensues after the harrowing and sudden experience of brain damage, or as a consequence of psychological or psychiatric disorders. The repercussions can last a lifetime, with language deficit and/or a changed self-concept proving to be a feature of the altered reality. Language impairment and/or reported identity change can arise from multiple neurogenic or psychogenic causes such as a stroke (cerebral vascular accident, CVA), traumatic brain injury (TBI) or psychosis. Various modalities and language systems may be affected. Many aphasics – those who experience difficulties in producing or understanding language post-brain injury or disease – report experiencing a significant change, an 'identity theft' (Shaddon 2005), the traumatic loss of a self once known. One of the major challenges facing those involved in remediation, rehabilitation and care, including professionals, clients and loved ones is how to facilitate and manage the renegotiation of a coherent and altered identity. In recent decades, clinical studies of individuals with acquired language and (degenerative) memory disorders have emphasized the importance of focusing on issues of identity in clinical practice and for client remediation, recognizing that understanding client experience from an emic perspective is fundamental to the planning, execution and evaluation of therapeutic interventions.

While there are many clinical cases that impact on discussions of identity (e.g. spasmodic dysphonia,[1] herpes simplex viral encephalitis[2] and capgras syndrome[3]), in this chapter we mainly consider studies of aphasic individuals, also briefly discussing a rare condition known as 'foreign accent syndrome' (FAS), as well as considering the impact of brain injury and memory degeneration on the 'storied self' and personal identity. The chapter begins with a short description of aphasia , before discussing studies which explore the renegotiation of identity by those experiencing aphasia and 'FAS' (see section 'The renegotiation of identity after acquired disorders'). This account is extended in the section entitled 'Narratives of aphasia and illness' which discusses the role of narrative in assisting aphasics with changes to identity. Towards the end of the chapter, we consider how narratives told by different patient types, aphasic and dementia patients (those with chronic neurodegenerative disease – Alzheimer's disease), can provide a window into the role of memory in supporting and constructing a sense of personal identity. We explore in the case of a mildly aphasic patient how his autobiographical accounts lacked a sense of personal ownership post-trauma. We also consider how disease, illness and/or injury can lead to disturbances in self-recognition and personal identity, albeit with different outcomes for aphasics and dementia patients in terms of self-reflection, recognition and potential recovery. We therefore consider research which views identity as both a discursive construction and accomplishment, as well as research which views it as a psychological/cognitive phenomenon.

Aphasia

Accounts of aphasia within clinical linguistics have traditionally focused on descriptions of medical aetiology and speech and language deficit – the client's post-trauma speech and language skills measured in relation to a premorbid target norm. Remediation, where possible, focuses on improved speech and language performance. Recently changes in clinical practice and models of treatment, in association with the influences of post-structuralist theoretical and methodological frameworks in communication studies, have caused a shift in focus to effective functional 'communication' and social interaction, rather than a stringent and narrow concentration on repairing the 'language system'. This shift in philosophy and practice, referred to by Christensen (1997) as a 'holistic' approach, incorporates a consideration of the client's retained communicative function(s), in addition to psychosocial and sociocultural dimensions of communication more broadly, considering how individuals use language to interact with their social world, while also considering how language (and accounts by self and others) is constitutive of the social world – the latter playing a crucial part in the nurturance of the 'self'.

This trend has blossomed in synergy with a professional aim to improve the quality of life of clients and their loved ones, with a recognition of the need to improve communication and client 'efficacy', 'self-advocacy' and choice with respect to post-trauma treatment and care (Mackay 2003; Shaddon 2005: 212). An appreciation of the need to harness an improved sense of self has led to the construction of therapies which are conducive to a renegotiation and reformulation of personal and social identities. It is recognized that in dealing with changed circumstances (including a changed sense of self), therapists must consider and manage both intra and interpersonal changes. One of the major challenges facing all involved is how to renegotiate and validate changed roles and circumstances in order to come to terms with the aphasic condition. A process likened to the stages of bereavement in which the sufferers and their loved ones and acquaintances must first address an altered reality, learn to adapt to the changed state and then 'renew' and reformulate their self-concept (Charmaz 1995, 2002; Miller 2010: 73).

In the following we discuss research that has focused on these issues, drawing on work predominantly seated within an interactionist, sociocultural framework, in which identity is viewed as dialogically negotiated and co-constructed, and studies in psycho/neurolinguistics and neuropsychology. Recovery for the patient is considered not only dependent on medical and/or technological intervention but also crucially contingent on social influences and systems which may support/validate or undermine/invalidate an altered identity. Research demonstrates that the identities resisted, adopted and 're'-negotiated are crucial to patient recovery. The aims of researchers and clinicians are to attend not only to an improvement in the quality of life of those with acquired disorders, but also those closest to them, who similarly face challenges to their personal identity.

Aphasia is the most common type of 'acquired' language disorder, that is, it is a disorder experienced by individuals who were, prior to brain damage, linguistically competent. It is reported to affect approximately 1 in every 250 people per year, with different patterns of impairment evident across the entire population. In any one aphasic, one or more language modalities may be affected: speech, understanding, reading and/or writing.

Global aphasia is the most debilitating condition with input and output modalities affected, leading to compromised ability to communicate in speech and writing (expressive aphasia) or to understand what is said or written (receptive aphasia). Individuals' spontaneous productions may be limited to just a few words or syllables and in the most severe cases, sufferers may be mute. Global aphasia is often diagnosed immediately post-trauma/ illness, and many recover sufficiently to regain some expressive or receptive ability. For those with damage to large areas of the brain, in particular to crucial language areas, global aphasia frequently persists without recovery.

Broca's and Wernicke's aphasia are two other types of aphasia. Broca's aphasia, named after Paul Broca, a French neurologist who provided a detailed case history and anatomical account of a neurolinguistic (brain-language) relationship in the 1860s following autopsy, identified cerebral damage to the lower regions of the frontal lobe of his patients (Obler & Kjerlow 2002). The speech of Broca's aphasics is non-fluent and agrammatic with characteristic omission of function words and bound morphemes (e.g. auxiliary verbs, determiners, verb inflections), frequent nominalization of verbs, reduced phrase length and complexity of utterances/sentences and an inability to use word order to indicate semantic relations.[4] Their speech production is often effortful, halting and slow, and they may experience additional difficulties in word finding and articulation. It is therefore an expressive disorder with language comprehension relatively spared, as illustrated in the extract below, a conversation between a patient and his speech and language therapist just a few weeks after a traumatic road accident (McEntee 1993: 398–399; also see, McEntee & Kennedy 1995):

> Therapist (T): *have you been in the ward the whole time or have you moved around?*
>
> Joseph (J): downstairs
>
> T: *did you go home at all?*
>
> J: Friday
>
> T: *you went on Friday and you came back this morning?*
>
> J: aye … (long pause) … a car crash
>
> T: *were you driving?*
>
> J: aye … (long pause) … on my spine
>
> T: *was anyone else in the car?*
>
> J: Dad, Mum … in backseats
>
> T: *did you have a job before the accident?*
>
> J: college . . . Arts
>
> T: *Arts and Technology?*
>
> J: yes
>
> T: *can you tell me what you did at the weekend?*
>
> J: sleep
>
> . . . .

T: *whose is that bed?*

J: don't name

T: *you don't know the name?*

J: yes

In contrast to Broca's aphasia, Wernicke's aphasia, discovered by the German neuropsychiatrist Carl Wernicke in 1874, following identification of damage to an area in the left temporal lobe, is characterized by impaired receptive ability. Sufferers have great difficulty in understanding what is said or written. Although speech appears to be fluent with no apparent articulatory difficulties, it makes little sense to listeners who perceive it as lacking in coherence and empty of meaning. Patients experience dissociation between words/sounds and their meanings and have word-finding difficulties, often substituting words. Frequently Wernicke's aphasics, in contrast to Broca's aphasics, who often experience low mood and frustration with their inability to express themselves, appear unaware of their condition and demonstrate comparatively less emotional angst at their inability to communicate effectively or to understand what is being communicated to them. They also do not react to their communicative partners' inability to understand what they are saying, or understand that their response may be inappropriate or inadequate.

Global, mixed and Broca's aphasia are more common, with anomia often remaining once other linguistic systems recover. As with all other types of aphasia, Broca's and Wernicke's aphasics may experience different and changing degrees of severity affecting different modalities post-trauma and following remediation over a long period of time. Many experience permanent changes to their communicative abilities for the remainder of their lives.

The renegotiation of identity after acquired disorders

Following trauma, '[i]t is important to recognize that persons with aphasia and their significant others are involved in renegotiation of identity, and the success of their recognition work ['what' and 'who' they are] may be a major predictor of adaptation to aphasia' (Shaddon 2005: 221). Shaddon and others (detailed below) assert that the nature of this 'recognition work' and the path to remediation, recovery and/or acceptance, is not only dependent on 'repairing' linguistic deficit but also contingent on social influences which have the power to validate and legitimize the self. Therefore, attention must be paid not only to the management of retained and improved function but also to the social contexts in which interaction will take place. In constructing a 'new', changed self, the aphasic subject must confront, manage and interact with dominant discourses and social actors who may appraise and 'position' their former and altered identity/ies in particular ways. The impact of this interactional relational enterprise can be significant for successful adjustment to aphasia and, as we shall see in the studies reviewed below, can have both positive and negative effects on the well-being and recovery of the aphasic. In the following, we consider how different interactional events, negotiated positions and contexts may impact on successful adjustment post-trauma and how treatment approaches which incorporate a consideration of 'identity', 'social embeddedness' and the 'co-construction of competence' (Shaddon & Agan 2004, Shaddon 2005) may serve to enhance the lives of those affected by aphasia.

The sensation of 'losing [one's] sense of self' (Brumfitt 1993: 569) or *anomie*[5] after brain injury and the difficulty of reconciling a new identity with one once 'known' is frequently mentioned in the research literature (e.g. see Christensen 1997; Gracey & Ownsworth 2012; Holland & Beeson 1993; Währborg 1991 and research reviewed below), as are better overall health and well-being outcomes for those able to accept and adapt to their post-injury self. However, this success (as mentioned previously) is not necessarily determined by the individual themselves but also dependent on the sense of self they derive from contact with others, which may promote sometimes conflicting feelings and evaluations.

Clinical encounters offer their own challenges for identity work with aphasics. Detailed analyses of conversations between therapists and clients (Horton 2007) have illustrated the limitations of particular approaches in therapy which position interlocutors in particular ways. Conversation analyses (CA) and studies of 'membership categorization'[6] and 'category-bound activities'[7] have highlighted how the generation and maintenance of topics and activities related to impairment in speech and language therapy build identities in particular ways, positioning subjects in specific roles and relationships – particularly, as 'expert' (therapist) and 'patient' (aphasic). Therefore, emphasizing and attributing individuals with skills or deficiencies, competences or incompetences. Horton (2007: 295) illustrates the difficulties arising from this practice for the client and professional in which shifts in roles and conversational footing prove to be constrained, leading to a power imbalance and an emphasis on an aphasic identity of 'impairment' rather than competence: 'It may be that therapists are so preoccupied with the complexities of "Doing therapy tasks" and associated work that they tend to reinforce the values associated with "improving language" rather than those of competent communicator'. Such a practice wrests control of the conversation (overall management and content) away from the client who may take a comparatively passive role in the speech event. It also ascribes and reinforces a restrictive identity of 'patient' which may prove detrimental to subsequent recovery. This research emphasizes a need for clients and therapists to collaborate in the therapeutic event: to establish equality via shifts in role and footing and encourages changes to conversational management and content in order to nurture improved communicative ability and social participation internal and external to the clinical setting – and therefore to recognize the complexity of personal and social identity.

Successful collaboration between client and therapist is illustrated in Purves et al.'s (2011) exploration of the relationship between 'literal' (physical) and 'metaphorical' (the interactional, intersubjective) voice in aphasia. The approach taken in this therapeutic project was novel, not only in its content but also in the fact that an aphasic individual initiated the project and became co-author of the subsequent publication. Noting the impact of aphasia on both literal and metaphorical voice, the authors report on a case study of the third author (a person with aphasia and apraxia), who collaborated with a student clinician in order to use a computer program ('SentenceShaper®') which facilitated the recording, manipulation and playback of his own speech. The program allowed the user to record short segments of speech, later using these to construct sentences and narratives in a way in which he wished to present himself using sentence frames. Skip (the subject of the article and third author) sometimes constructed well-formed utterances with sections of unintelligible speech or with prosodic manipulation, for example using intonation to mark humour, in order to present a recognizable and preferred revoicing of himself. This work was undertaken over many months. A qualitative analysis of the process is described drawing on ethnographic notes, written reflections and the recordings themselves. As illustrated in studies of foreign accent syndrome (see below), the article points to the importance of 'literal' voice for identity, creating 'an authentic link between person and message' (p. 688) and the impact of its loss and reconstitution by the sufferer. The study underlines the salience of incorporating a social dimension to therapy – making prominent the social interface – in order to support the rehabilitation of literal and metaphorical 'voice'. It also points to the importance of recovering a positive self-perception – particularly reconstituting a competence sense of self. SentenceShaper® enabled Skip to hear a well-formed and grammatical reconstruction of his voice that could be played back and performed not only to himself but to others also.

'Tools' for remediation and self-recognition post-injury do not have to focus solely on language and may be constructed by significant others, as well as the aphasic subject. Christensen (1997) illustrates how identity can be personally and socially mediated via other semiotic processes and products. Discussing the case of an aphasic who suffered a stroke at the relatively young age of 37, she details how art served to validate and negotiate the subject's identity. Following her stroke, sufficiently recovered to describe her ordeal to her husband, the aphasic individual in Christensen's study describes how her husband drew a series of sketches depicting stages in her illness and recovery which acted as recognizable representations of her changed status thereby legitimizing her post-stroke identity. Some years later, she attended art classes and lectures at a museum. The activities engendered a reflection on the control (or lack of control) of interactional activities and the difficulties experienced in understanding and contributing to discussions, in contrast to the ease of her relationship and interaction with the 'language' of painting, which served to promote and support a positive sense of self and well-being:

> After my stroke, paintings took on new meaning. When I am with others and they speak to me I have to understand what they say right away, otherwise it is too late – the subject of discussion will have gone on to something else. With the paintings it is not so – they do not change. I can look at a picture as long as I want…. . To understand painting more than just experiencing beauty or effect – it has a language that can be learned. (Christensen 1997: 730)

The role of the spouse/'significant other' in constructing a coherent identity, based on a former self, is similarly highlighted in Shaddon (2005: 217) who describes the case of a spouse who wrote a 'guide book' detailing important aspects of her husband's life (career, hobbies, travelling experiences) when he was hospitalized for an extended period. The text is reported to have facilitated a mediated representation of his identity for staff who were then able to engage in meaningful personalized conversations with her husband despite his communication difficulties.[8]

Shaddon (2004, 2005) emphasizes the significance of supportive social places as well as 'significant others' for the facilitation and successful renegotiation of identity. Aphasia support groups are noted to be particularly successful sites of identity reformation and negotiation, distinct in their focus on competence from clinical or other social contexts which may, as illustrated above, position and construct the aphasic as 'impaired' and disempowered.[9] In support groups, aphasics experience long-term, continuous reinforcement of a positively evaluated 'self' situated not in the past but in the present and future. It is a safe space in which to engage in narratives and ascriptions which challenge negative self-perception and dominating social discourses of 'disability'. The role of conversational partners in facilitating this support is emphasized.

In adapting to a new reality, post-stroke or post-traumatic brain injury (TBI), attendant conversational partners have an influential role in '[re-]presenting' the individual to the aphasic and to others, and a significant role in reconstituting the relational dynamic. As noted above, the centrality of significant others in post-trauma rehabilitation is crucial for the legitimization of the individuals' pre-aphasic identity, and in the validation and renegotiation of their post-trauma self. Guise et al. (2010) point to the fact that these representations might not always be positive and sufferers may orient to the negative representations made by their loved ones/

carers in conversation, not always challenging the constructions presented. However, the changed circumstances also have a significant effect on the supportive partner who finds her/himself having to adapt to new roles and new interactional practices and experiences – sometimes riling against and/or struggling to renegotiate their changed (sometimes disliked 'new') persona without the validation of the one they most love. A 'loss of self' can be felt as keenly by the partner as the aphasic; as one spouse reports, 'He's gone. He always reflected back positive energy for me. He used to adore me. I don't know what to do' (Shaddon 2005: 219).

A particularly rare, but nonetheless striking acquired language disorder, 'FAS' is very relevant to our discussion so far. Unlike Broca's aphasia, the resulting speech is not considered 'pathological' in the sense that it does not violate the regular sound structures or rules of language but rather the patient begins to speak in an apparently 'non-native' accent. FAS can arise from neurogenic (brain damage, e.g. stroke, TBI, multiple sclerosis) and/or psychogenic causes (e.g. schizophrenia or bipolar disorder), with some subjects, in the latter case, experiencing the new accent alongside episodes of psychosis. These may subside or disappear once the episode recedes. FAS may be temporary or persist permanently whatever the cause, sometimes intermittently long after initial onset. While scientific analysis (Dankovičová et al. 2001; Gurd et al. 2001; Miller et al. 2011) has proven that speakers do not actually adopt the precise articulatory and acoustic properties of the perceived accent they now seem to 'own', with productions also frequently inconsistently realized (e.g. sometimes pronouncing 'this' as 'zis'/'sis' or 'this'), they are frequently perceived by listeners to be speaking with a consistently recognizable foreign or changed social/regional accent (e.g. perceived as speaking in an Eastern European or Oriental accent). This judgement is further reinforced by the fact that the speech of many also appears to sound like that of a second language learner due to variation in articulatory accuracy. In reality, patients are experiencing changes to the motor planning and coordination of speech sounds (apraxia). Many strangers therefore believe that those with FAS are 'foreign', while close family, friends or acquaintances who still find speech intelligible, often perceive the sudden onset of a strange accent, in the absence of any other disability, as a sign of psychiatric illness even if the disorder arises from a neurological source. This has implications for the personal and social identity of the FAS person, who may experience a sense of bewilderment and displacement, not recognizing the alien voice and persona they now inhabit and equally wrestling with the attitudes and responses from others, which may challenge in unfamiliar and uncomfortable ways.

Miller (2010) and Miller et al. (2011) detail the rather negative effects on self-validation and authentication experienced by individuals with FAS. Miller (2010: 72) asserts that '[r]eactions to the person with FAS may be benign or malign'. Socio-psychological attitudes, stereotypes and prejudices held by community members towards speakers with particular

accents means that the FAS speaker may encounter stigmatization and/
or enjoy privileges or reactions not formerly encountered prior to the
onset of their condition. '[These] may range from positive engagement to
denial, distortion or denigration of identity and intentions. The person
with FAS may be perceived variously as befriendable, exotic, hostile,
threatening, guilty, an outsider, less employable, uneducated and difficult
to understand' (Miller 2010: 72). Some report being positively evaluated
as they speak with a highly prized or positively rated accent; for example,
a girl perceived as speaking in a French accent reported, 'The girls [her
friends] they all love the accent', while others report being less favourably
received in their speech community (Miller et al. 2011: 1061). Miller
(2010) and Miller et al. (2011) also provide examples of people with FAS
receiving offers of help to navigate their way around their local area or
receiving unwanted and unsolicited advice on local customs or currency,
positioned by their interlocutors as naïve foreigners in a new environment.
Identifying the speaker as a particular nationality or from a particular
region, interlocutors are even reported to switch to the perceived 'first
language' of the FAS person (e.g. French, Romanian), despite assurances
by the FAS person that this is not their 'native' language. Reactions may
have more serious consequences: individuals report being excluded from
public entitlements, such as health services, assumed by providers as non-
nationals and therefore not 'eligible'. Others experience rejection at the
hands of their social community and family and friends: for example, 'I'm
no longer British in my own Britishness and that's a very strange thing to
say because I can no longer be true to myself ... sometimes you get fed
up being foreign' (Miller et al. 2011: 1069). More distressing is the case
of 'Astrid L , who was perceived to sound German after a head injury in
World War II Norway, [and] was ostracised by her community on suspicion
of fraternisation with the occupying enemy' (Monrad-Krohn 1947) and
the case of one individual 'EJC', 'My friends? They went away, you
know. They couldn't take it, how I was. Maybe they were afraid' (Miller
2010: 72–73). Many find their roles, relationships and responsibilities
permanently changed in their personal, work and social life. A sense of
disempowerment is evident in many accounts with informants in Miller
et al.'s (2011: 1057) study reporting being treated as 'mentally unstable',
'crazy' and even 'drunk'.

As the examples above illustrate some FAS sufferers experience alienation
and distancing, their neurological condition unrecognized by strangers
and/or their accent considered fake by those who formerly knew them.
Responses by sufferers to this changed condition are various. For example,
some have sought out communities which now align with their new identity,
'Last summer we went to Dubrovnik and that slightly felt like going home'
(Miller et al. 2011: 1058); some have decided to isolate themselves from
their native community, losing confidence in their ability to communicate
and fearful of the negative feedback and challenges to identity; some listen

to old recordings of their former selves in order to reclaim a situated and 'known' identity; while others accept or decide not to challenge the identities others choose to bestow upon them and/or reformulate a 'new' sense of self (Charmaz 2002; Miller 2010). Not all experience 'loss' or such extreme reformulations as listed above, reconciling themselves to their accent and enjoying some aspects of their changed status (Miller et al. 2011: 1064).

The study of FAS provides a unique opportunity to explore how identity may be destabilized after the onset of a clinical condition and continues to be so by social influences. It draws into focus, even magnifies, the vulnerability, incongruity and dissonance between the individual's understanding of self and other's attributions and assignations. In non-FAS subjects, the manipulation of accent (e.g. switching from regional to more standard forms) is often unconsciously employed to project multiple and distinct 'selves'. While the negotiation of a 'preferred' identity may be challenging and challenged dialogically, this does not compare to the experience of the FAS person who may experience a daily struggle with misattribution or misrecognition, even denials of a professed or 'felt' self. As noted by Miller (2010) and Miller et al. (2011), studies of individuals with FAS highlight a need for clinical assessment and support to focus on psychosocial issues as much as language remediation, helping those with FAS and their significant others to adapt to their changed circumstance.

Research such as Guise et al. (2010), Miller (2010), Miller et al. (2011) and Shaddon (2005) emphasizes the importance of the social environment in reconstitution work. One's identity is understood, in part, through interaction with others and the stories that they and we tell. In the following section, we consider how narratives assist in supporting identity work and in renegotiating physical and emotional recovery following brain injury.

Narratives of aphasia and illness

Narratives told to and by the self, and by others, facilitate chronological and temporal continuity for the individual, shaping past, present and future identity and as argued by Ricoeur construct coherence in life stories (see discussion of Ricoeur's position in Chapter One). As illustrated above, aphasia and illness can disrupt an individual's life story[10] and destabilize 'self-concept'[11] leading to uncomfortable comparisons between a former and current status, as well as initiating an elevated anxiety about an uncertain future (Cantor et al. 2005; Ellis-Hill & Horn 2000, Ellis-Hill et al. 2000; Hill 1997; Nochi 1998). In recovery, narratives prove to be important instruments through which to mediate and negotiate a changed self-concept. However, it should be noted that narratives may not always serve the aphasic population well, especially narratives circulating in the public sphere which elevate the voice of the professional and construct a representation of aphasia based on stereotypes and judgements which run counter to the experience of many aphasics. For example, narratives which represent the aphasic population as predominantly aged and disabled (Armstrong et al. 2011). The latter notwithstanding, narratives can function as important media for adjustment to identity change following illness.[12]

Story telling supports the expression of emotions, attitudes and speaker stance, and facilitates the evaluation of experience and the construction and reproduction of value systems. In assessing the ability of mild-moderately impaired aphasics to exploit evaluative language in narration, Armstrong and Ulatowska (2007) identify its significance for remediation and identity mediation, noting in particular that damage to the left hemisphere gives rise to greater fluency when discussing emotional issues (Borod et al. 2000, in Armstrong & Ulatowska 2007: 764). Their study contributes to a growing body of research investigating narratives of illness and illustrates that although aphasics employ similar strategies to non-brain-damaged individuals in their expression of evaluative forms, their linguistic realizations, lexically and syntactically, are somewhat restricted in number and complexity which may impact on interactional fluency and self-perception. Despite the latter, they argue that therapy should, along with enhancing functional ability (e.g. encouraging clients to practise service encounters), facilitate the expression of emotive and evaluative narratives since these address a speaker's need to express his or her preferences and attitudes. This is crucial not only for self-concept but also for the successful negotiation and maintenance of relationships outside of the clinical context.

The narrative approach also provides a window into the phenomenological and metaphysical world of aphasics – ' "personhood" is bound up with [a] metaphysical ownership of body' (Murray & Harrison 2004: 814) – and often brain-injured individuals experience a severance or disruption to the 'self-body' relationship; the body becoming uncooperative, unknown and distant, a subject of discursive objectification. Narratives prove useful vehicles for the expression of this misalignment and the reimagining of a self with changed physical capabilities. Discussing the 'self-body split' in recovering stroke patients, Ellis-Hill et al. (2000) illustrate the protracted nature of this experience long after recovery for the majority of informants. They detail the perceived and experienced negative consequences of physical disability on identity, including a loss of completeness: 'It's er you sort of think good Lord I'm only half a person' (p. 728); or a sense of detachment of self from the body expressed via the appropriation of third-person pronouns ('it'/'they') – 'I can move it [arm] about a bit you know I keep lifting it up do my bit of exercises I let go and it drops (laughs)' (p. 729).

The fluid nature of a self-body relationship is noted to be situationally contingent, however, with informants reporting variation in attitudes towards their disability and sense of 'self'. For example, 'Mrs Robinson' asserts positive alignment to her past self as she recounts a daily routine in which she sits in a chair reading: 'but sitting here like this I feel just as I used to, but it's when I get up to walk' (Ellis-Hill et al. 2000: 730) that she becomes cognizant of her disability and changed situation. A sense of comfort and 'normality' engendered in such contexts, in contrast to the alienation felt in other settings may lead individuals to seek out similar experiences, often severing ties with activities and people external to the home which prove challenging to their preferred personal and social identity. Many report defining themselves and being defined in terms of their impairment[13] (Ellis-Hill et al. 2000; Murray & Harrison 2004). Successful 'adaption' to impairment, it is argued, can lead to successful 'reintegration' of 'self-body' concept and social re-engagement: 'chronically ill people who move beyond loss and transcend stigmatising labels define themselves as much more than their bodies and as much more than an illness' (Charmaz 1995: 660).

Personal identity and memory

A theme recurring throughout much of our discussion so far has been the desire to maintain and/or renegotiate a consistent, integrated, albeit multidimensional sense of self. Narratives, as we have seen, facilitate the expression and understanding of a past, present and future identity, contributing to a durable, continuous rendering. However, interruption to one's autobiographical account, brought about through illness or injury, appears to lead to a 'disturbance' in self-recognition. In this section, we consider clinical studies which incorporate the study of memory and extend beyond an examination of individuals with aphasia to consider those with a progressively degenerative disease – Alzheimer's disease[14]. The studies we review are framed within the discipline of neuropsychology and while adopting different theoretical, methodological and analytical approaches to those described above, equally highlight the importance of the linguistic expression of narrative for the continuity and integrity of personal identity.

In Chapter One we made reference to the philosophical writing of John Locke, noting how drawing on an account of memory can be used to define personal identity. He asserted that we are who we are through the memories which constitute us, or more personally, I am the same person as that remembered in my past. Others have critiqued this perspective (e.g. Butler, Hume, Reid) and the view that personal identity is consistent over time, suggesting instead, for example, that memory mediates an imaginary sense of continuity. Although many have debated the illusory power of memory for identity representation, psychologists have striven to determine its systemic nature and the bearing of this on a 'sense' of personal identity.

Recent research on long-term memory in psychology suggests that memory serves a very important role in the maintenance of personal identity and is composed of two fundamental systems – declarative and procedural memory. The latter involved in the learning and maintenance of 'motor, perceptual and cognitive skills' and the former in 'facts and beliefs' (Klein & Nichols 2012: 679). Declarative memory, particularly relevant to our discussion of personal identity, is constituted of episodic (or incident) and semantic memory. Semantic memory stores knowledge which is decontextualized and not dependent on one's having personally experienced an event/episode (e.g. knowledge about one's birth date, mathematical calculations, general world knowledge), whereas episodic memory stores memories of personal episodes and events including situational and temporal information. Accounts alluding to personal, autobiographical identity have largely drawn on discussion of episodic memory, for it is argued that it is this which provides the resources from which we construct our life narrative and develop a 'sense' of continuity; although as discussed below, semantic memory also plays a part.

The effect of memory on personal identity is investigated in a study of forty Alzheimer's (AD) subjects and matched controls (Addis & Tippett 2004). Defining 'identity' in terms of self-knowledge (e.g. perceptions and descriptions of personal traits) and a coherent, continuous life story (drawing on theories of 'psychological continuity' and 'narrative self'), the researchers argue that 'autobiographical memory' underpins and enables the construction of identity via the association and condensation of separate storied events/experiences ('moments [of] consciousness' p. 58) into a coherent self-narrative. Referencing the 'reminiscence bump' (p. 58), the authors also argue that memories established in early adulthood (between the ages of 16 and 25 years) are particularly salient and intense, often acting as a yardstick for narrative construction. Accordingly, loss of memory leads to loss of or significant disturbance to one's sense of self.[15] Unlike previous qualitative studies of identity in AD and other types of dementia (Crichton & Koch 2011; Orona 1990, 1997), Addis and Tippett administered quantitative tests of autobiographical memory (testing episodic and semantic memory) and identity (using The Twenty Statements Test[16] and the Tennessee Self Concept Scale[17]). Findings revealed that in comparison to the matched control group, the AD subjects experienced significant disturbance to both semantic and episodic memory. They were comparatively impaired in their ability to generate statements of 'who' or 'what' they were, producing fewer and more abstract statements. A recency effect was also found to be more pronounced in the control group, which was more able to recall incidents in their recent past in comparison to the AD group. Not all measures were identified as important to identity; however, a correlation was found between the quantity and quality of responses given on the Twenty Statement Test and episodic memory in childhood and recall of names in early adulthood: the greater the impairment to the latter, the greater the effect on identity, pointing to the importance of memories from early adulthood on the integrity of identity. While memory is noted as important to the integrity of personal identity, other cognitive functions are also acknowledged.

In a more recent exploration of the significance of past memories on personal identity, and continuing to debate the continuity perspective in personal identity, Klein and Nichols (2012) report on a mildly aphasic, brain-injured individual capable of recalling episodic memories while experiencing a disengagement from them: 'I was remembering scenes, not facts … I was recalling scenes … that is … I could clearly recall a scene of me at the beach in New London with my family as a child. But the feeling was that the scene was not my memory' (p. 687). Despite this dissonance, he asserts that 'Intellectually I suppose I never doubted that was a part of my life' (p. 694). 'R.B.' provides evidence for differential memory processes – processes which separately provide material of the experience and those which provide a distinct sense of 'mineness', that is, an engagement with the incident. 'R.B.'s recollections during his "unowned" period can be explained in the context of the view that there is a specialized neural machinery that inserts the conceptual element *self* into the agent slot of an episodic memory attribution' (p. 689). Episodic memory, it would seem, contains different representations of self. The narratives elicited enabled the scholars to contribute to the philosophical and psychological debate about the relationship between and constitution of 'quasi-memory' and a speaker's sense of an integrated, continuous self.

Conclusion

This chapter illustrates how identity has become salient to clinical research and therapy for individuals with speech and language impairments, as well as individuals experiencing memory deficit. This research has led to developments in theoretical frameworks and significantly for those affected, and has also led to changes in clinical practice, notably influenced by a reconceptualization of the client as a competent social actor in therapy, and recognition of identity 'changes' as an intra- and interpersonal phenomenon. In a return to a philosophical discussion of the impact of memory and narrative on identity continuity (see Chapter One), the chapter also reviewed more recent research on the systemic representation of identity and the processes involved in its constitution and expression, illustrating the significance of memory to a storied representation and understanding of self.

CHAPTER FOUR

Forensic Studies

All of the work and all of the theory that I had developed since Martha's Vineyard flowed into the testimony that I gave in court to establish the fact that Paul Prinzivalli did not and could not have made those telephone calls. It was almost as if my entire career had been shaped to make the most effective testimony on this one case.... By means of linguistic evidence, one man could be freed from the corporate enemies who had assailed him, and another could sleep soundly on the conviction that he had made a just decision.

WILLIAM LABOV (1997)

Introduction

Advancements in forensic linguistics have contributed to the outcome of some significant legal cases. Among the most notable is the case of Paul Prinzivalli, an alleged disgruntled employee accused of making bomb threats to his employer, Pan Am Airlines, but cleared of all charges following the expert testimony of dialectologist William Labov (Labov & Harris 1994). Through a detailed analysis of the phonetic features of the incriminating recordings and the speech of the defendant, Labov demonstrated how the voice on the recordings could not be that of Prinzivalli since the perpetrator had the defining characteristics of a New England (Boston) accent, while Prinzivalli spoke with a discernible New York accent. Labov's testimony was accepted by the court and the suspect freed.

It is a truism to state that stakes are high when attempting to identify an individual or individuals who are responsible for crimes in legal cases. Expert testimony can influence judgements and lead to the incarceration and/or, in some jurisdictions, the death of the accused. A plethora of cases and research studies have shown how linguists have a role to play in legal cases. It must be acknowledged, however, that while their expert opinion and testimony may guide law enforcement officers, intelligence personnel and the courts, it may not always be considered admissible, and/or once admitted, not heeded by judges or jurors (e.g. see Tiersma & Solan's 2002 account of the United States). Nevertheless, the field of forensic linguistics has grown exponentially in recent years and forensic linguists increasingly called upon to offer their expert opinion, applying sophisticated linguistic theory, methodology and analyses to a range of legal contexts.

Linguists have acted as expert witnesses and advisors in *inter alia*: disputes or queries over authorship of spoken and written texts (e.g. terrorist threats, suicide or ransom notes) and issues broadly pertaining to communication and meaning, for example, the interpretation of a term in a particular language,[1] educational provision for minority groups and trademark cases. They have identified the unique interactional and linguistic characteristics of legal contexts/texts and played an important role in calling attention to the disadvantages meted on those who are not able to communicate effectively in and/or are disadvantaged by the legal system. It has become an established field of research and part of the criminal justice system in many countries, for example, Australia, Germany, Spain, Sweden, United States, UK (Olsson & Luchjenbroers 2014).[2]

In this chapter, we are unable to consider the multiple strands of forensic linguistics that impact on issues of identity; however, we will explore some of the approaches, methods and analytic frameworks applied to the identification of speakers and writers by forensic linguists, incorporating examples of disciplinary expertise in forensic dialectology, phonetics, stylistics and discourse analysis. We also review work that has focused on the identities 'brought to' and 'brought about' in the courtroom and throughout the legal process. We begin with a consideration of authorship identification of spoken texts for, as noted by Grant (2008: 216), these are often afforded priority in investigations where a voice recording is available.

Authorship identification: Spoken texts

Occasionally, forensic investigation demands the identification of suspects or victims based on speech samples. Investigations such as Prinzivalli are illustrative of terrorist or hoax activity; however, the need for identification extends to a broad array of other cases too, such as the analysis of recordings in kidnapping, murder or drug dealing enquiries.

Research findings point to the potential unreliability of evidence provided by untrained/naïve 'ear witnesses' in the identification of a voice previously heard in an incident, and even the unreliability of trained phoneticians in identifying an unknown and/or even a familiar voice on recall, or without transcription or instrumental analysis (see Watt's 2010 account of Ladefoged & Ladefoged 1980). The reliability of witness testimony has been noted to be hampered by such variables as the age of the ear witness (e.g. see Clifford et al. 1981 who report greater success in identification among 16–40 year olds in comparison with older-age informants), memory limitations (the latter sometimes affected by the trauma of the event), emotion and unfavourable conditions at the time of the hearing (e.g. extraneous noise, whispering/shouting, limited speech). Some have also highlighted the confounding influence of methods used by police forces to elicit witness testimony[3] when no recording is available. Others (e.g. Hollien et al. 1983 in Olsen and Luchjenbroers 2014: 102) have asserted, based on experimental evidence, that when carried out correctly, ear witness testimony can prove to be a faithful and accurate identification mechanism.

The availability of speech recordings has enhanced methods of speaker identification. Advancements in forensic phonetics and acoustics, and speech and audio analysis have led to scientifically informed and arguably more robust indicators of speaker identification by professional phoneticians. The sharing of this work internationally via the International Association for Forensic Phonetics and Acoustics (IAFPA) and peer-reviewed publications such as the *International Journal of Speech, Language and the Law* (formerly '*Journal of Forensic Linguistics*') has also enhanced the replication of procedures and promoted improvements in the validity and reliability of techniques used in forensic speech analysis (Schiller & Köster 1998; Watt 2010). Science has not advanced sufficiently to enable 'voice prints' to accurately distinguish speakers with the certainty of DNA or fingerprint analysis, and until researchers understand the distribution of speech features across the general population this may not be possible (Nolan 1997; Watt 2010). Nor are there the means at present to facilitate 'Identikit' reconstructions using voice synthesis in a way similar to visual representations of assailants in which witnesses are asked to describe a perpetrator based on their memory of the event in order for a professional to reconstruct a pictorial representation (Jessen 2010). However, there are a number of significant, 'testable' parameters along which voices vary which enable experts to make informed judgements via the identification of a cluster of distinctive and consistent features. These variables enable forensic analysts to 'profile' or 'compare' samples of data.

Some of the parameters along which voices are noted to differ include the following (Watt 2010: 78ff): *anatomy*, such as the size, shape and position of the teeth, soft and hard palate, and thickness, condition and length of the vocal folds; *physiology*, such as the movement of the vocal tract, including, for example, the favoured positioning of the velum, which may, if raised, create a voice which sounds like a speaker with adenoid problems, and if lowered, may sound rather nasalized. Also the degree of *vocal fold (cord) closure* which determines the quality of sounds emitted, for example, a husky or whispered voice. Some distinguishing characteristics may also arise from *social influences*, such as a particular accent; or due to a particular *pathology* (e.g. cleft palate or lip); or *personal style*. Watt (2010: 79) details the case of twins who despite sharing identical anatomical and physiological characteristics, and extremely similar developmental and socio-cultural influences, still varied in their speech production, illustrating how speech production may be influenced by speaker choice (see Chapter Two).

In their analysis of speech data, the aims and methods employed by phoneticians differ somewhat depending on the nature of the data available to them and the stage of the investigation. If the speaker is unknown, a profile/voice analysis is developed in order to construct a description of the person drawing on biological, social and geographic classifications and indices, such as age, sex, region of origin, social status as well as any distinguishing phonological, anatomical or physiological features (e.g. high/low pitch, nasal articulation, stuttering, speed of delivery). The analyst may also note any noticeable emotional, psychological or physical traits, for example, anger, psychosis, intoxication. In this way, both social classifications and individual characteristics are accounted for. Figure 4.1 details the 'domains of forensic speaker classification' (Jessen 2010: 381) used in investigations to date.

These descriptions can be useful to police in their attempts to track down a suspect. If there are previous recordings of the speaker (e.g. voice messages) or a defendant/suspect is willing to be recorded after the event, a speaker/voice comparison is made in order to identify features of similarity or difference, thereby ruling a suspect in or out of the investigation. The scientist in this instance may be able to design the content of the subsequent recording in order to control the data gathered to match the recording/s. This may not always be possible and may not always be preferable as it can compromise the integrity of the data; for example, speakers may attempt to disguise or alter their voices. Elicitation procedures may also interfere with the quality of the data (e.g. lack of spontaneity and natural prosody) if,

Body size	Medical conditions	Age	Sex/ gender	Sociolect	Regiolect	Foreign accent (L2)/ethnolect	Language (L1)

←———

| Organic/biological (anatomy and physiology) | | | | Social | | Grammatical (linguistic system) | |

FIGURE 4.1 *Speaker classification domains (Jessen 2010: 381)*

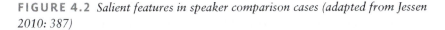

Organic	Idiolectal	Habitual
i. Average fundamental frequency (f0)[4]	i. Sociolect, regiolect and foreign accent	i. Articulation rate
ii. (Long-term) formant[5]	ii. Linguistic-phonetic details (e.g. glottalization)	ii. f0-variability
iii. Voice quality (e.g. breathy/ creaky/nasal voice)	iii. Forensic linguistic features (idiosyncratic, syntactic and lexical features)	iii. Dysfluent behaviour (e.g. (un)filled pauses, impediment)

FIGURE 4.2 *Salient features in speaker comparison cases (adapted from Jessen 2010: 387)*

for example, the informant is asked to produce less spontaneous speech by reading or repeating passages (Jessen 2010: 379).

Features that have proven to be salient in speaker comparison cases are shown in Figure 4.2 and elaborated on in Jessen (2010).

Some investigations can involve initial speaker profiling and later speaker comparison, as in the infamous case of the Yorkshire Ripper in the UK (Ellis 2013; French & Harrison 2006, also summarized in Watt 2010 and Jessen 2010). This was the case of a serial killer whose crimes of murder and attempted murder in the north of England extended over two decades (1970s and 1980s) before final conviction. Early in the investigation, police and press received written and spoken confessions from an individual claiming to be the Yorkshire Ripper. A voice analysis was carried out and it was determined that the speaker originated from Sunderland in the north east of England (Ellis 1994). Specific phonetic variants, such as the long vowel /uː/ and the diphthong [ai], were identified as indices of the speaker's regional origin. Further comparisons with recordings of men from the local area were made to establish regional variants. In 1981 Peter Sutcliffe, who originated from Yorkshire, was convicted of the crimes. In 2005, DNA evidence retrieved from the envelope of one of the confession letters identified John Humble, a man who had originated and been educated in the Castletown area of Sunderland. On arrest, Humble admitted that the calls and letters had been a hoax. He was subsequently imprisoned for his crimes. His acts, many argued, led police to waste valuable time in identifying the murderer.

The analyses undertaken by phoneticians can be both auditory and acoustic. The former involves listening to recordings and transcribing the auditory characteristics, including consonants and vowels (segmental features), prosody, intonation (suprasegmental features), disfluencies (e.g. pauses), etc., and also any non-standard or idiosyncratic features.[6] Voice quality, for example, can be difficult to assess acoustically due to the quality and frequency of the speech signal (particularly when mediated by the telephone) and is therefore often determined auditorily (Jessen 2010: 391). An acoustic analysis demands instrumental methods such as spectral analyses and these can prove very useful in identifying both social and individual characteristics. The measurement of formant frequencies is increasingly noted to be particularly important for speaker identification, particularly since they arise from the individual characteristics of a speaker's vocal tract and articulatory movements. Nolan and Grigoras (2005) report on the success of this technique in the case of a series of obscene telephone calls made to a female bank employee in London. They carried out a two-stage analysis of vowel (and diphthong) formant frequencies (F1 and F2), enabling them to rule out the voice of a suspect based on a comparative analysis of the telephone calls and recordings of the suspect's speech.

While the tools and techniques available to identify speakers have advanced significantly in recent decades, there is still progress to be made. As noted by Watt (2010: 84), '[a]nalysts are duty-bound to inform legal professionals, jurors and the general public of the limitations of these methods, an obligation necessitated further by the "CSI effect", whereby laypeople's expectations are raised to unrealistic levels by the misleading portrayal of forensic speech analysis in television and in film'. Not only is the absence of population statistics (which point to inter and intra-speaker tendencies) detrimental to unique speaker identification, other factors continue to prove testing to analysts, for example, disguised voices (Eriksson 2010), multiple voices, poor recording and voice quality, background noise, to name but a few.

Authorship identification: Written texts

Authorship identification is equally complex when considering the analysis of written texts, not least because these may be developed by more than one author. There is also, like voice recordings, no 'bank' of written texts gathered across a general population which can be used for comparative 'linguistic fingerprinting' and the texts under investigation may be limited in length or quantity. Most letters or notes are reported to be below 200 words with a significant number below 100 words (Coulthard 2004: 432). Nonetheless, linguists agree that writers display a style – an idiolect – marked by consistency (with some variation) and distinctiveness.[7] Working with this assumption, they have developed increasingly sophisticated qualitative and quantitative methodologies involving manual and computational techniques which enable them to determine and offer opinions on issues relating to authorship.[8]

Opinions have been offered on written material across a range of genre and forms, including hand-written and electronically mediated texts, such as, ransom/suicide/threatening notes/letters; disputed confessions, wills and witness statements; text messages; intellectual property and trademarks. Expert testimony has also included advising on the semantic, pragmatic and/or lexico-grammatical complexity/ambiguity of texts in, for example, insurance policies (Prince 1981), jury instructions (Levi 1993) and statutes (Kaplan et al. 2013) (e.g. see Coulthard 2007 for an interesting review of these cases).

The first forensic examination of a written text was made by Jan Svartvik in 1968. It was he who first coined the term 'Forensic Linguistics' incorporating it into the subtitle of his volume: *The Evans Statements: A Case for Forensic Linguistics.* This was a case study in which he demonstrated, via an analysis of police statements submitted to a public enquiry at the Royal Courts of Justice in London (1965), that confessions of murder, allegedly dictated to police in two locations, Merthyr Tydfil, Wales, and Notting Hill, London, in November and December 1949 by Timothy John Evans, were not accurately recorded and did not bear the idiolectal features of the accused in their entirety. They were therefore potentially unreliable.

Evans had been convicted of the murder of his young wife and 14-month-old daughter and was subsequently hanged for the crime in March 1950. In 1953 John Christie, who had occupied the same house as the Evans's family at the time of the murders, was convicted of the murder of his own wife. She and other female remains were found under the floor boards and kitchen by a new tenant. A private enquiry was convened in 1953 led by Scott Hendersen Q.C. While the Scott Henderson inquiry did not find Christie guilty of the Evans's murders, a subsequent public enquiry was less certain and in 1966 the home secretary issued a posthumous pardon to Timothy Evans. During the public enquiry, many had questioned the validity of the statements claimed to have been made by Evans in his initial confessions, particularly given the fact that Evans was reported to have been illiterate. Svartvik subjected the small corpus of four statements (two made in Merthyr Tydfil and two in Notting Hill), consisting of only 4,861 words to linguistic scrutiny, and also compared Evans's performance in the witness stand to the written data. He demonstrated through an examination of features such as time statements (e.g. one fifty five versus five to one) and standard versus non-standard forms (e.g. negation, verb forms, pronouns) that sections of the statements bore the characteristics of his speech; however, there were also uncharacteristic features of an 'idiolect of an illiterate' (p. 24), including complexity in sentence length (analysis extended to the number of finite verb clauses per sentence) and combinations of clause types. Svartvik was cautious in his conclusion noting that 'at least three factors ... thwart all hope of reaching any firm conclusions ... the small size of the material ... the highly artificial linguistic situation ... a policeman ... giving a graphic rendering of the speech of an illiterate [and] ... our inadequate knowledge of how language is used in different situations'. Nevertheless differences between the disputed and undisputed text were considered 'too remarkable' (p. 46) by Svartvik to be overlooked.

Many years intervened until further work progressed in Svartvik's newly established field (Shuy 1993) but many of the authorship and methodological issues highlighted by his study are still debated today. For example, questions as to: whether one or more individuals are responsible for the construction of a text; the type of person/people involved in the production of a written sample/s; the nature of text production, for example, in investigations of originality or plagiarism; and, where a queried/ unknown text and a comparative/known text(s) are available (e.g. a series of text messages purported to be from the same person), whether these bear resemblances/differences which may be of significance to an investigation (Grant 2008). A variety of analytic approaches and procedures have been developed and critiqued since 1968, with an increasing tendency in the profession (as in speech analysis) for analysts to work towards the development of replicable, valid and reliable instruments and analyses. We consider these issues and critique, through an exploration of case studies, diverse approaches to the analysis of written texts in investigations of the identity of authors.

Determining the identity of writers and the 'originality' of texts can be crucial in disputes over claimed authorship. The concept of 'fabricated authorship' extends to cases of plagiarism, child grooming online (Grant & Macleod 2016), investigations of police tampering in the recording of statements or interviews, as illustrated in Svartvik's study, and even the fabrication of wills (McMenamin 2002). A question often asked of texts is: 'who is/are the author/s?' Why this may be relevant obviously differs according to the investigation. It may be that academics are attempting to determine whether a student has plagiarized, or police are attempting to 'profile' a suspect, or it may be that a court is attempting to determine if the evidence presented before it is a faithful representation of suspect/victim/ witness testimony previously made to law enforcement officers.

A more recent legal case of disputed authorship, not dissimilar from the Evans's case, involved the reanalysis of police statements submitted to court in connection with the murder of a young school boy, Carl Bridgewater. The statements related to an interview and confession made by one of four men accused of Carl's murder in Staffordshire, UK, in 1978 (Coulthard 2004, 2007; Coulthard & Johnson 2007; Coulthard et al. 2010). It is believed that Carl disturbed burglars when on his paper round and was shot to death. The accused were jailed on the basis of the confession made by Patrick Molloy, who later withdrew his confession and argued that he had been coerced into making it by police who had physically and verbally abused him and had told him what to say. The police responded by submitting a handwritten document of an interview purported to have taken place prior to the confession which contained an uncanny similarity in content and form to the details of the confession.[9]

These can be seen in the extracts below, reproduced from Coulthard (2004: 436–437). Identical phrases are represented in **bold type** and paraphrases in *italics*. Malloy argued that the interview never took place.

Extract of Molloy's statement

(17) **I had been drinking and cannot remember the exact time I was there but whilst I was upstairs I heard someone downstairs say be careful someone is coming.** (18) **I hid for a while** and *after a while* **I heard** *a* **bang** *come from downstairs.* (19) **I knew that it was a gun being fired.** (20) I went downstairs and **the three of them were still in the room.** (21) **They all looked shocked and were shouting at each other.** (22) **I heard Jimmy say, 'It went off by accident'.** (23) I looked and **on the settee** I saw the *body of the boy.* (24) **He had been shot in the head.** (25) **I was appalled and felt sick.**

Extract from disputed interview with Molloy

P. How long were you in there Pat?

(18) **I had been drinking and cannot remember the exact time I was there, but whilst I was upstairs I heard someone downstairs say 'be careful someone is coming'.**

P. Did you hide?

(19) Yes **I hid for a while** and then **I heard** the **bang** I have told you about.

P. Carry on Pat?

(19a) I ran out.

P. What were the others doing?

(20) **The three of them were still in the room.**

P. What were they doing?

(21) **They all looked shocked and were shouting at each other.**

P. Who said what?

(22) **I heard Jimmy say 'it went off by accident'.**

P. Pat, I know this is upsetting but you appreciate that we must get to the bottom of this. Did you *see the boy's body?*

(Molloy hesitated, looked at me intently, and after a pause said,)

(23) Yes sir, he was **on the settee.**

P. Did you see any injury to him?

(Molloy stared at me again and said)

(24) Yes sir, **he had been shot in the head.**

P. What happened then?

(25) **I was appalled and felt sick.**

The defence and prosecution teams interpreted the similarity between the two texts in their favour: the defence that this could only suggest police malpractice and the prosecution, that the similarity bore the markings of two texts produced by the same individual, that is, Molloy. At appeal in 1997, the texts were submitted to forensic analysis. Coulthard (2004: 439) reports 'there was in fact not one single word in the Molloy's statement, neither lexical nor grammatical, which did not also occur in the interview record. I have only seen that degree of overlap on one other occasion, when two students had in fact submitted identical essays for assessment'. Based on previous research (Hjelmquist 1984; Hjelmquist & Gidlung 1985) and experimentation by Prof. Clifford in 2003 in a separate trial involving police collusion, Coulthard determined that it would be most unusual for an individual to use exactly the same wording on two separate occasions (also see Solan & Tiersma 2005), leading him to determine that either one text was derived from the other, or that both texts were sourced from a third text.

Further evidence of fabrication came in an examination of the interleaving of question forms in the interview text. Examination of cataphoric and anaphoric referencing appeared to reveal the insertion of questions into a text that had already been created (i.e. the supposed 'confession'); for example, the use of the verb 'said' in the interview question 'Who said what?' fits uncomfortably between lines (21) and (22) in which the verb 'shout' is used. A more plausible utterance would have been 'who shouted what?' Further, 'grammatical misfit' was identified when statements were transformed into the interview text; for example, in the question 'Did you see **the boy's body**? Yes sir, **he** was on the settee', Coulthard argues that it would be more usual for the pronoun 'he' to be realized as 'it'. This along with other evidence was used to demonstrate that the interview text was derived from the statement. Coulthard reports that 'sadly, it was not possible to test the acceptability and persuasiveness of these arguments in court, as the Crown conceded the appeal shortly before the due date when compelling new evidence ... emerged to convince the judges of the unsafeness of the conviction' (p. 440).

In a reversal to the practice illustrated above in the Bridgewater case, Coulthard (2002, 2005) makes reference to a number of investigations in which dialogue has been reconstituted into monologue – alleged statements/ confessions initially derived from interview data. Sometimes, these 'statements' have been manipulated or added to so that they misrepresent or subvert the original utterances, therefore undermining the reliability and validity of the evidence submitted to court. Examples include the Birmingham Six Whiteway and Bentley cases in which it has been shown, via cross-examination and linguistic analysis, that the defendants could not have uttered the quotations recorded in the police statements, at least not in the form represented. In the Whiteway trial, a detective, Detective Hannam, confirmed in court that the nature of the police recording of the suspect's words attributed utterances to him that were not his own:

> I would say "Do you say on that Sunday you wore your shoes?" and he would say "Yes" and it would go down as "On that Sunday I wore my shoes" (Court transcript p. 156, cited in Coulthard 2005).

Coulthard's work on the Bentley case led to the posthumous pardon of Derek Bentley, who had been tried and found guilty in 1953 of involvement in the murder of a police officer. He had been convicted partly on the basis of an alleged written confession to the crime. Coulthard found the confession to have identifying lexico-grammatical features consonant with police discourse and a narrative structure and content (Coulthard 2005) that made the confession 'unsafe'. Using corpus analysis, he compared the discourse of police reports to witness statements recorded without police involvement and found particular features of the confession that did not appear in other witness statements but were apparent in police reports, for example, the use of 'then' in statements such as:

Chris **then** climbed up the drainpipe to the roof and I followed

'Then' recurred every 78 words in police reports, in contrast to every 930 words in witness statements. When drawing on a corpus of spoken English, it was found to appear every 474 words. In Bentley's confession, the figure revealed an unusual and unexpected frequency of use, closer to that realized in the discourse of police officers, measured as appearing once in every fifty-eight words. It was not only the frequency that was unusual but also its syntactic placement. In everyday usage, we generally use 'then' at the beginning of an utterance, before the specification of the subject, for example, 'Then I ran', whereas police, Coulthard found, generally favour the use of 'then' after the subject, for example, 'I then ran'.

The methods employed in these case studies built upon work in forensic stylistics and plagiarism. Issues of authorship attribution and the concept of idiolect proved fundamental to early studies of collusion detection and 'borrowing' from sources. Johnson's (1997) work was the first account of a comparative statistical analysis of student texts using a concordance program – CopyCatch – (formerly created by Woolls; see Woolls 2010) and opened the field to the possibility of complementing qualitative stylistic analyses with computational analyses. It also allowed researchers to identify the directionality of copying from source to derivative text(s) (Coulthard et al. 2010; Turell 2008). Rather than investigating sequences of lexical items, Johnson's analysis focused on the incidence of overlap in individual lexical items. Woolls (2003) subsequently refined this work by demonstrating not only how a high degree of lexical overlap indexed collusion but more importantly a high percentage of shared unique occurrences of lexemes (known as *hapax* or *hapax legomena* if they occur once, *or dis legomenia* if they occur twice) marked high degrees of similarity between texts. Copycatch has permitted researchers/expert witnesses to provide 'base-line or threshold levels of similarity' (Turell 2008: 287) between texts. Turell (2004) suggests that up to 50 per cent similarity may not be unusual; however, above this figure some degree of plagiarism or collusion has taken place. Increasingly the implementation of sophisticated software in institutions, coupled with close qualitative analysis, is argued to be having a positive effect, deterring individuals from plagiarism and collusion (Coulthard et al. 2010). Woolls (2010: 588) reports on the success of such detection programs in the case of the Universities and Colleges Admissions Service (UCAS) in the UK, noting that 'the number of serious cases requiring UCAS notification of applicant and admissions tutors dropped by 26% between January 2008 and January 2009'.

The practice of comparing 'queried'/known texts with 'comparative'/unknown texts can be crucial in police investigations. Grant (2012) discusses the comparative analysis of mobile text messages by Malcolm Coulthard following the disappearance of a teenager, Jenny Nicholl, in the north of England in 2005. Not long after her disappearance, family and friends received messages from her telephone. Police, in an attempt to determine if they were dealing with a murder or missing person enquiry, requested help from Coulthard to determine if the style of messages known to have been sent prior to the disappearance bore any resemblance to those post-disappearance, and to the text messages produced by their suspect, David Hodgson. Changes were found in the style of the texting, particularly in the realization of certain lexical forms; for example, in the case of pronominal realizations, Jenny had a preferred style of self-reference, using 'my' and 'myself' – in contrast to Hodgson's style which echoed a north-eastern pronunciation 'me' and 'meself'. Changes in style proved to be consistent with the time of disappearance. At trial, David Hodgson was convicted of murder.

Coulthard's account did not rely on statistical analysis of the data presented to him; however, Grant (2012) demonstrates how a methodologically rigorous approach to stylistic analysis can be achieved using as a case study the evidence he was called to work on in the case of the suspected murder of Amanda Birks. This led to a comparison of her text messages with those of her husband Christopher Birks.

Amanda Birks's body was recovered from a bed in the attic of her home in Stoke-on-Trent (UK) following a house fire in January 2009. Despite being able to rescue his sleeping children from the lower floors of the house, Christopher Birks was unable to rescue his wife. Forensic tests post-mortem indicated limited traces of carbon monoxide in Amanda's lungs and therefore evidence that she was not breathing when burned by the fire. Also fibres on her body indicated that she was wearing day clothes despite being recovered at night. No definitive cause of death was determined. Christopher Birks reported that his wife had been home all day prior to the fire and an employee of the couple claimed to have seen them both at home in the morning when they came to the house on business. Christopher was reportedly out of the home in the afternoon when Amanda allegedly sent a number of SMS text messages to her husband, family and employees (later recovered from the recipients as her telephone was destroyed in the house fire). Grant notes that the messages to her husband made reference to the 'state of their relationship and that she was going to bed early "relaxing with candles" in the attic room' (p. 468). However, despite Christopher's claims about his wife being home all afternoon, analysis of their burglar alarm showed no movement within the property.

In light of all of the evidence above and police access to the couples' texts messages in which suspicions were raised about changes in the style of texting from approximately 12 p.m. on the day of the fire, Grant was asked to act on behalf of the prosecution team and analyse the text messages of the couple. He had access to two small corpora consisting of messages sent several days prior to the fire by both parties. In total, just over 200 messages sent from each telephone were available for analysis. The analysis focused on vocabulary choices and variation in spelling. It also included a number of other features, such as spacing between words, letter and number substitution and accent markers (e.g. 'ad' for 'had'). Only features that occurred ten or more times across the entire data set of over 400 texts were analysed. Twenty-eight features were finally compared. Grant notes that 'for neither author can these lists be considered identifying in an absolute sense. The features contained in these lists are not linguistic "fingerprints" identifying individuals against a population. Rather, they demonstrate a relative consistency of habit and a pairwise distinctiveness which thus can be used to stylistically discriminate between messages of the suspect and the victim in this case' (p. 480). Following both a statistical and qualitative analysis of the data, he concluded that it was not possible to definitively identify the husband as the author of the final messages sent from his wife's telephone on the afternoon prior to her death; however, he noted that the couple did have different texting styles and identified that the last messages sent by Amanda were stylistically different to those she had sent in the days and morning prior to her death. The final messages sent from her telephone were consistent with those of her husband. Based on this evidence, as well as the other circumstantial evidence detailed above, Christopher Birks was found 'guilty' of the murder of his wife, arson and the endangerment of his children and firefighters. He received a life sentence.

A further comparative analysis is that of the Unabomber case in the United States (Coulthard 2004; Frantzekou et al. 2004; Grant 2008). Over a period of seventeen years (1978–1995), bombs were posted annually to individuals working at universities or airlines (hence the prefix 'Un'-'a' bomber). In 1995, several newspapers received a manuscript from someone claiming to be the bomber, requesting that it be published and promising that if published all bombings would stop. In the summer of 1995, the manuscript was published by the *Washington Post* and sometime later the FBI received correspondence from a member of the public who suspected that the author of the text was his sibling. He drew attention to a particular phrase used by his brother – 'cool-headed logician' – an unusual term noted by Grant (2008: 433) to index 'idiolectal preference'. Following the arrest of the suspect, the FBI carried out further analyses of texts found in the home of the assailant and concluded that the manifesto had been written by the 'Unabomber'.

Sometimes, experts have very little information to draw on. They may be presented with a written sample and asked to profile the writer of the letter in order to provide law enforcement officers or intelligence services with a sociolinguistic and/or psycholinguistic profile of the writer. In a few cases, post-conviction (re)analyses of texts have taken place. For example, Grant (2008) refers to two: the analysis of the letters sent by John Humble, the fraudulent Yorkshire Ripper (discussed above), and Foster's (2001) reanalysis of the UNABOMBER manifesto. In the former case, based on Humble's admission to police that he had been inspired by the letters of Jack the Ripper (an unknown serial killer active in London in the late nineteenth century), a comparative analysis of the texts revealed lexico-grammatical parallels. Grant acknowledges that this information may not have driven the enquiry forward at the time; however, it did provide some clues as to 'the psychology and interests of the letter writer' (p. 219). In contrast, Foster's (2001) analysis of the UNABOMBER text draws on sociolinguistic expertise to track down the written precedents/sources, or as Grant refers to them (drawing on Love 2002), 'influences [of] … precursory authorship'. Focusing on the linguistic and thematic content of the manifesto, Foster deduces not only the books but also the libraries visited by the author.

A final area of written/semiotic text analysis, briefly considered in this section, is that of trademark law. An increasingly large area of law in many nations, demanding the expertise of linguists in offering scientific advice and sometimes expert testimony in court in relation to three main areas of contention impinging on issues of identity: the possibility of confusing one trademark for another, the 'propriety' of a mark and the 'strength' of the trademark (Butters 2008, 2010; Shuy 2002). We consider only the first issue here but see Butters (2008, 2010) for a detailed account of the other two.

The potential for confusion between the identity of trademarks can occur at different linguistic levels – sound, meaning and visual representation (i.e. spelling, typography, etc.) – and as illustrated by Butters (2008: 233ff) in the case of *Aventis v Advancis*, can involve all elements. In this case, Butters acted as a consultant for Aventis, a pharmaceutical company, concerned that a new company trading under the name of Advancis bore a mark too closely resembling that of their own. Butters undertook a linguistic analysis and determined very close similarity between the trade names across various parameters, including 67 per cent similarity in the letters and close similarity in their positioning,[10] and very close phonological and semantic overlap.

Another case hinging on morphological similarity between an established and new trademark is that of *McDonald's v McSleep* motels (Tiersma & Solan 2002: 228). The key linguistic conundrum here was whether 'Mc' is unquestionably associated with 'McDonald's' or whether 'Mc' is a morpheme that can be productively invoked by any other trader. Testimony in this case concentrated on the meaning and use of 'Mc' in different contexts. The court decided in favour of McDonald's concluding that 'Mc' was too closely associated with its trade name to warrant appropriation by the McSleep company.

In the next section, we shift our focus away from issues of authorship identification to a consideration of actor identity in legal proceedings, focusing first on the identities of judges and lawyers before discussing witness, victim and defendant identities.

Courtroom identities: Judges and lawyers

Analyses of questioning and opening/closing arguments in courtroom contexts reveal how judges and defence/prosecution lawyers shape and reflect their identities in professional practice (Gibbons 2003; Felton Rosulek 2010). For example, focusing on the questioning of lawyers by six judges during the 'oral argument' stage in the hearing of *Hernandez v Robles*, a case brought before the New York Court of Appeals regarding same-sex couples' right to marriage within New York state, Tracy (2009) illustrates how style, frequency, content and structure of questions leak and perform different types of judicial identity/'personality'. These identities range from aggressive/oppositional to balanced and judicious. At one extreme, she focuses on the identity work employed by Judge R. Smith 'who repeatedly pursued appellant's assertions that the state did *not* have a rational basis' (p. 212) for distinguishing between same-sex and opposite-sex couples, and at the other extreme, she details the performance of Chief Judge Kaye whose contributions to the proceedings were comparatively 'even-handed and measured' (p. 216).

Judge Smith is described as taking an oppositional stance to same-sex marriage and shown to ask repeated follow-up questions to the petitioner – questions used rhetorically to promote his favoured argument against same-sex marriage and to undermine the validity of the opposing argument. He employed the discursive strategies of 'extreme case formulation' (Pomerantz 1986) and interrogative questions in order to frame and foreshadow a negative answer (e.g. 'can you think of a case where something that was that well accepted for that many centuries was found unconstitutional?', p. 214). Tracy (2009: 214) asserts that 'Judge R. Smith's questioning does the identity work of portraying him as not only likely to vote against the appellants, but as a politically conservative person who did not favor gay rights'.

In contrast, Chief Judge Kaye's questioning style was less adversarial and rhetorical in form, found to be 'information-seeking' (p. 215) rather than leading. Questions were also comparatively shorter in length and less pursuant than the questions posed by other judges. Her interpersonal stance was comparatively respectful, marked by polite address terms when speaking directly to the attorneys. 'Judge Kaye's talk constructed her as a judge working to be even-handed and measured. Rather than an argumentative, position-displaying style, which Judge R. Smith enacted, Judge Kaye's talk constructed her as pursuing an unbiased-as-possible identity during oral argument' (p. 216).

While recognizing the importance of verbal skills and rhetorical style in persuading listeners, Hobbs (2008) claims that a key factor often overlooked in discursive studies of courtroom interaction is the perceived legitimacy of a speaker's identity and personality as shown in the case of 'Mohammad'. Mohammad acted as a *pro se* defendant in his own murder trial. Hobbs undertook a comparative analysis of the opening statement made by John Allen Muhammad in the 'Beltway Sniper' trial, with statements made by well-known successful legal professionals.[11] She establishes that although the discursive strategies employed by Muhammad reflected the sophistication evident in similar texts (e.g. impact statement; thematic thread; employment of poetic devices such as analogy, parallelism and repetition), the identity and personality of the defendant served to undermine his case. Hobbs concludes that '[a]ccordingly, it would appear that the expectation that Mohammad, with no legal training and only a high school education, would be incompetent to conduct his own defense resulted in the negative interpretation of his opening statement' (p. 245). Drawing on the concepts of 'voice' and categorization, Hobbs asserts that the defendant 'cannot produce [a] legal voice' (p. 245) since this is the preserve of qualified lawyers who have the credibility and authority to carry it off. His lack of 'ethos' determines that the potential for a successful outcome to his trial is significantly undermined.

However, where a lawyer's professional legitimacy is established their language use may not conform to the formal expectations of the setting or their role. In some instances, non-standard, vernacular forms have proven successful in exercising authority and in symbolically enacting a shared identity with jurors and judges. For example, Hobbs (2003) details the case of an African American lawyer who rhetorically appropriated the style of African American Vernacular English (AAVE) in a brief (three-minute) rebuttal in court. Through such devices as synthetic personalization (Fairclough 1989/2014),[12] AAVE phonology and 'proverbial statements and cultural references' (p. 283), she is shown to enact cultural and ethnic solidarity with a predominantly black jury and judge (e.g. appropriating the slogan of the black comedian Arsenio Hall 'Things that make y'go "Hmm!"' p. 283) in a bid to align herself with the majority of her audience and undermine the defence attorney's closing argument.

Lawyers have also been shown to appropriate 'character voices' (Koven 2002, cited in Felton Rosulek 2010: 223) or direct and indirect speech in other contexts too, recontextualizing the words of others, particularly the words of authoritative voices, for example, expert witnesses, in order to bolster their claims and/or refute the position forwarded by the original speaker or the opposition. Felton Rosulek (2010: 225) provides the example of a prosecution lawyer who repeats the words of a doctor who testified to the fact that injuries sustained by an infant while in the care of a day care facility could not have been attributable to a fall from a high chair: 'And she said it was *impossible*, that was her word, *impossible*[13] for these injuries to result from a short fall based on her experience'.

Witness, defendant and victim identities

In developing opposing positions, lawyers and judges have the power and motivation to construct the identities of witnesses, defendants and victims in competing and often binary ways, drawing on circulating discourses and interpretative frameworks and multimodal means of communication (see Matoesian 2008 with regard to the latter). McKinlay and McVittae (2011: 127) argue that lawyers 'enter the courtroom with a variety of ready-to-hand descriptions of the identities of the people they are going to represent'. This occurs not only in courtroom monologue but also in written petitions (see discussion of Hobbs 2007 later). Devices often employed in this endeavour include, for instance, categorization work, metaphor (Cotterill 2003; Luchjenbroers & Aldridge 2007) nomination and impersonalization, all exercised to index and imbue particular representations of social actors in the service of their argument.

In a critical discourse analysis of defence and prosecution lawyer's closing arguments in five criminal cases, Felton Rosulek (2009) explores the systematic oppositional framing of individuals via 'frequency of reference' and terms of reference. A quantitative and qualitative analysis showed that prosecution lawyers referred to witnesses, defendants and victims in their closing arguments whereas defence lawyers were found to 'silence or background' (p. 9) individuals if reference to them undermined their case. Terms of reference differed markedly: defence lawyers personalized their client using formal or semi-formal nominations, for example, addressing them by their full name or title and surname, whereas prosecution lawyers avoided personalization, making reference to defendants by means of functionalization, for example 'the defendant'. In contrast, prosecution lawyers referred to the victim using nomination, thereby humanizing the victim for the jury in the same way that the defence attempted to 'humanize' their client. The study demonstrates how terms of reference may be used rhetorically to index particular social identities and roles, thereby activating particular mental schemas and associated ideologies in the minds of the jurors or judge, serving to promote the strategic goals of the lawyer.

Hobbs (2007, cited in Felton Rosulek 2010: 128) similarly details how lawyers working on behalf of the US government, and lawyers working for detainees imprisoned in Guantanamo Bay since the 2001 conflict in Afghanistan, differently construct the identities of those detained in order to argue for prolonged detention or the right to legal process. This is achieved partly through selective categorization practices, for example, the government lawyers depicted the detainees negatively as 'war criminals' and 'enemy aliens', whereas the lawyers working on behalf of the detainees referred to them positively as 'citizens of our closest allies' and as victims 'without legal process'.

Categorization work is further explored by Titus (2010) in his consideration of how offender identities may be ascribed in courtroom discourse in order to morally validate the sentence given. Through conversation analysis, Titus illustrates how membership categories[14] of 'paedophile' and 'sexual predator' are activated and 'reconstructed with monster status' (p. 1) by the district attorney and judge in opposition to the category of 'youthful offender' (p. 13) ascribed by the expert witness in the case of a juvenile sex offender. The case hinged on whether or not the youth should be classified as able to be rehabilitated or not. By rejecting the attributes of a youthful sex offender and therefore unlikely to reoffend following rehabilitation, and making salient the attributes of a predatory paedophile likely to relapse, the judge justifies his decision to sentence the individual to an eight-year term of imprisonment.

A large area of forensic linguistic research focuses on vulnerable actors (as illustrated above) and the disadvantages which may be experienced by them when subject to the legal system, particularly the adversarial system (Aldridge 2010). Cases involving children, the disabled, asylum seekers and minority group members have been discussed throughout the research literature. Underpinning these discussions is an acknowledgement that many of these individuals are linguistically/communicatively disadvantaged and/or disadvantaged by stereotypical attitudes/ignorance prevailing within societies, and by extension within the legal system itself. Such actors often find themselves at the wrong end of the power asymmetry unable to adequately participate or be 'heard' within the legal context. A case in point is the Deaf community (Eades 2010: 183ff) whose first or preferred language is sign language (see Chapter Ten). A lack of understanding surrounding the culture, communication and language of the deaf can and has led to police and judicial malpractice (Castelle 2003; Mather and Mather 2003). Disadvantages meted on numerous other minority groups litter the literature (e.g. see Eades 1994, 1996, 2007, 2008; Findlay et al. 2005 and Walsh's 2008 accounts of the Australian aborigines and Eades 2005; Fraser 2009; Jacquemet 2009 and Patrick's 2010 accounts of language analysis in asylum seeker cases). The latter notwithstanding research has shown that changes to legal practice in relation to some groupings and individuals, such as children (Aldridge 2010), can lead to more successful outcomes, including the empowerment of witnesses and the strength of evidence submitted to court. Deckert (2010), for example, demonstrates how child witnesses in the United States are empowered through forensic interviews to construct and resist the identities ascribed to themselves (e.g. as 'victims') as well as ascriptions given to the perpetrator.

Conclusion

This chapter has considered diverse areas of forensic linguistic research impacting on issues of identity and identification. With an increased movement towards improving evidentiary standards (particularly in the United States in light of the Daubert criteria), we have witnessed increased sophistication in the methods and analyses employed. The field is proving invaluable to legal professionals in many jurisdictions, and most importantly to the lives of those they represent. Controversies and disagreements still abound, however, between researchers and between researchers and legal practitioners – some of whom refuse to admit linguistic testimony in court. However in the short time that the field has existed, it has made a significant contribution to questions of authorship and our understanding of how identity/ies impact(s) on the structure, form and process of legal practice and legal language.

CHAPTER FIVE

Youth Studies

To capture the process of meaning-making, we need to focus on a level of social organisation at which individual and group identities are being co-constructed, and in which we can observe the emergence of symbolic processes that tie individuals to groups, and groups to the social context in which they gain meaning ... one might most profitably think of identity as a process of engagement (and disengagement) – and the study of meaning in sociolinguistic variation is a study of the relation between variation and identity.

ECKERT (2000: 34–35, 41–42)

Introduction

Adolescence is a time in which youths innovate stylistically across multiple modes of self-expression and become sensitive to peer influence as well as larger social and political pressures. It is a significant life stage in which social status and community belonging become acutely salient. Distinctive personas evolve through social engagement as participation is negotiated within and across social communities and contexts. Style becomes a resource for, and symbol of, group identity and once reified gives rise to recognized personae in local contexts as well as identifiable social types (Moore & Podesva 2009: 449).

Recent research on youth language has prioritized the study of youth practices, in particular, repertoires and styles of speaking and writing in context. This work has pointed to the contingency and fluidity of youth style and the value of exploring intersecting identifications across and beyond boundaries via the use of multiple linguistic resources (Kerswill 2013). The focus of this chapter is on the study of 'active' and 'transgressive' acts of identity formation and is seated within a sociocultural linguistic approach to the study of identity/identifications,[1] combining the tenets and approaches of linguistic anthropology (including ethnography, indexicality and language ideology), variationist and interactional sociolinguistics.

We seek to explore how teenagers, predominantly in school and youth group settings in European and American contexts, discursively construct, reproduce and/or challenge their own and/or others' identities. Also how they negotiate, resist and interpellate 'stable' social systems and categories (such as class, ethnicity and gender) in order to index group affiliation/disaffiliation and ideology through the use of variant and multiple linguistic forms. Discussion focuses on how identities are cast or altercast and become jointly produced and transformed within these contexts via shifts in style and indexical markers of stance.

As in Chapter Two therefore, the concept of 'style' provides a useful operating variable in the study of youth identity/identification; it assumes an agentive and relational influence arising through social practice and operating across many linguistic levels – phonology, lexicon, morphosyntax, discourse. It is defined here using the definition of the Half Moon Bay Style Collective as 'a socially meaningful clustering of features within and across linguistic levels and modalities' (Campbell-Kibler et al. 2006, in Moore & Podesva 2009: 448). Although youths are subject to cultural influences, and at times, restrictive ideologies of category membership, they can manipulate and disrupt these through the creative and reflexive appropriation of forms which carry established/routinized social meaning, derived from multiple sources. However, styles only become meaningful in context, when a contrast can be determined within the semiotic space of a community. A style is therefore defined via its distinctiveness (Irvine 2001), and it is the distinctive constructions and negotiations that we are interested to explore. Flexibility in self-expression enables actors to construct novel cultural practices and styles, sometimes, as we'll discuss below, through a process of 'Styling the Other ... us[ing] language to index group affiliations in situations where the acceptability and legitimacy of them doing so is open to question, incontrovertibly guaranteed neither by ties of inheritance, in group socialisation, nor by any other language ideology' (Rampton 1999: 422). Style is therefore a semiotic resource through which identity/ies are constructed via the particularities of personal experience, trajectories and connections with social influences (cultural, economic, historical, political, etc.) and it is a medium through which social categories and language intersect.

Many of the studies reviewed here have been selected due to their prominence in the research literature; however, others serve to illustrate the breadth of contexts and linguistic variables studied. The review is differentiated into geographic areas for convenience of reporting, although the reader will determine that work on both sides of the Atlantic has exposed a multitude of youth styles and identities in response to varying circumstances. Space will only permit a review of a small number of studies; however, the reader is encouraged to consult more recent work on youth language (e.g. research on youth language in multicultural cities and youth language and the media[2]), and work which moves beyond a discussion of style to consider, for example, the impact of complementary schools on 'multicultural, heritage and learner identities' (Creese et al. 2006).

We begin by briefly outlining the framework of 'Community of Practice' (CofP) – a framework appropriated by some of the seminal studies we are about to review in order to represent and understand the social organization of youth groups and the processes of meaning-making which take place within them, including the (co-)construction and contestation of individual style and identity.

From speech community to communities of practice

Research on youth language has predominantly (although not exclusively[3]) focused on the major sites of socialization, that is, school and youth group settings (clubs/neighbourhoods). Some of this work has appropriated the concept of 'CofP' to account for the processes of meaning-making and identity formation by individuals and groups whose engagement in a less than neutral linguistic setting is sufficiently constant and sustained. The framework recognizes the role of individual agents in the construction of meaning through mutual engagement in shared endeavours with others in their community. This mutuality is a source of identity. Through ethnographic observation and analysis of distinct and diverse communities of practice, researchers have been able to identify intra- and intercommunity stylistic variation and the social significance afforded to linguistic structures. They have also been able to explore how individuals negotiate their participation within multiple communities. The examination of local dynamics, individual status (e.g. core or peripheral member status) and what people are 'doing' is the starting point for these studies, with extensive and intensive attention to the practices of the 'natives' before any generalizations about the 'group' are drawn. A focus on local 'practice' therefore marks this framework out as distinct from the concepts of 'speech community' and/or social networks[4] as appropriated in other research on language variation which have been considered as inadequate in explaining the association between broad social categories (such as class, ethnicity, gender) and meaning construction by agents in situated engaged language practice (Eckert and McConnell-Ginet 1992: 464). Through the study of meaning construction in local contexts, an association between the individual, group and broader social categories/ structures can be analysed. Linguistic performance can be interpreted as a function of this association (Eckert 2006).

CofP was first developed by Lave and Wenger (1991) in support of a social theory of learning incorporating the components of 'meaning', 'practice', 'community' and 'identity': 'a way of talking about how learning changes who we are and creates personal histories of becoming in the context of our communities' (Wenger 1998: 5). It was introduced into sociolinguistic investigation by Eckert and McConnell-Ginet (1992: 464) in their study of language and gender. Drawing on the work of Lave and Wenger, these researchers define it as:

> An aggregate of people who come together around mutual engagement in an endeavor. Ways of doing things, ways of talking, beliefs, values, power relations in short, practices emerge in the course of this mutual endeavour. As a social construct, a CofP is different from the traditional community, primarily because it is defined simultaneously by its membership and by the practice in which that membership engages.

Three salient characteristics denote a CofP therefore: 'mutual engagement', participation in 'a joint negotiated enterprise' and 'a shared repertoire of negotiable resources accumulated over time' (Wenger 1998: 76). Salient indices include, among others:

- 'sustained mutual relationships – harmonious or conflictual'
- 'shared ways of engaging in doing things together'
- 'substantial overlap in participants' descriptions of who belongs'
- 'mutually defining identities'
- 'certain styles recognised as displaying membership'
- 'specific tools, representations and other artifacts'
- 'local lore, shared stories, inside jokes, knowing laughter'
- 'a shared discourse reflecting a certain perspective on the world'

(Wenger 1998: 125–126)

Linguistic research appropriating this framework focuses on the importance of contact and participant status (incorporating a consideration of belonging and the ability of the individual to effect change and shape meanings within the community) and focuses first at a local level on how language may be used to mark group affiliation and/or distinction as illustrated in the studies below.

Youth studies in Canada and the United States

Eckert's (1989, 2000) ethnographic study of white adolescents at 'Belton High', a high school in the suburbs of Detroit, United States, and her description of two CofPs within that school – the 'jocks' and the 'burnouts' – drew the Labovian-filtered sociolinguistic lens away from a focus on determining large-scale statistical tendencies of speakers of different social and regional dialects, to a focus on the linguistic repertoires and practices of individuals in local communities of practice, thus moving from a structural to an ethnographic, agentive and practice-based model of variation.[5] Her aim was to examine social order within the school context and to determine the boundaries of local ('native') categories through the practices that make variation in speaker style meaningful for category differentiation by participants. Rather than assuming associations *a priori*, 'bottom-up' observation enabled her to link patterns of variation to macro sociopolitical and sociocultural influences such as class, gender, locality and linguistic markets and the interactions that prevailed between them. She illustrated how linguistic variables carry interactional meaning and are employed creatively and fluidly as individual stylistic resources and markers of identity in CofPs. Meaning was derived from the close study of interaction, and for the interactants, from ideological bases – in particular, knowledge and perceptions about the activities, lifestyles and personae of people who participate in particular places and inhabit particular geographic and social spaces.

The distinctive styles of the jocks and burnouts are discussed. These styles are recognized as class-based cultural resources expressing different alignments with respect to the institution of the school, the local community and personal trajectories. Moreover, these alternative styles and CofPs mark different ways of 'being' male or female – that is, as a male or female jock or burnout. The jocks are described as 'an institutional, [middle class] corporate culture; while the burnouts are a [working-class] personal, locally oriented culture' (p. 3) – the former aspiring to a college education away from the local area and the latter seeking employment in the local area. They 'utilise just about every resource in and out of the school to construct their mutual opposition: space, movement, demeanor, adornment, participation, consumption, human relations' (Eckert 2000: 140–141).

Eckert's ethnographic approach, which involved milling around hallways, cafeterias and the environs of the school, observing and interacting with students during free periods and after school, enabled her to provide a rich analysis of students' own perspectives of their place in their social order and subjectivities in relation to the local and global context. Her analysis demonstrates how linguistic variables are indices of practice rather than necessarily category membership (such as class or gender) and therefore how social meaning in variation can relate to interactions between different and multiple social variants. Those who engage in similar practices act in similar ways (e.g. language, dress, gesture, use of space) and are able to recognize and use their distinctive practices as markers of affiliative and oppositional stances.

Eckert's analytic foci included six vocalic variables (the mid and low vowels participating in the Northern Cities Vowel Shift[6] and the backing and raising of the nucleus of /ay/[7]) and one syntactic variable – negative concord. She found that these variables patterned differently across gender and style categories, as shown in Figure 5.1.

Burnout girls led in the realization of five of the phonetic variables and were also 'runners up' (Eckert 2008: 458) in the remaining two variables. The burnouts (boys and girls) were ahead in their use of newer variants associated with the urban setting, 'embedding a linguistic opposition between city and suburb within a community to support a local opposition between urban- and school-oriented kids' (2008: 458). This style contrasted with the jocks who adopted a 'preppy' speech style. However, both jock and burnout girls used the older, now stable suburban phonetic features of the shift marking a gender distinction. Eckert was at pains to assert, however, that use of these forms did not simply index a claim to gender or urban/suburban identity; rather, it indexed an affiliation with lifestyle and character traits. Detroit, she claimed, was marked by segregation and predominantly populated by African Americans. White kids who survived in this urban setting were perceived as 'autonomous, tough, and street-smart' (2008: 459). The use of the urban linguistic variables by suburban adolescents marked an alignment to these traits.

Further subdivisions within the jock and burnout groupings were identified. In particular, the burnout girls clustered into two further networks

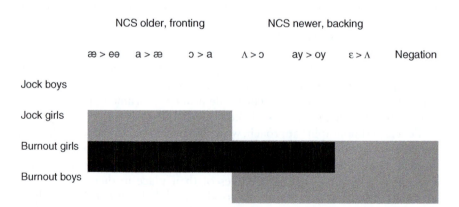

FIGURE 5.1 *Use of Detroit variables involved in the Northern Cities Shift (NCS) by gender and social category. Black = greatest use, gray = second greatest use (derived from Eckert 2008: 459).*

of the 'burned out burnout girls', who were 'wilder, more alienated, and more urban-oriented' (2008: 459) and the 'regular' burnouts. As predicted perhaps (based on Eckert's previous conclusion), the burned out burnout girls exceeded all others, boys and girls, jocks and regular burnouts, in their use of the urban phonetic and syntactic variables.

Overall, Eckert's findings illustrate that the use of particular linguistic features does not neatly correlate to some pre-specified social category or location but can represent a construction and (dis)alignment to the traits or qualities of speakers who are positioned socially and geographically in ideological space. This positioning renders the traditional decontextualized and non-practice-based correlations using static demographic categories unstable, and points to the importance of ethnographic approaches for the study of the local construction of meaning-making and the indexical value of linguistic variables for individuals and communities occupying distinct ideological spaces. A focus on CofP also contributes to an understanding of the social order and the acquisition and maintenance of linguistic features for the (indirect) signalling and recognition of category membership.

The language of 'white kids' was also prioritized in the work of Mary Bucholtz (1999a, 2011) who, like Eckert, carried out extensive ethnographic fieldwork in 'Bay City High School' in the United States in the mid-1990s. She explored how white minority teenagers exposed to multiracial influences at school positioned themselves stylistically and racially in relation to their peers through linguistic and other semiotic resources. A multitude of linguistic styles were identified marking alignment with specific racial groups and positioning within a landscape in which white status was less valued. The salience of racial identity within the United States is made evident in this work, not only through the analysis of individual language performance but also through the way in which students discussed issues of race.[8]

Bucholtz determined that the styles adopted by the European American youths reflected and reproduced an orientation to hip-hop.[9] Three styles were identified and examined: 'cool,[10] nonmainstream hip-hop'; 'cool, mainstream preppy style' and 'uncool, mainstream nerdy style' (2011: 43). Unlike the jocks and burnouts, no single white style was determined as dominant and there was greater fluidity in group boundaries. Through an examination of various linguistic features (e.g. quotatives, labels, slang, grammar), Bucholtz illustrated the complexity of 'whiteness' and the proliferation of stylistic repertoires, realized by the coordination of multiple linguistic features in addition to dress and social geography. A 'cool' youth style (in opposition to a 'nerdy' style) could be constructed in speaking and writing by an alignment to local African American culture marked by the co-occurrence of slang[11] and non-standard grammatical forms appropriated from African American Vernacular English (AAVE). An utterance such as 'haven't seen ya for *hella* long' (Bucholtz 2011: 71) is typical of such realizations distinctively marked by the slang quantifier and intensifier 'hella' ('hell of'), in combination with non-standard second person 'ya'.

The use of such forms served to re-indexicalize their meaning. As did the appropriation of the slang term 'nigga', which, while drawing on racial stereotypes and discourses, attempted to subvert its racial association by marking a 'laid-back' cool stance (p. 75).[12] Such realizations were avoided by the 'nerdy' students who deliberately rejected non-standard forms, instead using 'super-standard English' (p. 150), that is, formal phonology; lexicon, grammar and playful/humorous use of language, in their display of intelligence. Through such analyses and descriptions, Bucholtz illustrates how 'cool' versus 'non-cool' identity is founded on stylistic associations between race and class.

Preferences were also noted in the use of certain linguistic features, for example, quotatives and hip-hop. Quotatives were noted to be liberally used by preppy girls in the school as an important stance-taking resource and also utilized by non-preppy girls to mark negative stance. A 'bricolage' (Eckert 2002) of hip-hop features were employed to denote a 'cool' masculine status,[13] realized through the selective and non-fluent realization of AAVE variables (e.g. slang, address terms; basic phonological and grammatical forms). However, Bucholtz (2004, 2011) stresses that stylistic preferences do not mark gender differentiation but rather difference in orientation to 'youth-cultural style' (2004: 131). A case study (2004) of two Laotian girls revealed how they differently negotiate their identities at school – one appropriating a 'nerdy style' and negatively orientating to AAVE and slang, while the other displayed a 'cool' identity via a positive alignment with AAVE and slang.

With a similar practice-based and school-oriented focus, Mendoza-Denton's (1997, 2008) study of bilingual (English/Spanish) Latino gangs (the Norteño and Sureño gangs) explores how rival groups can be linguistically differentiated along multiple levels. Her investigation of code-switching lends further credence to the study of micro-interactional data and how such data invokes macro-ideological stances/ideologies. The youths under investigation appropriated the 'voice(s)' of adults/out-group members in order to shift footing and mark alignments/stances towards their interlocutors, story characters and the subject matter of the conversation. 'Revoicing' enabled them to index the linguistic repertoire, social personae and values of the characters they invoked and thereby position themselves ideologically with respect to the subject under discussion. This is illustrated in the excerpt below, in which two Spanish-English bilingual girls engage in a conversation about marriage:

1 Christy: My parents said that if I got married to a guy and he treated
me bad,

2   me pagaba o alga,
          if he hit me or something

3   that I couldn't go back home . . .

4 Pilar: You know, I mean,

5   if you make a mistake, what –

6   you're going to have to pay for your mistake?

7   I don't believe that, you know,

8   if you got married,

9   and your husband is beating you,

10   I'm sorry but leave him!

11   I mean, **nomás pore no estar pecando** or whatever, how can you . . .

     just so you won't be in sin

12   Cristy: **O nomás porque,** you know,

     Or just because, you know,

     porque tus padres te enseñaron a seguir eso . . .

     your parents taught you to follow that . . .

13   doesn't mean **que te tienes que estar ahí.**

     that you have to stay.

             (Mendoza-Denton and Osborne 2010: 118)

Both girls switch between English and Spanish in their discussion of marital fidelity. In positioning herself in opposition to the stance of her parents, Pilar, in line 11, invokes a parental/mature Spanish 'voice', marked through exaggerated intonation in order to overtly index the stances of both her parents and the traditional Catholic Church with respect to the sanctity of marriage ('for better or worse'). The girls' opposition to this creed under the circumstances of marital abuse is overtly stressed through their use of English rhetorical questions ('you're going to have to pay for your mistake?'), assertive statements of cognition ('I don't believe') and directives realized as exclamations 'I'm sorry, but leave him!'. We therefore see how voicing 'the other' (enacted and marked via code-switching) serves to link the micro-interactional, meso (parental ideology) and macro (religious ideology) levels of meaning.

Therefore, distinctive codes can be invoked in conversation to enact particular stances and reference larger systems of evaluation or judgement. They construct and index identities which in turn delineate group boundaries, a phenomenon similarly determined by Bailey (2001) who documented the linguistic versatility of second-generation Dominican-Americans, residing in Providence, Rhode Island. Dominican Americans are 'Hispanic, American and largely of African descent' (p. 190) and are competent in multiple varieties of English and Spanish, including Standard and Vernacular Dominican Spanish and English, AAVE and hybrid forms. These are appropriated in their production of and resistance to ethnic and racial boundaries, as illustrated in the excerpt below (Bailey 2001: 195–196):

Two girls, Isabella and Janelle, are chatting in high school after lunch. Isabella ate at a nearby diner and is describing the sandwich she ate:

J: Only with that turkey thingee //*ya yo (es)toy llena.*

"I'm already full"

I: //Two dollars and fifty cent.

J: That's good. That's like a meal at //Burger King

// That's better than going to Burger

King, you know what I'm saying?

. . . .

I: //But it's slamming, though, oh my God, mad ["a lot of"] turkey she puts in there

We witness how Dominican American youth identity is constructed via a combination of codes (Spanish, English and AAVE) into a distinct Dominican American repertoire. However, Bailey also reports on the selective use of codes by Dominican Americans in order to construct particular alignments and identities. He describes 'three nested levels' (2001: 192) of boundary marking as Dominican Americans are able to:

1. construct 'non-white' identities and establish solidarity with other non-white (low-income and minority) groupings, through the use of AAVE and the mocking use of white English varieties;

2. perform a 'non-Black' Dominican identity through the use of Spanish, thereby creating a boundary between themselves and others of African descent and an identification with a 'Dominican-American' ethnolinguistic ascription; and

3. mark intra-group boundaries between those Dominican-Americans born in the United States and more recent immigrants from the Dominican Republic.

Such 'hybrid or syncretic repertoire(s)' (Bailey 2000: 560) serve to challenge and renegotiate established ethnic and racial categories in America.

This is further illustrated in a separate case study of one Dominican American boy, Wilson (Bailey 2000). Wilson and his peers subvert the established 'phenotypically based' black/white dichotomy of racial categorization by defining his racial identity in terms of language. Through the study of peer interaction in one class period at Wilson's high school, Bailey illustrates how ethnic/racial identity was momentarily constructed and performed in the turn-by-turn talk of peers and how alignments to different social categories were established situationally. The use of Spanish determined that Wilson was 'Spanish' and 'Dominican'. At the same time, although not defining himself as 'black', Wilson and his peers appropriated AAVE, aligning with the low-economic and political status of African Americans and therefore making this relevant to their social identity. Their language use therefore invoked and disrupted larger static racial categories (i.e. black versus white) often imposed by circulating master narratives[14] about racial identity in America.

Rather than challenging dominant discourses, we see how an alignment to them can be achieved, if desired, by subjects encountering new fields of action. We see this in a study of French-speaking immigrants and refugees from continental Africa acculturating to Canadian society and having to learn English as an L2. Ibrahim (1999) documents the experiences of African youths who on entering high school in Ontario found themselves already positioned within a *social imaginary* (p. 349) of African American black identity and culture, despite the fact that such identification did not align with their domestic discourse or self-concept. The way in which they were positioned and treated influenced who the students associated with and the language and culture they adopted. As a consequence, black American English and hip-hop formed part of their stylization. They assimilated these consciously as part of their 'embodied subjectivi(ty)' (p. 350) and belonging via exposure to sites of popular culture (e.g. TV programmes, music videos, films). It was through their exposure to and active learning of black English that the youths developed and performed a black American identity.

Crossing (Rampton 1995, see below) into a nontraditional code consistently can bestow the language user with capital (including discursive resources), as previously highlighted in the studies above and reinforced in the work of Alim (2009), Chun (2009) and Igoudin (2013) (as discussed below). However, the nature of that 'capital' and its sphere of influence can differ. In an account of the linguistic repertoires of Asian and American girls in a high school in the United States, Igoudin (2013) illustrates how the girls only employed AAVE in order to advance themselves within their peer group in order to gain popularity, switching to Standard American English, for example, when with teachers. Their appropriation of AAVE was argued not to mark a 'proto-political' stance towards broader racial hierarchies or ideologies but rather to index a strategic choice which was motivated by personal advancement.

In another study of Asian American youth identities in a high school in Texas, Chun (2009) focused on the relationship between immigrant and non-immigrant identities. She explored how fluent English-speaking Filipino and Korean American students 'revoiced' stereotypical linguistic forms associated with Asian immigrants in order to perform oppositional rhetorical acts – accommodation and mocking – and thereby position themselves in alignment or disalignment to others in the cultural market of the school, construing similarity and/or difference.

Studies in the UK

We have seen in the studies above how identification gives rise to active and transgressive modes of linguistic performance, particularly in multi-ethnic contexts and this is further evidenced in the work of Rampton (1995) who first introduced the term 'crossing' into the linguistic lexicon to describe the way in which adolescents used linguistic forms more usually associated with ethnic or social groups to which they did not belong, to strategically mark a local group identity and resistance to adult authority. His focus was on the multiracial recreational activities of a school and youth club in the urban setting of the South Midlands of the UK. The activity of crossing enabled the teenagers he studied to traverse ethnic boundaries, to strategically position themselves interactionally and construct heterogeneous identifications.

Rampton documents examples of Panjabi used by speakers of Anglo and Afro-Caribbean descent; Creole by Anglos and Panjabis and stylized Asian English (SAE) by all three groups. However, each of these varieties were reported to index class and race differences and stereotypical linguistic/trait associations – SAE, for example, connoting 'linguistic incompetence and deference'; Creole 'toughness, quick wittedness and opposition to authority' (p. 56); while Panjabi was noted to be less easy to stereotype due to its interracial use.

Despite the stereotypical associations listed above, SAE crossing was reported to be used mostly by those experiencing difficult relationships with adults in authority and therefore appropriated to mark an oppositional disrespectful stance. The object of the oppositional stance could not be definitively determined – it could have been a reaction to the interlocutor, an act to rile against the institution that positioned the adult in authority, the value-laden framework of the institution and society that placed white above Asian or possibly all three. What was determined however was that SAE was used by those in subordinate positions to mark nonconformity. Crossing into Panjabi, in contrast, was noted to be used mostly with peers rather than with adults and often used for provocation. Linguistic competence in Panjabi by black and white speakers was limited to a lexicon of approximately twenty to thirty words and phrases – its use symbolic rather than predominantly communicative. Crossing into Creole took on a very different status to SAE or Panjabi, used in both peer and adult interaction to exercise power and support positive evaluations. It was also said to be much more closely tied to class and youth identity.

Speakers were sensitive to their legitimacy in invoking specific codes and negotiated this throughout interactions. Non-black speakers tended to avoid crossing into Creole with Afro-Caribbeans in order not to be considered 'pretentious' in their language use. While many also avoided using SAE with Panjabis in order not to insult Asian speakers. These sensitivities underline a recognition of ethnic boundaries; nevertheless the act of 'crossing' into and out of different codes, Rampton (1995: 297) argues, involves the development of 'new ethnicities ... the construction of a politics' which (drawing on the words of Hall 1988: 28; also see Chapter One) 'works with and through difference, which is able to build those forms of solidarity and identification which make common struggle and resistance possible but without suppressing the real heterogeneity of interests and identities'.

With a different emphasis – a focus on vowel change in the East End of London – Fox (2007, 2010) explores the role of religion, ethnicity and friendship networks on language use among working-class Bangladeshi, white and mixed-race adolescents. In 2010, she reported on findings elicited from extensive ethnographic observation and interviews carried out in a youth club in the Tower Hamlets area of London, in which she identified variation in the pronunciation of the PRICE and FACE vowels by male Bangladeshi youths, determining that the social practices of these youths (including their orientation to academic, cultural, friendship, kinship and religious matters) influenced their language use.

The younger boys in her study (aged 12–14) were reported to socialize among themselves at the youth club and attend schools predominantly populated by other Bangladeshi and Muslim children. They were also quite strongly oriented to academia and maintained strong religious ties. In contrast, the older boys (aged 15–17) were noted to engage in more mixed friendship groups within and outside of the youth club setting – many also participating in 'street subculture' (p. 153) and gangs, including antisocial and illegal behaviour. Some had left school and were now unemployed, mixing with other white youths in the same predicament. Similarities in social practices were found to correlate with the articulation of phonetic variants. In their articulation of PRICE, the older Bangladeshi and white boys used the centralized [ɐɪ] variant the most frequently, followed by the fronter [ɑɪ] and [æ] variants. These phonetic realizations differed from those most associated with vernacular Cockney English – [a:]. A similar pattern was found in the articulation of the FACE variable.

In further dividing the informants into individuals with a strong or weak Muslim identity (determined by their activities and self-report), Fox found the [ɐɪ] variant to index weak Muslim identity; however, she concludes that rather than marking religious affiliation per se, this variable indexed an association 'with a group of people who engage in social practices related to street culture, regardless of their ethnic background' (p. 154). This is a conclusion reminiscent of Eckert, in which a direct correlation between social category and language use would appear to be simplistic and possibly fallacious. Rather, as Fox concluded, an indirect association may be determined in which alignment to a particular lifestyle and social network (even community/ities of practice) may be a clearer marker of language preference.[15]

Such a conclusion is similarly drawn by Emma Moore who undertook a long-term ethnographic study of forty girls (aged between 12 and 15 years) in a high school, 'Midlan High', in Bolton, north-west England (2003, 2004). Her study documented the gradual differentiation of social groups within the school which manipulated both distinct and similar stylistic variables in the construction of their sociolinguistic identities. Like Eckert, Moore spent time with the girls outside of the classroom at lunchtimes, hanging around with them as they ate lunch, participated in dance practice and congregated in the environs of the school yard. Her recordings were informal and mainly focused on the activities and interests of the girls.

Two distinctive CofPs are documented as becoming particularly salient as the girls reached 14–15 years of age: the *Populars*, a group of girls who engaged in some school activities such as dance and talent shows and also less conformist activities, such as smoking (in and out of school) and drinking alcohol; and the *Townies*, a more extreme and rebellious version of the *Populars* who practiced drug-taking and sexual activity. They engaged less with school and enjoyed greater contact with the local community, frequenting local parks and streets. Although these girls once mixed more readily with one another when they were younger and all tended more towards an 'anti-school' stance, the division between them became marked as their social practices and preferences diverged. This became evident in their language use too, particularly in their realization of three linguistic variables: non-standard *were*, tag questions and negative concord. While there was not an exclusive use of any of these variables by any CofP, tendencies were identified, with the Townie girls realizing a greater proportion of non-standard forms from the local area, in particular, negative concord and non-standard *were*. Moore determined that this arose as a consequence of their greater integration in the local community in comparison with the Populars. The Populars were also exposed to these forms in and outside of school; however, they tended to use them to a lesser extent due to their greater alignment with school culture. Populars were found to use a higher proportion of tag questions, which indexed their engagement beyond the institution of the school. However these were subject to less stigmatization since they were not vernacular/local features.

Interestingly, the two CofPs continued to negotiate their distinction from one another via the stances they took towards these shared variables. For example, in the case of the non-standard 'weren't' tag (e.g. 'It were that new t-shirt, *weren't it*?' 2004: 391), as the Populars began to expand its usage within their linguistic repertoires, the Townies began to avoid it, recognizing this as a feature now denoting 'Popular' style. The same linguistic features therefore marked fluid social meaning. These were employed differently in the repertoires of the two CofPs. Moore concludes, 'When the Popular girls use nonstandard *weren't* tags, they don't simply borrow a Townie variant, but manipulate their use of the nonstandard *were* in such a way that they absorb the variant into their own linguistic style … when the Townie girls reject the use of nonstandard *weren't* tags, they are not rejecting a Townie variant, but simply reconstructing their use of nonstandard *were* in order to signal their difference from the Popular CofP in a context where group identity is at stake' (2004: 392–393).

The use of tags by four of the CofPs identified by Moore in her larger study is further detailed in Moore and Podesva (2009). Two of the CofPs included the Townies and Populars (as described above), the other two were comparatively more school-orientated; these included the 'Geeks', who are described as engaging in activities such as orchestra and sport and maintain friendships largely through networks within school (including platonic friendships with boys). They are also described as having a 'practical approach to their appearance' (p. 455). The other CofP, the 'Eden Village', is described as adopting a 'trendy "teen" style' and spending their free time in all-girl friendship groups, dancing, shopping or staying over at each other's houses (p. 455). The study affords a stylistic analysis of the stances and characteristics of CofP members, marked through their use of tags in conversation. Three different identity frames are identified as being indexed through the use of this feature: 'micro-social stances [e.g. rebelliousness]; macro-social types [e.g. working class] [and/"via"] meso-social personae [e.g. Townie]' (p. 453). The authors report on both quantitative and qualitative analyses of the amount and type of tags used by each CofP, including a consideration of topic/content, phonetic and grammatical positioning. For example, Townie's prototypical tags were used in conversations about themselves as a group. They realized *he* in subject position more frequently than others and adopted non-standard grammar (e.g. *h*-dropping and *t*-deletion). In contrast, Popular tag use occurred in self-reference to their own group, mainly with the second-person inclusive *we* pronoun and third-person feminine *she* in subject position, with slightly less non-standard grammar in comparison to the Townies.

Drawing on Silverstein's (2003) model of indexicality (see Chapter Two) and Eckert's (2008a) indexical field analysis, the authors determine that tag questions mark group personae and CofP identity through the repetitive marking of stance. As depicted in the diagram below, tags function to construct: the Eden Village girls as polite, collaborative and friendly; the Geeks as intelligent and authoritative; the Popular girls as critical and 'cool' (a trait which they also share with the Townie girls, as denoted by the dotted line) and the Townies as independent and experienced. Connections between tags and macro-category level identities are also indicated in the figure via the italicized words *female* and *working class*. The Eden Village girls' use of tags aligns quite directly with the dominant representation of a feminine speech style; whereas, the Townie's appropriation aligns with a working-class social category. However as the authors point out, an association between these larger category identities can only be made by

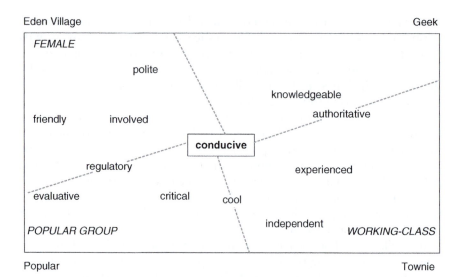

Eden Village   Geek

Popular   Townie

FIGURE 5.2 *Indexical field for tag questions at Midlan High (appropriated from Moore & Podesva 2009: 478).*

the person interpreting the behaviour, assuming that they share the same ideology concerning social status, in the same way that any hearer may interpret a tag uniquely or synchronously as, for example, polite, regulatory or distinctively feminine (Johnstone & Kiesling 2008; see Chapter Two). The indexical field therefore carries social meanings at different conceptual levels (micro/meso/macro) and these may be resonant in unison or singly depending on the interpretation afforded.[16]

Other European contexts

In this final section, we explore research on youth language and identity in other European contexts, in particular, studies undertaken in schools and youth clubs in Belgium, France, Germany and Spain. Some of these studies (as Rampton, Bailey and Fox, see above) are illustrative of contemporary interest in the effect of language contact between and within 'immigrant' and indigenous groups in inner-city and suburban multicultural and multi-ethnic contexts, and the impact that globalization and transnationalism has had on their speech repertoires, styling practices and identities within their local contexts (see also, among others, Appel & Schoonen 2005; chapters in Androutsopoulos & Georgakopoulou 2003; Blommaert 2010; Heller 1999; Quist 2008).

In his exploration of the linguistic practices of Moroccan-Flemish students in a secondary school in Antwerp, Belgium, Jaspers (2008, 2011) critiques the analytic category of 'ethnolect',[17] arguing instead that the linguistic practices of the youths he studied are less an attribute of their heritage and ethnicity and more a feature of reflexive and conscious stylization. His study focused on their exploitation of a repertoire of linguistic varieties employed to subvert and reproduce the linguistic and social hierarchy for rhetorical and playful affect. The students were described as highly competent multilinguals in standard and vernacular Arabic, Berber, Dutch as well as English, French and Spanish. They prided themselves on their linguistic prowess, especially in contrast to 'illegals' (a blanket term derived from 'illegal refugees'), a category encompassing a variety of referents, for example, 'recent immigrants, political refugees, older immigrants … East European guest workers' who are renowned for their use of 'illegal Dutch' (Jaspers 2008: 95), a variety that belies their 'non-native' status. The Moroccan-Flemish students were reported to often stylize 'illegal Dutch' overtly appropriating and strategically employing the variety used by these comparatively marginalized and less fluent individuals in conversation among themselves and in mocking interactions with their Turkish peers in class, and with unfamiliar white adults, with whom they wished to provoke a negative response towards their supposedly poor command of standard Dutch. Once again in reviewing this work, we witness how the study of local stylistic practices and the social meanings attached to specific linguistic codes/features inform our understanding of the linguistic creativity of youths and their agency in reproducing and subverting broader social and political ideologies. Through their stylistic acts, we also see how they enact group solidarity and (dis)affiliation.

The latter is also demonstrated in a study of insulting address forms, as discussed by Günther (2013) in her account of solidarity marking among migrant youths in Germany. Focusing her discussion on the impact of 'transmigration'[18] on the disruption of social and political structures (such as national belonging/languages), Günther illustrates how language contact brought about through globalization has led to more fluid and heterogeneous linguistic codes, collective identities and CofPs. Moreover, as highlighted in the studies above, she emphasizes the importance of honing in on local contexts and activities to explore member's interpretations of identities and social relationships, including such demographic categories as class, ethnicity, gender, etc. Data was collected in youth centres in Germany over a five-year period and the focus of analysis was the stylistic appropriation of insulting address forms, particularly in Turkish. These, Günther notes, were used in the negotiation of status and hierarchy within the group as a subcultural resource shared by migrants and predominantly employed to construct a masculine persona and 'we-code' among members, invoking an aggressive, dominant and yet cool stance (p. 19).

Agency in linguistic style is also discussed by Corona et al. (2013) in their account of 'the emergence of new linguistic repertoires among Barcelona's youth of Latin American origin'. Through an ethnographic study of the language practices of Latin American adolescents (originating from different geographic regions in Latin America) in two secondary schools in Barcelona, they sought to determine the impact of peer socialization on the development of multilingual repertoires and how these youths reformed and adapted the indigenous varieties of 'Catalonia's Castilian' and Catalan, in addition to their own Latin American varieties of Spanish, in order to develop a collective identity. They argued that this reconfigured code, which drew on similarities between the different varieties, was motivated by a need to develop altered identities within their new territory of belonging. Their performance was described as a 'translinguistic Latino repertoire' (p. 186). The study contributes to current interest in exploring new hybrid patterns of language variation and identity performance (including the consideration of 'translanguaging') in multilingual, multicultural settings, and the integration of 'global' practices in 'local' spaces of interaction due to mobility (Blommaert 2010; Creese & Blackledge 2010; García & Li Wei 2011; Hornberger & Link 2012; Li Wei 2011). It also contests the notion of 'speech community' exploring instead how a global community of practice is constructed via the development and exploitation of 'shared transnational[/translocal] repertoires' (p. 191). As an illustration, we see below an extract of a conversation between a 16-year-old Bolivian boy, Oscar (OSC), and the researcher Manuel (MAN), undertaken in the playground at school. Oscar exploits the use of various linguistic features assimilated from different varieties of American Spanish and some words from Catalan. Ecuadorian is indicated in **bold**, Caribbean in *italics*, Peruvian via <u>underlining</u>, peninsular Castilian in ***bold italics*** and Catalan is in Courier New Style:

13. MAN: por qué te expulsaron?| ósca:r_ (1.8)

  why did they expel you?| Osca-.r (1.8)

14. OSC: le quité el balón a **un man_** (1.1)

  I took the ball from a guy (1.1)

15. y luego_él tam_o sea_ que_a jugar en la pista vino ***cogió el balón*** (.)

  and then_he al_ well_ to play on the pitch he came he took the ball\ (.)

16. le dije- ***tío déjamelo*** (.)

  I told him- man give it to me (.)

17. MAN: aja\ (.)

  uh huh (.)

18. OSC: él no quiso me empujó y de allí yo lo empujé_ me dio un <u>puñete</u>\ (.)

  he didn't want to he pushed me and then I pushed him_ he punched me\ (.)

19. he metí uno en la cara (0.2)

   I punched him in the face (0.2)

20. *(laughter)*

21. OSC: le metí en la cara y se fue\ y como el padre estaba ahí\ (.)

   I punched him in the face and he went off\ and since his father was there (.)

22. vino acquí y **se chivó** al cap d'estudis\ (.)

   he came here and he snitched to the head teacher (.)

   . . .

In combining features from different varieties of Latin American, Oscar performs the identity of a '"Latino in Barcelona"' (p. 187). This is achieved phonologically and lexically, for example, there is no articulation of [θ], realization of aspirated [s]; [r] and [l] are noted to be assimilated at the end of a word and 'in the consonant group', thereby crossing into and constructing a Caribbean accent; words are derived from different varieties with a number derived from 'peninsular words' which provide the resonance of a working-class status. His performance obscures a connection with any particular national group (Bolivian, Catalan, Dominican or Spanish), instead marking an identification with a global community of Latinos. This speech repertoire is used with peers and teachers and is complemented by a command of other repertoires too, such as Catalan (learned at school) and Castilian (used in their neighbourhoods.)

The authors also document the case of a boy of Pakistani origin, who had recently immigrated to Barcelona and crossed into a Latino accent in class. They report on the teacher's negative response to this and assert that this performance extends to many other students of non-Latino origin who socialize with this group. They argue that the appropriation of 'the Latino repertoire emerges in contexts of transgressive practices (Corona 2012), in which its use obtains a counter-school value' and emerges after a period of socialization and alignment with certain adolescent groups (p. 189).

We complete our discussion of research on youth identity by moving across the national border from Spain to France, picking up on some of the issues discussed above in relation to the manner in which multiethnic working-class youths[19] carve out a 'third space' (Bhabha 1990, 1994) and shared social identity through the appropriation of a distinct linguistic repertoire – in this case, Verlan. Verlan is variety of French marked by syllabic inversion (e.g. 'soirée 'a party', 'an evening' > realized as 'résoi'), borrowings from different languages and prosodic and phonemic variants (Doran 2004: 96–98). It is said to be spoken predominantly by marginal male adolescents and indexes an anti-establishment stance – a tough street mentality with criminal overtones. Doran (2004) undertook a longitudinal ethnographic study and made recordings of a group of youths centred mainly in an after-school tutoring programme in a southerly suburb of Paris – the town of 'Les Salières'. She was particularly interested to explore how a transgressive identity might be enacted in conversation and in combination with other varieties of French.

Her analysis determined that Verlan was indeed just one code embedded in a repertoire of resources available to these youths, which included vernacular and standard French and heritage languages. Verlan is shown to have a distinct position and purpose, employed by these individuals: to construct an in-group identity, to positively mark racial and ethnic boundaries (including a distinction with the ideal 'French'), to negotiate class and cultural difference and to distinguish their culture from other street cultures, especially *la racaille*, a group considered as uneducated and extremely anti-establishment.

As a group language it was depicted as a code for peer interaction, to be used in social spaces which were devoid of adults, and in which one could be creative in one's expression and through which one could show alignment to one's class and value system. Its use was therefore somewhat distinct from *la racaille* who used it in almost all domains and did not accommodate to the demands of the social context or their interlocutor. It was not deliberately used to exclude others, rather to reinforce internal bonds among friends. It was also, however, a code employed to disrupt the hegemonic discourse of a homogeneous (mono-ethnic, monocultural, unilingual) French society and a code used to reject an upper-class, individualistic 'bourgeois' stance. Verlan terms were employed pejoratively to distance the user from *les Français* (e.g. 'the Gauls'/*les Gaulois*; 'white cheeses'/*les fromages blancs*, p. 113) from whom the students felt disaffiliated and rejected. In contrast, the students deliberately orientated to discussions about race and ethnicity, teasing and insulting one another, using Verlan terms (e.g. *feuj* for Jew; *cainf* for African) in a manner that would be deemed unacceptable in mainstream discourse. Doran argued that such acts were legitimated within this group since multiple ethnicities defined their social identity; reworking the terms of reference (such as 'feuj') stripped them of their negative meaning in other contexts, simultaneously therefore subverting the dominant perspective evident in social and political narratives about French identity, while constructing through these acts, and the borrowing of features from each other's languages, a 'self-defined [multiethnic/cultural] identity' (p. 109) for the CofP.[20] Verlan enabled these youths to strategically construct a shared identity, to occupy a 'third space' – situated at variance to the *bourge* at one end of the continuum and the *racaille* at the other.

Conclusion

The focus of this chapter is in line with other contemporary studies of 'youth' as a life stage which pay close attention to the specifics of locality and culture, and the fluidity of social relations, in which semiotic resources (beyond the linguistic e.g. appearance; features of consumption) are employed by the young in a process of stylistic bricolage in the construction of personal and social identity/ies. We have seen how youths are able to challenge their social inheritances and construct identities for themselves, marking out an individual and social space through language choice. Contemporary researchers are intrigued by the manner in which youths appropriate, reproduce and reconstruct linguistic variables from within and outside of their domestic, ethnic, racial, class-based (etc.) communities in order to 'style' themselves into being and position themselves ideologically within a local and global frame of reference. The complexity of these resources has been illustrated in the studies above, and has the fluidity and complexity of identity categories. Young people are, to a degree, agents of their own making, drawing on their personal histories and experiences to project their own and others' social identities/identifications, while subject to community and structural forces. An abundance of linguistic resources is at young people's disposal; what they choose to utilize depends on multiple individual and social factors.

CHAPTER SIX

Workplace/Professional Identities

*Historically discourse research tended to centre around seeking out, analysing and teaching, 'the language of work' associated with becoming a competent, or perhaps a critical, worker. . . . But our work now focuses on discourses that centre around expressing and negotiating being, doing and talking at work **about** work. Such discourses are both reflective and reflexive. They are reflective because they talk about what I do and how I do it. They are reflexive because they put my identity at risk to myself and to others.*

IEDEMA AND SCHEERES (2003: 334)

Introduction

Sociolinguistic interest in workplace interaction began in earnest in the 1980s, emerging from an interest in the role of talk at work to enable goals to be achieved and workplace relationships to become established and maintained. Scholarly interest in the linguistic enactment of transactional and relational goals by leaders and workers, as well as the interaction between experts and lay people entering into institutional/professional domains, became an object of study for many, and their analyses have revealed a complex understanding of diverse workplace settings and linguistic performances in different national and international contexts (see e.g. Bargiela-Chiappini & Harris 1997; Candlin & Sarangi 2011; Clyne 1994; Drew & Heritage 1992; Handford 2010; Holmes et al. 1999; Koester 2011; Sarangi & Roberts 1999 and the proliferation of literature arising from the 'Wellington Language in the Workplace Project' [LWP] in New Zealand).

In recent years, attention has turned towards the discursive enactment of identities at work (e.g. see Angouri & Marra 2011a for a book-length introduction). The aims of this chapter are therefore to review and represent a selection of this research, exploring identity construction and performance in diverse workplace settings (including institutional and professional[1] contexts) and genre. A vast array of theoretical and analytical approaches have been applied to this study, and as will become evident, scholarship in this relatively young field of investigation has applied the tenets and frameworks of varied approaches: ethnography, conversation analysis, corpus linguistics, critical discourse analysis, interactional sociolinguistics, pragmatics, metaphor analysis and narrative analysis, to name but a few.

The sections below discriminate between scholarship that has prioritized different issues: the first two sections consider workplace roles; the third reviews what is now a large area of interest in workplace research, gender studies (Baxter 2010; Holmes 2006; Mullany 2007, 2010) and the final section addresses the increasingly pertinent question of the impact of globalization and 'transnationalism' on workplace identity/ies.

Apprentice, worker and professional/institutional identity

In this section, we consider the discursive enactment and (co-)construction of apprentice, worker and (temporary) professional/institutional identity. In the case of 'temporary' identity/ies, we review research that has explored the performative and sometimes temporary/multiple roles that individuals perform in workplace contexts, such as when acting as 'mentor' in corporate or academic contexts, or as 'expert witness' in a law court. We begin with studies that have mapped the terrain of the apprentice/newcomer as they enter into new communities of workplace practice. As will become evident, researchers have explored different work sites (blue/white collar[2] etc.) and applied different analytic tools to their investigation of worker integration and identity.

As we enter into any new setting, we are often confronted with patterns of behaviour that challenge our sociopragmatic and sociolinguistic frames of reference. In the workplace, integration into a new community of practice[3] can be testing as we are confronted with an established community of professionals. As a novice, we have to acquire the necessary technical expertise along with the concomitant linguistic 'know-how' in order to pass as 'one of the team' and/or be an effective employee. This process of assimilation is played out in multiple work sites. For example, Holmes and Woodhams (2013) report on a detailed case study of Rick, a novice 'blue-collar' apprentice to a construction site, who finds himself not only having to learn about the trade but also the interactional norms of his new workplace in order to progress from peripheral to core status within the builder community. Through an analysis of directives, jargon, small talk and humour, the authors juxtapose Rick's behaviour with that of another, more established intern, Max, who has worked with the same mentor, Tom (the site manager) for two years. Comparing conversations and the reactions by Tom and the other builders to the behaviour of the apprentices, the norms of interaction become evident and the status of Rick as a 'new boy' and Max as an increasingly accepted member of the group becomes salient.

Max are Tom are determined to often 'confirm and echo each other's comments, indicating and co-constructing their relationship as members of a CofP, with extensive shared knowledge, experience and assumptions about "ways of doing things, ways of talking ... in short practices"' (Eckert & McConnell-Ginet 1992: 464; Holmes & Woodhams 2013: 286). Max's steady integration into the community is marked by the ease with which he initiates humour[4] and the way in which his fellow workmen happily tease him. Tom is also noted to readily shift from transactional to relational talk while getting the job done – an unmarked feature of builder interactional skill.

In order to 'fit in' and progress to core status, Rick must acquire these skills and orientate to the practices of his new colleagues – something he does not always manage to achieve. His peripheral status is marked by a number of linguistic and behavioural features. Under Tom's tutelage, he is subject to far more directives and explicit requests than Max and is also the victim of far more criticism by his co-workers about the standard of his work and his attitude towards it. Sometimes, such criticism serves to create solidarity between fellow builders as they discuss their shared stances and values towards the practice of 'being a builder'. Through their acts of criticism Rick is positioned as a novice, on the margins of the group, lacking a recognizable builder identity and therefore easy fodder for their jokes. For example, the workmen criticize him for leaving work early:

Tom: oh young rick

Max: yeah young rick

Tom: fuck, he doesn't have many days
    where he stays here all day does he [. . .]
    doesn't often get through a full day [. . .]

Max: probably got sick of sweeping up in the [laughs]: morn-:
                                    (Holmes & Woodhams 2013: 291).

Through reference to micro (i.e. interactional), meso (i.e. company) and macro (i.e. New Zealand) social values, it becomes evident how norms of behaviour impact on the construction and development of blue-collar worker identity and how deviation from these norms highlights exclusion from community belonging and the construction of an 'inauthentic' identity. Discussion of novice transgressions and explicit instruction by core members of the community serves to police and position young neophytes within the community of practice and reinforce community norms and member identity.

As Max, white-collar workers similarly experience marginalization as they enter into new communities of practice. Richards (2011) provides a detailed account of the difficulties experienced by a new teacher entering into an established group of professionals. Richards uncovers the manner in which the newcomer attempts to establish his competence by making reference to his previous experience and status when confronted by interactional acts of exclusion (e.g. boundaried use of 'we' by other teachers).

In a more explicit examination of the experiences of new teachers' perceptions of their identities over a period of months, Thomas and Beauchamp (2011) report on a study of forty-five new Canadian teachers who were asked to metaphorically describe their professional identity immediately post-graduation and later in their first year of teaching (Tsui 2007[5]). Informants were found to shift from metaphors of preparedness and strength (e.g. 'The offensive line in a football team. The teacher protects the classroom, and the students in the class.' 'A coat hanger: Everything hangs on you and you need to support everything and everyone. If not it fails.' [p. 765]) to metaphors of survival as they ventured from students into the teaching profession (e.g. 'Some days you have really calm waters, you love being out there and there are other people on the ship that really help you out. Other days you feel like you are on that ship all by yourself, the water is rocky and you wonder, "Why am I on this boat? I didn't sign up for this"' [p. 765]). The authors conclude that 'new teachers struggle to develop a professional identity during their first year, and that this development process is gradual, complex and often problematic' (p. 762), and therefore the subject of professional identity for new teachers should be explored in pre-service training programmes (as similarly argued by Tsui 2007) – a suggestion that may be applied to novices in other professions also.

Metaphors prove not only useful analytic tools but also of benefit to the integration and socialization of new members in the workplace. They help to convey the sociopragmatic norms of the community, in addition to member and organizational identity (Kram et al. 2012; McEntee-Atalianis 2011, 2013b), and also aid in the acquisition of workplace skills. This is evident in a detailed case study of a skilled Chinese migrant in a New Zealand accounting firm (Woodhams 2014). Metaphor proves crucial to the mentoring discourse of the team leader, who uses it to convey workplace norms and the identity of the organization. Leo (the mentor) compares the work of his department with that of a 'hospital'. The extension of this source domain permits him to exploit various mappings, including describing himself as a 'nurse', the work of the department as a 'patient' in need of treatment and medication, and his superiors as 'surgeons'. This exploitation of cross-domain mappings permits Leo to emphasize the importance of the work of his department, which he compares to the life-saving work of a hospital, stressing the dependence of others on the skills he is imparting to his intern (Isaac) and the care with which they must mutually work to ensure the survival of their company. Moreover, his use of the ubiquitous JOURNEY metaphor reflects and constructs Isaac's peripheral status and represents the culture of the CofP (which is 'driven' by incoming work, not by higher-ranking officers), as well as the predicted difficulties (e.g. 'obstacles') that the intern may encounter as he acculturates to the processes and systems of his new work setting. Metaphor becomes a teaching tool and the linguistic realization of a discursive, rhetorical strategy to bestow the organization and employees with a recognizable status and role. Becoming part of the CofP demands aligning with the conceptual metaphors proffered.

Developing a recognizable and convincing professional identity requires therefore the appropriation and use of culturally relevant content and form; this can range linguistically from particular grammatical forms and pronunciations, to speech acts, figurative language and stories. Narratives are recognized as important relational and transactional tools in the workplace, used by employees and leaders to index professional status and expertise. Competent renderings are recognized as necessary ammunition in any leader's or newcomer's arsenal for rallying the troops, representing authentic identities and/or oiling the process of integration (Holmes & Marra, 2011; Juzwik & Ives 2010). Their power is partially derived from the status that they bestow on the orator. Stories construct identities via their content and by the manner in which they position their story characters and the narrator (Bamberg & Georgakopoulou 2008; De Fina 2003; Georgakopoulou 2007; Mullany 2006). They are therefore crucial and powerful resources in the representation of individual and group identity. Being able to effectively master the skill of narration can make one an effective employee.

This is discussed by Holmes and Marra (2011)[6] in an account of stories told by skilled migrants of non-English-speaking backgrounds in a workplace internship in New Zealand during their participation in a 'Workplace Communication course'. They draw attention to a sensitive and ubiquitous situation apparent in many globalized workplaces – the difficulties experienced by skilled migrants integrating into culturally and linguistically alien contexts. They conclude that in training non-English-speaking personnel, ESOL (English for speakers of other languages) teachers should incorporate storytelling into their curriculum in order to 'empower students in their efforts to negotiate high-stakes environments such as workplace settings' (p. 510). Their analysis exposes the way in which interns exploit stories in order to build rapport with their co-workers and construct a competent persona of a skilled, informed worker – thereby 'doing professional identity through workplace narratives' (p. 521). Through the analysis of one case study, we see the reflexive and agile capability of one Russian employee, Andrei, who finds himself having to adapt to the New Zealand workplace. Andrei discusses the cross-cultural differences between the two national settings and in so doing constructs himself as an authoritative and highly competent professional and cultural consultant, drawing on his past and present experience in so doing:

> And: and er in Russia they so and they behave the boss
>
>   if he's the boss he behaves quite bossy
>
>   you should this this this and this
>
>   . . . .
>
> All: [laugh]
>
> And: you're a boss you are here
>
>   you get your money you get your salary
>
>   so do as according to your position according to
>
>   . . . .
>
>   **because I was a team leader for more than four years**
>
>   **and everybody just stick to my to my er to my demands**
>
>   **you know**
>
>   **because I report also to report it to the director of the**
>
>   **Division similar to Eileen Eileen so it's er . . .**
>
>   **[New Zealand culture] it's different . . .**
>
>   **[laughs]: I'm talking to client:**
>
>   **It's more it's more indirect //[laughs]\ (p. 524)**

Andrei discusses his former status using comparisons with recognizable roles in this current context, for example, he makes reference to a senior colleague, 'Eileen', in his present company. He also details the need to adjust to the pragmatic norms of interaction in New Zealand, which requires a greater degree of indirectness, in contrast to Russia. He effectively exploits narrative in order to subtly convey his meta-awareness of cross-cultural differences and invoke aspects of his former workplace identity. His personal narrative allows him to subvert his novice status and enhance his current position.

As employees, we often switch professional hats taking on different institutional responsibilities and roles (e.g. meeting chair, mentor) which are recognized and authenticated within our workplace establishment. Externally, we may be called upon to convey our expertise to other professions or to lay/non-specialist audiences. In all of these roles, our professional identity is argued to emerge from ours and others' discursive practices; we do not just claim an identity but negotiate it, and different identities may be moulded in different workplace contexts.

In an analysis of mentor identity in white-collar and academic settings, Chiles (2007) investigates the variety of ways in which mentors '"do mentoring" in the workplace' (p. 730) and how the goals of the mentoring programme influence content and interactional engagement. Analysing twelve meetings between mentors and mentees in four workplaces, the study focuses on the type and amount of work and non-work-related discussion. She found a difference between mentoring and mentor identity in corporations and academic institutions, noting that 'overall, corporate mentoring pairs are more likely to use "on task" core business talk than the academic mentoring pairs' (p. 736). Non-work-related talk appeared mainly at the beginning of corporate mentoring sessions (if at all), whereas in the academic setting, it appeared to be interspersed throughout sessions and readily taken up by mentors when introduced by mentees. They determine that it is the organization's goals for the programme which determines the structure of the exchange and the way in which mentors construct their identities, as highly task-focused (corporate mentor) versus 'holistic' (academic) (p. 740).

Professional expertise may be called upon in institutional settings that are less familiar to the normal 'run-of-mill', everyday work undertaken by the professional. The courtroom, and in particular the witness stand, is one such setting in which experts may be called upon to provide their opinion. The subject of 'identities and the law' is increasingly occupying the interests of researchers (e.g. see Chapter Four and Tracy 2011 for a discussion of the identity of an appellate judge) and it has been shown that expert witnesses are afforded unique status and discursive rights within law courts. It has been found, for example, that they command the conversational floor for up to three times longer than other witnesses and contradict attorney questions or assertions in a manner not permitted by other witnesses on the stand (Chaemsaithong 2012; Cotterill 2003; Heffer 2005).

In a study investigating the performance of expert witness identity in a historical murder trial – 'The Trial of Alice Clifton' – Chaemsaithong (2012) analyses the discourse of an expert witness invoking the concepts of footing (Goffman 1981) and the framework of stance and engagement (Hyland 2005, 2008) and concludes that the expert does not just assert his authority, but rather constructs it through explicit self-identification and via alignment with other participants. He lexically self-identifies as a medical expert and invokes category-bound (Sacks 1995) references which locate him within the medical fraternity, for example, 'I was called upon by the Coroner and the Inquest', 'there are too many circumstances of evidence, which would confirm the justness of the conclusion drawn by Doctor Jones and myself' and 'the blood of children is much finer and more fluid than that of men' (p. 481). He carefully attends to impression management, constructing a moral persona in order to ward off potential objections to his opinion and makes explicit reference to the scientific and stepwise diligence of his work on the case, which subsequently led him to contradict previous diagnoses. Throughout his testimony, he addresses anticipated questions and alternative positions conveying sensitivity to his audience and other potential opinions. It is through these 'moment by moment' (p. 482) discursive acts that he successfully pulls off his expert status.

Worker/professional identities are not only constructed through talk but also in written texts and these can often belie a less than objective rendering of their subject matter. Critical discourse analysts have been at pains to highlight inequities in representations of individuals or social groupings through detailed analyses of texts. They highlight the impact that these constructions may have on the subjects represented, as well as the author(s) of the texts. This work has been instrumental in challenging natural or 'taken-for-granted' perspectives of identity/ies, instead demonstrating and arguing for the contingent nature of identity construction as influenced by political, sociocultural and historical factors (see e.g. the work of Fairclough 2001; Krzyzanowski 2010; Van Dijk 2006, 2010; Wodak et al. 2009; etc.). This research has brought into the spotlight issues of inclusion/exclusion, rights and privileges, discrimination, etc. which motivate much of this work.

Ainsworth and Hardy (2007) explore the construction of the identity of the older worker in texts arising from an Australian public parliamentary inquiry. The inquiry was motivated by government concerns about declining numbers of older workers in the labour market in Australia and its goal was to determine why older workers were leaving and/or not returning to the workforce when made redundant. The study investigates how the identity of the 'older worker' is constructed throughout the inquiry and discusses the policy implications of these constructions. They determine that particular identities are privileged (men), while others (women) are silenced or disadvantaged. Men are constructed as lacking in self-esteem and therefore in need of help from the state in the form of welfare and employment. Women, in contrast, are depicted as willing to accept low-paid and low-status jobs and therefore not in need of any policy protection. These uniform reductionist renderings of gender categories provoke a specific, narrow reading and response to the national problem and highlight the production and reproduction of particular institutional discourses and structures which serve to privilege certain sectors of the national population.

The relationship between structure and agency and the power of rhetoric in constructing work group identities has also been explored in public and employee-facing texts, such as mission statements or annual reports from companies. Koller (2011) undertook a systemic-functional (grammatical), attribution (of characteristics/qualities) and an Aristotelian rhetorical analysis of corporate mission statements, investigating how corporate identity serves to create a collective and 'ideal employee' identity (p. 106). The power of the corporation (structure) to mould and shape employee identity and the manner in which that identity is taken up by the employee (agency) forms part of an interactional act. She determines that the genre of mission statements functions as a device employed by management to project the goals and values that they place on the organization. These qualities are laminated onto the 'ideal' depictions of employee identities within the text.

Mission statements, letters to stakeholders or customers, one might argue, demand a particular rendering of company identity; however, contemporary markets, work patterns and practices may be subject to global demands (see section entitled 'Transnational contexts' below), competitive influences and public scrutiny and therefore demand that employees are flexible in the way in which they communicate about their work within and across public, organizational, departmental and hierarchical boundaries. As noted above, many of us now step outside of our usual work habitus to engage in contexts and discursive events which demand a shift in the way in which we talk about or practice our work. Such movements also mean that we construct dynamic speaker positions of accountability, flexibility, interdependence as well as the adoption of strategies which serve to constitute and reconstitute different ways of 'doing' and 'being' a worker; 'these strategies are part of a new textualisation of work ... and represent ... the "reflexivization" of worker identity' as alluded to at the start of the chapter (Iedema & Scheeres 2003: 316). Discourse studies recognize these challenges and contemporary researchers do not just report on the discourse of a particular work context (e.g. the language of the law court) but also on how speakers negotiate their roles and ways of talking about, as well as doing, their work in different settings and for different purposes. Iedema and Scheeres (2003) argue that learning to be a worker is no longer about learning to move from marginal to core status, rather it 'can be a long, arduous and contorted' (p. 332) journey as one comes to identify with the discourse of work and different identity positionings, some of which are 'not all necessarily sanctioned by their original occupation and profession' (p. 332).[7] Conflicts in constructions, representations and performances, which may arise due to the dissonance between the individual and other's understanding of conventional ways of being (also due to the less 'circumscribed' nature of identity representation), can cause stress for the individual, but may also pose new exciting opportunities and challenges through talking or writing about one's work in a different context – perhaps coming to new understandings and imaginings, and facilitating interaction and relationships with communities and people outside of the workplace/space that one might not have previously encountered.

Leadership identity

Research on the discursive enactment of leadership identity in the workplace has given rise to an understanding of the constitution of (effective) leadership/leadership style and the importance of its validation and co-construction by fellow employees. Many studies have reported on microanalyses of conversational data and some have made business meetings – when the corporate leader takes on the role of the meeting chair – their focus of study (Angouri & Marra 2011b; Svennevig 2011). While such studies occupy a large part of the research landscape, others have explored more diverse genre, such as email messages (Ho 2010) and speeches (McEntee-Atalianis 2013b) and considered less hierarchically determined management practices. A number of salient linguistic, pragmatic and discursive features are noted as fundamental to attaining leadership goals and a range of different styles are evident – some indexing and reproducing broader sociocultural categories, for example, culture,[8] ethnicity, gender and social class. The latter in turn influencing the way in which leadership is 'done'.

The relational nature of leadership work is fundamental to its success. The manner in which leaders interact with colleagues is both reflective and constitutive of their professional identity and is under constant negotiation. In enacting leadership, pragmatic considerations have to be attended to, including the importance of attending to co-workers' face needs. Face work has been identified as fundamental to relational success and the identity construction of any speaker (Spencer-Oatey 2007).[9] Attending to interlocutor face needs involves taking up particular stances/positions which may reflect alignment or disagreement. The management of this has been recognized as a momentary undertaking and indexes shifting identity positions.

In taking a critical stance towards leadership, a stance in which leadership is considered as a distributed co-responsibility, Schnurr and Chan (2011) discuss how leadership identities are built and negotiated via the face-threatening act of disagreement in meetings between employees in two workplaces – an IT Consultancy and a paint manufacturer – in Hong Kong. Leadership identity unfolds as a 'moment by moment negotiation of power relations' (p. 205) between a more senior leader and a subordinate as each takes the floor and challenges or concedes to their co-worker. These fluid and dynamic exchanges construct momentary 'leader' (senior) and co-leader ('second-in-command') status, which sometimes contradicts the prescribed hierarchical organizational structure. We see this in the extract below in which QS (CEO) and Danny (managing director) disagree about the involvement of a member of staff (Lilly) in a marketing event:

> *Context*: … QS [CEO, Senior], Danny [Managing Director, 'second-in-command'] and Lilly (one of the meeting participants) are discussing an upcoming marketing event that Lilly is supposed to prepare.

1 QS: so I was just suggesting um Lilly's upcoming marketing activity

2 Danny: uh they she is not ready

3   so this oh she wouldn't

4 Lilly: I'm not ready yet

5 QS: [laughing] no I know you're not ready;

6   but if I if I there are lots of them that are coming up

7 Danny: yeah we need to at first see the marketing event er calendar

8   looking for ()

9 QS: I'm I'm talking to the VP of marketing

10 Danny: I'm talking to my help-

11 QS: [in agitated tone of voice]: I don't care I I'm talking to//VP of marketing\:

12 Danny: [in agitated tone of voice]://()\\:

Overt threats to face are indexed through explicit markers of disagreement and an aggravated tone as the speakers battle to take the upper hand. At first, QS asserts his authority over the decision to involve Lilly in the marketing event but Danny repositions himself as 'leader' and in control of Lilly's workload countering his senior's opinion, before the pendulum swings back once again to QS before Danny's final retort (although his reply was not audible). Neither leader appears to concede his position.

Differences were found in the nature of the disagreements in the two companies studied by Schnurr and Chan (one being less confrontational than the other) and in the linguistic strategies adopted (e.g. the type and extent of mitigation strategies); however, most employees attempted to mitigate or forewarn interlocutors of their disagreement, for example, employing laughter or silence tactically. In both companies, leadership status was found to be negotiated momentarily through the continual management of face work.[10]

Humour is found to be an important discursive resource in mitigating threats to face and constructing leadership identity. It is invoked by leaders in order to achieve diverse relational and transactional goals, for example, to establish collegiality and solidarity, to initiate ideas and to convey information (Holmes et al. 2007; Rogerson-Revell 2011). However, subverted humour, in the form of jocular insults, can also act as threats to face and serve to maintain power within the workplace.

In an exploration of gendered leadership language style in an Asian context, Ladegaard (2012) reports on the appropriation of what are often considered 'normative'/stereotypical masculine management styles, that is, direct, aggressive, confrontational styles, by two women leaders in a small factory in Hong Kong. The study focuses specifically on their use of jocular insults within a team meeting. The women are shown to frequently make direct and aggressive face-threatening acts (e.g. swearing and insulting colleagues) in order to shock, entertain and humiliate their subordinates. Drawing on an interpretation of Chinese cultural values, in which, face and group harmony are cherished and 'subordinates are required to be deferential and obedient to their superiors' (p. 1673), the author concludes that the behaviour of the women bosses in this CofP 'becomes possible because the autocratic leader has cultural and social legitimacy in the community' (p.1674), and as such these discursive devices are used as an instrument of power to maintain their superiority and leadership status. Status differences are further marked by the indirect and silent reactions of their inferiors to their provocations which are marked by embarrassed laughter, humour and lack of response. The author suggests that this unmarked face-threatening behaviour may reflect, and indeed reproduce, the cultural milieu of Hong Kong society.

Ladegaard's account reflects the current post-structuralist perspective in gender and language research which argues against a binary or essentialist reading of male versus female language performance (see Chapter Nine). In enacting leadership, men and women adopt diverse discursive and linguistic strategies and resources (including normatively feminine and masculine styles), often shaped by the CofP in which they operate (Holmes 2006; Mullany 2007). Therefore, as illustrated in the account above, a number of factors have to be taken into consideration when exploring leadership identity including, at the very least, the sociocultural and interactional context.

Women are significantly under-represented in leadership positions however, and some suggest that their communication strategies may affect their professional performance. Holmes (2007) reviews research on gender and language in the workplace and details the 'double bind' often experienced by women in leadership positions who may find, due to the 'repressive, predominantly masculine, discourse norms in their workplaces' (p. 605), the need to adopt a stereotypically masculine discourse style and in so doing transgress the borders of femininity. However, she also notes that if they adopt a feminine style, they may also find their performance as a manager less effective. As a consequence, women often switch between different styles according to changes in context and the cultures endemic to the CofP in which they operate. She also notes variation in behaviour depends on individual choice – with some women choosing to adopt more masculine styles of behaviour and workplace contexts, while others preferring more feminine, and yet others alternating between normative male or female gender styles. She notes the latter to be important as it points to the transformational nature of workplace interaction: '[b]y appropriating normatively masculine discourse strategies to "do power", it can be argued that women in leadership positions contribute both to de-gendering the leadership role as well as the discourse strategies they use to enact that role' (p. 605).

Baxter (2011) contends, however, that within Western contexts senior businessmen and women in mixed-gender groups differ with respect to the extent to which they self-monitor and regulate their speech in response to interlocutor feedback. She finds women do this to a greater extent than men and hypotheses that within male-dominated corporations self-monitoring and regulation may exclude women from senior leadership positions. Appropriating Bakhtin's theory of 'double-voicing' (DvD),[11] she argues that women's greater use of double voicing 'may be partly driven by the visibility and conspicuousness of their minority position' as leaders in the business world and as 'an expression of a judgement call, a kind of linguistic "second guessing" of the intentions of other speakers which enables senior women to constantly adjust their language in order to make the right "impact" on their colleagues' (p. 236–237). She contends that DvD serves four main functions for the women employees in her study; it enables them to anticipate and avoid impending criticism, exercise power in threatening situations, repair speech where they may have made an error and help them to reduce the impact of taking an authoritative stance, enhancing rapport with their co-workers. Baxter argues that through DvD women leaders find a way to 'survive' in a male-dominated work environment.

However in a subsequent critical linguistic study, in which the reasons for the under representation of women in leadership positions are further explored, Baxter (2014) investigates how women 'do' leadership in all-female groups in order to highlight 'the multiple and diverse ways in which women's leadership identities emerge and are enacted' (p. 25). Basing her study on the analysis of interactions in a simulated leadership team task between six female middle managers attending a Master of Business Administration (MBA) course, Baxter discusses the shifting egalitarian nature of the leadership role among the group and the diversity of discursive and linguistic strategies used in its enactment, including markers of politeness, humour, praise and the adoption of authoritative stances. No clear gender pattern can be found in the data; rather, the women 'perform multiple and at times competing identities' (p. 35), shifting between more powerful and authoritative subject positions to less powerful and vice versa. Indeed, her findings are corroborated by others (Mullany 2007; Peck 2006; Sung 2011) who find that women adopt multiple mixed-gender leadership styles and employ sophisticated linguistic strategies in their multiple and fluid workplace encounters. She contends, however, that the preference for a distributed and at times competitive and 'chaotic' management style, rather than a top-down hierarchical management structure, was not necessarily beneficial to the group since it slowed down decision-making and the successful accomplishment of the task. She cautions that if this behaviour is indicative of interaction in the wider sphere of the workplace, women may not succeed in taking up authoritative leadership positions or being supported by their colleagues in contexts where a clear hierarchical structure is enforced or necessary.

Gender and the workplace

As evidenced in research on leadership, the issue of gender and the workplace has certainly become a vibrant topic of research and applied interest. Researchers have explored various workplace contexts such as business settings (examples above), call centres (Cameron 2002), courtrooms/legal contexts (Ehrlich 2006), health care encounters (Rees & Monrouxe 2010; Sarangi 2010; West 1998) and Parliament/politics (Shaw 2006). In synergy with changing perspectives in the broader field of language and gender (see Chapter Nine), many studies originally focused on examining binary differences in the linguistic performance of men and women in workplace interaction, as well as the domination, subordination, marginalization and exclusion of women in the workplace (e.g. see chapters in Barrett & Davidson 2006). Although this tendency has not fully abated, more recent work (as evidenced above) has become interested in exploring the multiplicity of gender identities as discursively performed in different professional contexts and the impact of globalization on the development of service industries which have led to the feminization of linguistic workplaces. Studies have explored the agentive potential of men and women to perform their identity in the workplace while also being subject (sometimes unequally) to cultural, professional and structural constraints (as discussed above). As an illustration of this research, in the following, we explore three distinct thematic orientations and investigations, considering how women perform success and power in different professional spheres and genre, how gendered communities are constructed and boundaried and then, taking a pragmatic focus, we consider the role of humour and laughter in performing femininity and masculinity in the workplace.

As highlighted in the review of Baxter's work, feminist linguists take a critical stance towards the way in which language, in synergy with other social practices and structures, influence and maintain gender divisions in society. However, discourse studies also reveal the way in which men and women employ language to challenge stereotypical gender ideologies. For example, in a comparative analysis of 'Midwestern congresswomen's self-presentation' in online biographies, Lee (2013) recounts the way in which female politicians describe their personal characteristics, emphasizing masculine traits, including words and metaphors marking strength and leadership – language which is less evident in the biographies of their male counterparts. Backgrounding her analysis in a discussion of the historical under-representation of female politicians in the United States and the continuing pervasive negative attitudes towards their performance and skills by voters and mainstream media, Lee suggests that female politicians adopt these communicative strategies in order to counteract harmful gender stereotypes about female 'weakness' in a strategic bid to emphasize their equality. Further, visual representations of congresswomen depict them engaging in professional pursuits, whereas male politicians often present themselves in private contexts, at leisure or with their family. Lee concludes that this 'was consistent with the literature ... male politicians often emphasized their compassionate and nurturing characteristics whereas female politicians tended to downplay their soft sides in favour of rough traits' (p. 311). She contends that given the already established dominate masculine discourse around politics, male politicians do not need to construct a masculine self-image in order to establish their competence, whereas the female politicians do, responding to social pressure and circulating gender stereotypes. 'These self-constructed emergent identities designed for the consumption of the general public are a joint product of the congresswomen and society. Thus they are shaped through a "social positioning of the self and other"' (Bucholtz & Hall 2005: 585).[12]

In a further exploration of the multiplicity of femininity and its realization within a public context, Sznycer (2010) employs a critical discourse and pragmatic analysis in the examination of the self-presentation of winning female tennis players in post-match press conferences in Europe and the United States. She finds their conversational style to be 'aggressive, adversarial, confrontational, uncooperative, impolite, self-assured, ego-enhancing, exaggerated, marked by a high level of affectability and extremely efficient in affect management' (p. 474) – a style which empowers their player identity and contradicts the traditional stereotype of women being powerless, cooperative and in search of solidarity.

e.g.

'Non-co-operative'

(1) Q: What did you say? ((on the court to the referee))

SW: ((drinks)) What did I say? (.) You didn't hear? (.) (US Open, 12 September 2009)

'Disagreement'

(12) Q: Good match despite the conditions?

DS: (3.0) Good match? (U.S. Open 5 September 2008)

'Persuasively powerful self-characterisation'

(23) SW: (....) believe me I'm gonna be number one sooner or later.

(US Open, 3 September 2008)

Their identity performance is contextually and pragmatically influenced, enhanced by the genre of the confrontational nature of the post-match interview, structured for entertainment as well as informational value in line with the competitive style of the sporting event. However, the players successfully combine aspects of the 'conventional discourses of femininity and masculinity', for example, combining affect and intensifiers with disagreement, in the construction of a powerful discourse. Snzycer argues that '[t]hrough creative transformations, recontextualisations and articulations, the emergent novel notion of a female identity violates ideological expectations concerning gender and power, which may augment its persuasive appeal. The naturalized links between linguistic forms and social categories become significantly weakened or undermined by innovative identities' (p. 476). Such studies undermine an essentialized reading of gender identity and point once more to the significance of interlocking variables, such as, context, genre, power and positioning in identity performance and construction.[13]

Although recent research on gender identity (see Chapter Nine) has destabilized the notion of distinct female and male interactional styles – recognizing the capacity of both men and women to take up discursive and linguistic strategies and features traditionally marked as 'feminine' or 'masculine' – it is acknowledged that all are subject to the social pressure of hegemonic gender discourses. These can be confronted and resisted, as in the case of the congresswomen and tennis players; however, often they become naturalized and remain unchallenged, serving to construct boundaries between men and women and even to construct representations of segregated gendered professions (e.g. see Ashcraft's 2007 discussion of gendered representations of commercial airline pilots).

In a return to our earlier discussion of builder identity, we draw for illustrative purposes on Baxter and Wallace's (2009) study of the impact of male hegemonic discourses on the linguistic behaviour and identity performance of white working-class male builders in the UK considering how this discourse reinforces a hegemonic perspective towards women. Through an analysis of builder talk in transit (while travelling to various building sites), Baxter and Wallace uncover the linguistic features that shape builder discourse and the variables which construct a boundaried hegemonic discourse, including, a lack of reference to women. Their analysis concentrates on four features: 'us/them' boundary marking in which the builders set themselves apart from their 'snobbish' clients and 'rival builders', the demonization of immigrant builders, 'collaborative talk' and the exclusion of women. Builder identities, they argue, are built on masculine dominant discourses and solidarity marking. However in their silencing of women, the authors find that 'women are viewed as so unthreatening to male experiences in the building trade that they do not even qualify for a place in the 'out-group' (p. 423). This absence reinforces and reproduces discriminatory hegemonic cultural behaviour making it difficult, the authors argue, for women to penetrate the building profession.

Gender and sex are salient themes provoking humour and laughter in the workplace. Their thematic invocation often enacts and reinforces discriminatory stereotypes about men and women, for example, 'men as communicatively incompetent ... women as objects of sexual titillation at work' (Holmes 2006: 47). However, stereotypical propositions, particularly when negative, are also frequently challenged and resisted. These apparently contradictory positionings – reinforcement and resistance – are sometimes realized in the same interactional encounter and have been found in diverse workplace contexts. For example, Rees and Monrouxe (2010) report on the role of laughter in co-constructing power, identity and gender in medical bedside learning encounters in UK hospitals. Identifying the role of teasing and the rhetorical potential of laughter to construct gender, identity and power, Rees and Monrouxe (2010) argue that through laughter men and women are able to construct their masculinity and femininity – either reinforcing cultural assumptions or subverting them. Focusing their study on masculinity, they report on the way in which male patients and consultants tease male and female medical students while making bedside consultations in order to 'perform masculinity and enact control' (p. 3386). Sexual teasing is enacted as a coordinated masculine performance aligning male consultants and patients as powerful allies in opposition to the students. In the case of one event in which two female students are being assessed, the authors illustrate how sexual teasing, initiated by the consultant, serves to mark a boundary between the male figures in the encounter and the female students, whose status as novice professionals is degraded by the men to a sexual role.

In the following extract, the students are asked to check the patient's heart. The consultant first describes the procedure to the patient:

MD1 [Consultant]: ... Now (.) what they're going to do. ALL they're going to do is listen to your heart

MP1 [Male patient]: Right

MD1: That's all they're going to do

MP1: No problem

MD1: If they do anything else, you let me know ((says playfully))

MP1: Huh huh huh huh (.) I should be lucky [ha ha ha ha

The students are noted to proffer no response to the exchange, marking their 'disapproval' (p. 3396) and resistance towards their discursive positioning as sexual beings.

Teasing is not only directed at the female students but also the male students. In one extract in which a student is being teased for having cold hands while examining a male patient, the patient engages in a sexual jibe. The authors suggest that the teasing performed by the patient functions to construct him (the patient) as an authoritative 'witty' figure, in control of the interaction and consultation. Moreover, it is through the enactment of this 'competitive play frame' (p. 3396) that the patient's masculinity is forged. Interestingly, in this encounter, a female student laughs along with the patient, reinforcing the 'patient's subjugation of her male peer (and herself)' (p. 3397); however, neither the male student nor male consultant respond, instead choosing to regain ground and authoritative control of the situation by shifting to a more serious tone and focus on the consultation itself.

Teasing and the initiation of laughter is therefore shown in this study to mould affective, 'intelligent, witty and powerful' (p. 3397) identities, sometimes employed to subjugate less powerful interactants (even playfully) and used by others, particularly by the less powerful students, to resist and rebel. Patients appear to employ self-deprecating humour in order to counteract threats to face and construct a positive affective identity. Sexual humour appeared to construct a stereotypical hegemonic masculine identity, reproducing cultural discourses of masculine potency. These were differently received and responded to by male and female interactants who chose on occasions to either entertain or reject them.

In a seminal study of humour in government and private companies in New Zealand, Holmes (2006) questions whether the gender of workers influences the type and style of humour adopted and she explores the role of humour in constructing gender identity. She finds, as Rees and Monrouxe, that 'gender stereotyping underlies a great deal of workplace humor' (p. 41) reinforcing cultural stereotypes (sometime negative or simplistic stereotypes); however, this does not always remain unchallenged by employees. Examples are provided of 'gender-typical' humour and constructions which 'reinforce typical, conservative, and conformist gender identities'; for example, in the case of humour among all female employees, examples are found of pragmatic alignment (affiliative and supportive stances) – the adoption of a collaborative discourse style and a focus on subject matter typically associated with the concerns of women (e.g. appearance and dress). In contrast, some all-male jokes were found to be competitive, non-collaborative and propositionally focused on stereotypical male subject matter (e.g. fighting). However equally, examples are found of contestations to these stereotypical behaviours and constructions and in one case female employees are found to rile against humorous suggestions about how women should behave at work, contesting the gendered depictions constructed by their male counterparts.

The construction of gender identity remains a rich area of study and a topic that we will return to in Chapter Nine. In the remainder of the chapter, we'll briefly consider research that has focused on issues of identity in increasingly transnational workplaces.

Transnational contexts

Processes of globalization and transnationalism, including the movement and networking of people, goods and practices physically and virtually, have led to complex scenarios of multilingual and multicultural contact. These have had a significant impact on the negotiation and construction of collective and individual identities, which are argued to be more unstable and fractured than previously and also more dynamic and malleable. As workers in multilingual, multicultural contexts, many have to establish their social positions and identities within dynamic and shifting encounters and there is often a blurring of personal and professional behaviour and identification. Research has explored the impact of 'globalization' on local practices ('glocalization') and the nature of linguistic performance on identity construction in 'de-territorialized' sites of engagement, for example, the use of English as a lingua franca (Gu et al. 2014). Scholars have investigated the way in which transnational processes and contact impact on the way in which individuals and groups understand and enact their identity in social situations and the influence that this has on their linguistic performance, even on 'unofficial' language policy (Hatipoğlu 2007; Hazel 2015; Zhang 2005). Transnational flows have therefore had a major impact on traditional notions of workplace social order and destabilized previous understandings of community belonging and affiliations, as well as the 'norms' of interaction within workplace settings. As employees working in 'globalized' workplaces, many of us now find that we have to navigate multilingual and intercultural communication practices on a daily basis – this can be both rewarding and testing. For some (e.g. immigrants), as we'll discuss below, these situations can be especially challenging.

The successful and fruitful negotiation of identities in workplace interaction is discussed by Moody (2014) in his analysis of the interactional accomplishments of an American intern in a Japanese company. Moody illustrates how David (the intern) negotiates his outsider, 'foreigner' ('Gaijin') status as a 'non-Japanese' employee through his use of English and humour – thereby linking micro with macrocultural stereotypes about 'foreigner' identity (as outsiders) and also as an English speaker, as a possessor of 'valuable cultural capital' (p. 77). The English language and the appropriation of humour are used to gain attention and interactional privileges. It is the discursive construction of his foreigner status by himself and his Japanese colleagues that permits him to disrupt interactional norms in order to accomplish workplace goals and manage the intercultural demands of his transnational workplace. For example, his repeated playful interruption of colleagues using an English greeting (despite colleagues not being fluent in English) in order to seek advice is not considered face-threatening but received warmly and humorously.

David: Hi.

Ikeguchi: ((look up at David)) Hi.

David: How are you?

Furuta: [hahaha

Ikegucha: [Oh (.) haha

David: I nee:d your help.

Ikegucha: Oh. (.) OK:: (.) na- nani? ((unintelligible))

            what

           Wh-what? (p. 79)

English marks his outsider status and contextualizes the exchange as playful, while Japanese (a language in which he has fluency) indexes work-related content. The authors note that whereas repeated interruptions would normally not be tolerated in this context, David gets away with this behaviour due to his playfulness and foreigner identity. Further, his colleagues affect his style in order to mock him, 'in a way that is positive, friendly, and contributes to the strengthening of their social relationships' (p. 83), thereby actively co-constructing his *gaijin* status. They argue that '[i]t is not the fact that he is *gaijin*, but rather how he discursively presents himself as *gaijin* that achieves his goals' (p. 85). This behaviour enables him to reposition himself as integral to the workplace setting rather than just a peripheral member.

In contrast to the positive consequences of David's enactment of a foreigner identity, critical discourse analysts have highlighted the darker side of globalization and in particular the power of a dominant culture's 'otherization' of foreigners in workplace contexts to impose national cultural homogenizing norms on outsiders. They have even identified barriers restricting access to jobs by foreigners due to differences in the way in which they identify with their workplace in contrast to the 'locals' (e.g. separation of personal and professional roles/values[14]) and how this identification is expressed in discourse.

For example, Campbell and Roberts (2007) critique the demands of contemporary UK interview protocols which they find to be especially discriminatory to foreign-born candidates who lack the necessary experience to 'synthesis[e] … work-based and personal identities'(p. 244) and as a consequence are often unsuccessful in garnering posts (see Chapter Eight for more details). Interviewers reported to the researchers that 'some candidates were seen to produce rote-learned "textbook" answers … which did not employ their own voice. On the other hand, candidates were seen to be overly personal and informal in their style of self-presentation and therefore "unprofessional"' (p. 244). Candidates are expected to combine personal values, history and motivations with those of the organization, for example, demonstrating the ability to be a team worker, self-organized, etc. 'They are expected to attain native-like "preferred" British stylistic and narrative competence in order to construct a preferred subjectivity and produce a "strong authorial voice"' (p. 254). This is noted to be particularly difficult for many foreign candidates to attain however. Many have experienced long-term unemployment or employment in ethnic minority workplaces which differ in discursive practice to British workplaces. Moreover, many interviewers fall victim to the dominant culture's negative attitudes towards foreigner identities. Access to and operation within the 'globalized' workplace is therefore shown to be highly regulated and controlled.

Conclusion

In this chapter, we have reviewed an array of literature focusing on the discursive construction of workplace/professional identity. While research questions, goals, orientations, methods, subjects and CofPs are varied, it is apparent that most studies try not to reify identity/ies or contexts but rather treat them as co-dependent, dynamic, multiple and discursively constituted. Many studies have explored the moment-by-moment evolution of identity construction in the workplace and some have also attempted to link the micro-conversational/linguistic emergence of identity with macro/ cultural ideologies and stereotypes, sometimes highlighting the impact of power dynamics (imposition and resistance) on identity construction. The act of 'doing' and 'being' a worker/professional, it would seem, demands acquiring and activating sophisticated linguistic, cultural and professional knowledge; however, it is also dependent on the perceptions, performances and positioning of us by others. Contemporary demands, such as switching between workplaces and workplace roles, and shifting ideologies, lead to the continuous constitution and reconstitution of workplace identities and identifications.

CHAPTER SEVEN

Social Media and Identity

By facilitating new modes of productivity, representation and socialisation, technology has helped transform the stage on which language and identity is performed.

RON DARVIN (2016: 526)

Introduction

In 2015, the average daily use of social media (SM) by global Internet users amounted to 106.2 minutes[1] – a figure increasing year on year. In September 2016, Facebook (FB) was the most popular network internationally – accumulating 1,712 million active users over a fourteen-year period. Other SM platforms also reached high levels of participation at this time, for example, WhatsApp, 1 million; Tumblr, 555,000; Instagram, 500,000; Twitter, 313,000 and the photo-sharing site, Snapchat 200,000. Contrary to lay opinion, current increases in SM usage are not restricted to teenagers but extend to older generations too. What was once considered a trend that predated the noughties has now morphed into a desired leisure and necessary professional pursuit for many, enabled technologically by the evolution of the collaborative and participatory capabilities of Web 2.0.

For the purposes of this chapter, SM is defined as any Internet-based application that facilitates the development, sharing and exchange of 'user-generated content' on mobile or Web-based technologies (Kaplan & Haenlein 2010: 61). Interaction between users can be synchronous (e.g. Internet Relay Chat – IRC) or asynchronous (e.g. Web logs/'blogs') and may lead to ephemeral (e.g. WhatsApp) or more permanent exchanges/

productions. Online activities and communities may or may not intersect with offline activities, communities or contexts.[2] The various types of SM applications can prove difficult to classify; however, a useful framework proposed by Kaplan and Heinlein (2010) lists six: Web logs/(micro)blogs, collaborative ventures, content communities, social networking sites, virtual game worlds and virtual social worlds. These applications are ordered along the dimensions of social presence/media richness and self-presentation/self-disclosure, as illustrated in Table 7.1.

SM applications differ markedly from one another in structure and form. Users are subject to varying affordances and constraints in generating content and in engaging with the user/follower interface. This can affect agency in self-representation/autobiographical reporting and updating, and in drawing audience attention to information that can be interpreted.[3] For example, some applications offer the potential for private exchanges or postings where the content is restricted, while others are semiprivate and many have some degree of public access. Users can share their real names (e.g. on FB) or use false names or nicknames (e.g. IRC). Some applications are reciprocal (e.g. FB, LinkedIn) while others not. FB offers multimodal presentational possibilities using pictures, video, written text and provides an established framework of self-classification, inviting users to (optionally) supply a profile picture and detail demographic and personal information. Status updates may consist of 'embodied' representations of the self and/ or others (shared) in photographs/videos, or a simple rendering of a text written by the poster or another FB user and 'shared' on the poster's own page. Access to accounts and/or content may be restricted. In contrast, Twitter home pages are public and offer limited biographical information.

Table 7.1 Classification of social media by social presence/media richness and self-presentation/self-disclosure (adapted from Kaplan & Haenlein 2010: 62)

Self-presentation/ Self-disclosure	Social presence/Media richness		
	Low	Medium	High
High	Blogs	Social networking sites (e.g. Facebook)	Virtual social worlds (e.g. Second Life)
Low	Collaborative projects (e.g. Wikipedia)	Content communities (e.g. YouTube)	Virtual game worlds (e.g. World of Warcraft)

Posts are restricted to small text contributions ('tweets') of between 140 and 280 characters.

All SM applications have the potential to distort conventional dimensions of time and space, allowing us to interact across time zones, (a)-synchronously, and in a multitude of contexts with multiple audiences. In its daily use, the boundaries between public and private worlds and personae become blurred. Local and global networks may become less discrete, less bounded, and deterritorialized, and features of contextually bound offline interaction are often found to combine with elements of broadcast media. The term 'context collapse' (Marwick & boyd 2011) has been coined to describe the way in which followers on, for example, FB and Twitter merge online in a way that is rarely encountered in offline settings. Friends, family, acquaintances and even strangers may all access the same material on user accounts which can make managing self-presentation difficult for the user. Furthermore, platforms such as Twitter have the potential to collapse front and backstage (Goffman 1959) performances, supporting among other things, the potential for the generation of 'pseudo-intimacy' between the poster and recipient through the sharing of select private details with a public audience. Crandall (2007, cited in Lee 2014) argues that the propensity to draw attention to the self via publicly shared images and information is all part of a newly formed 'presentational' culture. However, as noted by Lee (2014: 93), there is often a conflict for the individual between different versions of the self – the '"actual self" (aspects of identity that one possesses) ... [the] "ideal self" (what one wants to possess) and [the] "ought self" (what one should possess) (Higgins 1987) ... (I)dentities in social media are not just about *who we are*, but also *who we want to be to others* and *how others see us* or expect us to be' in our networked lives. A challenge many confront offline as well as online. Indeed, similarities and differences between online and offline identity performance and interaction have been debated. Deumert (2014) asserts that online/offline identities are best conceptualized as a continuum rather than as discrete entities or polar opposites. While Page (2013: 16) argues that analysts need to take into account 'the ways identity work online connects with the identities that are performed offline', Georgakopoulou (2013: 20) asserts that SM 'afford[s] opportunities for sharing life in miniaturized form at the same time as constraining the ability of users to plunge into full autobiographical mode'. As discussed below, technological affordances (and/or constraints) may alter interactional events and practices; however, contemporary research points to many similarities in the contingency, multiplicity and fluidity of identity performance in face-to-face and online encounters.

SM platforms are recognized as increasingly important sites for the creation of 'networked individualism' (Darvin 2016: 526) and (imagined) communities of 'networked publics' (boyd 2014) who share similar interests and invest in the negotiation of shared values, behavioural norms and desirable social identities. Many studies have identified variation in the multi/

translingual specificities and communicative affordances of different media and social networks, illustrating too how semiotic practices and shared indexicalities may be employed to demarcate community boundaries online (Barton & Lee 2013; Jones & Hafner 2012; Thurlow & Mroczek 2011).

In this chapter, we consider research which has focused on SM that affords both 'high' and 'low' possibilities for self-presentation (see Table 7.1) within a community of users, that is, micro and video blogs, notably Twitter and YouTube, as well as social networking sites such as FB and chat rooms. We approach the discussion of SM (Lappänen et al. 2014, cited in Seargeant & Tagg 2014: 131) as 'environments which enable activities, interaction and the emergence and sharing of an active "prosumptive" participatory culture'. We largely focus on studies carried out in the second wave of 'computer-mediated communication' (CMC) research (Androutsopoulos 2006a), which embed ethnographic, discourse analytic, multimodal and sociolinguistic insight into explorations of how identity is discursively and dialogically performed within or for a community of users. Taking a user-centred approach, we therefore seek to explore the affordances and constraints of new technologies; the types and varieties of identities (discourse, personal and social) built within/via SM (communities) and discuss the technological and contextual potential for the enactment of '(in)authentic' identity presentation. The chapter aims to incorporate a discussion of research from different applied linguistics areas in order to illustrate the breadth of research focus.

The 'authentic' self

Early SM applications, including those with limited audio, visual or contextual detail, led some to suggest that there were significant differences between the performance of online and offline identities. Early work focused mainly on analyses of user profiles/homepages and suggested a greater potential online for anonymous, fictive, 'inauthentic' self-portrayal. The liberating potential of the Internet for the user to play in a carnivalesque manner with alternative social roles (e.g. gender switching), or the ability to 'hide' identit(ies), has been illustrated in social-psychological research (Turkle 1995). It was suggested that CMC provides a unique space for identity play – the wearing of alternative masks to those worn, borne or constructed 'offline' (Danet 1998). However, 'second-wave' CMC work has suggested that such a discrete separation does not necessarily exist and that the multiplicity of identities performed online and offline bears more resemblances than differences (Androutsopoulos 2006a, b; Page 2013). Indeed, accounts of acts of identity 'play'/'switching' are rather anecdotal and infrequent (Herring & Stoerger 2014). The boundaries between 'authentic'/'inauthentic' and on/offline performances are instead rather hazy: hoaxes and identity play can occur just as readily offline as on, and efforts to perform a recognized, 'preferred' social identity can be just as demanding on SM (as illustrated in the case of 'Frape' below) as in face-to-face encounters.

In an exploration of narratorial identities, Page (2013) points out that the concept of 'authenticity' has recently undergone critical reflection, particularly in sociolinguistics, and asserts that 'the ambiguities of online representation lead us to a heightened awareness of how authenticity is played out across a spectrum from the apparently genuine to entirely fictional constructions … inauthentic identities are a crucial resource for making visible the processes by which authenticity is constructed' (p. 165). Current practices of selective and, on occasion, idealized self-presentation, she argues, challenge the boundaries between the 'fictional' and 'real' (p. 166). Some (Seargeant & Tagg 2014) argue that users have to be more industrious in their construction of an authentic, credible identity online, while others suggest that CMC offers greater opportunities for performing authenticity than face-to-face interactions (Del-Teso-Raviotto 2008). Herring (2003) and Herring and Zelenkauskaite (2009) assert that user identities are readily evident online in a similar vein to offline performance with audiences picking up indexical cues, such as linguistic style, to identify user status (see discussion of gender and sexual identity below).

Defining 'authenticity' is challenging since it superficially draws on associations with notions of stability, uniformity, polarity (with 'inauthenticity') and 'truth' – concepts which are troubling from a postmodern perspective. For the purposes of this discussion, we view 'authenticity' as a socially determined, localized and temporally situated *construct* which allows us to account for the different presentations of self in diverse contexts. An 'authentic' self is therefore not a stable or 'true' representation but rather multiple and complex. Moreover, authenticity is not only performed but perceived by others, and is therefore open to evaluation and challenge. These characteristics are incorporated in Coupland's description of 'authenticity' (Page 2013: 167ff) which provides a suitably nuanced lens through which to analyse research in this area. He lists five characteristics drawn from traditional definitions of the term: ontology, historicity, systemic coherence, consensus and value.

Ontology refers to the ontological status of the entity – whether it is artificial or natural, fictional or nonfictional. *Historicity* relates to the history of the entity and its connection with historical roots. *Systemic coherence* refers to the positioning of the entity in the social world and in particular in relation to contextual constraints or values, for example, 'a religious order might attribute different authenticity to scriptures than might a literary class' (Page 2013: 168). *Consensus* demands mutual agreement among experts who are in a position to corroborate authenticity and *value* is attributed to those who are in a position to authenticate (in contrast to those who are not, and who may as a consequence of their ignorance lose face should they be duped).

In the remainder of this section, we explore these features considering how individuals and groups establish their own authenticity online, and/ or, as audiences, determine the authenticity of others. Appealing to systemic coherence, we first consider how online groups establish authentic identities that may challenge mainstream (hegemonic) constructions and how membership within these groups is contingent on performing a recognized 'authentic' identity which attunes with the values and behaviour of the online community. Support group websites are a suitable initial example since they provide a space for individuals to negotiate a status which may be challenged in other online/offline contexts.

Different types of support groups have been studied and findings suggest that while not 'reductively Cartesian' ('I [post], therefore I am') (see Chapter One and Murthy 2012: 1062, 1063), SM facilitate processes of preferred self-construction and self-affirmation. User validation is however dependent upon acceptance within dialogic communities; participants must develop 'authentic' identities by enacting authenticating processes in alignment with other members. Individuals may be 'rumbled' or ignored if their contributions and identity performances do not align with those of the group (McKinlay and McVittae 2011: 192ff). For example, Guise et al. (2007) illustrate how myalgic encephalomyelitis (ME) sufferers often struggle to have their debilitating condition recognized by medical professionals or lay people in the absence of objective evidence. They therefore seek identification with, and validation by others experiencing similar struggles through online support group discussion. Through a process of alignment in their subjective reporting, they authenticate their identities as sufferers of a valid condition.

In a somewhat different vein, a study of online 'self-harm' discussion groups has shown how contributors invoke counter narratives to the mainstream in order to validate their self-injurious behaviour by framing it as positive action. Through a supportive network, they construct a legitimate identity for themselves which is at odds to the positioning of them as being 'at risk' or 'ill' as evident in health care/medical discourse (McVittae et al. 2009). Through these forums participants establish a supportive and bounded community, building desirable identities for their membership.

Opposing constructions of the same medical condition are poignantly evidenced in Riley et al.'s (2009) account of 'pro' and 'anti' anorexia nervosa websites in which 'pro-anorexia' contributors build accounts that are supportive of weight loss and the actions and values associated with this, in contrast to 'anti-anorexia' website contributors who identify anorexia nervosa as a medical condition in need of remediation. Authenticating and negotiating one's preferred status within such support groups is vital for inclusion. Adopting a stance at variance to the group leads to rejection.

Moving from a discussion of illness/health forums to sports forums, we can also see how the gatekeeping practices of established members can influence the identity construction of novice participants (see Chapter Six for similar accounts of workplace encounters). Page (2013) invokes the concept of 'second stories' (Sacks 1995) in her illustration of how social hierarchies are established in a Body Builder discussion forum through interactive accomplishments. She illustrates how through naming practices (e.g. 'newbies', 'expert') and narrative interaction, posters to the forum establish their position and authenticity within the group. New members often seek the support and advice of established and experienced body builders ('historicity'). However, the responses received by the neophytes can vary between 'face-threatening' and 'face-enhancing' speech acts (/second stories). Face-threatening acts are reported to negatively impact on the new member, leading to social isolation or exclusion from the group, while face-enhancing responses establish rapport and acceptance, facilitating the development of authentic bodybuilding personae for new members and the enhancement of their self-esteem. The study illustrates the socially determined nature of online authenticating practices and its dependence on hierarchies of power.

The salience of asymmetries of power and 'ambient affiliation' (Zappavigna 2013) to perceptions of online authenticity is further evidenced in work investigating the role of self-branding and 'micro-celebrity' by corporations, celebrities and lay users on the micro-blogging site, Twitter. Page (2012) discusses the role of hashtags in differentially positioning and authenticating corporations, celebrities and non-celebrities. Celebrities exploit the medium to self-brand and promote their 'front-stage' (Goffman 1959) status through their alignment with products/campaigns/promotions of their own work. Their individuated performance contrasts with lay tweeters, whose use of hashtags demonstrates more affiliated identities (e.g. as community members or fans). These findings align with Zappavigna (2013) who reports on how ordinary users of Twitter exploit hashtags to establish social bonds and an 'ambient identity' (p. 210), that is, bonds and values which denote 'networks of fellowship' (p. 223) and Twitter personae.

Different types of identity work undertaken by corporations, celebrities and ordinary users (acknowledged to exist on a continuum since even lay people can 'self-commodify') are shown in these studies to reflect and reproduce offline social and economic hierarchies. Indeed Marwick and boyd (2011) point to the salience of the network (as noted in studies above) in authenticating and collaborating in the content and identity of the Tweeter. They note however that '(m)icro-celebrity practices like interacting directly with followers, appealing to multiple audiences, creating an affable brand and sharing personal information are rewarded ... in a Twitter culture' (p. 127), although sometimes are perceived as 'inauthentic' by audiences used to a marketing culture.[4]

Inauthenticity is often equated with impersonation. The potential for impersonating identit(ies) has long been considered an issue in online interaction (as noted above) and can range from relatively playful acts[5] to more serious instances of identity theft. In more serious cases, concerns beyond the material include challenges to face and reputation should one be a victim. Responses to 'Frape' cases – where a person takes over the FB account of another user and posts material without his or her permission – and reactions to the construction of fictional characters in YouTube video posts illustrate the sophistication of audiences to detect 'false' identity claims. Moreover, as discussed below, the reactions of some within the YouTube community to finding out that a poster is in fact an actor rather than a 'genuine' contributor, challenge notions of subject authenticity as a necessary factual ontology; rather, fictional characters can be perceived and treated as just as 'authentic' as real people.

'Frape' can take different forms, from posting updates on the victim's page, altering profile information (e.g. relationship status, gender) or interacting with readers of posts. It can provoke different responses, from humour to significant embarrassment, depending on the severity of the action and the manner in which the 'frapists' manipulate (often negatively) the 'authentic'/'preferred' identity of the victim. In cases where a Frape is not identified or where a victim suspects that some of their audience may have been duped, significant harm can be done as the victim may feel that their online and offline identity has been violated and compromised. Frape challenges 'systemic coherence' but lends 'value' to those who can identify it. For a 'frape' to be successful, the audience must deem the action to have been undertaken by the 'legitimate' FB member. However, for a Frape to be identified it has to 'draw attention to [itself] as [an] inauthentic speech act[s] … [so that] the "frape" creates a gap between the impersonation and the target reality of the victim's authentic identity' (Page 2013: 178). This may be determined by the 'expert' due to their offline as well as online knowledge of the poster. For example, Page (2013) provides the example of a wife taking over her husband's FB account and 'liking' posts to his wall – something that would be completely out of character, as identified by his daughter.

Unlike FB, the identification of online authenticity is perhaps less straightforward on sites such as YouTube. Lonelygirl15 is a well-known example of an online impersonation – a 16-year-old American character, called Bree, who initially duped many as she narrated stories about her daily life as the home-educated daughter of religious parents (Page 2013: 170ff). Despite similarities in the production of her blogs to regular amateur bloggers (e.g. recordings made close-up to camera in her bedroom), the character was exposed as an actress. After a brief period of online video postings, her authenticity was questioned by a number of 'expert authenticators' who identified violations of what they deemed to be conventional methods of self-presentation on YouTube at the time of its production in 2006, in addition to inconsistencies in the character's self-report and storytelling practices (Page 2013: 172). Her blogs used orchestrated lighting, editing and sound effects – techniques not regularly used by 'genuine' bloggers, and her narratives aligned more with fictional storytelling, for example, a propensity for conflict and suspense. Contact with her audience reflected a micro-celebrity status rather than one of a novice blogger in touch with her peers. The 'scam', as perceived by some, was designed by a corporation claiming to support a new venture of online interactive storytelling. They argued that their endeavour was a creative, community-minded act, designed to exploit the potential of YouTube. The 'controversy surrounding the disclosure of Lonelygirl15 arose because of the values of self-expression in the early days of YouTube where the "vernacular creativity" and assumed authenticity of amateur video-ship was positioned ideologically in opposition to commercial models of mainstream media production' (Page 2013: 170). This online phenomenon led to a series of responses and reflective accounts which further authenticated the social identities of her audience (Page 2013: 174). Some viewers reacted negatively to the perceived deception feeling devalued and misled, rejecting the action as deceitful. Others provided a different reading, perceiving the posts as not an intentional conceit but as performance art in which they had willing played a role. This bolstered their social standing since they recognized the ontological status of Bree as a fictional character and continued to participate in her fictional life by continuing to watch her posts. A further category exploited the 'out(ing)' (Page 2013: 174) of Bree by constructing satirical blogs of their own based on a caricature of the fictional character. They in turn accrued status, tapping into the fan base already present on the Web. Their actions further challenged notions of authenticity, for, as noted by Page (2013: 184): 'it seems that the meaning of authenticity associated with ontology has been supplanted by the equation of authenticity as a participatory fiction or insider joke'.

Online gender and sexual identity

Issues of authenticity are no less salient in online studies of gender and sexual identity, research which has questioned whether gender is visible online and whether it acts as a meaningful social category in SM; whether offline gendered performance, ideologies and values translate to online contexts; and given that there are reportedly more women than men engaging on some SM sites (Herring & Stoerger 2014), whether SM affords a more democratic and egalitarian space in which to interact.

Early research on identity in CMC focused on gender as a salient social category determining that stereotypical discursive and linguistic markers for gender were visible online and that marked differences in practice could be detected. Asymmetric identity performances online have been identified in the work of Cherny (1994), Herring (2003) and Selfe and Meyer (1991), for example, who reported on differences in male and female participatory acts, discourse styles and vocabulary in synchronous and asynchronous modes. In asynchronous CMC, women were noted to write fewer posts, less frequently and also receive fewer responses. They adopted a more affective, polite style, aligning with and supporting their audience, employing neutral and emotional vocabulary, emoticons and laughter – also preferring to qualify or justify assertions and they were reported to be more willing to assert appreciation or apology. Men, by comparison, were found to adopt more assertive, less polite and adversarial, aggressive styles, employing profanities, insults and verbs of violence. They posted more frequently and extensively, opened and closed discussions in mixed groups and received more responses. However, Herring (1996) also determined that majority gender status effected language use: groups dominated by women led male members to align more readily with the group than in male-dominated communities, and women in male-dominated groups tended to adopt more aggressive styles. Such conclusions complemented other gender studies at the time exploring 'offline' interaction (Coates 1993; Tannen 1990) and these have been partially supported by later CMC work (Fullwood et al. 2011; Koch et al. 2005; Thelwell et al. 2010; Tossell et al. 2012).

Indeed, recent research continues to point to a disparity in practice, particularly the way in which users respond to male and female posts and the way in which men and women use the Internet. Mens' blogs and tweets are found to be taken up to a greater extent than female posts in online communities and by the media (Herring & Stoerger 2014), whereas women are the victims of a higher proportion of online harassment and violence, as evidenced in Hardaker and McGlashan's (2016) analysis of rape and death threats directed on Twitter at the feminist campaigner Caroline Criado-Perez, following her petition to the Bank of England to retain a female figure on a UK bank note. Their study illustrates how particular discourse communities and identities can form around the shared linguistic and discursive production of 'rape, misogyny, racism and homophobia' (p. 92). Moreover, gender stereotypes are reported to carry over into the 'products, services and entertainers' that are 'liked' on FB by men and women; in the topics that are discussed; and their motivations for doing so, for example, to support flirtation (Herring & Stoerger 2014: 12).

In a study of online sexual and gender identity in dating chat rooms, Del-Teso-Raviotto (2008) argues that authentication involves a necessary validation achieved through a process in which posters draw on offline sexual and/or gender stereotypes. He analyses texts in which performances of gender and sexual identity are discerned through self-descriptions, screen names and age/sex/location schema (in the absence of aural or visual evidence). Identities are demonstrated to be locally managed and performed drawing on hegemonic social and cultural discourses, for example, 'genderisation of online identities … is … achieved in some occasions through the depiction of bodies using letters and diacritics', for example, '(@) (@)' (p. 258) to denote female/masculine forms. Screen names align with feminine or masculine features (e.g. *little male devil, Ms Georgia Peach*). Stereotypical features and traits of feminine or masculine interaction, such as a greater propensity to demonstrate affect, are noted to be afforded by female posters who use a greater proportion of emoticons, while gay participants appear to adopt a style of self-attribution more aligned with personal ads. Stereotypical differences in gendered style and identity performance are therefore found to translate from offline to online performance, as also found in a study of support groups by Page (2013).

Page (2013) reports on an analysis of a set of blogs posted by ten female and ten male cancer patients and the 'rupturing effect of illness and its treatment on the narrators' gendered identities' (p. 62). She observes that women had a greater tendency to offer supportive posts and affective anecdotes, in contrast to men who offered medical information and recounts of events. Women's posts were generally longer, more responsive to other female bloggers, they received more comments, with more hyperlinks, and were more evaluative than men's posts. Women, she argues, exploited the online space for emotional support while men sought and exchanged information. However, as Page acknowledges, the findings illustrate tendencies rather than absolutes and reflect a possible North American bias in data sampling.

In a further discussion of FB posts, Page (2013) continues to argue for the salience of gender as an indexical category in CMC and the greater propensity for women to post and receive responses, especially from other women. She identifies the transference of offline values and behaviour to online interaction, asserting that:

> The linguistic trends found in status updates suggest that gender differences in Facebook are becoming reified, where expressivity as performed sociality continues to be an index of playfulness associated with young, Western femininity... in line with other recent studies that depict Facebook as a heterosexual marketplace in which women are particularly sensitive to the needs of self-presentation in order to compete for attention. (p. 90)

Other studies trouble the descriptive and interpretative stability of sex/gender categories however. Correlations between linguistic/discursive features and gender are seen to be unstable and opaque; intersectional variables such as age, culture (as noted above), social network, style and genre may on occasion more accurately account for patterns of performance, rendering gender less salient or simply one of many variables which can act as a correlational and/or explanatory variable. For example, Herring and Paolillo (2006) discovered that when blog genre was considered – in particular taking into account differences between personal diary and 'filter' blogs (linked to external content) – gender differences in grammatical word frequency were not apparent. Guiller and Durndell (2007) found few linguistic indices for gender in student discussion groups, although they did find differences in style. Whereas Bucholtz (2002) found professional women posters to a technology website displayed styles typically associated with men and women, these were both adversarial and supportive in form. Further, in a computational analysis of the relationship between gender, linguistic style and social networks, Bamman et al. (2014), who analysed a corpus of 14,000 individuals on Twitter, argued for the importance of considering intersectionality in interpreting cluster results asserting 'the impossibility of pulling different dimensions of social life like gender, race and affect into different strands' (p. 146). The analysis revealed 'quantitative patterns [that] suggest repertoires that mix identities, styles, and topics' (p. 147) and produce multiple stances, styles and personae. While they found many clusters to strongly correlate with gender, their linguistic performance did not always correlate with 'population-level language performance' (p. 135). Gender, they argue, while acting as an important structural concept in social life, is more than a binary rendering of male and female categories; rather, the topic of the post played a vital mediating role between gender and linguistic forms. Men were more likely to talk about careers and hobbies which yielded higher percentages of named entities. They argued that there was not a general preference for greater 'explicitness' or 'informativity' by men and affectivity by women; rather, performances of gender identity intersected with other stances and personae 'e.g. sports fanatic' (p. 148) revealing a multiplicity of gendered styles (as found in other 'offline' work e.g. Eckert 2008a, see Chapter Nine). Moreover, gender homophily and audience design were found to influence language choice such that individuals would often adopt and accommodate to gender-marked forms used by others in their social network, if their network was populated by a significant number of same-gender contacts (see Herring 1996, above).

Language learning and second language identities

The impact of gender and sexual identity on language learning and second language identities has been explored by a number of scholars (King 2008; Nelson 2009; Norton & Pavlenko 2004). In line with work discussed above, these studies do not consider gender or sexual identity as binary categories (as just male or female); however, they do consider them as existing in 'a system of social relationships and discursive practices that may lead to systemic inequality among particular groups of language learners, including women, the poor minorities, the elderly, and the disabled' (Norton & Toohey 2011: 425). Issues of intersectionality and hybridity become salient to interpretations of linguistic and sociocultural practice. In writing about a long-term study of six 'Haafu'[6] female adolescents in Japan, Kamada (2010) describes their battle for recognition and acceptance as 'half' by mainstream Japanese society in and out of school – their gender identity intersecting with their mixed ethnic status. A situation similarly reported by adults in Shaitan and McEntee-Atalianis (2017). Menard-Warwick (2009, see

Norton & Toohey 2011: 426) examines the influence of immigrant women's life histories in California on their English language learning experiences as adults and as mothers. Although noting similar experiences, differences are also reported within and across groups of women who are subjected to the effects of Latin American immigration to the United States (e.g. poverty, marginalized status). Other scholars such as King (2008), Moffatt and Norton (2008) and Nelson (2009) explore the ways in which teacher materials and pedagogic practice (including use of the Internet and SM) can be more inclusive to accommodate and respond to a range of sexual and gender identities by questioning and troubling the normativity of hegemonic heterosexual discourses and materials. The development of inclusive materials leads to greater learner 'investment' in the learning experience and positive outcomes for language learning and learner identity (Norton 1995; Peirce 1995).

Psychological factors alone cannot explain learner success or failure. Factors such as motivation or personality type exclude the important relationship between the language learner and their social world, including interaction on SM, and its subsequent impact on the language learning process and identity formation. Economic and sociocultural factors impinge on potential success; themes of power and conflicting ideologies, including those in relation to, for example, class, gender and race, are noted to be important in negotiating learner identity and affording opportunities in/ through learning environments (Norton & Toohey 2011).

Drawing on Bourdieu's notion of 'habitus',[7] Darvin and Norton (2015: 46) assert that learners are positioned and position themselves in relation to capital: 'What learners desire can be shaped by habitus; however, it is through desire that learners are compelled to act and exercise their agency ... Imagination allows learners to re-envision how things are as how they want them to be'. Digital technology and SM act as positive platforms for language learning and socialization for through 'Internet connectivity, and SM, learners are able to traverse transnational spaces ... and oscillate between online and offline worlds ... Because of the dynamic nature of these spaces, and the increasing diversity of those who occupy them, the asymmetric distribution of power no longer rests on the simple dichotomy of native speaker and language learner' (Darvin & Norton 2015: 41). Nevertheless, as illustrated in the contrasting case studies of two young people, a young female language learner called Henrietta in Uganda and a young male Filipino immigrant (Ayrton) in urban Canada, we see how differing aspirations and habitus give rise to disparities in the attainment of digital literacy and cultural, economic, social and symbolic capital associated with learning and using English.

Henrietta is stymied by her socio-economic circumstances in Uganda. It challenges her ability to acquire language practices that are necessary to function in the knowledge economy and enter competitive online and offline spaces – not least because of the poor technical infrastructure in Uganda and her economic circumstances which make engagement with transnationals and the development of appropriate literacies, including high-level competence in English, very difficult. 'Henrietta positions herself as inadequate, as one who is not sufficiently "knowledgeable"' (p. 49). Her use of the Internet is limited, denying her the opportunity to access materials for language learning. She uses it mainly to establish friendships; however, this bestows her with limited capital. In contrast, Ayrton's opportunities far outweigh those of Henrietta. He lives in a comparatively wealthy economy and family and is empowered through his socio-economic standing – including ready access to the Internet and a good command of English to engage in online fora which endow him with the opportunity to garner capital. His enrolment in an online currency trading course enables him to interact with high-functioning adults. His linguistic and pragmatic skills afford him the opportunity to garner economic and symbolic capital and develop an identity, despite his young age, which aligns with that of successful professionals. These two students illustrate the varying impact of socio-economic circumstances on learner identity formation and negotiation.

For those lucky enough to have ready access to the Internet in the developed world, computer-mediated environments afford alternative opportunities for students to extend their learning and be accepted as competent language users. Lam (2000, 2006) reports on the multilingual competences and identities of immigrant youths in the United States and notes how their online experiences offer enriching opportunities which cannot be experienced in the classroom, where they often face discrimination, inequity and feelings of incompetence. Lewis and Fabos (2005) similarly describe the benefits of instant messaging for the development of social networks and enhanced social identities. They illustrate how SM supports the enactment of multiple identities by students and the development of literacy practices not available through formal education. Others (Pahl & Rowsell 2010) have shown how teachers have successfully combined student interest in SM with class work in order to enhance engagement and develop positive learner identities, even in contexts where access to the Internet is more challenging. And Norton and colleagues (Early & Norton 2014; Norton et al. 2011; Norton & Williams 2012) have illustrated how investment in digital technology and the learning of English in Uganda has led to the social and cultural development of both students and teachers and the imagining of identities that extend beyond the confines of their local context.

However, Norton and Toohey (2011) note that not all research has shown a positive correlation between the use of digital technology and identity enhancement. Citing Kramsch and Thorne (2002) who studied (a) synchronous communication between learners of English in France and learners of French in the United States, they note that students did not fully understand the cultural context in which their interlocutors were functioning and this often led to difficulties in communication and by extension the development of positive learner identities.[8]

Diasporic and multilingual identities

Despite the difficulties mentioned above and the dominance of English on the Internet, SM platforms have supported the emergence of global multilingual networks and the display and negotiation of dual/hybrid identities. They provide a forum for the exchange of news, cultural information, and permit contact with friends, family and strangers in host, home and global contexts. Moreover Web-based forums offer a space in which diasporic/multilingual identities can converge, develop and be (re)imagined, as shown in Sharma's (2012: 485) account of the 'construction of cosmopolitan personae' by Nepalese youths mixing English and Nepalese on FB (also see Dovchin 2015 and Christiansen 2015). They also facilitate the preservation and 'negotiation between the poles of an original home and a newly acquired host culture' (Sinclair and Cunningham 2000: 15) for immigrants.

In a study examining language choice and code-switching in seven websites targeting different ethnic groups in Germany (Indian, Persian, Greek, Asian, Moroccan, Turkish and Russian), Androutsopoulos (2006b) demonstrates how multilingual codes function to convey and negotiate diasporic identities. In an analysis of debates about identity in discussion forums, he identifies the way in which code choice and mixing are strategically invoked to mark boundaries between members and to 'negotiate the relationship between language preference and ethnic identity' (p. 536). As Sebba and Wootton (1998), he argues that an analysis of the 'we' and 'they' codes (Gumperz 1982) needs to extend beyond a consideration of the host and home language to their situated salience within threads. For example, a contributor to the Greek forum rejects a previous poster's preference to solely socialize in Greek cafés in her area. She simultaneously marks her disdain towards this ethnocentric act and indexes her preferred multicultural identity via a switch to German:

Greek forum, 'Wo kommit ihr eigentlich alle mal her???' ('Where do you all come from?), post 39; *[Greek in italics]* <u>German underlined</u>

Nai exoumai eipa ellinika kafe. Alla giati vgeneis mono se ellinika me liges eksereseis? ego pantos vgeno pantou. Den kleinomai mono se ellinika na vlepo ton idio kosmo kai tous idiou tuxous. <u>Bin nun mal multikulti</u>.

Yes, we have Greek cafés, as I just said. But why do you only go to Greek cafés apart from a few exceptions? I for my part go everywhere. I don't lock myself up in the Greek ones to always stare at the same people and the same walls. <u>I happen to be multicultural</u>.' (p. 536).

Through code-switching, she aligns with a cosmopolitan social category. For her the German language does not index a 'they' code, the language of the 'other', the dominant majority in Germany, but rather authors her multilingual and multicultural subjectivity.

In another example in which discussants debate the preferred linguistic medium of interaction on the forum, Androutsopoulos illustrates how language and ethnic identity is invoked, both coupled and decoupled, via the different identity positioning of contributors. The German language is the dominant medium of communication in the Greek forum due to member preference and the fact that some participants do not understand Greek; however, some contributors object to this. The initiator of the discussion thread asserts his objection to the use of German. For him, 'Greek is *the* essential "we code" of the Greek forum. He criticizes the predominance of German over "your language", and calls its users *Fritzified* ("Germanised") – a nonce formation that implies excessive assimilation' (p. 538). Three responses follow: the first reinforces the reasons for the dominance of German as simply a language preference of the group, making no reference to ethnic associations; the second responds in Greek but rejects the position of the initiator of the post, again disassociating language and ethnic identity in his interpretation of the linguistic status quo. Rather, as in the example above, he supports the use of 'whatever [language] comes naturally' (Respondent C, p. 538) thereby constructing a multicultural persona for himself and the group. The final respondent replies in mixed code (a strategically marked language choice in comparison with his other posts), rejecting the initiator's stance and supporting a 'multicultural' identity for himself and the group.

Linguistic means of self-presentation are also evident in the analysis of screen names and message signatures. Almost two-thirds of screen names (total of 340 analysed) on the Greek and Persian websites were in the home language, seconded by a preference for English. Androutsopoulos 'read the strong preference for a home language screen name(s) as an index of ethnicity' (p. 539). He notes a preference for the denotation of personal traits over 'collective membership' however, with users 'rarely making ethnicity or regional origin explicit' (p. 539). Contrary to expectations, the language of message signatures did not necessarily correspond to screen names or indeed the language of the discussion. Some users were reported to even have bilingual signatures, for example, English/Hindi, and others to employ languages other than the home language, German or English. Hybrid realizations become fused to index a multitude of sociocultural associations. The study reveals how multilingual repertoires are exploited in situated practice across different modes of virtual space and how users not only draw on their host and home languages but others too in the discursive negotiation and strategic presentation of self.

In an analysis of code-switching between Standard Modern Greek (SMG) and the Greek-Cypriot dialect (GCD) in Internet Relay Chat by Greek-Cypriots, Themistocleous (2015) further shows how CS is utilized by participants in their performance of different roles and identities and how it is influenced by factors pertaining to the medium of interaction ('synchronicity and the "speak-in-writing" character of IRC' p. 12) as well as macro-sociolinguistic and micro-interactional norms. Contributors are shown to 'play' with identities in a humorous fashion, changing their nicknames and playing imaginary characters (e.g. 'ninja instructor') which invoke styles and codes associated with 'real-life' personae functioning in the Greek-Cypriot speech community. For example, characters are shown to appropriate SG when adopting a teacher/instructional style, or switch between SG to GCD when pretending to be interviewers. Even a change of nickname can lead to a change in language use. One female character switched from the nickname of 'Princess' to 'Zina' (aka 'warrior princess'); as 'Princess', she adopted the more prestigious SG code whereas as warrior princess, she appropriated the vernacular GC. Themistocleous concludes that '[o]verall, CS in digital writing in combination with the social- and medium-specific characteristics of IRC allows Greek-Cypriot Internet users to gain access to different roles and identities … switches seem to be associated with stereotypical modes of language use within the Greek-Cypriot speech community' (p. 13).

Themistocleous's study illustrates how CS permits a flexible, fun performativity, authenticated by the appropriation of stereotypical features known to informants; however, code choice is also dependent on audience, user perceptions of themselves and others and their technical histories, as also found by Lee (2014) in an investigation of the online behaviour and language awareness of twenty multilingual Hong Kong University students using techno-biographies. Techno-biographies, as the name suggests, involve reflexive accounts reported in interviews and ethnographic observations of users' technological life histories. Lee's study points to some shared and consistent behaviours/reports within and across students as well as individual differences. For example, all informants reported a preference to use specific codes when addressing and positioning themselves in relation to different audiences for various functions, for example, Chinese when interacting in a Chinese-based online forum, while code-switching between Chinese and English in a Hong Kong forum. However, individual relationships with technology at different times of their life reveal idiosyncratic language performance online. The case study of Tony, a third-year trainee teacher, is illustrative and reveals how his linguistic practices on FB at the time of data collection were influenced not only by other participants but also his self-perception and his perception of others in different settings, as well as his historical online practices in other more traditional media (Instant Messenger, IM). Salient among his identities is reported to be his national and ethnic identities which determine the codes he perceives as appropriate in different forums. He reports avoiding English in Chinese-based forums since he would neither wish to mark his Hong Kong identity nor 'offend the mainland Chinese forum participants' (p. 104). However, his teacher/student identities also influence his online choices; he reports having two FB accounts in order to accommodate different audiences (his friends/colleagues versus his students while on teacher practice). He invokes a multilingual repertoire (Cantonese, Standard Chinese English) in posts to friends, marking his student status as an English major and his identity as a

Hong Kong resident – although he reports, as others, that his use of English is sometimes employed with trepidation since he is aware that he is not fully proficient in the language. His language choice reflects his past preference for language mixing in IM when conversing with friends. In contrast, he posts entirely in English on the FB page designed for his students, adopting an 'academic discourse style' (p. 106) in a bid to encourage students to use English for themselves. He reports being anxious that his students will find his other FB page in which he performs a different 'version' of himself: *I was worried that if my students discovered my 'real' Facebook account, I had to reshape my identity for them.* In sum, Lee demonstrates how SM users negotiate their online identities in relation to their historical and contemporary relationships and linguistic practices on and offline and how their 'preferred' means of self-presentation influence language use.

Conclusion

In this chapter, we have discussed research that has focused on issues of identity in SM. We have considered the affordances and constraints of different technologies, different types and varieties of identities evident in the research literature and considered the salience of 'authenticity' and identity categories in discussions of online identity presentation. We have witnessed the role of SM in translating and authoring (Turner 2010) identities online and considered the relationship between offline and online performance. As in offline performance, we see that identities are context-dependent and context-creating, constructed in particular cultural, economic, historical and social settings and often motivated by perceptions of the self and the other. The salience of the 'network' in authenticating and legitimizing identities is evident. Identity work online is shown to reflect, reproduce but also challenge offline hierarchies and stereotypes. While studies of SM are comparatively new in identity research, they have much to offer contemporary theorizations.

CHAPTER EIGHT

Ethnic and Religious Identities

*Ethnic and religious identities concern where we come from and where we are going – our entire existence, not just the moment to moment. It is these identities above all that, for most people, give profound **meaning** to the 'names' we identify ourselves by, both as individuals and as groups. They supply the plot for the stories of our lives, singly and collectively, and are bound up with our deepest beliefs about life, the universe and everything.*

JOSEPH (2004: 172)

Introduction

Many studies have examined the relationship between ethnicity, language use and change, as well as the ways in which individuals' ethnic identity/ies[1] are constructed and negotiated in and through discourse. 'Ethnicity' is a contentious and elusive term with multiple definitions which often appeal to overlapping categories such as 'race', 'nationality' and 'religion' (Cohen 1999; Eriksen 2010). There is often difficulty in separating out such categories. Often religion and ethnicity intersect, each depending on the other, although there may be many different ethnicities observing the same religion. Many accounts of national identity also appeal to the category/ies of ethnic identity/ies (see Chapter Eleven) although these often prioritize political autonomy and boundedness, rather than cultural heritage or common descent[2] (Joseph 2004: 162). Moreover, many nations house different ethnic groups, while individuals sharing the same ethnicity can be spread across the globe, unbounded by national borders. Further, 'race' is sometimes used interchangeably with ethnicity, especially since its definition as a socially constructed category rather than a biological or genetic 'given' has become commonly accepted (Cokley 2007).[3] As such, this chapter acknowledges the blurred boundaries between these categories but has nevertheless prioritized the examination of work identifying and declaring 'ethnicity/ethnic identity' as a key/convenient analytic variable or object of study, with 'religious identity'/'identification' treated as a characteristic feature of ethnicity or as a separate analytic category in its own right.

We refer broadly to an ethnic group as 'a collectivity or community that makes assumptions about common attributes related to cultural practices and shared history. Thus, religion, language[4] and territory are all included in the term ethnicity' (Phoenix 2010: 297) or 'a sense of group identity deriving from real or perceived common bonds such as language, race or religion' (Edwards 1995: 125). At the same time, we acknowledge that recent work conceives of ethnic identity as a social construction, an outcome of interactive engagement based on salient values and categories which mark cultural differences and groups (e.g. 'us' versus 'them' dynamics) rather than stable or predetermined differences, internal heterogeneity within ethnic groups and ethnicity as a dynamic performance and not therefore something that individuals 'have' or simply 'are' but rather are constructions related to particular times (including historical trajectories), contexts and situations (Anthias & Yuval-Davis 1992; Brubaker 2004; Eriksen 2001).

For the purposes of this chapter, we conceive of ethnicity as both a self-concept/subjective understanding and as a process of individual/group performance and experience of identification. This calls for an appreciation of both psychological and social processes and frameworks of investigation. The aim of this chapter is to highlight the theoretical, methodological and analytical diversity in the study of ethnic identity which has impacted on or been developed within applied linguistics and the influences therefore of different disciplinary perspectives and research questions. The chapter first examines traditional research on language maintenance and the role of ethnic identity with respect to this before discussing more recent concerns in sociolinguistics and discourse studies. More specifically in the section 'Ethnic identity and ethnolinguistic vitality', we explore social-psychological and sociolinguistic approaches to the study of the relationship between ethnic identity and language. We begin by discussing the theory and approach of ethnolinguistic vitality (EV), exploring the application of 'Social Identity Theory' (see Chapter One) to the study of language maintenance in minority groups and some of the difficulties encountered by researchers in this endeavour. We describe and critique the framework and its application and consider ways in which the study of language maintenance by minority groups in language contact situations may be informed by discursive studies of identity. We also discuss research which has not invoked EV but has nevertheless explored the relationship between ethnic identity and heritage language maintenance. The section 'Ethnolects and ethnolinguistic repertoires' explores the explanatory validity and power of two notions prevalent in sociolinguistic research: 'ethnolect' and 'ethnolinguistic repertoire' (ER), discussing in particular shifts in recent work towards the appropriation, development and exploration of the latter. The following two sections turn to the discursive realization of ethnic and religious identity: in the section 'Macro-level discourse studies I: Narrative approaches', we discuss studies appropriating critical discourse analysis, performative and positioning theories and some types of narrative analysis and in the section 'Micro-level discourse studies II: Discursive psychology and interactional sociolinguistic approaches' research approaching the study of identity/identities via ethnomethodological and conversation analytic micro-analyses, including work from discursive psychology and sociolinguistics is explored. We therefore review both macro and micro approaches to the study of the discursive negotiation and construction of ethnic identity in order to identify their differing assumptions, theoretical bases, methods and approaches and demonstrate how and why ethnic identifications and stances towards them are significant to study theoretically and practically.

Ethnic identity and ethnolinguistic vitality

The subject of ethnic identity – defined in the cognitivist paradigm of social psychology as a subjective affective and cognitive understanding of belonging to a real or imagined ethnic group with common ancestry and origin – and its relationship to group/group language maintenance has featured in both social-psychological and sociolinguistic research for some years. Members of ethnic groups are considered to affiliate or align with a common sense of belonging and being, tied to a shared sense of ancestry/kinship including cultural and historical understandings. A social-psychological reading of identity considers both personal and social characteristics, with ethnic identity functioning as one component of an individual's social identity/self-concept, both ascribed (determined by birth) and situationally determined and achieved. Since the mid-twentieth century, as contact between ethnic groups has increased due to globalization and mobility, changing patterns of intergroup relations and language practice have afforded new avenues of investigation, including studies into the (linguistic) vitality of minority groups, explored by some through the lens of Ethnolinguistic Vitality Theory (EVT) (Yagmur & Ehala 2011). The 'vitality' of an ethnolinguistic group is defined as 'that which makes a group likely to behave as a distinctive and active collective entity in inter-group situations' (Giles et al. 1977: 308). The strength of group identification with in- or out-groups is considered pivotal in determining the maintenance or loss of members' language. Indeed, shifts in speech style are considered partially or mainly dependent on ethnic identity.

EVT has been prominent in investigations of complex intergroup relations between communities with different linguistic repertoires and applied to issues and studies as varied as age vitality (Giles et al. 2000), language maintenance and shift (Gogonas 2009; Hatoss & Sheely 2009; Komondouros & McEntee-Atalianis 2007; Yagmur 2009), language loss (Landry et al. 1996) and revitalization (Yagmur & Kroon 2003, 2006). A large body of work has emerged as separate works and collections of studies (Allard & Landry 1994; Kindell & Lewis 2000).

Within EVT, three related sociostructural factors are considered to influence group vitality: status (economic, linguistic, social, socio-historical), demography (number and distribution of group members within a region or nation, plus consideration of birth rate, marriage – endogamous/exogamous and migration patterns) and institutional support (formal and informal representations, e.g. in education, government services, mass media, politics, religion). In addition to these objective measurements, subjective perceptions of societal conditions and in- and out-group vitality are also considered to influence group vitality and shape ethnic identity (Bourhis et al. 1981) as measured by such tools as the Subjective Ethnolinguistic Vitality Questionnaire (SEVQ). Assessment of objective and subjective parameters (with various variables measured for each) provides an indication of low, medium or high group vitality. If high, members are considered likely to maintain their language and cultural autonomy; if low, they are more likely to be assimilated into the dominant (or host) group such that they are no longer considered as a distinctive collective and there will be language attrition and loss, unless they are able to counteract the pervasive social conditions and negative perceptions of community members. The main assumption of EVT is that there is a two-way relationship between ethnic/ social identity and language behaviour and that sociostructural factors impact on an individual and group's language and sense of identity.

Although there has been strong empirical support for the social-psychological conceptualization of objective and subjective EV (Abrams et al. 2009; Brown & Sachdev 2009; Willemyns et al. 1993) and many developments to the framework, analytic tools and their application, its heuristic, ontological and instrumental value continues to be questioned and scrutinized (Abrams et al. 2009; Edwards 1995; Ehala 2011; Ehala & Niglas 2007; Ehala & Zabrodskaja 2011; Hogg et al. 1989; Husband & Saifullah Khan 1982; Johnson et al. 1983; Tollefson 1991; Karan, 2011; Yagmur & Ehala 2011; Williams 1992; Yagmur 2011; papers in a special issue of the Journal of Multilingual and Multicultural Development 2011, Vol. 32 (2)). Some have queried the determination of ethnolinguistic groups without consideration of other intersecting variables (e.g. age, gender, social class, mixed ethnicities), others the conceptual clarity, definition and comprehensiveness of sociostructural and demographic variables and a tendency to emphasize the importance of mainstream institutions/ social structures in determining EV at the expense of minority group social structures and institutions (e.g. heritage schools, religious centres; see Yagmur 2011) or factors such as the impact of emotional attachments on collective identity (Ehala 2011).[5] Others have suggested that a tendency to read identity as a stable internal state rather than a dynamic external construction simplifies categories and underestimates the status of group vitality. In the following, we discuss some of these criticisms focusing our discussion mainly on how traditional studies of EV treat the concept of 'identity' and the difficulties that may arise as a consequence of this. We then discuss studies which have not directly invoked EVT but explored the relationship between heritage language maintenance and the maintenance of ethnic identity.

One of the key concepts of EVT is ethnic/social identity, which is noted to interact with a number of other variables to determine group vitality. The notion of identity invoked in EV studies relies on an interpretation drawn from Tajfel and Turner's 'Social Identity Theory' (SIT – see Chapter One and Reicher et al. 2010 for a more detailed description) which proposes that people categorize themselves and others into memberships and groupings based on beliefs, norms, values and patterns of interaction. This sense of group belonging is determined to be one's social identity. Members may positively or negatively evaluate themselves and others in light of psychological processes of social categorization, identification and comparison. SIT theorizes how psychological dynamics function within different social contexts. Its application allows for an exploration of when, why and how these psychological dynamics influence group behaviour and proposes that when group boundaries are weak, members within low-status groups may have the opportunity and mobility to transfer to high-status groups. If boundaries are fixed, other strategies of positive self-evaluation may be invoked. Distinctions can be marked linguistically such that speakers adopt forms which index their preferred in-group membership. The strength of one's group identification with in- or out-group members is considered important to ethnolinguistic identity and vitality: if one's ethnic identity is weak, one is more likely to shift to the linguistic behaviour of an out-group; whereas if it is strong, one is more likely to retain one's in-group language/ speech style.

The Social Identity Approach (including SIT and Social Categorization Theory; Turner 1982) considers the cognitive process of self-categorization as essential and primary in understanding group processes and relations. Individual and social structures are conceived as independent with individuals undergoing socialization through social contact. Social identity provides a psychological framework in which individuals conceive of themselves as social and cultural entities. The sociocultural meanings connected to any social category thereby influence subject behaviour. Within SIT, identity categories are considered as biological and social categories and used by EVT researchers as independent variables to explain and predict the behaviour of speakers. Identity construction is therefore conceived as a product of cognitive, evaluative and categorization processes influenced by mental structure and perception (Postmes & Jetten 2006; Postmes et al. 2006; Tajfel 1986; Tajfel & Turner 1979).

This view of identity, embedded within a cognitivist approach, has been considered as too limiting by some (including those studying EV); for example, Billig (1995, cited in Phoenix 2010: 302) rejects the notion that individuals self-stereotype in order to align with an ethnic group as this appeals to a static view of identity, others that prioritizing the cognitive process of self-categorization in order to understand and explain group behaviour may underplay the importance of discourse in identity construction. Moreover, McEntee-Atalianis (2011) argues that while the tripartite framework of EVT in assessing subjective and objective vitality is useful, EV studies must account for the hybrid and fluid nature of identity performance and therefore in developing methodologies and analytic frameworks – a consideration of the latter must be taken into account.

Drawing on a study of language attitudes and shift among the autochthonous Greek Orthodox community of Istanbul, Turkey (Komondouros & McEntee-Atalianis 2007), McEntee-Atalianis (2011) demonstrates how the treatment of intergroup relations can be too simplistic and essentialized in interpretations of community members as homogenous and bounded, in addition to being over-deterministic in their consideration of the relationship between identity and language use. Rather, she argues that researchers should engage theoretically and methodologically with the complexity and heterogeneity of identity performance/claims/conceptualizations as well as social and ideological influences. Moreover, she posits that rather than emphasizing the primacy of social identification as an internal psychological state/process, its discursive accomplishment should also be considered. Further, as others (Pavlenko & Blackledge 2004), she critiques the methodological bias for questionnaire data collection alone in assessing subjective vitality, noting such difficulties as the 'distillation of complex issues and experiences into a limited number of assessable constructs; the assumption that all informants will equally understand and engage with the concepts/constructs assessed …; and the "over-reliance" on subjective evaluations, which may not reflect actual performance or account for the variables which influence language use in reality' (p. 155). She also notes that in the study of EV and intergroup relations, languages and communities are treated as discrete entities such that bilingual/bicultural individuals are considered as the sum of two (competing) monolingual/monocultural identities rather than as hybrid and complex which may not reflect or constitute informant experience or performance. She instead recommends the adoption of a constructionist perspective in the development of EVT methodological and analytic tools illustrating this via a metacritical analysis of her study with Komondouros (Komondouros & McEntee-Atalianis 2007). For example, she highlights differences in informant reports according to the methodological approach adopted by the researcher. Questionnaires are reported to have elicited the following reports of ethnocultural identity among the Greek Orthodox community of Isanbul (Komondouros & McEntee-Atalianis 2007: 382ff) (Table 8.1).

The majority (89%) of informants reported feeling 'completely Greek or more Greek than Turkish' in response to ID1 and pride in being an 'Istanbul' Greek (ID3, 78%); more than two-thirds (72%) considered it necessary to have command of Greek in order to be a 'Constantinopolite' (an Istanbul Greek), with very few considering a command of Turkish to

Table 8.1 Identity questions

	Valid *n*	Not at all or more Greek than Turkish (%)	Equally Greek and Turkish (%)	Completely or more Turkish than Greek (%)	Mean	Standard deviation
ID1: How Turkish do you feel?	53	78.3	10.0	0.0	4.4[a]	0.69

	Valid *n*	Agree or strongly agree	Indifferent	Disagree or strongly disagree	Mean	Standard deviation
ID2: To be a true Istanbul Greek, it is necessary to speak Greek	60	71.7	16.7	11.6	3.9	1.09
ID3: I feel proud to be an Istanbul Greek	58	78.3	11.7	6.6	4.2	1.02
ID4: Speaking Turkish weakens our identity	58	11.6	10.0	75.0	3.8	0.99

Note: Percentages are of total sample, not just of valid responses.
[a]Indicates statistical significance at the 5% level.

impact on their distinct ethnic identity (ID4). When a two-factor analysis of
the effects of age and main language was undertaken on ID1 and ID2 (see
Table 8.2), a significant effect of main language was found on the strength
of self-perception as more Greek than Turkish (F1,52 = 8.0, p = <.01) with
no effect for age. This suggested that greater competence in Greek led to
stronger feelings of Constantinopolite Greek identity.

As a more complex picture emerged in subject self-reports, the analytic
focus shifted to the role of discourse (as social practice) in the construction
of social identities and processes. Evaluation and categorization were
viewed as discursive accomplishments rather than cognitive states. In
contrast to the questionnaire which presented informants with binary,
polarized and stable representations of the Greek and Turkish language
and ethnic identity, interviews yielded alternative representations and
'self-naming' practices by informants. Respondents referred to themselves
as 'Istanbulites/Constantinopolites', describing a hybrid identity enacted
via fluid linguistic repertoires (including use of both Greek and Turkish
elements in exchanges). These reports were also observed and confirmed by
ethnographic observations within the community. Questionnaires therefore
limited category choice and appealed to bounded 'essential' notions of
standard language and identity. Interviews and observations opened up a
more complex picture of multilingual practice and identity performance.
McEntee-Atalianis also reports that interviews provided a space for
informants to relay narratives about their life in Istanbul. These proved to
be sites of contestation and negotiation in which variable positions were
taken up by respondents towards their linguistic repertoires and ethnic
groupings with respect to such issues as historical events and sociocultural
norms and activities. She asserts that '[i]nformants almost uniformly
reported that they were Istanbul Greeks and Turkish nationals, which gives
them a distinct ethnocultural identity described as consisting of hybrid
characteristics, including the Greek language, Greek culture and traditions,
and the Greek Orthodox community, but also significantly that they were
proud members of Istanbul, with deep roots and historical ties to the city
and to Turkish society' (p. 161). Many informants also reported differences

Table 8.2 Marginal means for feelings of identity by main
language

Best language	Mean	Standard error	95% confidence interval	
			Lower bound	Upper bound
Turkish	4.190	0.141	3.903	4.477
Greek	4.889	0.279	4.321	5.457

in linguistic accent, style and 'character' between themselves and mainland Greeks. She contrasts this with the questionnaire which she notes provided a 'crude and insensitive instrument of measurement … when compared against informants' own characterisations' (p. 161), failing to account for the 'multiplicity and recombinant nature of "Constantinopolite/Istanbulite" identity as narrated by informants in interviews' (p. 163).

Her research (with Komondouros) points to the importance of first understanding the sociopolitical and cultural context of investigation prior to subjecting informants to standardized measures of assessment, for these may or may not be applicable, nor indeed suitably nuanced, to account for the complexity of the situation/community under investigation.[6] However, it also supports and critiques methodological triangulation in the assessment of ethnolinguistic vitality and arguably highlights the benefits (and disadvantages) of a synthetic approach which draws on different theoretical stances (cognitivist versus discursive).

One of the key findings arising from the Komondouros and McEntee-Atalianis (2007) study was a significant relationship between perceived and actual competence in the Istanbul Greek variety and strength of feeling with regard to Constantinopolite Greek identity. Greater competence and use of Greek correlated strongly with a sense (and discursive positioning) of Greek ethnic identification and heritage. Research since the 1980s has found a strong effect of heritage language(s) (HL) maintenance and ethnic identity[7] (where both are considered as mutually constitutive); in instances where HLs wane, so too do perceptions/self-reports of ethnic identity. Studies are difficult to compare due to differences in research foci, research contexts, competence and use of HL by informants, demographic variability from study to study of the target groups under investigation (e.g. differences in age, gender, social class, racial background) and differences in measures of ethnic identity. However, a meta-analysis[8] of studies undertaken by Mu (2015) reports on an investigation of forty-three data sets taken from eighteen studies (journal articles [thirteen], theses [four] and a conference paper). It found a 'significant moderate positive correlation' between the HL proficiency and ethnic identity of fourteen ethnic groups in English-speaking countries (Australia, Canada, UK and the United States). In other words, heritage language use/maintenance and ethnic identity are neither completely dependent on one another nor completely independent – a number of individual and social factors may influence their relationship such as age, family, gender, race, social class and sociocultural variables. Mu notes, as McEntee-Atalianis (2011 in relation to research of EVT), the limitations of the theoretical and methodological approaches adopted in many of the studies examined in the meta-analysis which take an 'inside-out' (p. 251) cognitive perspective towards ethnic identity and 'draw on an individualistic position to quantitatively predict the linear relationship between ethnic identity and HL' (p. 250), thereby simplifying a picture that is far more complex. Calling for a complementary post-structuralist reading of the relationship between ethnic identity and heritage language maintenance, Mu highlights the difficulties and challenges faced by heritage language learners/users in majority language contexts for they are often positioned in contradictory and sometimes negative ways by different actors (family; friends; peers; community).[9] They may also differ in their motivations for learning and maintaining their heritage language and may not only wish to align with the practices of their ethnic group but also transform them. Ethnic identity construction is therefore concluded to be 'a diverse, heterogeneous and ultimately precarious hybridity (Ang 2001)' (p. 250) which needs to be investigated through a consideration of both internal and external (social/discursive) conditions.

The complexity of the ethnic language and ethnic identity link is further demonstrated in investigations of bi or multiethnic individuals and groupings – studies which may also refer to 'mixed-race' individuals, where one parent is of one (or more) ethnicity and the other of another ethnic type. To date, there has been some research on mixed-race individuals, particularly black/white individuals in the United States and the UK, although work included in volumes such as Edwards et al. (2012), King-O'Riain et al. (2014) and Fozdar and Rocha (2017) extend to other nations/continents – the latter in particular focusing on the Asian context.

Noro (2009) is an example of scholarship investigating the role of language on the formation of ethnic identity in children of mixed heritage – specifically children of mixed Asian-European heritage acquiring Japanese in British Columbia, Canada. Taking an ecological perspective, in which the situational context is deemed to affect how an individual views his/her identity, Nora explores the role of family, heritage language schools and the cultural environment in influencing ethnic identification. Comparing two cohorts of children (aged between 5 and 12 years) in Vancouver and Victoria, Nora reports on differences in ethnolinguistic vitality and self-identification. Children in Vancouver were found to have higher rates of Japanese oral proficiency and 'clearer self-identification' (p. 12) in comparison to those in Victoria. While some differences were found in the management of the heritage schools and in the number of children attending them (more children attended the school in Vancouver), both cohorts received almost identical contact hours and teaching methods and materials. Reasons for differences were determined to be largely ecological. First, children in the Victoria cohort were slightly younger than those in Vancouver which may account for lower levels of proficiency and greater ambiguity in self-identification; and second, the Japanese language and culture were noted to be more salient in Vancouver with many opportunities for children to hear and see the language in the linguistic landscape. Further influential factors included the language choice and cultural influence of parents; in the study over 90 per cent of the non-Japanese parents were fathers but their degree of acceptance and use of Japanese with their spouses and children and acceptance of Japanese cultural mores had a significant impact on children's language use and self-identification.

The surrounding social environment was therefore found to have a significant effect on the children's construction of their (mixed) ethnic identity.

Ethnolects and ethnolinguistic repertoires

The distinctive code used by an ethnic group is often referred to by sociolinguists as an 'ethnolect' or an ethnic variety, dialect or system (Androutsopoulos 2001; Carter 2013; Clyne 2000; Fought 2006; Labov 1972a; Leap 1993; Mendoza-Denton 2008; Newmark et al. 2016; Szakay 2012). However, as noted by the scholars referenced above and others (Benor 2010; Coupland 2007; Eckert 2008b; Irvine 2001), there are difficulties in determining boundaries between varieties, dialects and systems, and when studying identity, difficulties in teasing apart ethnicity from other social variables. There are also difficulties in accounting for fluidity of language performance in intergroup/speaker and intra-speaker variation. This means that uniform and consistent inventories of identifiable linguistic/discursive features are often difficult to map within and across group members in all contexts of use. 'Ethnolect', as a theoretical construct, has been considered by some as a problematic notion and concept.

Nevertheless, studies have explored the intersection between ethnicity and other social variables in structuring social practices and in building matrices within which systems of identification evolve. Recent examples include Kirkham's (2015) discussion of the intersection between ethnicity and social class in a community of British adolescents, Rosowsky's (2012) account of the teaching and practice of religious classicals in diasporic ethno-religious settings in the UK and Baker-Smemoe and Jones (2014) study of the intersection between religion and ethnicity in the Mexican Mormon colonies in border towns on the US/Mexico border.

In seeking to tackle the difficulty of attempting to identify distinctive language use by ethnic groups, that is, that not all speakers use the ethnic variants, and if they do, not all of the time, Benor (2010) proposes the concept of ER, which she defines 'as a fluid set of linguistic resources that members of an ethnic group may use variably as they index their ethnic identities' (2010: 160). Influenced by work in sociocultural linguistics, the concept addresses what she considers as five 'theoretical problems with the notion of "ethnic language variety" as a bounded entity: ... intragroup variation; intra-speaker variation; out-group use; delineating the ethnic group; [and] delineating "ethnolect"' (2010: 160). Using data from her research on Jewish Americans in addition to research by others on African Americans, Latinos and other groups, she sets out the ER approach, which she argues is equally applicable to other spheres of social organization (e.g. 'profession, social class, sexual orientation and region'; Benor 2010).

Within this approach, greater agency is afforded to speakers than traditional variationist studies which correlate pre-established social categories with language use. Rather, identity work including alignment or distancing is actively achieved through the adoption and selection of 'distinctive linguistic features' (p. 160) from an arsenal of elements ranging from the phonetic/phonological to morpho-syntactic, lexical and discursive. On Benor's own admission, the concept of ER is influenced by studies of individual monolingual and multilingual repertoires, including recent work on style in which speakers exploit a range of sociolinguistic resources in their practices of 'bricolage' (see Chapter Two).

Within-group variation may occur, Benor argues, as a consequence differences in speaker's social networks, ethnic activities, stances and ideologies towards these, as well as towards social categories and language. For example, she found in her research on Jewish Americans that Jews with a high number of Jewish friends scored higher on a scale of loanwords and constructions than those with few (see Table 8.3). Also, Jews who reported active participation in religious life (particularly Orthodoxy) reported using Hebrew and Yiddish loanwords and Yiddish constructions, marking out an identity as observant Jews.

ER circumvents the need to differentiate individuals into speakers or non-speakers of an ethnolect, or the need to determine how many features, or which combination of features, need to be used by a speaker in order to establish their use of a particular variety/dialect. Rather in examining identity performance, investigators can explore the selective use of ethnically marked forms from a distinctive repertoire alongside the use of other linguistic resources by individuals in particular interactions and within different ethnic landscapes.

The approach is appealing in accounting for intra-speaker variation across contexts and over time (including across the life course). In the case of the former, Benor argues that rather than appealing to such notions as code-switching (CS) or style-shifting to account for different patterns of

Table 8.3 Jews' use of loanwords and constructions according to social networks (Benor 2010: 163)

Close friends who are Jewish	Mean score on 23-item index (range: 0–100%)
None	30
Some	35
About half	41
Most	49
All or most all	56

linguistic realisation even in one speaker exchange, an account based on the notion of ER more adequately accounts for behaviour (compare with studies discussed in the section 'Micro-level discourse studies II: Discursive psychology and interactional sociolinguistic approaches' below). For example, she analyses an excerpt taken from Jacobs-Huey (2006: 42–43), in which an African American woman talks about the work of a cosmetologist:

Extract 1

4   You want them to be satisfied and that's your work and your

5   talent that you let walk out the door and ... when somebody asks her

6   who did her hair, she's gonna ... -You know I was in a grocery store

7   yesterday in [name of city]. I was at Winn Dixie shopping and

8   bo::y it was two ladies standing at the – two black ladies standing at

9   that counter. I don't know WHO this cosmetologist was or you know

10   that they go to to get they hair done but boy they was dogging her

11   name in the grocery store . . .

63   And don't try to rush your client 'cause a lot of people do not need you

64   and you know for yourself when you do a rush job, you gonna do a

65   bum up job

If one treats this as an ethnolect, one might analyse the shift in line 8 as an example of a CS from Standard English (lines 4–7) to African American Vernacular English (AAVE – lines 8–11); however, she notes that there is some difficulty in then accounting for the behaviour seen in lines 63–65, as there appears to be a switch back to Standard English with marked copula deletion in line 64. Therefore, rather than accounting for patterns of CS, Benor argues that the speaker is using one code but stylistically varying the amount of African American features from her repertoire.

Intra-speaker variation across the life course is further demonstrated in the case of Jews who become Orthodox in adulthood. As they mix within new social networks, they become exposed to a distinctive and different repertoire marked by loanwords from Hebrew and Yiddish, semantic and syntactic forms from Yiddish (e.g. 'staying *by* us', 'If I see him, *so* I'll let you know' p. 167) as well as some phonological features (e.g. word-final /t/ release). Speakers vary in the use of these forms – differences between them linked to the adoption of particular ideological stances. For example, in a comparison of three speakers, Benor notes that one informant adopted many of the Orthodox features, to the point that others within the community believe her to be 'even more *frum* ("Orthodox, religious")' (p. 167) than those who originated in the community; another speaker used loanwords, marked intonation and final devoicing but not semantic or syntactic influences; and finally, a third speaker only appropriated Hebrew/Yiddish loanwords. These realizations mark differences in motivation and awareness influenced by cognitive, linguistic and social variables. In this example, and others, we see how the repertoire approach accounts for the adoption of resources from one group's linguistic repertoire by another and therefore the fluid, multiple and constructed nature of ethnic group boundaries and ethnic group membership by individuals, and the potential for the linguistic and stylistic realization of 'mixed' ethnicities (e.g. African American and Latino or black and white). Speakers may use various resources to identify themselves at a particular time with others or to convey a particular stance or style. Listeners too may determine markers of ethnic identity via perceptual cues (Szakay 2012; Thomas & Reaser 2004).

The approach of ER has been assessed, taken up and extended by some researchers in recent times. For example, Sharma (2011) argues for its salience in the study of dialect variation in urban contexts. She compares a variationist approach to a repertoire approach in an examination of socio-phonetic features in the speech of lower-middle-class British Asians living in Southall, London, who combine elements from British and Indian English dialect systems. She concludes that her findings support ER rather than the notion of 'ethnolect'; however, she also addresses the claim often made about ER that repertoires are broadly fluid and dependent on individual agency. She develops a typology of hybrid repertoires realized under different social conditions and structures.

Sharma's ER approach facilitates the investigation of clusters of variables in different speaking contexts which lead to marked differences in the generalizations that can be made about social meaning and language change within the Punjabi community studied. The variationist analysis adhered to a standard format of exploring only one variable – retroflexion of /t/ – elicited in sociolinguistic interviews, whereas the ER analysis focused on the realization of three more variables (the FACE and GOAT vowels and coda /l/) across a range of speaking situations and took into account speakers' social networks, calculated using a 'Diversity Index'. Results from the first analysis (variationist) revealed no gender difference in use of retroflex /ʈ/ among the older generation, in contrast to the younger generation. Young women were found to hardly use the form, favouring a [t] realization instead. On the surface, the results leant themselves to a traditional interpretation of younger women favouring standard forms for their prestige value but it did not account for differences across the generations nor the historical and contemporary experiences of those living in the Southall community. Four case studies of older informants (one male and one female) and younger informants (also one male and one female) in different interactional contexts, also taking into account their social networks, revealed a more complex picture in which two types of repertoire were determined: the first, 'flexible and highly differentiated' (p. 481) characterized the speech of older men and younger women; the second, 'more fused and invariant' (p. 481) evident in the speech of older women and younger men. Expanding data collection beyond the sociolinguistic interview showed that women use the Asian retroflex form in the home context and that older men strategically varied their use of ethnolinguistic features in comparison to younger men. A simple explanation of variation in use according to audience design or speech accommodation cannot account for intersubject variability, and age and gender do not neatly correlate with repertoire types; rather, they are linked not forged by them. An explanation can however be found in the fact that older men and younger women maintain contact with more diverse groups within their social networks leading to greater diversity in their ERs. A single ethnolect was therefore not apparent but a repertoire of feature selection corresponding to the 'relative complexity of social worlds that individuals develop' (p. 487).

Other research invoking ER has focused on different linguistic/discursive devices and levels of analysis. For example, D'Arcy (2010) investigates the ways in which young male Maori and Pakeha English speakers employ systems of direct quotation, drawing on shared linguistic resources in constructions of dialogue. She reports on how quantitative and qualitative differences in quotation lead to the enactment of Maori and Pakeha ethnic identity in Aotearoa/New Zealand. Negrón (2014) investigates the Latino ER in New York and the performance of 'latinidad' (a shared sense of Latino identity) in conversations between Latinos from New York City, thereby extending the framework of ER and analysis to discourse analysis and panethnic groups.

The complexity of Latino panethnicity in the United States is evident in the fact that there are nineteen dialects (or more) and speakers come from different racial and sociohistorical backgrounds with varied immigration histories. This leads to the negotiation and positioning of multiple linguistic and ethnic identities. On first meeting, Latinos have to determine their interloctor's standing (Latino and national identity) among a number of cues (phenotypical features, language and dialect, etc.). The Latino ER equips them with the necessary resources to flexibly and contextually adapt their self-presentation to other Latinos along a continuum ranging from 'micro-regional cultures' at one end, 'cultural nationalism' in the middle and 'panethnicity' at the other, using a variety of linguistic features from English (New York English, AAVE and other varieties) and Spanish (multiple dialects) to mark collective identity.

Benor's original framework of ER has therefore been extended by research within different contexts and communities. These studies point to the importance of investigating local/community beliefs and ideologies[10] and also the ways in which social meaning is attached to particular linguistic/ discursive features to strategically perform alignment, construct relationships and shared ethnic identity. They also uncover systematic realizations of sets of (nested) repertoires used by members of multiple subgroups and illustrate the fluid nature of performativity as subjects select and invoke different types and combinations of resources (marked linguistic and discursive features) in self-presentation and for the purpose of achieving interactional goals across different situations.

Macro-level discourse studies I: Narrative approaches

In the following two sections, we continue our discussion of the discursive enactment and negotiation of ethnic and religious identities but move away from our previous focus on ER. In this section, we consider studies which have explored how individuals or groups adopt or take on available positions in discourse and/or how individuals or groups may be positioned. These include studies which have drawn on the approaches and principles of critical aspects of narrative analysis, performativity and positioning theories. The latter conceive of identity as being culturally and historically influenced and socially constructed, and therefore often invoke an understanding of this via analyses which tie together both fine-grained investigations of text and talk with macro conditions (contexts/institutions) of discourse creation, investigating how discourses are forged within and by social structures and influenced by ideology – therefore investigating the ways in which social reality is at the same time constituted and reflected in discourse. Ethnicity and religious identity is therefore conceived as alignment to a social identity – membership within one or more social groups. It is considered as a dynamic, interactive accomplishment within specific economic, historic and political contexts, influenced by the dynamics of power relations and circulating discourses.

In the following, we initially discuss how storytellers position themselves (and others) in interaction and within the story world that they create in order to convey and construct an ethnic or religious identity. We then return to a consideration of subject 'authenticity' (see Chapter Seven) in order to discuss how ethnic identity is constructed via authenticating discourses and also how and why the inability to construct an 'authentic self' may have significant personal consequences for foreign-born minority ethnic individuals seeking settlement and employment in a host nation.

An oft-cited question posed to individuals who in some way look or sound as if they are different from the host community is, 'Where are you from?' (Zhu Hua & Li Wei 2016), a question often met with a mixed response, depending on who is asking and the context in which the question arises.

Such questions often demand subjects to provide narrative accounts of their status or dismiss the question as irrelevant. Hatoss (2012) discusses this very issue in relation to Sudanese people with refugee backgrounds in Australia, drawing on subjects' self-reflective accounts in semi-structured interviews. The case of the Sudanese living in Australia is noted by Hatoss to be particularly interesting since they are phenotypically distinct from the mainstream community and hypothesized to have a strong connection with their ethnic heritage (as found in other ethnic minority groups e.g. Phinney 1992; Windle 2008). The study emphasizes how in interethnic interaction the salience of where one is from and the need to define membership categorization becomes a routine practice. Adopting positioning theory (Davies & Harré 1990), the study explores the way in which informants position themselves (reflexive positioning) and others (interactive positioning) in their story world and within the interactional site, 'in such a way that these "locations" or "positionings" reflect their attitudes, emotions and other embedded cultural meanings based on higher level institutional and macro-social events" (p. 50). The author explores the identity labels and referential categories appropriated, determining that participants used multiple identity labels but that these were noted to be context dependent, also reflecting how they were used in Sudan. Many labels referred to country of birth, nationality, colour and ethnic group membership. For example, the 'Dinka' label is noted to provide a broad classification of many ethnic groups; however, a tribal and government system of identity classification was also invoked, for example, 'a member of the Dinka ethnic group can be a member of the Dinka Bor dialect group, and he/she can also be a member of the Twic county, the Lith and Adhiok communities and the Nyanthieth "clan"' (p. 56). A dynamic and fluid appropriation of identity labels is reported to be negotiated on a daily basis, the most salient relating to physiological and racial characteristics. Informants report that their blackness is readily associated with their refugee status, marking them as outsiders.

When questioned how they respond to being asked by other Australians about where they are from, half of the respondents reported that they were cooperative in providing a response; however, three (of fourteen) reported that they were often uncooperative and four (out of fourteen) that it depended on the context. Analysis of the narratives provided by informants about their encounters with mainstream Australians unearths a more detailed and complex picture of how they are positioned by themselves and others. For example, one informant (Ajang) describes his feeling of being positioned as a stranger when asked about his place of origin; however, he also indirectly reports on how he renegotiates the ascribed identity labels and constructs a past self which is spatio-temporally distinct ('from Sudan') from his present self ('Australian') (p. 59; also see, Merino et al. 2017 for a discussion of the time-place chronotope in narratives of the ethnic Mapuche). Analysis of specific discursive, linguistic and paralinguistic features within the reporting of his story reveals how difficult the question is for Ajang's sense of self and how much work he has to do in order to establish an in-group identity within the Australian context.

Others shift between the world of their accounts/stories and the interactional exchange with the interviewer. One subject (Duom) is described as employing direct quotations as a strategy to distance himself from the overt marking of evaluative judgements, a feature noted to arise in other anxious and fearful immigrant accounts (De Fina 2003, cited in Hatoss 2012: 60). Another (Jacob), in an act of resilient self-positioning, describes how he turns the tables on his enquirers to ask where they are from, since, 'Australians who are not Aboriginal cannot be fully Australian' (p. 63).

The study highlights the tensions between establishing a strong ethnic self-concept and a desire to be a member of the host country. It also points to marked differences between reported feelings about being positioned as a foreigner within the interactional event of the interview and narratives of actual encounters; more specifically, when directly questioned, subjects often downplayed the extent of 'otherization' by mainstream Australians; however, conflicts became evident through the stories told.

Narratives, as noted previously, are important sites of identity construction and in the case of religious identity can mark both the individual and social religious experience (McKinlay & McVittae 2011a: 46ff). Dumanig et al. (2011) document the role of conversion narratives in the construction and reinforcement of Christian identity in Malaysia. These narratives are shown to take on a particular pattern of performance which indexes a marked transition from a pre-Christian identity to that of 'Christian'. These distinct identities are built through the ritualistic performance of public testimonials. Their analysis focuses on the rhetorical moves and lexical choices made by speakers as they testify to their changed, positively evaluated Christian personae. The stories represent replicable genre, moving through three steps: life prior to conversion, how and why conversion took place and life following conversion. Lexical forms shift to features recognized within the Christian faith and the speaker's community of practice, with individuals professing responsibility for their conversion, marking this through the appropriation of self-referential linguistic forms (e.g. first person pronouns). After conversion, they construct an identity that aligns with Christian values of goodness while rejecting the negative characteristics of a past non-Christian self.

Other studies focusing on narrative accounts (in many cases 'small stories' or micro-narratives within interview data) include, for example, Jaspal and Cinirella's (2010) investigation of the negotiation of the religious identity of young Muslim gay individuals in which they report on the manner in which their Muslim faith frames their interpretation of their sexuality as a 'temptation' to be resisted (p. 10), a test from God, and Figgou and Condor's (2007) account of how Greeks categorize members of the Muslim minority in northern Greece as 'Turks', appealing to reports they claim to be made by the Muslim Turks themselves in order to distance themselves and disavow the minority of civil rights.

The rhetorical process of 'otherization' enacted via such means as membership categorization and negative stance marking can lead to racism and discrimination. These are issues discussed in the work of Wood and Finlay (2008) and Lindgren (2009). Racism and discrimination can have not only emotional but also practical and material consequences for ethnic minority members who do not have command of the necessary discursive skills to gain access to mainstream institutions and their advantages. Many face discrimination as a consequence of their inability to present an 'authentic identity' in settings such as job interviews as discussed in Chapter Six. As also discussed previously (see Chapter Seven), authenticity is not only performed but perceived by others and is therefore open to evaluation and challenge; if one is in a less powerful position, this can have significant (negative) consequences and outcomes.

Campbell and Roberts (2007, previously cited in Chapter Six) report on the difficulties faced by foreign-born ethnic minority individuals who are unfamiliar with the requirements/genre of a competency-based interview in the UK, in particular the need to synthesize work-based and personal identities in order to demonstrate competence, trustworthiness and belonging to an institution, and who as a consequence fail to access jobs within the mainstream market. Combining interactional sociolinguistics, critical discourse analysis, organisational discourse analysis and narrative theory they illustrate the discursive skills honed by successful candidates in the construction of an authentic worker subjectivity and contrast their performance with those who are unsuccessful.

Successful candidates produced a desired 'synthetic personality' using three methods: 'personalized and idiosyncratic language ... used to describe how [they] implemented institutional procedures'; 'the employment of personal history, linked with an analytic overview, to demonstrate the candidate's internalisation of institutional values and skills such as getting up early or customer service' and 'strategies of euphemization to put an institutional gloss on personal experience, recasting a frustrating or upsetting experience as "challenging"' (p. 251). Unsuccessful candidates were perceived by interviewers as less authentic, producing text-book answers and 'buzz words' (e.g. 'teamwork') suspected to be rote-learned rather than adapted to the interactional context or interpreted through their own 'voice', and were considered as 'overly personal and informal in their style of self-presentation and therefore "unprofessional"' (p. 244). The authors determine that in the majority of interviews, a 'disproportionate number of candidates who were born abroad were unsuccessful' (p. 244) and note that without awareness of the new demands of the new work order foreign-born candidates will be doubly disadvantaged because they will be forced into often low-paid work supported by their own ethnic group and as a consequence not be exposed to the discourse of the mainstream workplace; and society will also negatively evaluate them, leading to negative ethnic stereotyping.

The issue of 'authentication' as an ethnic minority group member is equally important within the permeable boundaries of one's group. For example, Shenk (2007) illustrates how authenticating discourse, which draws on hegemonic ideologies in casual and very playful exchanges in a bilingual Mexican American group of friends, can be used to perform and argue for an ethnic identity. This is strategically achieved by appealing to purity of heritage, purity of nationality and fluency in Spanish. These themes are invoked and negotiated throughout conversational exchanges through stance acts serving to position subjects with respect to their cultural authenticity.

In the remainder of this chapter, we explore how ethnicity as a social category is constructed, legitimated (for self and others) and negotiated in talk exploring this in the next section, first through the lens of discursive psychology (DP), an approach which applies the principles of ethnomethodology, conversation/discourse analysis and rhetoric to topics in psychology (Edwards & Potter 2001), before turning to consider other sociolinguistic accounts.

Micro-level discourse studies II: Discursive psychology and interactional sociolinguistic approaches

Despite its psychological orientation, its emphasis on discourse has meant that DP as an approach has drawn on some of the tools created by anthropologists, sociologists and linguists, while it, in turn, has influenced work in applied linguistics. Within DP, in contrast to the cognitivist psychological viewpoint, discourse is not considered as a product or reflection of the mind but as a field of social action serving various functions and therefore worthy of interrogation. Emphasis is placed on examining accounts of the world: how individuals categorize and construct the world, and how these accounts may inform and influence attitudes, beliefs, dispositions and values – the latter making actions accountable. Three important characteristics of discourse inform how it is analysed in DP; these include its *situated status* – how it is 'occasioned', that is, oriented to and invoked, or silenced and subverted by interactants in situ and in sequentially managed interaction, and how participants employ defensive and offensive rhetorical devices in managing evaluations; *action orientation* – how discourse performs actions and how representations/evaluations are occasioned within situated talk, and therefore how they are variable and fluid; and its *constructed nature* – how particular actions are performed/constructed through the appropriation of particular linguistic and discursive features and also how representations of the world are developed to perform particular actions in interaction (Edwards & Potter 2001).

Within DP, ethnicity is therefore considered as a discursive accomplishment which is locally performed and negotiated in talk and text through the use of linguistic and rhetorical devices. Of significance is how these constructions are built and what versions of 'reality' are presented.[11] As in social psychological theories of identity (e.g. 'Social Identity Theory', Tajfel & Turner 1986, see above), processes of social categorization and comparison/ contrast are considered fundamental to identity performance (Verkuyten 2005). However, in contrast to SIT, analysis begins with discourse and processes of evaluation and categorization are primarily seen as discursive accomplishments. Discourse may be flexible, even contradictory, creatively (co-)constructed via the appropriation of social and cultural categories and repertoires, involving the 'endless work of forming and dismantling, claiming, reminding, identifying, re-establishing, [and] rejecting' (Wetherell 2009: 4) claims/positions/constructions. DP therefore aims to explore the relationship between the inner world of thoughts and the outer world of experience in examining how people talk and account for themselves and their actions in different contexts and situations. It employs conversation analytic tools also used by interactional sociolinguists.

Studies focusing on the fine-grained analysis of ethnic minority identity construction include, for example, Verkuyten's (1997) examination of Turks residing in the Netherlands and his later study with De Wolf (2002) exploring Chinese people's accounts of their identities also in the Netherlands, Davydova and Heikkinen's (2004) examination of accounts by ethnic Finns in Russia prior to their return to Finland and Sala et al.'s (2010) analysis of differences in presentation between different generations of Italian immigrants in Australia. Studies of 'hybrid' ethnic identities have included Ali and Sonn (2010), Bélanger and Verkuyten (2010) and Malhi et al. (2009). In the following, we discuss two recent studies which have adopted DP and CA, selected for their comparative and contemporary interest: one which examines the discursive construction of ethnic minority status within a majority culture, the case of Mapuches in Chile (Merino and Tileagă 2011), and another, the case of Finns residing in Russia (Varjonen et al. 2013). The latter focuses on ethnic identity construction prior to and following migration by individuals who 'return' to their country of ethnic origin, in some cases after several generations of initial emigration. Both research projects address how ethnic social categorization is legitimated, categorized and justified by participants and to others, and reveals the fluid and accomplished nature of situated identity construction over time and space.

Merino and Tileagă (2011) examine the ethnic self-definition of young urban Mapuches from Temuco and Santiago in Chile in semi-structured interviews with an adult Mapuche.[12] Mapuches are reported to have experienced social prejudice and discrimination evidenced in political and public discourse and educational texts and practices. They argue that identity construction is a product of practical and interpretive reasoning, built through the flexible appropriation and negotiation (including resistance) of group attributes, categories and characteristics in talk. They examine the significance and importance of minority ethnic identity for the young 15–20 year olds and the way in which ethnicity is 'occasioned' – 'how identity is *at* and *in* play' (p. 87), and its significance as a social category in action for ethnic minority self-definition and in-group membership and for sociopolitical aims. The analysis focuses on an in-depth qualitative analysis of two individuals (Sergio and Jessenia) responding to the question, 'What is it like for you to be a young Mapuche in Chilean society today?' (p. 91). Answers to the question appear as qualified accounts as illustrated in the excerpts below.

Extract 2

1 Carmen	… What is it like for you to be a young Mapuche in the Chilean society?
5 Jessenia	Eh::: first (.) well (.) it is kind of cool,
6	it is (.) all the same it is (.) good (.)
7	but, sometimes it is (.) nevertheless (.) it
8	is like (.) 'oh, she is Mapuche' and (.) like
9	(.) they reject you but that has never
10	happened to me (.) it is like I have been
11	accepted everywhere (.) that is (.) I mean
12	(.) I don't know whether it is because I get
13	along with everybody easily, that I am good
14	at making friends with people (.) but I have
15	noticed that other persons (.) yes=
16 Carmen	Right
17 Jessenia	=that it has happened to them (.)
18 Carmen	But you have been lucky
19 Jessenia	Yes (.) I get along well with everybody and
20	they kind of like me (.) and accept me
21 Carmen	That's good? (.)
22 Jessenia	In (.) in my my class (.) it is like
23	everything is all right (.) No (.) there is
24	<u>no</u> discrimination at all (.)

25 Carmen   Well (.) then (.) Okay (.) so you feel good

26   being a Mapuche (.)

27 Jessenia   Yes (.) and what's more (.) I like the things

28   they do (.) traditions and stuff (.) (p. 95)

Jessenia orients to the interviewer's question and acknowledges in her response the difficulties that may be encountered culturally by others in being positioned and categorized as a Mapuche. However, to the surprise of the interviewer (line 18), her personal experience runs counter to this. She explains that this may be due to her sociable personal qualities (lines 12–15, 19–20), positioning herself therefore within the category of a particular 'type' of person. Moreover, she also claims that she has not witnessed discrimination in her class (lines 22–24). The interviewer probes further:

Extract 3

110 Carmen   Do you know your name in

111   Mapuche?

112 Jessenia   Yes

113 Carmen   But (.) how do you know that you are Mapuche?

114   Is it only because of your surname (.)

115 Jessenia   No (.) it is that my family on both sides

116   they are Mapuche (.)

117 Carmen   Okay

118 Jessenia   And because my mother has a second last name

119   which is also Mapuche and (.) I don't know

120   (.) also my body build (.) I don't know (.)

121   like (.) my shape (.) my body build is like

122   that of the Mapuche people (.) all Mapuche

123   people look somewhat alike (.)

124 Carmen   Right::

125 Jessenia   I have noticed that

126 Carmen   Really? (.)

127 Jessenia   Yes (.) they all look alike (.) (pp. 96–97)

Later in the interview, the interviewer (Merino and Tileagă argue) sets up an opposition between public (external) and private (personal) facets of ethnic self-definition. Naming is considered as a public act of self-definition and associated with a group of culturally determined 'category-bound attributes and features' (p. 97), whereas 'knowing' one is Mapuche is a private undertaking. However, Jessenia extends the markers of ethnic self-definition and identification beyond that of have a Mapuche surname to heritage (lines 115–116) and physical appearance (lines 120–123), calling upon these in her construction of Mapuche ethnic identity.

The analysis of Jessenia's account (and that of Sergio) demonstrates how ethnic self-definition and social identification is a collaborative negotiation between the interviewer and interviewee drawing on shared and personal category-bound knowledge of attributes, characteristics and understanding of what it means to be Mapuche in Chile. The CA style of analysis reveals the interpretive and sequential development of identity construction as the participants attend to the local, interactional negotiation of meaning and further reveals how they draw on particular qualities/traits/attributes/categories to index ethnic membership and identity.

In contrast to the cross-sectional nature of data collection illustrated in the account above, Varjonen et al. (2013) report on a longitudinal study of ethnic Finns, prior to and following migration to Finland from Russia. Motivated by increasing social science interest in the impact of migration and globalization on intergroup relations and ethnic identity construction and negotiation, they focus on the interesting phenomenon of the 'return' migration of individuals who share the same ethnicity as the majority population of the receiving country. The authors note that 'migration to the country of ethnic origin can have an even greater impact on migrants' ethnic identities than migration to an ethnically alien country' (p. 111) and report on the changing nature of their subject's self-concept in light of their changed experience. Their analysis examines participants' use of category labels, rhetorical devices, interpretative repertoires[13] and other linguistic and discursive features garnered from semi-structured interviews within focus groups conducted in Russia, prior to migration and Finland, after migration. Analysis reveals that ethnic identity construction is variable both within and across time and space intra/inter-individually and used to perform different functions during the process of migration. General patterns emerge however: prior to migration, subjects mainly identified with one category label, that of 'Finn' imbuing this with positive characteristics and pride in being Finnish, drawing on a biological repertoire and marked by a comparison with Russian people. Finns are described as honest, calm, thoughtful, with an attention to detail and 'morally superior' to Russians (p. 118) as illustrated in the account below:

Extract 4

1 Viktoria   (. . .) They don't know how to lie. Well, they don't know

2   how to lie, not how to talk nonsense, not how to scheme.

3 Oleg   **

4 Viktoria   They're more straightforward. They are like more honest.

5   That's the trait, that doesn't please everyone, you know.

6   They don't know how to scheme, like at all. They're not

7   capable of deceit. That's why I think, that Finns, are very

8   clearly different from say, Russians. I for instance, am

9   proud, that I'm a Finn. I'm proud, that I, Finns aren't

10   capable of deceit (2) (p. 116)

However post-migration Finnish identity shifts and is found to be problematized, subjects often experiencing and reporting on 'otherization' and exclusion in intergroup relations, and as a consequence noting the invocation and ascription of a plethora of identity labels (e.g. Finns, Russians, Ingrian[14] Finns, Ingrian Russians, partly Russian, people from Russia, immigrants, 'never Finnish in Finland') – the most common self-label being 'Russian'.

The migrants' identity construction in each context is shown as dependent on interaction with the others, evident in the type of talk invoked. In the pre-migration setting (in Russia), participants used a 'biological repertoire' to refer to their Finnish ethnic heritage, indexed by reference to such terms as 'blood, roots and genes' (p. 126), in addition to asserting differences between themselves and the majority Russian population with respect to moral and mental traits. These unifying characteristics are used rhetorically to justify ethnic pride as well as the right to migrate to their country of ethnic origin, where they expect to adapt and align with the traits and practices of their ethnic brethren. In addition, a repertoire of 'socialization' is noted to be drawn on by informants, with references made to their Finnish upbringing involving exposure to Finnish cultural influences (including language) practices and values, leading to a sense of being 'Finnish' within Russia. Acknowledgement is also made, prior to and following migration, of the influence of Russian socialization, which they anticipate and demonstrate sets them apart from others in Finland. The influence of the majority culture on ethnic identity construction is also apparent in their use of 'a repertoire of intergroup relations'. Informants discuss the influence of the majority culture in each context on their sense of ethnic identity. In Russia, the repertoire is invoked resourcefully to build a Finnish group identity marked by differences with the majority population and feelings of 'otherization'. In Finland, however, the repertoire establishes an ascribed Russian identity. In both national contexts, the repertoire is argued to 'position ethnic Finnish migrants as a powerless minority when it comes to the possibility of defining their own ethnic identities … These types of constructions give the impression of a double minority position as the unavoidable fate of returning migrants' (p. 128).

Despite these general patterns, results also point to agency in subject positioning, with some informants reporting on their positive experiences in combining cultural influences, rejecting ascriptions or reinterpreting those afforded by others. Migrants were able to perform both insider and outsider positions; indeed, the study highlights the practical as well as emotional significance of identity labels and insider/outsider positioning. To self-identify and be recognized legally as a Finn prior to migration endowed the individual with capital – the ability to move from one nation to another and to avail themselves of the opportunities afforded to other Finnish citizens, while at the same time being positioned by the Russian majority as 'different'. However to be recognized and received within the country of ethnic origin, it is important to be socially accepted and recognized on equal terms, something, the Finnish migrants found difficult to accomplish, at least at the initial stages of their settlement.

The study reinforces the view that constructions of ethnic identity are very much individually, temporally and spatially/contextually determined and subject to the forces of power relations. Although the DP approach is influenced by the tenets of CA (assuming therefore the dialogic production of identity in ongoing talk), it is equally important to take into account broader historical, social and cultural contexts/influences on identity construction[15] (as discussed in the section 'Macro-level discourse studies I: Narrative approaches' above).

Sociolinguistic researchers (as discursive psychologists) adopting social interactional approaches argue that ethnic and religious identity cannot be abstracted from concrete social practices. Research (beyond that discussed in the section 'Ethnolects and ethnolinguistic repertoires' above) has focused on the linguistic resources employed by speakers to project and shape ethnic identity in ongoing talk. For example, Schilling-Estes (2004) combines variationist quantitative analysis with CA in her investigation of a triethnic community in southeastern United States, showing how two informants appropriate linguistic features to shape and reconfigure (inter)-personal and group identity. In so doing, they orient to their ethnic identities but also mark ethnic distance between one another. The study finds that despite slight shifts in identity performance, the two informants also display relatively fixed ethnic identities (that of 'Lumbee' and 'African American'), and this stability is marked by the ethnolinguistic patterns displayed in their speech (assessed quantitatively). These findings contribute to an understanding of the relationship between and the constraints imposed by agency versus social institutions.

Sociolinguistic research has also identified the relationship between speech community/Community of Practice membership, CS and the discursive construction of ethnic identity. De Fina (2007) combines ethnographic observation with CA in an analysis of the construction of Italian ethnicity in interactions between members of an all-male card playing club. She identifies CS as fundamental to the building of a collective identity among the group and notes that switching into Italian is particularly important in the execution of particular practices, notably socialization practices in relation to the game being played (see Extract 5) and in the official discourse used by the club president to his membership.

Extract 5

01 Lino: Have you got a *briscola?* [trump]

02 Dave: No *briscola* [trump]

03 Lino: Have you got a *carico?* [high trump]

04 Franco: *Io c'ho quelli là.* [I have those]

05 Lino: Let's take a chance.

06 John: *Ah accidenti!* [Oh damn]

Within the club, all members, whether or not they speak Italian, are expected to use Italian terms for cards and moves when cards are in play. In Extract 5, Dave is the only player of Italian heritage who was born in America and does not speak Italian fluently, and yet he orients to the term first used by Lino in line 1 to describe the status of his game. Further analysis reveals the way in which established club members teach new members the terms and moves in Italian and how they stress the importance of learning Italian in order to display a competent player identity and membership within the club. Even those who are not competent in the language work hard to 'cross' (Rampton 1995) into the Italian language to display an authentic identity and alignment with the group. As such 'ethnicity is negotiated as a central category defining the collective identity of [the] card-playing club ... among which code-switching into Italian has a central role' (p. 389). The study shows how ethnicity becomes a frame of reference for a collective made up of individuals with diverse backgrounds and language abilities and how the study of its constitution provides a window into the 'the social mechanisms through which relevant inventories of identification are created and enforced as part of the social life of groups' (p. 390).

CS is also invoked as a mechanism in other stance-making displays, appropriated to evaluate moral positions and to convey category memberships for speakers and interlocutors given participant roles (e.g. author/animator). Lo (1999) analyses a conversation between two American men of Asian background in Los Angeles as they take up a moral stance towards a woman who is not present in the interactional exchange. They discuss the desirability of Chinese, Korean and Vietnamese women using CS to build stances characteristic of particular ethnic groups and also appropriate CS to align or disalign from each other's positions. Once more their study illustrates how ethnicity is interactionally achieved through the development and negotiation of category-bound characteristics/attributes and stances taken towards these.

The role of affective and epistemic stance-taking in evaluating speaker attitude towards ethnic groups and in the construction of subjectivities within institutional settings is evident in a study by Mara and Holmes (2008). They examine the way in which Māori ethnic identity is discussed and constructed in workplace conversations in a New Zealand media production company. The workplace discussion revolves around a recent media awards ceremony in which the presenters had to pronounce certain Māori words and phrases. The authors assert that the pronunciations used by non-Māori speakers often belie their attitudes towards Māori people – those who adopt a more affiliative stance take on Māori pronunciations, in contrast to those who do not and who appropriate more anglicized articulations. The authors discuss the case of one Māori staff member who criticizes the anglicized pronunciations of the presenter and the manner in which other staff member align with her evaluation, concluding that the interactants not only display a professional expertise in their evaluation of the event but also mark the ethnic distinction between mainstream white New Zealand identity and ethnic Māori identity.

The constraints of institutional structures and frames of reference can be inhibiting in defining and discussing ethnic categories. For example, Wilkinson (2011) analyses the influence of the social context on the production of official statistics about ethnicity. Using CA, she examines how an organization monitors and records statistics about ethnic affiliation via telephone surveys. The study shows how self-categorization is determined by the categories listed on the organization's monitoring form and by the structure of the questions posed to informants. Constraints on subject agency in self-definition are brought to light as informants orient to the demands of the organization's categorizations. Such a study appeals to the practical implications of such constraints for informants and organizations.

Conclusion

This chapter has considered ethnicity as both a self-concept and as a process of individual/group performance and experience. It drew on multiple definitions and frameworks of analysis – from the social-psychological to sociocultural and sociolinguistic in its aim to explore a range of perspectives. The chapter began with a consideration of EV and discussed the application of 'Social Identity Theory' to the study of language maintenance and loss. We described and critiqued the EV framework and its application and considered ways in which the study of language maintenance, and the role of ethnic identity in relation to this, might be enriched by invoking an ethnographic and discursive approach. We further reviewed studies which have focused on the relationship between ethnic identity and heritage language maintenance and discussed the complexity of the ethnic-language–ethnic-identity link and its investigation. In the section 'Ethnolects and ethnolinguistic repertoires', we explored the concepts of 'ethnolect' and 'ER', noting how these concepts have informed work in sociolinguistics and also illustrated the currency of 'ER' in studies of identity/identification in sociolinguistics. As in critiques of EV, these studies point to the importance of studying local conditions (beliefs/ideologies/practices) in order to investigate and understand the way in which social meaning is attached to particular linguistic/discursive forms in interaction, the maintenance of relationships, the development of (shared) ethnic identity and identification. While some of the studies mentioned in the sections 'Ethnic identity and ethnolinguistic vitality' and 'Ethnolects and ethnolinguistic repertoires' drew on discourse analyses, the following sections turned to a more detailed consideration of the discursive realization of ethnic and religious identity, exploring both macro and microanalytic approaches. Some of the themes and issues discussed in other chapters came to the fore including sociostructural and interactional constraints on self and other definitions, issues of 'authenticity' and how the inability to perform an authentic (ethnic) identity can have emotional, practical and material (negative) effects. We also discussed issues of discrimination and racism and the impact of migration and globalization on intergroup relations and (ethnic) identity.

CHAPTER NINE

Gender and Sexual Identities

Gender and sexuality are part of a person's identity, along with many other components (age, social class, ethnicity, religion, health or ableness . . .) . . . while all of these components interact in a variety of ever-changing ways to construct an individual's identity, the interaction between gender and sexuality is special – it has a saliency that is worth highlighting and investigating in detail.

BAKER (2008: 8)

Introduction

At a recent academic conference (unrelated to topics on gender or sexual identity), I congratulated a colleague on the birth of their first child and enquired in a routine and glib fashion about its sex: 'Girl or boy?' I asked. In response to the banality of the question and perhaps also in light of their obvious sleep deprivation, I received a terse and unexpected response: 'It's one of those' and after a very lengthy pause, a monotone, 'It's a girl'. My flippant and somewhat unreflective query undoubtedly mirrored that of numerous other enquirers – its repetition obviously wearing for the hearer. However, my colleague's marked and somewhat irritated response also caused pause for reflection and pointed to the (arguably) unnecessary importance placed on identifying and categorizing an individual according to their sex, even from birth. What difference did it make whether the baby was male or female? And yet my question, at least in a Western context, was pretty routine and poignant – sex and gender identity does become a salient, even primary topic of enquiry prior to and/or from the moment a baby is born for its parents, extended family, friends and acquaintances, who frequently ask about a baby's sex in order to provide culturally appropriate responses which often materialize in the gifts received (often a plethora of either pink versus blue outfits or gender-determined toys). Sex and gender identity also affects the way in which an infant is spoken to and about ('such a doll!' 'what a bruiser!'), the names given and the social expectations and experiences later encountered as the child forges an understanding of their gendered self and their presentation of it. But to what extent are such binaries constraining, lacking in representativeness and too simplistic? To what extent do they become attached to social and cultural ideologies and expectations about masculinity and femininity? How else might one construct and perceive of sex and gender identity, and crucially what role does language and discourse play in thinking about and performing gender and sexual identity?

In this chapter, we consider how language both communicates and constructs gender and sexual identities focusing our discussion on overlapping concerns and themes in the fields of language and gender and language and sexuality research[1] – notably heteronormativity,[2] hegemonic masculinity and performativity. Both fields recognize the role and significance of studying the influence of power, regulatory structures and agency on subject positioning, and the impact of the latter on ideology, linguistic practice and identity construction. These issues are explored in the sections that follow but we must first define three key terms, which were used interchangeably above and foundational to our subsequent discussion; these are 'sex', 'gender' and 'sexuality'.

'Sex' and 'gender' prove difficult terms to define due to their multiple definitions and often synonymous appropriation by lay people and scholars alike. *Sex* is commonly used to refer to a binary biological (anatomical/physiological) distinction between females and males – the majority are born male or female – this polarization erasing the fact (as illustrated above) that some are also born intersexed. However, some researchers (Bem 1993; Bergvall et al. 2016; Butler 1990, 1993; Eckert & McConnell-Ginet 2003: 44[3]; Nicholson 1994; Zimman & Hall 2010[4]) argue that *sex* should not be treated as a biological binary but a continuum and a socially constructed category. In this way, the term can account for differences in physiology, sexual orientation, culture and behaviour and therefore distance itself from a basic dichotomy.

For linguists, the term *gender* is perhaps most frequently associated with grammatical word categories; however, for gender theorists, it refers to the way in which people enact their roles as males or females in society (masculinities/femininities) in accordance with or in contravention of 'normative' patterns of behaviour via such signals as language, dress, hair style, gait and other forms of self-expression. As discussed below, this gives rise to socially constructed semiotic markers of identity – differences recognized by members of a society. As will be discussed below, post-structuralist theorists argue that gender categories are fluid and multiple, socially acquired rather than biologically determined. Individuals grow up and develop in communities in which femininity and masculinity may be differently expressed and understood within the same community and/or in comparison to other societies; individuals may shape, style and change their gender identity over time and space differing from one occasion to the next or even within the same interaction.

Another feature of identity related to and overlapping with sex and gender identity is *sexuality* – how individuals behave as sexual entities, what they desire and how they express and understand themselves as sexual beings; connected to this is sexual orientation (preference). Sexuality according to Bucholtz and Hall (2004: 470) is 'the system of mutually constituted ideologies, practices and identities that give socio-political meaning to the body as an eroticised and/or reproductive site' – a definition which they assert also draws attention to the nature of current research on language and sexuality (as discussed below) which has moved beyond a concentration on marginalized identities (e.g. gay, lesbian, transgender individuals) to a variety of other issues, such as investigations of cultural and institutional discourses of heterosexuality and heteronormativity, sexual harassment/ violence, sexual labelling and linguistic marking of (non)normative sexual identities, to name but a few – far too many topics to mention or review in one chapter.

It is recognized that sex, gender and sexuality are overlapping and connected components of identity and worthy of joint consideration. While not advocating a unified framework or approach to the study of language and gender, Baker (2008: 9) notes that 'sex, gender and sexuality map onto each other to form a triangle of connected identity components'. Moreover, Cameron and Kulick (2003: 72) assert that 'a performance of heterosexuality must also be in some sense a performance of gender, because heterosexuality requires gender differentiation. There is no such thing as a generic, genderless heterosexual: rather there are male and female heterosexuals' and Cameron (2005) further asserts that 'sexual identities, like gender identities are … culturally and locally variable. Yet, in fact, these are intersecting rather than parallel developments, because sexual and gender identities do not only inflect one another, they are to a considerable extent mutually constitutive'. Many argue that gender norms are clearly tied to sexuality norms which may in turn lead to false assumptions and stereotypes.

As discussed below, although much early work in the field of sociolinguistics focused on comparisons of (predominantly white middle class) heterosexual male and female subjects, a burgeoning area of interest, in light of developments in queer linguistics (Barrett 1997, 2002; Hall 2003; Livia 2002; Livia & Hall 1997), has been a focus on 'queer' identities, that is, 'non-normative' heterosexual and homosexual identities. Feminist linguists, queer linguists and sociolinguistics have sought to investigate such issues as how identity categories become reified and inextricably linked to power structures and hegemonic forces/discourses, how subjects conform to and/or resist powerful discourses of hegemonic masculinity and heteronormativity and the nature of the heterogeneity and multiplicity of identity performance across and within communities/groups and individuals. The (comparatively) more recent focus on language and sexuality has sought to trouble the notion of heterosexuality and bring into relief the way in which language is used to sustain and impose heteronormativity and construct non-heteronormative categories and identifications. These issues among others will be examined in a limited fashion in the sections that follow.

We begin with a brief historical overview of research on language and gender in the section 'Historical overview: 1920s–1980s' in order to highlight past approaches and their influence on current work. This precedes a discussion in the following section ('Historical overview: 1990s onwards') of two interrelated and influential theoretical models which have had a significant impact on language and gender and language and sexuality research since the mid-1990s: performativity and queer theory. Then in the section entitled 'Linguistic performance of gender and sexual identity(ies)', we review illustrative studies which have appropriated these and other theoretical models examining the performance of gender and sexual identities, before turning in the final section to a consideration of discourses of (hetero)normativity and gender and their impact on individuals and groups.

Historical overview: 1920s–1980s

The rise of sociopolitical movements and campaigns for sexual equality (e.g. the Suffragette Movement, Women's Liberation Movement, Gay Liberation, Stonewall), in addition to advancements in fields such as technology and philosophy[5] throughout the twentieth century, challenged traditional views and attitudes about gender and sexuality bringing them to the forefront of social scientific enquiry. Although some significant changes and advancements have been made in the way in which gender and sexual identity is viewed, it cannot be denied that the influence of traditional perspectives and structural inequalities still perseverate – for example, in the West, there is still a significant pay gap between men and women; few women hold senior positions in organizations; many report the experience of being placed in a 'double-bind'[6] and/or hitting a 'glass ceiling' in the workplace; some lesbian, gay, bisexual, transsexual and queer (LGBTQ)[7] people report that they prefer not to disclose their sexual identities in some contexts for fear of judgement, discrimination or even ill-treatment (e.g. see Baker 2008; Derks & Ellemers 2016; Gianettoni

& Guilley 2016; Mullany & Litosseliti 2006; and see sections 'Linguistic performance of gender and sexual identity(ies)' and 'Discourses of (hetero) normativity and hegemonic masculinity' below for discussion of these various issues). In line with these social and political movements and work in other areas of the social sciences, linguists throughout the twentieth and into the twenty-first century sought to investigate the relationship between language and gender and language and sexuality, more recently investigating the linguistic and discursive construction and perception of gender and sexual identity and the impact of gendered discourses and ideologies on people's lives.

In this section and the next, we examine the influence of evolving (Western) understandings of sexual and gender identities in studies of language, we consider linguists' research questions and findings from work emanating from the 1920s onwards, and in the process detail evolving theoretical perspectives – deficit, dominance, difference and social constructionist theories – which mirror the sociopolitical movements of their time. Significantly, as discussed by Cameron (2005) and summarized prior to our account in Table 9.1,[8] we witness a paradigm shift in the 1990s, away from a conceptualization of gender difference (a 'modernist' perspective) to diversity (a postmodernist/post-structuralist perspective) in identities and practices, and an evolving and increased interest by some researchers to explore sexuality and its relationship to gender.

Early (pre-feminist) writing treated gender as a binary categorization. It presented two different perspectives about men's and women's language use, that it indexed biological difference and it signalled distinct gender roles within society (Litosseliti 2006). Jespersen (1922), is credited with being one of the earliest linguistic commentators on the subject in the twentieth century. He pointed to the former perspective arguing, without empirical support, that women's language use was inferior to men, marked by such features as less extensive or innovative vocabulary, overuse of hyperbole and incomplete sentential and syntactic formations (due to cognitive limitations). Echoes of Jespersen's assertion appeared in 1973 in Robin Lakoff's now classic feminist account 'Language and Woman's Place'. Relying on observation and introspection (particularly with respect to media stereotypes of men and women's language use), Lakoff argued that women were disadvantaged due to their inferior language use (marked by such features as overpolite forms, hesitancy, empty vocabulary, overuse of tag questions, etc.); however, she argued that this was not a result of biology but a consequence of their early socialization. This perspective was soon discredited by many authors (Cameron & Coates 1989; Fishman 1990; Holmes 1986, 1990) who pointed out the need to gather empirical evidence and explore such features as the relationship between linguistic form and communicative function, strategic language choices and power dynamics (e.g. use of politeness to warrant gains), cultural dependence of forms and use and the intersection between gender and other social categories (such as age, class, ethnicity,

Table 9.1 Approaches to language and gender (derived from Cameron 2005: 484)

'Modern' feminist approach	'Postmodern' feminist approach
Gender is built on the foundation of sex: *One is not born, but becomes a woman* (Simone de Beauvoir 1949). Gender (socially constructed) is distinguished from sex (biologically based), but the latter is implicitly assumed to provide a grounding for the former.	The foundational status of sex is disputed: *Are there women, really?* (Simone de Beauvoir 1949). The sex/gender distinction is questioned on the grounds that sex itself is not 'natural', but constructed; so-called 'biological facts' are always filtered through social preconceptions about gender.
Socialisation: gender identities and gendered linguistic behaviours are acquired early in life; gender is something you 'have'.	Performativity: gender identities and gendered behaviours are produced ongoingly; gender is something you do or perform.
Difference: research presupposes the existence of two internally homogeneous groups, 'men' and 'women', and looks for differences between them.	Diversity: research assumes an array of possible gender identities or positions, inflecting or inflected by other dimensions of social identity; intra-group differences and inter-group similarities are as significant as differences between groups.
Big stories: linguistic gender differences are explained in terms of overarching social structures, for example, male dominance or separate gendered subcultures; some researchers are interested in discovering cultural universals.	Local explanations: masculinities and femininities are produced in specific contexts or 'communities of practice', in relation to local social arrangements. No assumption that the same patterns will be found universally.
Mainstream focus: subjects conceived as generic 'men' and 'women' – implicitly or explicitly often white, straight, middle-class, monolingual.	'Liminal' focus: more interest in non-mainstream and 'queer' gender identities, and in relation of gender to sexual identities and heteronormativity.

etc.). Despite the subsequent criticisms, Lakoff's publication is credited with destabilizing an androcentric perspective in sociolinguistic research by introducing a feminist agenda to issues of language, thereby launching a plethora of studies which sought to empirically investigate the relationship between language and gender.

Towards the end of the 1970s and into the 1980s, researchers continued to conceive of gender identity in a binary fashion, in terms of a speaker's biological sex, focusing on how women and men used language differently. This research, in tune with the sociopolitical movements of the time, sought to answer such predetermined questions as: how and why do women and men speak differently? How does language use reflect male dominance? Biological sex differentiation also played into studies of sex preferential language use in variationist research in sociolinguistics (Cheshire 1978; Horvath 1985; Trudgill 1974, 1978).[9]

In the 1980s, researchers began examining interaction in single- and mixed-sex groups. For example, Spender (1980) argued that women's language was not deficient; rather, a patriarchal perspective in society meant that men were dominant within the social order. She (among others, e.g. Bodine 1975) argued that the male perspective was naturalized by language use: lexicalized in such forms as 'mankind', 'man-made' and a preference for the use of male pronouns to mark the generic form. Male hegemony was also evident in mixed sex conversations as men tended to dominate the conversational floor. Studies investigated the differential use of such linguistic and discursive features as back channels, hedges, interruptions, politeness forms, questions and responses, topic control and initiation, turn length and floor holding within mixed-sex exchanges (DeFrancisco 1991; Fishman 1980, 1983; Herring et al. 1995; Swann 1989/2011; West 1984; West & Zimmerman 1983). All pointed to the comparative dominance of men in conversation and the expected social role of women to support and facilitate conversation. However, as pointed out by Litosseliti (2006: 37), work within the dominance paradigm fallaciously correlated gender with specific forms of language/discourse without 'attend[ing] to the effects of conversational contexts, topics and genres, objectives, styles and rules for speaking, when examining specific forms' and assumed a straightforward correlation between linguistic form and function. Despite these limitations, work within this paradigm brought sociocultural issues to the forefront and attempted to base conclusions on the analysis of data, albeit (as noted by Litosseliti 2006), data derived from the study of predominantly 'white middle-class heterosexual couples'.

For dominance theorists, differences in male and female language were seen as a consequence of male advantage and hegemony. Others (Coates 1993, 1996; Holmes, 1995; Maltz & Borker 1998; Tannen 1990) argued that these differences were due to differences in male/female socialization such that boys and girls/men and women are socialized into subcultures which display different patterns of linguistic behaviour. In this paradigm, women are not considered as inferior or dominated by men but part of a separate and different subculture. This work focused more intensively on all-female groups and pointed to the importance of all-female talk/gossip for establishing solidarity and the construction and negotiation of personal identity (Litosseliti 2006). Although no longer framing women as an underclass (as weak and inferior), this work still treated men and women as separate categories and did not acknowledge the variability and complexity that exists within, and the similarity between, categories (e.g. women can equally dominate a conversation; men are also prone to gossip). The work also silenced the issue of power and the sociocultural influence of patriarchy although relied on a dominance-based conceptualization of gender. As noted by Litosseliti (2006: 40), 'Ultimately, the problem with difference – and indeed with all traditional models in the field – is the *lack of a complex conceptualisation of gender* (alongside other variables), and, again, the *assumption of difference*, with the polarisation that ensues from it'.

Contemporaneous with this work was research on gay and lesbian language use in different languages, which sought to investigate such features as intonation, vocabulary/slang, grammar and interactional and discursive patterns that might index queer language (see e.g. Kulick 2000 for an extended review). This research conceived of lesbian/gay identity as also arising from socialization and integration into gay and/or lesbian communities with identifiable gay/lesbian ways of speaking/varieties of use. Speaker identity, determined by subject self-identification as gay or lesbian, was considered to be marked by distinctive social and linguistic practices; for example, Chesebro's (1981, cited in Levon & Mendes 2016: 3ff) text 'Gayspeak: Gay Male and Lesbian Communication' echoed the correlational nature of the difference approach seen in the work of other language and gender researchers of the time.

Although the difference and dominance paradigms are not completely discrete for they have much in common (Cameron 2005: 486), both are now considered by many as too simplistic in their aim to correlate linguistic form with function and to ignore the interaction between gender and sexuality and other sociocultural, socio-economic and contextual variables. Their emphasis on viewing gender as binary categories (male versus female) and sexuality as fixed categories is argued to be a simplification and problematic, 'First [such a view] ... defines mutually exclusive scripts for being male or female. Second, it defines any person or behaviour that deviates from these scripts as problematic – as unnatural or immoral from a religious perspective or as a biological anomalous or psychologically pathological from a scientific perspective' (Bem 1993: 80–81). Many of the research studies focused their data collection on limited samples of predominantly white middle-class heterosexuals in the UK and the United States or groups of self-identified gay or lesbians and overemphasized (as discussed above) differences rather than identified similarities across groups or diversity within them. A move beyond an essentialized, dichotomous and generic perspective of femininity/masculinity/sexual identity meant transforming the way in which researchers viewed gender and sexuality; a shift was needed from a consideration of them as an inherent property of individuals to a symbolic system.

Historical overview: 1990s onwards

This shift arose in the early–mid-1990s following the influential work of Judith Butler (1990, 1993; also see Chapter One) who argued, drawing on the philosophical writings of Austin (1962)[10] and others (e.g. Searle, Lacan, Derrida, Foucault), that 'there is no gender identity behind the expressions of gender … identity is performatively constituted by the very 'expressions' that are said to be its results' (1990: 25), and that '[g]ender is the repeated stylization of the body, a set of repeated acts within a highly rigid regulatory frame that congeal over time to produce the appearance of substance, of a "natural" kind of being' (1990: 32). She argued that cultural and historical understandings and expressions of 'appropriate' gender behaviour become naturalized through the repetition of performance within specific systems of power and as such, certain categories are privileged over others. She called for 'gender trouble', that is, the dissolution of traditional categories which lead to inequality, 'the mobilisation, subversive confusion, and proliferation of precisely those constitutive categories that seek to keep gender in its place by posturing as the foundational illusions of identity' (1990: 34).

An understanding of gender and sexual identity, informed by Butler's philosophical and political position, proposes that they are performed/ accomplished/brought into being through symbolic means within historical and sociocultural frames – a repeated *process* of appropriation, selection and negotiation rather than static, essential *states* or *products*.[11] Sociolinguists, feminists and queer theorists argued that language mediates between regulatory systems of power and agency. Through language, cultural ideologies are able to circulate as it becomes a primary site of social practice, fundamental to the production of sociocultural identities – individuals drawing on the linguistic and discursive symbols available to them in their sociocultural milieu (including engagements within Communities of Practice, Wenger 1998; see Eckert & McConnell-Ginet 1992; Eckert & Wenger 2005; Holmes & Meyerhoff 1999) to perform acts which constitute feminine/masculine/sexual personae. These are not usually consciously performed (although see discussion of the performance of gender identity by telephone sex workers, Hall 1995 below). Gender and sexual identity is also considered to be inflected by and tied to other social identifications (e.g. class or ethnicity) and contextual influences – subject to social norms and regulatory control/practices including regimes of power. Put simply, gender and sexual identity is conceived as complex, fragmentary, multiple and dynamic – produced, reproduced and negotiated in contextually and culturally relevant communities and within local sites of interaction – the outcome of momentary intersubjective practices and broader ideologies.

This perspective of gender and sexual identity as symbolic constitutive acts appeals to the complexity of gender and of sexuality work and has subsequently influenced investigations of identity performance. Rather than attempting to identify generic and apparently fixed or exclusive markers of heterosexual or LGBTQ speech, and therefore determine linguistic and social difference between groups, researchers have sought to examine the way in which gender and sexual personae are enacted locally in diverse ways through particular roles, stances, styles and activities – also how gender is culturally encoded and how this knowledge affects our perception of the linguistic behaviour of others (including the social force of stereotypical ways of speaking/styles normatively associated with gender categories). Rather than attempting to determine the exclusive use of specific linguistic or discursive forms by individuals or groups therefore, researchers seek to identify the operationalization of the same linguistic resources by different individuals and groups in order to perform stances or acts which carry specific social meanings. These linguistic features in turn can be found to cohere and accrete to construct styles related to recognizable personae. As such, it is argued that there are no male/female/gay/lesbian, etc. 'ways of speaking'; rather, there are multiple possible realizations.[12] Moreover, linguistic performance has been shown to challenge the oppositional and hierarchical conception of gender and the 'compulsory practice of heterosexuality' (Butler 1990:151).

Within this new paradigm, gender and sex difference is still salient but it is no longer considered that there are *a priori* generic, binary, exclusive, homogeneous or fixed categories[13]; rather, researchers ask instead if, how and why differences materialize? How they are constructed in and through spoken and written texts (discourse) and what is their relationship to macro-level (e.g. institutional/societal) processes and constructions as well as micro-level local (relational/interactional) events. There are a range of possible performances which may involve shifts according to setting (private/public), company (single/mixed sex; familiar/unfamiliar), interactional goals, etc. Moreover, what are the consequences of such linguistic performances? What are the norms/boundaries that subjects adhere to/confront/challenge? How are they perceived? How and why might identity categories be strategically and rhetorically essentialized (Spivak 1995), for example, to forward equality of rights, for commercial purposes, etc.?

In response to the influence and assumptions brought about by modernists viewing language and gender through a heteronormative lens, and in light of the influence of queer theory,[14] evolving sociopolitical movements, and increasing analytical refinement in studies of social identity (in sociolinguistics, linguistic anthropology and sociocultural linguistics, including what have been termed 'emergentist approaches' to language and gender and sexual identity[15]), a burgeoning area of interest has been an exploration of 'more peripheral or non-mainstream' (Cameron 2005: 489) sexually or gender-variant individuals/groups in a range of sociocultural contexts, for example, LGBTQ communities/individuals, straight-identified individuals engaging in same-sex relations or subjects working in sex-segregated occupations traditionally associated with one or other sex (see

McEntee-Atalianis & Litosseliti 2017, as discussed in more detail below).[16] Therefore, in addition to focusing on mainstream gender norms, some researchers have investigated those who deviate from them. In so doing, we see how certain linguistic and discursive practices come to be identified with and/or construct certain identities.

Some of this research has drawn explicitly on theories of indexicality, stance and style (Ochs 1992; Podesva et al. 2001; Silverstein 2003 and see previous discussions in earlier chapters) to suggest that the association between linguistic form and identity is mostly indirect. Podesva et al. (2001: 179) assert that '[a] style may be viewed as a collage of co-occurring linguistic features which, while unfixed and variable, work together to constitute meaning in coherent and socially intelligible ways. Style simultaneously gives linguistic substance to a given identity and allows identity to be socially meaningful' such that 'certain social meanings (e.g. stances, social acts, social activities etc.) ... in turn help to constitute gender meanings' (Ochs 1992: 391) within specific contexts of use. For example, a post-structuralist interpretation of interruptions and control of the conversational floor would suggest that they are not considered to directly mark masculinity but rather in their realization may index a stance of authority, which in turn may indirectly and stereotypically relate to a masculine style of speaking. The meanings derived by any realization have also been shown to depend on context and the moment of interaction. Eckert (2008a) has shown how meanings about a persona or social type are situationally determined. Interruptions may be invoked and interpreted differently according to the moment of realization, for example, they may express authority; however, they may also be invoked to enact humour or demonstrate conversational engagement and support. These acts may index different types of social/interactional identity. As such researchers have been increasingly carrying out close (ethnographic) studies of different communities, settings and the individuals who move between them.[17] They have also explored expectations and perceptions of gender normative behaviour arising from gender stereotypes and how certain linguistic behaviour may be perceived to be deviant. It has been determined that certain language styles, symbolic of social dimensions (categories/lifestyles), can be discriminated against and perpetuate inequality.

Scholars have sought therefore to examine the linguistic resources used to perform gender and sexual identity – also to analyse the regulatory/normative boundaries that determine the types of language or discourse that are considered possible in the performance of specific types of gender and/or sexual identity in specific settings. Related to the latter is the way in which hegemonic practices regulate identity through language and discourse and how determination of 'normativity' is contextually bound such that certain performances are legitimized and privileged over others in different situations. Illustrative cases are discussed in the sections below.

Linguistic performance of gender and sexual identity(ies)

As noted above, Butler's theory of performativity alludes to a 'repeated stylization' which serves to constitute masculine and feminine ways of behaving. Attending to different linguistic/discursive levels of analysis, researchers have been at pains to identify the nature of, and reasons for, these varying stylizations, including realizations which rupture the apparent naturalization or fixity of binary gender and sexual categories. Some of these studies have been described in other chapters (e.g. Bucholtz 1996, 1999a, b, 2002 account of 'Geek girls'; see Chapter Six). Below we briefly explore how gender and sexual identities are multiplied and stylistically brought into being. We consider cases which illustrate a performative adherence to heteronormativity as well as those which illustrate subversive/alternative ways of 'doing' gender or sexual identity. We witness how linguistic practice can arise from multiple, sometimes conflicting identifications and contextual, interactional and ideological influences and how individuals and groups shift and differ in their linguistic performance.

Some early studies of performativity investigated how masculinity/ femininity/sexuality is (variably) constructed and policed within social groups or Communities of Practice and identified certain motivations for particular stylizations and thematic foci, including the desire to be accepted within a homosocial group (Kiesling 2002/2011). For example, Cameron (1997/2011) describes how a particular type of masculinity is performed by a group of five American college friends who were engaged in watching and discussing a sports event via gossip about their sexual exploits and non-present actors who they identify as 'gay'. Cameron analyses the exchanges between the participants and describes how the students position themselves at a distance from the absent others, by critiquing in some detail their appearance, behaviour and sexual habits. In so doing, the subjects paradoxically have to display knowledge of styles, material and what constitutes an attractive male. She queries whether the characters discussed and constructed by the friends were actually homosexual, instead noting that 'the term "gay" [used by the friends to discuss the absent others] is not so much [about] *sexual* deviance as *gender* deviance. Being "gay" means failing to measure up to the group's standards of masculinity and femininity … conformity to gender norms can be a matter of degree' (p. 254). The performance of homosocial gender identity is therefore facilitated by positioning the self/group in relation to a different 'other'. The study highlights how it is not just heterosexuality which is normatively structured but a particular form of heterosexuality which is venerated over others (see Motschenbacher & Stegu 2013 and other papers in the special issue which similarly discuss cases of same-sex normativities).

Kiesling (2002/2011) also explores the construction of hegemonic masculinity and homosociability in his investigation of a group of men living in a university fraternity. He notes that in constructing gender hierarchies and status within the group, the men not only index their heterosexuality by drawing on differences between themselves and other gay men and women (see Cameron above), but they also discursively display dominance over these groups, positioning themselves as superior to other types of men and women. For example, they metaphorically refer to other men as women and enact particular narratives of heterosexuality (e.g. 'fuck stories', 'drunk stories'; see further Coates 2003 who discusses male narratives of hegemonic masculinity and female stories of 'ideal femininity'). 'Heterosexuality [he concludes] is thus not just about sexual object choice, but it also has a social construction that is primarily used by social actors to compete with same sex groups' (p. 285). Enactments of gender differentiation and domination are therefore a discursive strategy in the performance of hegemonic masculinity.

A more literal interpretation of 'performativity' and exaggerated stylizations of femininity and masculinity is evident in the work of Hall (1995) and Barrett (1995). Hall details the stereotypical linguistic markers employed by telephone sex workers in California to enact a variety of fantasy women of different personas and ethnicities for the enjoyment of male heterosexual clients. This case study is somewhat different in its subject matter to Cameron (above) and to others discussed below since the enactments and persona of these individuals are understood to be intentionally and deliberately 'performative'/'fantastical' for a reason. Hall reveals however the linguistic dexterity of the workers, some of whom perform roles which are far removed from their own status, for example, black women performing as white women; white women, acting as Latinos; even a man presenting himself as a woman.

Barrett's (1995/2011) study of African American drag queens also examines a dramatic 'performance' but demonstrates how imbalances in power can become renegotiated through the subversive enactment of hegemonic styles. These acts serve to destabilize heterosexist assumptions about how gay black men should behave. In their acts, Barrett found that the drag queens creatively switched between a stereotypical white woman style (polite/refined), a street variety of African American Vernacular English (AAVE) and gay male speech. The white-woman style indexed an 'ideal' feminine behaviour but this was deliberately subverted by the use of taboo words or switches into a stereotypically masculine voice. The 'polyphonous' nature of these stylizations facilitated the conveyance of varied and multiple meanings/identities. 'Successful' performances, Barrett concluded, typically included cases of signification.[18] For example,

Extract 2:

Drag Queen: Everybody say "Hey!"

Audience: Hey!

Drag Queen: Everybody say "Ho!

Audience: Ho!

Drag Queen: Everybody say "Hey! Ho!"

Audience: Hey! Ho!

Drag Queen: Hey! How y'all doin?

This typical call-response routine is noted to be a recognized rhetorical trope apparent in African American sermons and reported by Barrett to be frequently used in drag performances. '[It] relies on the polysemy of the word *ho* as both an "empty" word frequently used in call-response routines by drag queens and an equivalent *whore*. After leading the audience into the chant and getting them to yell "Hey! Ho," the drag queen reinterprets the word *ho*, taking the audience's chanting of *ho* as a vocative. The polysemy is dependent on the connection between the utterance and the context' (pp. 419–420).

A further example is taken from an interview with RuPaul and demonstrates the use of careful standard American English phonology marked by 'final high intonation on declarative sentences' (p. 422). This is an example of stereotypical women's language (see Lakoff). Barrett claims this performative indexes a white woman style which is fundamental to the drag queen performance – marking a sexual ambiguity and distinguishing the performer from other African American gay men. 'Thus it functions to index stereotypes of white femininity and to construct a unique drag-queen identity that appropriates and reworks the symbols of "ideal" femininity' (p. 422).

Extract 2: RuPaul (Barrett 2011: 422)

H – high intonation L – low intonation H* – pitch accent

L   H   L   H*   L

You guys, I wish there was a camera so I could remember

H*   L   H

all the love your're sending to me

  L   H

  and the...

L   H

the love energy from over here.

L   H*   L

You're absolute the best

Although the two accounts above (Hall and Barrett) relate to the literal 'performance' of sex and gender roles, they nevertheless point to the constructed and creative potential of gender/sexual identity. Numerous studies have investigated how individuals and groups actively negotiate their gendered identities in ways which are remarkably distinct and diverse, pointing to the multiplicity and context-dependency of gender and sexual identities. For example, Coates (2001/2011) discusses the conflicting and variable performance of masculinity, pointing to the dynamic nature of negotiation between speakers, and Ostermann (2003/2011) details the varied performance of femininity within two distinct communities of practice – an all-female police station and a feminist crisis intervention centre in Brazil. At an intrapersonal level, Podesva et al. (2001) present a case study of a gay attorney speaking on a radio programme. They carry out an acoustic analysis of five variables which were empirically and/or stereotypically associated with gay speech. Their findings contradict the assumption that there is 'a singular gay way of speaking' (p. 187). For example, their subject did not employ pitch or duration of /l/ typically associated with a gay style and he released final stops – a feature noted to be associated with a geek girl style. They note the fluidity of his performances and the influence of professional status and the formality of the context on his stylistic variation. Podesva (2007) later develops this analysis and argument in his study of a medical student, Heath, who he finds to enact different persona and styles of speaking in his workplace as opposed to other social settings (see Chapter Two).

These studies show how gendered identities are built through the often momentary process of enacting other social roles and stances. This point is also made by Kendall (2008), who analyses the meal-time conversations of a young family. She highlights the contradictory performances of the parents: the mother who performs the role of disciplinarian versus the father who enacts the role of joker. As shown in the extract below, the father's actions serve to undermine the stance of the mother towards the child's behaviour (p. 561):

Extract 3

1 Mark: You want another bowl? ((HOST))

2 Beth: Ew.

3 Mark: Hm?

4 Beth: No! They're disgusting.

5 Elaine: Excuse me? ((LANGUAGE MONITOR))

6 Beth: Sorry!

7 Elaine: Just say 'no thanks'.

8 Beth: No thanks!

9   ((6 seconds))

10 Mark: (chuckling, whispered) Disgusting.)

11 Beth: (scoffs)

12 Elaine: Go take your vitamin. ((CARETAKER))

Kendall suggests that in taking up these different interactional positions Elaine and Mark enact their gendered identities: Elaine, the disciplinarian, performs her role as caretaker and nurturer/mother in contrast to Mark who enacts his role as entertainer and father. Through the performance of one type of social identity, another is realized.

Pichler's (2008/2011) account of 'Traditions of Marriage in a Group of British Bangladeshi Girls' illustrates how the concept of intersectionality[19] has increasingly become central to many investigations of gender and sexual identity performance (e.g. see studies in Levon & Mendes 2016[20]). Within this study, Pichler not only highlights the constructed and fluid nature of gender but also the salience of the intersecting variable of ethnic culture in its performance. She discusses the identity work of five subjects, examining how they position themselves as British or 'Londoni' in the discussion of marriage, simultaneously indexing their Bangladeshi identities through an altered discourse about arranged marriage. They are shown to draw on and negotiate a range of (competing) discourses about culture and gender enabling them to construct hybrid British Bangladeshi femininities.

The fluid, socioculturally situated and momentary production of the gendered self is further apparent in the case of the Banaras hijras in India (also referred to as 'third sex') who are reported to habitually switch between the marking of Hindi verbs, adjectives and postpositional forms as masculine or feminine, for example, employing masculine forms when marking distance/power and feminine when marking solidarity. The hijra construct a self-identity which resists and subverts the gender order. They are considered as neither female nor male and yet must and do appropriate markers of both. Hall and O'Donovan (1996/2016: 229) note that 'it may be liberating to believe in the possibility of an alternative gender which is not limited by societal expectations, but even the hijra must create self-identity by resisting and subverting a very real and oppressive gender dichotomy'. They report that hijras are often brought up as boys and on entering the community become socialized in feminine ways (dress, gesture, language, etc.) and as such adopt a gendered bilingualism. While noting variability in performance within and between subjects, they report on an individual (Sulekha) who explains that when she dresses as a woman she adopts feminine marked verb forms as opposed to when dressed as a man when she employs masculine-marked verb forms. Choice of linguistic variable is often dependent on the context of interaction, including the status (and familiarity) of the addressee. Feminine linguistic forms signify solidarity within the group of hijra; however, when disputes occur between individuals, often male referents, including the male names of the hijra (the names they first entered the community with), are used as vehicles of abuse. Male forms may also be appropriated to index power, for example, Sulekha refers to herself as a 'landlord' (rather than a landlady) to indicate her status as a land owner – a privilege normally enjoyed only by men. The fluidity of linguistic performance is noted to mark their status as hijra – neither aligning with a male or female identity.

The hijra illustrate that the performance of socioculturally and ideologically linked gender styles of femininity or masculinity is not predetermined by a subject's biological sex. This is further reinforced by studies which illustrate how linguistic gender can be used as a conduit for a range of performative goals and practices (Livia 1995; Saisuwan 2016). Abe's (2004/2011) study of 'Lesbian Bar Talk in Shinjuku' in Japan explores the naming and identity construction of lesbian women in Tokyo.[21] These women are noted to self-identify as either 'rezubian' or 'onabe' – the former attracted to women who consider themselves female while the latter attracted to women who identify as male. Both groups frequent different bars in the city. Among different linguistic variables studied (e.g. commands, requests and sentence final particles), one of the most salient is pronouns. In Japanese, first-person pronouns are gendered. Abe identified consistent differences in practice. The rezubian tended to employ the pronoun 'watasi' – a form available to both men and women; however, the onabe used a reflexive pronoun 'jibun' – a form associated with male sportsmen or military men. (However, Abe records individual flexibility in the use of first-person forms which also demonstrates difficulty in asserting a binary lesbian identity.) The forms adopted index a rejection of linguistic variables that are considered 'too feminine', hence the use of neutral or masculine variables; however, Abe also asserts that their use did not symbolize an identification with a male persona, rather they were employed 'to express a variety of context-dependent meanings relating to their lesbian identity and relationships' (p. 383).

The intersection between language, masculinity and social class is further investigated in Hall's (2009/2011) account of lesbian identity in New Delhi, India. The subjects of her study were participants in an outreach project designed to educate women who were attracted to other women about sexual diversity and HIV/AIDS. Hall found some women positioned themselves within a more traditional, working-class frame of sexual desire as a heterosexual phenomenon, while others within a more Western frame. The former were insulted if referred to as women preferring to be addressed as boys, asserting a desire for sexual reassignment. These differing ideologies are marked linguistically. Hall shows how the subjects of her study code-switch between English (a language connoting education, status and imperialism) and Hindi (a language associated with tradition and working-class status) to index differing allegiances (see Extract 4) and divergent positions on sexuality. She found gender (masculinity), sexuality, social class and language to be frequently contested in exchanges between participants:

Extract 4
31 Liz: You're – you're also- you're a woman

32   but you are attracted to other women

33   That's not acceptable to society

34   but you are being like that,

35 Jess: <quietly rapidly> <*gali deti hai.*

mujhe woman [*boti hai.*]

Hindi translation – <she insults me she calls me woman!>

In this exchange, Liz 'interpellates' Jess's identity as a lesbian rather than as a boy. In marking an adversative emotional stance, Jess switches to Hindi. Hall determines that 'Hindi serves as a likely conduit for a localized expression of identity that challenges the ideas of a globalized English-speaking elite' (p. 389). She appeals to an ideology which determines that only men can be attracted to women.

The intersection between language and sexuality and the complexity of subject identifications is explored in work by Levon (2016). In his analysis of the strategic use of creaky voice in acts of stance-taking by an Israeli married man who engages in sexual relations with other men (Igal), he demonstrates how, through the adoption of contradictory footings, conflicting religious and sexual identifications are negotiated to develop a complex understanding of subjectivity. He argues that the different positions and stances taken by Igal do not belong to two distinct personae but rather construct different (/opposing) dimensions of the same subject through a process of layering/lamination (Goffman 1974).[22] Levon argues that Igal:

> doesn't use creaky voice to project a 'gay' or 'religious' self … rather to adopt a deontic stance … through which he reaffirms his commitment to Jewish laws and customs despite the transgression of these laws that his identification with same-sex desire represents … using creaky voice to take this stance … Igal is able to orient himself to homosexuality while simultaneously signalling an awareness of the impossibility of his orientation … through this linguistic process … Igal succeeds in materialising a multidimensional self of which both homosexuality and Orthodox Judaism are an integral part. (p. 215)

Levon's account aligns with recent work which points to the complexity of subject identifications and the fallacy of there being a singular essence. It also points to the importance of attending to speaker's motivational and interactional goals, while his variationist analysis successfully combines quantitative and qualitative approaches. Through quantitative analysis, he demonstrates how creaky voice is appropriated predominantly when Igal speaks about topics which are related to sexuality and religion; whereas the in-depth qualitative analysis identifies creaky voice as occurring when expressions of affective alignment with same-sex desire coincides with his positioning as an Orthodox Jew. Levon argues that creak is therefore a linguistic realization of Igal's conflicting identifications not a means of overtly marking a gay Orthodox identity.[23]

Discourses of (hetero)normativity and hegemonic masculinity

Igal's linguistic acts of conflicting identification point to the connection between personal and social experience and the regulatory constraints imposed by the rigidity of normative frameworks which often privilege certain identities (hegemonic masculinity) and subordinate or marginalize others (femininity, homosexuality). While the relationship between micro-contexts of interaction and broader social ideologies can be complex, there is evidence that individuals draw on broader/dominant discourses in the construction of their gendered identities. Although researchers in gender studies and queer linguistics have focused on linguistic agency and the creativity of social actors in constructing gender and sexual identities/identifications, it is also interesting to explore how they draw on and sometimes challenge dominant discourses about heteronormativity and hegemonic masculinity and how they confront and manage the 'gender order' (Connell 1987), 'the repressive ideology which ensures that deviation from gender norms ... entails penalties' (Holmes 2007/2011: 601).[24]

Sandfield and Percy (2003) interviewed women (aged between 20 and 48 years) who had recently ended a relationship and become single. Their analysis shows how the women developed gender identities that conformed to and depended on social discourses of 'heterosexist' norms, characterizing themselves negatively as being outside 'stable' relationships and blaming themselves for their current status – a status which they presented as temporary and objectionable.

This perspective was also found by Reynolds and Wetherell (2003) who determined that single women often feel compelled to defend their non-partnered status, often distancing themselves from negative characterizations which are potentially hurtful. In the following extract, one of their informants, Jay, alludes to the cultural influences which have impacted on her expectations and sense of self:

Extract 5
Jay: I think my images when I was growing up were largely negative ones ... the sort of Victorian image of the spinster in the family who had to be supported somehow by the men in the family. And who was erm,

not quite a whole person in some way. So I suppose I grew up with those images, erm, and with an expectation that it wasn't me, it wasn't going to be me. I was heterosexual I was erm at some stage going to get married and have children. (Reynolds & Wetherell 2003: 8–9)

The study found that some single women have to work to develop defensive discursive strategies to counter unfavourable inferences and assertions and position themselves with a normative heterosexual framework. However, others framed their independent status more favourably in positive ways (as also found by Coates 1996).

McKinlay and McVittae (2011) discuss the negotiated status of gendered identities within the constraints of traditional communities, notably the identities of fishermen's wives in a remote fishing village in Scotland. Their study reveals how these women are at pains to convey the blended identities of a financially dependent spouse with a modern lifestyle of independence and autonomy. However, while enjoying their independence and time alone while their husbands work, they distance themselves from a feminine identity associated with the women's liberation movement:

Extract 6

AD: how would you see yourselves (2)

VB: Um (.) certainly not women libbers

PM: (.) oh no

VB: No. We like to have a man to bring home the bacon

PM: Yes

VB: (.) em I don't think either of us would want a man coming in every night=

PM: = No

VB: That aspect would (.)

PM: (.) not after 24 years, no

VB: We think we've got the ideal situation where we (.) have a man part-time and the rest of the time we have complete liberty to come and go as we like

The authors note how the use of extreme case formulation, that is, 'the ideal situation' and 'complete liberty' serves to emphasize VB's positive evaluation of her gendered status which is associated with a particular categorization of having a 'man part-time' while also having the freedom to 'come and go' as they please.

The situated negotiation of gender identity and its dependence on the broader context of social meanings and ideologies is equally apparent in studies of men. A dominant social construction of masculinity is noted to be

that of the 'macho/'hero' man – a form of masculinity that many men have
to discursively attend to and negotiate (as shown in the section 'Linguistic
performance of gender and sexual identity(ies)' above). This has been
identified in a number of studies, such as Andersson's (2008) account of a
young man's heroic positioning of himself in narratives of violence through
his self-portrayal as courageous and tough, and Coates' (2003) account
of male stories of themselves as heroic protagonists in action narratives
(contrast this with her analyses of female stories of relationships and
connectedness; see McEntee-Atalianis 2013a for further discussion). Others
have demonstrated how constructions of a 'new' more sensitive man are
built via counter-hegemonic discourses and strategies (Edley & Wetherell
1999).[25]

Sociocultural constructions and perspectives of hegemonic masculinity
and heteronormativity can prove difficult to challenge particularly in social
institutions. Language and discourse positions men and women in particular
ways in professional contexts. Individuals may take up or challenge
certain constructions. For example, it has been found that when men enter
nontraditional ('feminized') occupations (e.g. primary school teaching,
occupational or speech therapy), performing an 'appropriate' gender identity
becomes especially important. Men in these settings have been found to
perform 'hegemonic masculinity' discourses (Connell 1995) in order to
enact and even exaggerate a masculine identity (Cross & Bagilhole 2002;
Francis & Skelton 2001; Simpson 2004). Bradley (1993) has suggested
that while women may experience 'compromised' femininity in 'male' jobs,
a 'compromised' (i.e. non-heterosexual or non-hegemonic) masculinity is
perceived as more of a threat. Dominant or hegemonic discourses may be
challenged but they may also become naturalized (e.g. see Ashcraft's 2007
discussion of gendered representations of commercial airline pilots). Some
have suggested that it is vital to question the nature of identities built due to
the varied positioning of individuals in relation to different discourses, and
the nature of inequalities created or maintained as a result (Baxter 2010;
Litosseliti 2006; McEntee-Atalianis & Litosseliti 2017).

Analyses have revealed the often subtle manner in which particular types
of identity (and roles inherent to them) become restricted and maintained.
Some have shown how a female perspective may often be overshadowed,
silenced and/or distorted by masculine discourses (e.g. see Ehrlich's 2006
account of a sexual assault trial). Harding (2007) reveals the binary and
stereotypical ideologies associated with male nurses working in different
specialisms; those working in mental health are considered 'macho', while
those in general nursing often are considered homosexual, and McEntee-
Atalianis and Litosseliti (2017) analyse narratives told by male and female
speech and language therapists (SLTs) investigating the tensions expressed
in the negotiation and performance of their gendered professional identities.
They show how small stories support professional identity construction
and rapport-building, as well as act as sites of contestation, employed to

(re)appraise the social order with respect to 'women's' and 'men's' work. Gendered discourses are shown to impact not only on the amount of men entering the SLT profession but also the specialisms and career paths that men and women pursue. The analysis points to the reproductive and regulatory power of gendered discourses on individuals' experience of their gendered subjectivity and professional identity. They find that dominant gender discourses, in which women are positioned as carers and nurturers suited to paediatric work, while men are positioned as potentially threatening to children and more suited to adult clinical posts and senior management positions, have an impact not only on the amount of men entering the profession but also the specializations and progression routes that men and women pursue (Litosseliti & Leadbeater 2013). The SLTs interviewed struggled to reconcile themselves with stereotypical gendered attitudes about their professional identity and noted its influence on their career. Their study draws attention to the potentially constraining influence of hegemonic discourse and the struggle for recognition within and outside of the profession especially when their roles and status challenge preconceptions. However, it also reveals that alternative interpretations and counter narratives/discourses can be voiced within specific local contexts and harnessed to support a different perspective to the mainstream – a finding also supported in the work of Baxter (2003), Holmes and Schnurr (2006) and Lazar (2005).

The regulation of sexuality by hegemonic sexuality has been of central concern to queer linguists. The manner in which 'non-normative' sexualities are constructed and negotiated in relation to the constraints of regulatory structures and discourses has been researched by many. Some have noted that identities which challenge binary, dichotomous or heteronormative categories are often subject to marginalization and erasure and subject to discourses of discrimination; however, others have noted an emerging competitiveness between heteronormativity and non-heteronormativity and an increasing tolerance for and use of progressive gender and sexuality discourses. Motschenbacher (2013: 590) details the case of 'constructions of non-heteronormativity at the European Song Contest press conferences', identifying a community of practice and space in which linguistic constructions and discourses of non-heteronormativity are prevalent and distinct from national contexts which assert comparative intolerance and lack of acceptance of sexual minorities, instead promoting discourses of heteronormativity. Motschenbacher identifies three dominant patterns of non-heteronormative discourse: 'non-heteronormative talk about love song lyrics and performances, the construction of male same-sex desire, and the challenging of dominant gender discourses' (p. 590). Heteronormative discourses are still found to operate but these are found to coexist with non-heteronormative discourses more readily than at national levels. Heterosexual discourses about partners, spouses and families were notably absent. In echoes of Cameron and Kulick's (2003) paper, the author asserts that 'the expression of heteronormativity in this community of practice is only rarely a matter of identity construction, but rather is more related to the construction of desire. Identity labels such as *gay* or *lesbian* hardly ever occur in such non-heteronormative constructions' (p. 610).

Conclusion

After a brief historical overview of work in the fields of language and gender and language and sexuality, in which we witnessed a shift from a modern to postmodern and post-structuralist perspective, this chapter considered three key issues in the study of gender and sexual identity: heteronormativity, hegemonic masculinity and the nature of subject performativity. The chapter pointed to the importance of studying the influence of power, regulatory structures, context and agency on subject positioning. We considered gender and sexual identity as linguistic and discursive constructs strategically and stylistically intersecting with other types of identity categories. These can be built as (unequal) binaries and/or as diverse, multiple and fluid entities. It was argued that there are no male/female/gay/lesbian, etc. 'ways of speaking' and studies of linguistic performance across different contexts and cultures challenge heterosexuality and the oppositional and hierarchical conception of gender. We did however witness how powerful identity categories (e.g. hegemonic masculinity) can be constructed, maintained and act as influential sociocultural and ideological forces leading to the subordination and marginalization of some – also affecting subject choice and lifestyle (including career choices). It is evident that certain behaviours and styles are still associated with gender and/or sexuality categories and these influence gender and sexuality norms and stereotypes. The latter notwithstanding, we also identified resistance to heteronormative and hegemonic patterns of behaviour and discourses.

Many of the studies reviewed focused on Western contexts (including their norms and perspectives), but it must be acknowledged that over recent decades non-Western contexts and cultures have enriched work in this area and reinforced an understanding of the culturally, ideologically and contextually bound nature of gender and sexual identities and the need for researcher reflexivity in approaches to data collection and interpretation of findings (Atanga et al. 2012, 2013).

While a post-structuralist approach reinforces the multiplicity and diversity within and across identity categories, many have noted the importance of maintaining 'strategic essentialism' (Spivak 1995) for political and humanitarian purposes. For in a bid to unravel and elucidate the complexity and variability within and across categories in order to dissolve false boundaries, some believe that a rejection of essentialism has meant that some crucial issues, such as women's or LGBTQ rights, may be downplayed or no longer seen as so important (Cameron 2005; Philips 2003). Others note (e.g. see Litosseliti et al.'s forthcoming discussion of the post-feminist sensibility and 'gendered neoliberalism') that despite challenges to hegemonic masculinity and the gender order, they nevertheless perseverate often in more subtle ways. As such language, gender and sexuality researchers must re-engage, they argue, with political activism by turning their attention to matters beyond who people 'are' or how they are brought into being within local linguistic practice in order to address extant structural inequities.

CHAPTER TEN

D/deaf Identities

*To naïve observers, deaf people are a little like the Borg in the
Star Trek films. Deaf people think alike, and have the same life
experience. You meet one deaf person, you've met them all. This
antiquated, one-size-fits-all approach persists, even in this day
and age.*

STEPHEN F. WEINER. FOREWORD TO LEIGH, I. (2009) 'A LENS ON DEAF IDENTITIES'

Introduction

Research on sign language and Deaf[1] communities, mainly, although
not exclusively, in North American and European contexts, has grown
exponentially since the mid-twentieth century. Tervoort's (1953) structural
analysis of the visual language of deaf children in the Netherlands, Lunde's
(1956, in Stokoe 2005: 11) sociological account of deaf people as a
'subculture' and Stokoe's (1960) influential first description of the structural
characteristics of American Sign Language (ASL) proved seminal. The
subsequent dictionary of ASL (Stokoe et al. 1965) documented the linguistic,
cultural and social properties of a distinct minority. This research and other
'emically' inspired linguistic, sociological and anthropological studies of
deaf people in the 1970s and 1980s (Erting 1978; Kyle et al. 1985/1998;
Padden & Humphries 1988; Woodward 1982) initiated a change in
attitude towards the deaf and Deaf communities and contributed to the
empowerment of Deaf people (De Clerck 2010).

In this chapter, we explore D/deaf identities predominantly from socio-
psychological, sociocultural and sociolinguistic perspectives – initially

considering the impact of different social, medical and culturo-linguistic perspectives on historic and current representations of D/deaf people and 'deafness'. In the section entitled 'Models/perspectives of d/Deafness', we focus on different models/perspectives of d/Deafness, in 'Linguistic and sociocultural manifestations of the Deaf community and Deaf identity' we consider linguistic and sociocultural markers of Daf identity and in the following section we discuss the implications of biomedical developments, in particular the introduction of cochlear implants, as well as new technologies on the identity and vitality of the Deaf community and deaf people. Finally, we consider current interest in the multiplicity of D/deaf identifications and argue in the 'Conclusion' for the importance of incorporating Deaf epistemologies – Deaf ideological and cultural frames, experiences and performances, informed and enacted via spatial and visual perspectives – into identity research.

Models/perspectives of d/Deafness

In her book *A Lens on Deaf Identities*, Irene Leigh critiques the concept of 'Deaf identity' detailing instead a plurality of D/deaf identities, arising from and seated within different personal, political and sociocultural histories, situations and choices. Diversity in personal circumstance includes, for example, age, age of onset of deafness, extent of an individual's deafness, familial and educational experience, opportunities for integration into hearing and Deaf communities, social networks, etc. An array of appellations are given as examples of this diversity and its influence on identification, for example, 'Deaf, deaf, oral Deaf, … hearing impaired, acquired hearing loss, hard of hearing, deaf with a "hearing mind", Black Deaf, Deaf and Hispanic' (Leigh 2009: viii) – labels which individually, or in combination, and interchangeably may be self/other-ascribed or displayed in response to diverse requirements or sensitivities.

Defining 'D/deaf' identity/ies is far from simple and contrary to lay expectation is not necessarily audiologically grounded, for some hearing people consider themselves to be culturally and 'attitudinally' Deaf (Baker & Cokely 1980) – for example, hearing children born to Deaf signing parents who use sign language and support the social and political rights of Deaf people.[2] Johnson (1994: 103) considers attitudinal Deafness as a form of ethnic identity involving 'paternity' (in the case of Deaf people, this relates biologically to deafness and also the paternity of other Deaf family members) and 'patrimony' involving shared customs and values.

The majority of deaf children, approximately 95 per cent, are born into and acculturated in hearing families and may only become aware of sign language and Deaf culture as they make contact with other Deaf children or adults when they enter school or penetrate Deaf communities. Others may never sign or integrate into Deaf communities at all. Sign skills and degrees of socialization into hearing or Deaf communities vary considerably. Others, albeit, the minority of deaf children, are born to culturally Deaf, signing parents and become introduced to the spoken and written language of the hearing community on entry to school. Yet, others may 'acquire' deafness with age, remain culturally and socially hearing and have no contact with the Deaf community or understanding of the political, cultural or linguistic interests of the Deaf.

While a continuum and multiplicity of D/deaf experience and definition is acknowledged, as highlighted above and discussed in the section 'The multiplicity and fluidity of D/deaf identities' below (see Leigh 2009 for a comprehensive account of the complexities of D/deaf identities), this chapter is initially concerned with the experiences of those who identify linguistically, socially, culturally and politically with the Deaf community and Deaf culture; these constitute only a small percentage of the overall population of deaf people. In the UK, for example, this is estimated to be somewhere in the region of 50,000–100,000 people, in contrast to approximately ten million people estimated to be deaf or 'hard-of-hearing'[3] (Action on Hearing Loss 2014). A burgeoning and active process of defining and researching Deaf culture and identity (including the bicultural existence of Deaf people) – termed as 'Deafhood'[4] (Ladd 2003) – has developed in recent decades. This has been precipitated in part as an emancipatory response to the detrimental conditions and deprivations experienced by deaf people over many years of oppression in hearing-dominant cultures but also due to significant academic interest in investigating a visual-gestural modality of communication and the social, cultural and political characteristics of (a) 'silent' and unexplored subaltern group(s).[5] This research has contributed to a growing acceptance and recognition of the community and rights of Deaf people in many national and international contexts and has led to a definition of 'Deaf' identity as a 'process' rather than a state (Ladd 2003).

'Deafhood' and a sociocultural/linguistic-cultural perspective of Deaf peoples' interaction with one another provides a necessary insight into the preferred communication and community involvement of Deaf people; however, hearing culture has for centuries influenced and determined the lives, identity and identifications of deaf people. Three models usefully represent historical and contemporary constructions of D/deaf people and deafness in local, national and international settings. Each model harbours and engenders discourses and perspectives which are salient to an understanding of contemporary emic and etic constructions of D/deaf identities. They represent influential ideologies circulating within societies which have not only arisen from the practices and discourses of hegemonic institutions and actors (such as the powerful institutions of medicine and education) but also from the work of enlightened deaf studies researchers and the activities of the Deaf communities themselves. Therefore, in order to appreciate the concept of Deaf identity and 'Deafhood', it is first necessary to briefly contrast the sociocultural/culturo-linguistic model of 'Deafhood' with medical and social models.

The 'medical' model constructs deafness as a 'problem', as a disability. Deaf individuals are perceived to be in need of a cure or remediation in the form of, for example, cochlear implants, hearing aids and lip-reading skills. Such intervention, it is hoped, will enable them to adjust and function within a hearing world and 'become' hearing to a lesser or greater extent. Individuals and the medical professionals who pursue this model attempt to find a means to eradicate deafness.

A 'social' perspective of deafness similarly conceives of it as a disability or impairment, but rather than being a medical problem and physical abnormality, it is conceived as a social challenge and, as such, it is the responsibility of society to remove the necessary physical and environmental barriers to full integration into the hearing community for the individual, for example, via the provision of interpreters; auditory aids, such as dogs for the deaf and flashing door lights; text telephones; etc. In this perspective, 'integration' into the hearing community does not necessarily involve eradication of deafness or denial of sign language but recognizes a need for assistance to function within a predominantly hearing culture. Emphasis in this model is therefore on social responsibility rather than individual change. The model does not however promote the notion of social bonds between Deaf people (McKee 2008) or recognize the status of a signing Deaf community.

In stark contrast to the medical and social models, the 'sociocultural or culturo-linguistic model' (articulated by Ladd 2003: 15ff) rejects the 'disabled' label and conceives of the Deaf community and Deaf individuals as unique cultural and linguistic entities, with a community history, customs, values, social structure and norms. Deafness, kinship, sign language and Deaf culture (including the arts) are seen as core values of the community and are positively framed. In this model, Deaf people are represented as members of a healthy and distinct cultural and linguistic minority[6] who function in a visual-spatial modality and communicate via their first or preferred language – sign language. A visual rendering of the world affords a particular way of 'seeing' and interpreting events. Members are also politically sensitive to Deaf rights – to full integration in society via sign language – and strive to deconstruct the pathological model of deafness which is responsible for socially constructing the Deaf as disabled, promoting their assimilation into hearing society via speech. Sign language, they argue, provides visual access to auditory information. Speech can be a barrier to communication, whereas sign language is a conduit and enables Deaf people to function in all spheres of life. The notion of eradication or 'cleansing' of deafness is therefore treated with disdain and repulsion.

Responses to these different models and perspectives are apparently complicated and conflictual. D/deaf people and parents of deaf children frequently have to confront the realities and tenets of these different perspectives. Many Deaf people argue that the medical model is oppressive and colonial in outlook. It fails to account for their unique and 'whole' linguistic and cultural status. They argue that a pathologized ideology promoted by this model has for many centuries led to their oppression and marginalization, and in some instances, even needless fatalities due to medical malpractice as they have been subject to experimentation or medical procedures to turn them into 'hearing' subjects. Some have even committed suicide – unable to cope in a society which positions them as 'abnormal'. The social model similarly assumes a 'lack' and a need to integrate and function within the oral/aural norms of the hearing community. Others, favouring a hearing or bilingual/bicultural status, argue for the importance of integration into the majority culture, rejecting an essentialist interpretation of Deafness and favouring medical intervention and/or assistive technology or speech training to do so, even if they too wish to integrate and identify with those who are culturally Deaf (see discussion in the section 'The multiplicity and fluidity of D/deaf identities' of the 'dialogue model' which attempts to account for this identity status – a transitioning within and between hearing and Deaf communities (McIlroy & Storbeck 2011: 497)).

Although these models are theoretical and artificially discrete constructs, they represent something of the rich and assorted history of opposing hegemonic and subaltern attitudes and experiences in various national contexts. As noted by De Clerck (2010: 154), it is important to acknowledge 'that the construction of deaf identity is also related to local sociocultural, political, educational and social policy constructions, and hence differs among countries', and even within them at different historical moments. Indeed, documented accounts of deafness and sign language use on the island of Martha's Vineyard, in the United States, in the eighteenth and nineteenth centuries, illustrate how deafness was such an unmarked phenomenon on the island due to the high incidence of genetic deafness, that both deaf and hearing people readily interacted in sign, until the population of deaf people declined so markedly that the vitality of the language and the propensity for signed interaction weakened and died in the middle of the twentieth century (Groce 1985; Woll & Ladd 2011; Wilcox et al. 2012). In this community, speech and signing, hearing and deafness were merely perceived as variant constructs. Fluidity in linguistic performance was comparable to other bilingual or multilingual nations supporting variant language practices. Comparable accounts of signing communities are reported elsewhere, for example, in Bali (Branson et al. 1996) and Mexico (Johnson 1984); Woll and Ladd (2011) report that currently twelve signing communities are in existence over the continents of Africa, Asia and America.

In many national contexts, however, policy decisions, particularly educational, have been formulated and enacted by hearing legislators and professionals (Wilcox et al. 2012) and have predominantly promoted a negative rendering of deafness, with support for the medical model, which has perseverated throughout the decades and undermined the status of

D/deaf people by comparing them against a hearing norm – positioning them as disabled, while perceiving of deafness as a 'lack' rather than a variation in status.[7] Lane (1992: 482) asserts that:

> We have come to look at Deaf people in a certain way, to use a certain vocabulary of infirmity, and this practice is so widespread among hearing people, and has gone on for so long, and is so legitimized by the medical and paramedical professions, that we imagine that we are accurately describing the attributes of Deaf people rather than choosing to talk about them in a certain way.

Part of this way of viewing deaf people has had profound effects on their education[8] and status in society. As asserted by Morris (2008: 17), 'Deaf people's experience [in the UK] includes the dual oppression of being a cultural-linguistic minority group, whose language society has only just recognized, alongside the treatment of Deaf people as a disabled group who should be normalised'. Indeed, the continued strength of the medical model in many Western contexts is evident in the advice given to parents pre- and postnatally with regard to genetic screening for deafness and cochlear implantation.

Deaf people nevertheless view deafness as a positive trait and associate themselves with a 'Deaf culture' – a distinct Deaf identity rendered in sign communication and cultural ways. Part of this culture involves a 'remembering' and transmission of Deaf history and experience. As such, Deaf identity and status is conceived in a positive frame. It is to a discussion of this that we now turn.

Linguistic and sociocultural manifestations of the Deaf community and Deaf identity

Signing communities are thought to have existed for 7,000 years or more in Middle Eastern and Western regions and developed into more formal systems of organization from the eighteenth century onwards via the establishment of residential schools for the deaf, and in the nineteenth century, through deaf clubs and religious societies (Woll & Ladd 2011: 159ff). Sign languages differ globally. There is not one international sign language used by all Deaf people. As noted previously, sign language is seen by Deaf individuals and Deaf communities as an important tool in the mediation and enactment of their sociocultural life and identity: 'the discourse of cultural and linguistic identity is considered by Deaf people to be essential to articulating a self-determined vision of their collective past and future' (McKee 2008: 520). Identification with Deaf experience is articulated through various genres including traditional forms of storytelling, poetry and jokes.

Signed stories are noted to be an important medium for the transmission of Deaf tradition to children and adults. Ladd (2003: 297ff) recounts the salience of the visual rendering of stories for children socialized into Deaf culture by their peers and Deaf teachers in residential schools for the Deaf between 1945 and 1960 in the UK. For them, stories not only served as a mechanism for cohesion but also served a pedagogic purpose. Often denied the opportunity to sign in class or the school playground due to strict oralist policies,[9] children would congregate clandestinely in hiding places or late at night in their dormitories to watch stories eloquently told by their signing peers: 'To tell stories, we'd hide, round corners, in the toilets, wherever. Or go downstairs, and one would keep their foot by the door so when somebody came by, they would feel that person's vibrations, and tell us, so we'd all put our hands down sharpish' (p. 306).

One former student recounts how important these stories were: 'Some of those boys would pass the same stories onto me. In the playground, we'd hide, to tell the stories, round any corners, *all learning so much from each other*' (Italics in the original, p. 308). And noting the status afforded to those who were fluent and engaging narrators:

> We'd get in a circle for storytelling; one or two we didn't want in, slow learners, would refuse. But one girl … she was brilliant. We'd all lap it up, mouths wide open in sheer rapture; you could believe these stories, the way they were told … If people saw her in conversation with someone else, *they would gravitate towards her* … knowing the story wouldn't be planned, it would just happen.

Wilson, a Deaf poet (2006, cited in Sutton-Spence 2010a: 267), born to a hearing family recounts the delight and draw of witnessing for the first time a rendition of a signed poem by a Deaf peer while at school: 'She signed a simple poem about a tree by the river, blowing in the wind. Watching it had a very powerful impact on me. I laughed for ages afterwards. I wasn't laughing at her but at the delight of seeing her poem. It was like a slap across the face – the first time I'd ever seen anything so clear'. The sight of this spectacle unleashed new possibilities and new freedoms of expression, understanding and satisfaction never before considered possible – a discovery that visual and embodied communication was a key to an enriched experience of the world and the performance of Deaf identity.[10]

Ladd (2003) reports that it was not only Deaf peers but also Deaf teachers who tapped into the visual world of young children, passing on their wisdom and stories of their community to the younger generation. A former pupil, Barry (Ladd 2003: 319), recounts how he learnt about the danger of smoking directly from an inspirational Deaf teacher:

> He was a chain smoker, then stopped. When I was 16, he called me in one day, and reached into a drawer and got out a white handkerchief,

breathed into it and showed it to me – wow – there was a big black mark. I never smoked after seeing that. See he knew Deaf Way – *visual proof*.

Sutton-Spence (2010a) similarly identifies the importance of narratives in learning about the values and expectations crucial to the development of Deaf identity and the development of sophisticated sign competence in young children. Through an analysis of interviews with British Deaf teachers and adults, and narratives recited to children in the classroom, she identifies aspects of British Sign Language (BSL) and British Deaf culture that interviewees and signers see as salient to pass on to the next generation including valuing their sense of vision, sign language and pride in their community. These values, she argues, have to be taught, since, as noted above, the majority of deaf children are not born into Deaf families. Of course for those acculturated to the Deaf world, such values are second nature, as we see in this story told by a Deaf child when realizing disappointingly at a young age that there was an alternative majority 'speaking' world:

When I was small I thought the world was full of deaf people. Yes, we were great! Because when I was small my parents were Deaf. At school I didn't know if my teachers were Deaf or hearing because they signed and to my mind they were automatically Deaf. The other children I mixed with signed. I signed with Deaf people at home. So everyone was Deaf ... One day my Mum and I were on a bus ... I said to my Mum "Those people are like grandmother – speaking," and Mum said, "Yes, they're hearing." So I picked up on the sign HEARING and asked what it was. She said, "Oh, hearing people can hear sound." "Am I hearing?" I asked. "No, you're Deaf." (Paul Scott in Sutton-Spence 2010a: 271)

Sutton-Spence notes how all Deaf adults acculturated into Deaf families can relay similar stories of discovering their Deaf identity.

Recurring themes in non-fictional BSL and ASL narratives include encounters, sometimes humiliating and frustrating encounters, with hearing people in public and private settings. Sometimes, these narratives coalesce into fictional moral accounts and become part of a folkloric tradition to teach neophytes about their culture and to engender pride in their Deaf identity. Sometimes, the Deaf protagonist is made into a hero or victim. Paul Scott (in Sutton-Spence 2010a: 297), for example, recounts the story of a Deaf traveller who in denying his deafness manages to publically humiliate himself on a flight by pretending to be hearing. The moral of the story is to be proud of one's Deaf identity and not hide it from public view. Cross-cultural differences are also noted between stories told in different sign communities; for example, in ASL, differences between orally and manually educated people are made salient in narratives in a way not seen in BSL stories (Sutton-Spence 2010a: 277).

Other fictional stories reflect the influence of hearing folklore on the bicultural status of Deaf people. Sometimes traditional tales, such as 'Little Red Riding Hood' are adapted to incorporate Deaf characters, Deaf cultural ways (e.g. seeking the attention of interlocutors by tapping them on their shoulder) and familiar objects (e.g. flashing-light doorbells), while the 'villains', such as the wolf, are represented as hearing (Sutton-Spence 2010a: 277). This resonates with Ladd's (2003) observation that Deaf identity is, in part, borne out of oralist discriminatory policies and enacted through acts of storytelling, in which hearing actors, in fictional and non-fictional narratives are positioned as the oppressors or villains while the Deaf are represented as allies and victims. Sutton-Spence (2010a: 283ff) asserts that many of the stories told by Deaf people relate to negative school experiences in which they are/were subjected to intensive speech and language therapy and denied access to sign language.

To be a good storyteller is, as seen in the extracts above, very much valued in Deaf culture. Sutton-Spence (2010a: 295) identifies key characteristics that denote a good narrator, including, for example, the embodiment of characters (role-shifting), the use of sign space and sophistication of articulation. Through well-told stories, 'facts, values, and circumstances ... may normalise, reinforce and validate [Deaf] culture' and identification with the Deaf. Humorous stories in particular are very much prized in Deaf culture, not only because of the enjoyment derived from clever sign play and code-switching but also for their content, in particular their ability to denote boundaries between the hearing (including disabled) and Deaf worlds and their ability to poke fun at in-group member behaviour, including those who contravene community norms (Sutton-Spence & Napoli 2012). The following jokes serve to illustrate this: the first, recited by Clark Denmark, reinforces an identification with the Deaf community and a disavowal of the disabled characterization 'by implicitly censuring the Deaf man's behaviour' (Sutton-Spence & Napoli 2012: 314) and the second, told by Richard Carter, further highlights the values of the Deaf community in rejecting cochlear implants (CIs), in a tale that resonates with Paul Scott's instructive story (detailed above) and draws on a well-known folk story of the genie in the lamp (Sutton-Spence & Napoli 2012: 333ff):

(1) '*A Deaf man, a blind man and a man in a wheelchair are all in the pub one evening, complaining that the beer is weak and the pub is too crowded. Just then God walks in and sees them looking miserable and dissatisfied. He comes over to the table and says to the man in the wheelchair, "Be healed!" The man in the wheelchair stands up and runs from the pub shouting, "Praise the Lord!" God says to the blind man, "Be healed!" and the man looks around him at everything he can now see. He runs from the pub shouting, "Praise the Lord!" God turns to the Deaf man but before He can*

say anything, the Deaf man says in panic, "No, please don't heal me! I don't want to lose my disability benefits!"

(2) *A shipwrecked Deaf man is washed up on a desert island. He finds a teapot in the sand, polishes it and out comes a genie who signs to him . . .*

"You can have three wishes."

"Three wishes? OK. I'm alone. I can't hear anything. I want to hear. If there is help coming from a boat . . . I want to be able to hear it too. OK I want a cochlear implant."

. . .

The genie grants his wish . . .

"OK you have two more."

"Hmm. OK, I don't want to sign now. I want to speak. Maybe when a boat comes to rescue me I can communicate." . . .

The genie grants his wish. . . .

The genie signs "Third wish."

The man says, "What?". . .

The genie disappears back in the teapot because he doesn't understand speech, so the man loses the last wish."

The threat of cochlear implants to Deaf identity and the very existence of the Deaf community are made salient through jokes such as these. Sutton-Spence and Napoli (2012: 314) note that many jokes relate to this subject matter, some playing on the artificiality and nature of the technology, such as the fact that the cochlear implant has a magnet to enable the external processor to connect to the head. They recount jokes of flying cutlery attaching to wearer's heads and babies whipped from their prams and thrust onto passing buses. These negative and bizarre images serve to reinforce and underline the perceived stupidity and danger of CIs to the culture, identity and health of individuals and the community. Cis, many argue, serve to construct a bogus normalizing hearing identity and support a deficiency and medically based interpretation of deafness – a disavowal of Deaf identity.

Technology, medicine and D/deaf identity

Many D/deaf people[11] express negative views towards CIs (King 2004; Ladd 2003, 2007; Lane 1994, 2005); however, others are more ambivalent, even positive, arguing for their ability to enhance bicultural and bilingual opportunities, and increase satisfaction with life (see references in Leigh

2009: 151 and those below). Psychosocial research has recently explored the impact of CIs on identity formation and individual adjustment to D/deaf identity, focusing on issues of self-esteem and psychological well-being. This research has been prompted by an increasing number of profoundly deaf children and adults choosing to be implanted (see www.bcig.org.uk for current statistics on implantation in the UK and http://www.nidcd.nih.gov/health/hearing/pages/coch.aspx for statistics on the United States). Research has largely focused on adolescence, since this is noted to be a time at which identity formation is particularly salient and argued to be dependent on the mode of communication for the deaf (Wheeler et al. 2007).

Leigh et al. (2009) investigated psychosocial adjustment in adolescents with and without CIs arguing that an investigation of social identity in these distinct cohorts is important since group belonging motivated by conscious affiliation relates to psychological health and positive self-esteem. This research drew on the work of others, for example, Bat-Chava's (1993) review of research which found a positive correlation between cultural Deaf identity and self-esteem in adolescents and adults; Glickman's (1996) 'Deaf Identity Development Scale'[12] which proposed stages of development and adjustment to bicultural identity and Maxwell-McCaw's (2001) extensive examination of over 3,000 informants, which found higher levels of self-esteem and psychological well-being among those acculturated into Deaf communities and/or were living a bicultural existence. This contrasted with 'marginal' members of hearing and Deaf communities who had the lowest levels of psychological health.[13] Leigh et al. (2009) report differences in acculturative patterning: those with CIs acculturating more into hearing communities, and those without, into Deaf communities; however, 'similar percentages of adolescents with and without CI endorsed a bicultural identity. This appears to support the idea that even in view of the stronger orientation toward hearing acculturation on the part of CI users, it is possible for CI users to have bicultural orientation' (pp. 255–256). They assert that psychosocial adjustment and well-being may be mediated by CIs, enabling deaf adolescents to access hearing social groups. However, what is important for psychological well-being is the experience of satisfying social relationships and the support given to adolescents by their families and schools to enable them to integrate fully into groups of their choosing. Such research emphasizes the possibility of multiple identifications to occur simultaneously and to be performed differentially in different cultural contexts.

Other studies have attempted to give voice/sign to adolescents with CIs. Preisler et al. (2005) interviewed deaf children about their experiences with CIs in Sweden – a nation championed for its progressive attitude towards the Deaf community and deaf children. They note that, unlike some other Western countries, parents in Sweden often choose for their children to be implanted, not in the hope that they will become hearing children, but that they will be given the opportunity to become bilingual and have access to both hearing and Deaf communities. Positive and negative experiences with CIs are reported by the informants; however, they were comfortable with their bilingual and bicultural status. The authors conclude this status contributes to their healthy psychosocial development. They, as Grosjean (2010), argue for the importance of introducing sign language to deaf children from a young age. Grosjean (2010) argues from a slightly different standpoint, that CIs are not always successful and denying a deaf child access to sign language from an early age may compromise their cognitive, linguistic and psychological well-being.

Wheeler et al. (2007) note the reported benefits of CIs for deaf adolescents. In particular, they report that they enable them to communicate with hearing family members. Only 21 per cent of their informants considered themselves to be 'hearing' – the rest deaf or bicultural. The authors conclude that their informants did not feel strongly Deaf or hearing, but recognized the difficulties as well as the benefits of CIs: 'As many people, identity for these young people is not a fixed concept, setting identity in a one-dimensional way but reflects the complexity of their experience, a complexity which for many is positive' (p. 311).

Many researchers argue that despite the increasing tendency for implantation, the necessity for a visual means of communication (especially within educational settings) and a sense of community among Deaf people will ensure that sign language will remain vital (Brueggemann 2008; Carty 2006; Moores 2006). Some also suggest that vehement stances taken against CIs by some within the Deaf community may serve to further marginalize it from the mainstream (Woodcock 1992/2001 in Leigh 2009: 156).

Beyond biomedical developments in the shape of CIs and genetic intervention (see Obasi 2008; Padden & Humphries 2005 and Leigh 2009 for a discussion of the latter), other technological developments have contributed to the construction of D/deaf identity. Technology, particularly the Internet, mobile telephones and television, have permitted D/deaf people to connect and perform in ways previously thought unimaginable and also opened up the world of the Deaf to hearing viewers through sign-supported programming or visual modes of interaction.

Some Deaf people, particularly the young, who previously met face to face in establishments such as Deaf clubs, societies or religious gatherings, now prefer to interact virtually – sometimes forming subcommunities or friendships which then meet offline in other venues such as pubs or sporting events. Changes to 'Deaf geographies' (Valentine & Skelton 2008) facilitated by sophisticated technological advancements have meant that the spaces and places of contact between D/deaf and the D/deaf and hearing people have altered also and led to an equally sophisticated and self-determined shaping and reshaping of D/deaf identities. The visual, synchronous nature of today's technology enables D/deaf people to interact with others nationally and internationally and to function via sign or writing without the aid of interpreter services.

Valentine and Skelton (2008) explore how the Deaf community in the UK has changed due to ICT and the opportunities afforded to Deaf people for the development of Deaf space. They note that:

> access to wider networks offers D/deaf people the opportunity to sidestep some of the cultures of surveillance and regulation that can characterise traditional place-based Deaf communities centred on Deaf clubs ... the Internet is creating a space on-line for the articulation of identities and differences which are marginalised within Deaf off-line community spaces ... [permitting] deaf people ... to escape some of the pressures to conform to some of the Deaf cultural 'norms' ... and to develop more specialised networks. (p. 475)

Networks include individuals with disabilities, such as those with Usher's syndrome, ethnic networks, gender- and sex-based networks and many more. These sites are argued to provide a safe and alternative place for interaction with others who share in similar experiences or life choices. They argue that despite declining attendance at Deaf clubs, the Internet, in particular, is facilitating new avenues of interaction, virtually and physically, by encouraging a broadening of social networks. The authors assert, however, that the Internet has not necessarily supported D/deaf people's integration into mainstream society and may even be leading to an increased separation from physical contact with the hearing world. Deaf informants reported that they use the Internet instrumentally to access mainstream sites (e.g. to buy products) but not necessarily to form contacts or relationships with hearing people. Indeed, 40 per cent of informants reported hiding their D/deaf identity online – some preferring to access services online rather than in person as this obviated any need to manage potential marginalization or discrimination. Some even reported a lessening of confidence in face-to-face interaction since using the Internet.

Overall, their study suggests that technology has facilitated more fluid modes of interaction and community development, enabling new structures to develop in diverse spaces on and offline nationally and internationally. However, traditional spaces of Deaf integration, in particular the Deaf club in the UK, are now populated predominantly by older members and may be in decline (as similarly reported by Woll & Ladd 2011). The Deaf community itself is therefore changing in configuration and constellation, incorporating identities previously marginalized, for example, the hard-of-hearing and other minority groups. The authors assert, however, that until society supports the visual needs of D/deaf people, including sign language via affordable new technologies, communication between D/deaf and hearing people will continue to be dominated by the written mode and feelings of marginalization and oppression will continue for the Deaf.

The multiplicity and fluidity of D/deaf identities

Studies of identity affiliation and performance on the Internet hint at the multiplicity and hybridity of D/deaf identities on and offline (synchronously and diachronically), and the importance of theorizing about the impact of 'D/deaf' geography ('space', 'location' and 'areas of contact') and history, including community and personal history – familial, educational, on situated identity formation and performance. As evident from the preceding discussion, to define D/deaf culture and identity/ies is complex; whereas previously, in 'first-wave identity politics' (Davis 2002, in McIlroy & Storbeck 2011: 496), a line was drawn between 'd'eaf and 'D'eaf – disability versus difference, oral versus sign – research in the second, postmodern, post-structuralist wave, points to the heterogeneity and fluidity of identity perception and performance recognizing too that no one aspect of identity can be considered in isolation (e.g. Deaf, deaf, gender, ethnicity). The concept of 'Deafhood' as a 'process' is purposively focused in this regard, as is McIlroy and Storbeck's (2011: 496) interpretative 'dialogue model' which offers 'a postmodern ontological framework within Deaf studies ... [defined as] reconciliation through critical self-reflective bicultural dialogue, which embraces postmodern tensions between contradictory identities'. As such, in more recent studies, identity is framed as 'a quest for belonging instead of a narrow quest for self-determination based on difference in terms of being deaf or Deaf' (McIlroy & Storbeck 2011: 495, drawing on Brueggemann 2009). Through this research, we see how D/deaf people index a belonging to different, sometimes conflicting social categories, including 'bicultural' statuses, and how variation in identification is contextually influenced. We also acknowledge, however, that although this research rejects an essentialist reading of identity, stable social categories are often used as a basis for the analysis of informant 'hybridity' and positioning. While there is an apparent tension here, this nevertheless acknowledges the salience of these categories for the performance of 'strategic essentialism' (see Chapter Nine) in lay/informant discourse and consciousness. Many studies therefore include an exploration of overlapping axes on identity dynamics, intersecting categories such as gender and sexuality, and ethnicity and age. In this final section, we briefly review work which has explored these dynamics to reveal a multiplicity of identities and contextual identifications that extend beyond a consideration of a binary Deaf-hearing conceptualization. We reflect first on work which highlights the impact of educational experience on bilingual and bicultural identity before considering research on minority deaf ethnic or racial groups.

Many have noted the salience of the educational context and educational experiences on constructions of D/deaf identity (Foster & Kinuthia, 2003; Ladd 2003; Leigh 2009; Nikolaraizi & Hadjikakou 2006; Sari 2005). They report an increased (although not absolute) tendency towards a 'hearing' identity in mainstream oral schools, a bicultural identity in total communication environments and a Deaf identity in special schools for the Deaf. All note, however, that levels of interaction and feelings of inclusion and integration, or exclusion and alienation, often determine close affiliation with one or both cultures. McIlroy and Storbeck (2011) analysed narrative accounts of nine South African deaf participants who attended mainstream and special schools for the Deaf and demonstrate that D/deaf identity is not an essential, stable state but fluid and transitory. They report that participants were largely unaware of their deaf status until entering school – at which point they were propelled on a journey of self-analysis and discovery. Many reported that on first entering school they experienced feelings of isolation and exclusion which led them to seek contact with other Deaf and to communicate in sign language. Transitioning into a different culture was reported as difficult for many, some detailing discomfort in existing in hearing and Deaf worlds – preferring or having to stay on the margins of one or both. Others report satisfaction in entering Deaf schools for they experienced a shift to a Deaf identity; some even stressing a desire to be associated only with a Deaf identity. Yet, others in mainstream schools reported continued feelings of isolation and alienation, also noting the positives of developing new social networks with Deaf people and the ability to establish a bicultural identity. All reported a preference to develop and maintain relationships with hearing and Deaf people and highlighted the situated nature of identity performance.

In contrast to the emic perspective adopted in McIlroy and Storbeck's (2011) study, McKee (2008) reports on the 'construction of deaf children as marginal bilinguals' in mainstream schools in New Zealand, exploring the discourses and resources available within these settings. Basing her conclusions on an in-depth case study of a 10-year-old boy with a CI in a mainstream primary school, she details how, despite the increasing national and international recognition of the Deaf community and sign language, he is still 'positioned as a marginal bilingual or defective monolingual by the aggregation of beliefs, decisions, interactions and resources that construct his educational context' (p. 519). She supports and appropriates a 'rights-based' discourse to education and argues for the inclusion of Deaf culture and sign language in mainstream schools to facilitate, support and enhance a bilingual/bicultural status for these minority children. Her account is illustrative of similar settings and cases internationally.

Age is noted to be a potential variable influencing identity status in schools. As reviewed previously, Wheeler et al. (2007) reported that although a cohort of adolescent CI informants (aged between 13 and 16 years) expressed a deaf identity, they did not profess a strong hearing or Deaf status, despite their bilingual tendencies. Leigh (2009) asserts, however, that in contrast to this study, older adolescents that she studied have a heightened interest in identity issues and expressed greater affiliation with the Deaf community in comparison to their younger peers.

Generational differences in educational experience have been identified as impacting on identity status and tendencies toward political activism as evident in case studies carried out in Ireland and Japan. LeMaster (2003) reports on an extensive ethnographic study of the deaf community in Dublin, Ireland, in which she found that the older generations, who had been taught through the medium of sign language, were more prone to interaction with the hearing community and less inclined to the promotion of minority discourses or Deaf activism. In contrast, a shift in identity status appears to have taken place in the younger generations who were exposed both to an enforced oral education and also developments in European and American activism as well as research on sign language and the Deaf community. The young appear more prone towards stressing a Deaf cultural identity and promoting emancipatory discourses. Nakamura (2005) details a similar situation in Japan: older deaf people were educated via sign language and reported to adopt bimodal forms of communication – signing and speaking simultaneously – while the younger generations are reported to have undergone mainstreaming which precipitated feelings and circumstances of social and linguistic marginalization. The young report feeling strongly about their right to a Deaf identity and sign language. The older generations, in contrast, are said to value speaking and signing, happy even to code-mix, and are less politically motivated.

With an interest in exploring the instantiation of multiple identities[14] and considering minority identity politics, many are seeking answers to such questions as: how does being deaf influence one's attachment to and membership within ethnic/gender/social class/age (etc.) groupings and vice versa? For example, Smiler and McKee (2007) report on the influence of the emancipation of the *Māori* and Deaf communities in New Zealand and the influence of 'context' (broadly defined) on self-presentation. They engage with issues of socialization in the culture and customs of the *Māori* and Deaf communities (and the difficulties experienced therein) and the impact of macro-level structures on identity, for example, the treatment of *Māori* or Deaf identity in educational institutions and therefore student's access to their ethnic or racial values and customs. They argue that *Māori* Deaf children experience a 'double-bind' (p. 100) – those educated in the mainstream were identified as *Māori* due their external appearance and yet were unable to access elements of the *Māori* curriculum which were presented in spoken English or *Māori*; those educated in schools for the deaf found their *Māori* identity inaccessible (see Foster & Kinuthia 2003 for a similar discussion of Asian, Hispanic and African American deaf children). The latter reporting that issues of ethnic identity were never salient in the Deaf school setting; only later, when meeting people who had been educated in mainstream schools did they realize that boundaries might be drawn between people of different ethnicities within the Deaf community: '*Māori* Deaf who were socialised in the hearing *Māori* world identified exclusively as *Māori* and not as Deaf, whereas those *Māori* Deaf who were socialised in the Deaf world and identified strongly as Deaf tended to be marginalised in terms of *Māori* identity' (p. 100). Difficulties in *Māori* enculturation intergenerationally are also noted. Since older *Māori* generally had a superficial and unformed understanding of *Māori* customs and values and did not necessarily have deaf offspring themselves, the *Māori* way of imparting its culture and identity from grandparents/parents to children was somewhat impoverished. Knowledge for the most part had to be gleaned by deaf children through observing the behaviour of hearing family members. However, this is noted to have led to a diminished understanding of *Māori*. When asked to describe the 'protocol of their *marae* (traditional meeting compound) at events such as *tangi* (funerals) and *powhiri* (ceremonial welcomes) [m]ost could describe visible, procedural aspects of events that took place, and practices around the gathering and preparation of food. Participants were, however, unfamiliar with concepts that inform a *Māori* world-view and underlie traditional activities and rituals' (p. 98). Some noted the mediating and instructional role of interpreters in helping them to understand *Māori* traditions and ways. The authors report however that 'participants expressed fluid identities, in which *Māori* and Deaf aspects are both central but foregrounded differently in interactions with hearing *Māori*, and the wider Deaf community' (p. 93) and that neither identity was separable from the other. Drawing on the work of Foster and Kinuthia (2003) who constructed a framework to explain the way in which Deaf people from ethnic minorities[15] conceptualize and articulate their identity/ies, they argue that perceptions and performances of identity are influenced and mediated by individual, historical, social and situational characteristics and circumstances. These may alter across an individual's lifespan. The authors therefore take a dynamic interactionist perspective arguing for the influence of social contexts on individual identity perception and performance.

Conclusion

The concept of 'D/deaf identity/ies' is complex to theorize, define and research – a subject of multiple enquiries from different academic perspectives. We began the chapter by exploring different models of 'deafness' and D/deaf identity, noting the power of hegemonic discourses to position deaf people medically and socially. We also explored the sociocultural and linguistic markers of those who identify with the Deaf community and reject a medical or social definition of 'Deaf' identity, preferring a sociocultural and culture-linguistic definition. In this regard, we explored the importance of narrative, poetry and jokes as vehicles of kinship and cultural identity. It would seem that the term 'deafness' is lacking in analytic specificity and perhaps, as argued by Obasi (2008: 7), a concept that is, or should be 'under erasure'.

It seems evident that the impact of changing sociopolitical and technological 'advancements' on Deaf culture and D/deaf identities has given rise to a multiplicity and fluidity of temporal and spatial realizations and rather than 'closing' down opportunities for contact with other D/deaf people, it has the potential to enhance new social networks. It seems too from the results of psychosocial research that CIs and technology can have a profound influence on self-esteem and self-concept. Nevertheless, boundaries between the D/deaf and hearing world are still evident and D/deaf people are still subject to feelings of alienation and discrimination and 'misrepresentation'. The studies reviewed appear to support Hall's (1996: 4) assertion that 'identities are about questions of using the resources of history, language and culture in the process of becoming rather than being ... what we might become, how we have been represented and how that bears on how we might represent ourselves' appears as relevant to D/deaf people as to others.

Theories such as 'Deafhood' remind us also of the unique status and worldview of Deaf people – the value of incorporating theoretically and methodologically a uniquely visual epistemological perspective and subaltern experience into identity research. This *sui generis* perspective can only serve to enrich our understanding of the embodied experience in the construction and perception of self and others. At the same time, the diverse experiences and statuses of D/deaf people impel a critical engagement and reflection on multiple dynamics and power relations – individual, social, situational, cultural, political – for these render multiple epistemologies for scrutiny. We are beginning to gain insight into some of these but there is still a significant amount of work to be done.

CHAPTER ELEVEN

Space, Place and Identity

In sociolinguistics and discourse studies, as in geography, researchers are moving from the assumption that place defines identity, to studies of the ways participants may make place relevant to their identities in situated interactions .... As Doreen Massey puts it, '"the identity of a place" is much more open and provisional than most discussions allow' (1994: 164). And it is richer, because it is not just a position in space but also a link to tasks, practices, everyday life.

MYERS (2006: 325, 339)

Introduction

Our physical and social relationship to space and place[1] can impact on our sense of belonging as well as our perception and portrayal of community and self-identity. The relationship between language, space/place and identity has been the focus of much sociolinguistic and discourse research. Since early dialectological studies, sociolinguists have been interested to explore the relationship between place, language and identity in situated language use. For example, they have investigated the nature of language variation and change within speech communities in localities endowed with specific histories, biographies and networks, as well as the nature and outcome of sustained language contact in specific locations (e.g. dialect levelling) – and in recent years, the impact of supralocal and transnational movement and contact (both physical and virtual) on the deterritorialization of language practices[2] and the reshaping of identity. This research has contested notions of 'local' varieties or 'national' languages as discrete categories and stable markers of identity; rather, investigations reveal marked fluidity and variability in group and actor performance and identification.

In synergy with a 'spatial turn' in the political and social sciences (Soja 1989; Urry 2003; Warf & Arias 2009), sociolinguists and discourse analysts have begun to conceive of place in relational and practice-based terms (Johnstone 2004; Llamas 2007).[3] Regions/spatial geographies however defined – local, supralocal, regional, national, supranational – are not considered as established bounded spaces but as discursively and interactionally constructed, open to change and variability through human contact. As such, languages and dialects are formed culturally by social groups that use and/or recognize specific repertoires as denoting and constructing a particular group (themselves and/or others) in relation to space/place. Britain (2010: 196) argues, for example, that:

> Dialectological 'regions' are formed as individuals interact while they go about their everyday lives, free to move but constrained in that movement by institutions of capital and the state … This approach forces us to recognise that space is not only physical, but also social and perceptual … Routine behaviours ensure that some 'paths' are well-worn … leading over time and on a community scale to the emergence of 'places' and 'regions'. Viewing places and regions in this way emphasises that they are shaped by practice, that they are processes rather than objects.

A sociolinguistics of place is therefore conceived and operationalized as a facet of identity which can be constructed in and through social practice. Frequently, sociolinguists investigate linguistic features associated with place in their investigation of intersecting variables (e.g. class, ethnicity, gender) and recognize that individuals choose linguistic features which are both available and meaningful to them (Becker 2009). Also, as discussed and illustrated in section 'Supranational space' below, a critical analysis of the behaviour and discourses of transnationalism and the politics of space and place reveals an orientation towards multiple and unbounded realizations of identity by some.

The study of the fluidity and multiplicity of language practices within, between and across spaces and places has fuelled the proliferation of theoretical frameworks and concepts, such as, 'Crossing', 'Super-diversity' and 'Translanguaging' (Blommaert & Rampton 2012; Creese & Blackledge, 2010; García & Li Wei 2014; Li Wei 2011; Rampton 2014). As patterns of physical and virtual contact have proliferated and changed, a greater awareness and sensitivity towards spatial multi-scalarity (the interaction between micro and macro contexts) in place identity[4] and in practices of identification have emerged in investigations of personal and group performance. Sociolinguists and discourse analysts have begun to rethink the tenets of such fundamental concepts as 'speech community', which for so long relied on the concept of geographic location to contextualize language variation across and within social groups in bounded space.[5] It is argued by some that a community is not something that can be predetermined; rather, it is a socially constructed category which should be investigated in its own right within the local context, rather than assumed by the analyst. As such, the term 'speech community' has been replaced in some studies by an emphasis on 'communities of practice' or networks of engagement with investigations focusing on how speakers invoke and perform place identity in interaction through linguistic and semiotic means.

This chapter takes a 'scalar' approach to studies of place identity moving from micro to macro, beginning with a discussion of (supra)local identity and ending with the consideration of supranational identity, and moving from a focus on the study of socio-phonetic variables to the discursive construction of identity. In the section entitled 'Local places', we examine the indexical association between linguistic variables and local identity drawing illustratively on the early dialectological work of Labov (1963), before moving onto more contemporary work drawing on Becker (2009) and Stuart-Smith et al. (2007) as illustrative accounts. We then consider the impact of mobility on dialect levelling and feature reallocation in local contexts through language contact. In the following section, we discuss a burgeoning area of sociolinguistic investigation – language and borders – focusing on how variation in language use relates to (self-)ascribed identity in borderland areas and how identity/identification(s) can be influenced and changed by personal, political and social phenomena. A discussion of national identity is presented in the section entitled 'National space', before finally turning to a consideration of globalization and mobility in the last section of the chapter ('Supranational space').

Local places

Many sociolinguistic studies have focused on the marking of identification to a locality through the appropriation of regional dialect features. Labov's (1963) seminal study on Martha's Vineyard, off the coast of New England, masterfully illustrates the correlation between place identity and socio-phonetic variation. Concentrating his analysis on the articulation of the diphthongs [aɪ] and [aʊ] by local inhabitants, Labov reported a marked centralization of these features by some members of the community, notably the 31–60 age group and the fishermen of an area called Chilmark. Taking into account social-economic and attitudinal factors, Labov concluded that these groups, more than others (older, 75+ and younger, 14–30 age groups), experienced the negative impact of the summer incursion of wealthy visitors to the island and the declining economy and therefore adopted a distinct pronunciation of these features in order to denote their belonging to the island and distinction from visiting 'outsiders'. He notes in particular that the fishermen's way of life and attitude to island identity served as a model to some of the younger generation who too distanced themselves from the lifestyle and identity of those from outside. However, Labov found more fluid and less concrete affiliations to the island by the younger 14–30 age group, which accounted for less centralized articulations of the diphthongs in their speech. Informants in this age category did not discount the possibility of moving to the mainland and had less strong feelings about their island identity. This influential study showed how variation in linguistic practice across generations and occupational groups functioned to perform agentive and social acts of 'authentication' (Bucholtz 2003) and territorial marking.

Since this study, many sociolinguistic accounts have focused on regional features and place identity in the United States and elsewhere, for example, a study of the Mount Pleasant District of Washington D.C. (Modan 2007); Pittsburgh, Pennsylvania (Johnstone 2004, 2009; Johnstone & Kiesling 2008, see discussion in Chapter Two); Michigan (Remlinger 2009); and the Lower East Side of New York City (Becker 2009) – and Delforge's (2012) recent account of unstressed vowel devoicing in the Spanish spoken in Cusco, Peru, a study combining attitude-perception with acoustic analyses of features. Some have continued in the methodological vein of Labov, undertaking quantitative analyses of linguistic variables sometimes combining these with, or focusing solely on, ethnographic and discourse analyses as shown below.

Walking metaphorically and geographically in the footsteps of another of Labov's studies, Becker (2009) revisited the salience of /r/ in the construction of an 'authentic' place identity for white inhabitants of the Lower East Side of Manhattan. This study provides an excellent example of shifting interests in sociolinguistics (see Chapters One and Two) towards a social practice approach to situated stylistic and sociolinguistic difference. Her study focuses on a neighbourhood experiencing social unease due to the conflicting economic forces of lack of investment and gentrification. These contribute to disagreements among community groups of different ethnicities and status. It combines historical and ethnographic insight with a variationist analysis of rhoticity, investigating shifts in the realization of a /r/ among the 'white ethnics'/self-ascribed 'Lower East Siders' (p. 639) who find themselves increasingly isolated and subject to the forces of socio-demographic and economic change within their neighbourhood. Becker reports that:

> [t]he Lower East Siders create a space within their community landscape that isolates them from other residents; they are distinct from minorities, from those poorer than them, from those wealthier than them. In a sense

they are threatened from all sides by neighboring groups they see as 'other.' As a result, they turn to a 'distributed memory' (Mendoza-Denton 2008: 180) of happier times on the Lower East Side in order to construct a group place identity'. (p. 643)

She finds that the occurrence of rhoticity correlates strongly with topic shift such that non-rhoticity becomes more salient when subjects address neighbourhood topics in contrast to other subjects. This is illustrated succinctly in the case of Lindsey (see extract below) whose overall rate of rhoticity in her speech (coded below as [r-1], as opposed to [r-0] for non-rhoticity) is noted to be 60 per cent. However, when engaging in a discussion about a neighbourhood topic falls to almost a third (22 per cent) of this.

Lindsey: It really has changed, and, I just **never**[r-0] thought it would get that high. But it has. And I'm **forty-five**[r-0], so I didn't really anticipate things getting so expensive.

Kara: Do you find, being in the neighbourhood hard, I don't know groceries, and things like that?

Lindsey: Well we only have, really have like one **supe**[r-1]**market**[r-0].

Kara: Where do you guys go now when you go out. I don't know restaurants or, [other place to go.

Lindsey: [We **or**[r-1]**der**[r-0] in. (laughs) Well we **or**[r-0]**der**[r-0] from Odessa's and that's a **landmark**[r-0], that's been here for years. (p. 650)

Becker argues that it is through alternations in the use of /r/ that speakers adopt a situated local and 'authentic' persona. 'These place-related shifts align with a Speaker Design model of style (Coupland 2007; Schilling-Estes 2002) which acknowledges micro-variation as a resource for speakers in the active construction of identities; in this case, a place identity' (p. 637).

Some 3,000 miles north-east of New York, Stuart-Smith et al. (2007) reported on the salience of locality to an interpretation of differences in pronunciation between working class adolescents and middle-class speakers in the city of Glasgow in Scotland. Although socio-economic and age classification proved difficult to incorporate methodologically into Becker's New York study due to the small sample size, they are identified as particularly important variables in the case of Glasgow. In an investigation of eight consonants, Stuart-Smith et al. illustrate how the vernacular of young 13–14 year olds is changing through the adoption of 'non-local' features and the recession of local, Scottish features. Despite the older speakers (40 years+) maintaining weaker social networks and enjoying greater mobility, including more contact with English speakers than the young, they have a greater tendency to maintain the established Scottish pronunciation. The changing face of the youth vernacular (which incorporates such forms as the lessening of post-vocalic /r/ realization and the articulation of TH-fronting – use of [f] for /θ/) is 'explained in terms of the construction of specific, locally situated identities which simultaneously signal their own identity and differentiate them from "posh" people' (p. 255). The authors assert that these new features are not 'perceived as supralocal' (p. 255) but are invoked in the performance of a local (Glaswegian) youth identity in response to locally shared age- and class-based language ideologies. The consonant changes observed in Glasgow are not necessarily a consequence of supralocal dialect contact therefore, nor necessarily a wish by the young to identify with youths or others from other regions; rather, they were invoked to distance themselves from others within their own locality.

Dialect contact within defined regions can lead to some interesting changes in language practice and identity building as evidenced in a body of research on dialect levelling – a process in which speakers of different dialects who come into long-term contact with one another reduce the amount of demographic or geographically marked variant features through a process of accommodation, eliminating minority variants in favour of the majority and the reallocation of meaning of linguistic features. Supralocal dialect levelling can 'result[...] from migration, mobility, and expansion in the tertiary economy and labour-market flexibility' (Torgensen & Kerswill 2004: 25) as illustrated below. The role of identity construction in dialect levelling and in the creation of new dialects has been illustrated, although not uncontroversially,[6] by a number of studies. For example, Watt (2002) asserts that young Geordies in Newcastle-upon-Tyne adopt supralocal regional forms in order to project a 'Northern' modern identity (not just a local 'Newcastle' identity).[7] Moreover, Dyer (2010) illustrates how the social meaning of a linguistic feature which once originated in one region may change over time when incorporated into a new contact dialect.

Dyer's study focused on Corby, England, which had grown from a village to a town at the beginning of the twentieth century due to its transformation into a major steel-making plant. An influx of Scottish workers from Glasgow and Lanarkshire meant that the percentage of Scottish-born Corby residents reached a peak of around 30 per cent by the 1970s. These inhabitants were not initially welcomed into the new region by the locals and were somewhat separated by their place of residence from local residents, but nevertheless over time the communities mixed and the 'koiné now spoken in Corby is a distinct mixture of Scottish and established and innovatory Anglo-English features, although outsiders often perceive it as a form of Scottish English' (p. 209). The older Corby dialect is now relegated to the annals of time and heard only in the speech of the oldest inhabitants. Dyer reports on changes to the indexicality of the vowels in the lexical set 'GOOD/FOOD' and argues, based on an apparent-time study of the dialect in 1998 and a real-time study of data collected in 2006, that the Scottish pronunciation, which is marked by a merged pronunciation, continues to be stigmatized by the older generation but is increasing in the local dialect. It has taken on a less stigmatized status by the young for whom its social meaning has shifted from a marker of 'out-group' Scottish identity to a 'locally-based Corby identity' (p. 215). The accent now marks differentiation from closer localities, for example, Kettering.

Watt's and Dyer's studies illustrate how localities and regions are not pre-given, stable, defined spaces but are formed through the social practices and ideologies of those who inhabit these spaces and in studying contact situations it becomes apparent how linguistic variables which once carried particular associations can take on different meanings for their speakers in a new context and time. Britain (2010: 203) notes that 'we should look more readily to *spatial practices* wherein we will find differing intensities of local, supralocal and regional engagement' and we will also find different linguistic forms that are derived from different scales of engagement and contact with others, either via our mobility or that of others. As such, language contact may lead us to adopt some variables which carry supralocal or more local meaning. 'We draw our spatial identities from the routinized practices we engage in space and the ways those practices connect (or not) with those of others. In turn, these identities contribute towards the creation of contexts for subsequent spatial behaviour' (Britain 2010: 203); this can be seen no less in borderland regions.

Borderlands

Social scientific interest in identity construction and negotiation in borderland regions has escalated in recent years (Diener & Hagen 2010; Donnan & Wilson 2010; Watt & Llamas, 2014; Wilson & Donnan 2012). Sociolinguistic studies have focused on identifying how patterns of variation in borderland regions index self or other-ascribed identities, linking this to issues of nationalism and localism on the one hand, and stylistic/strategic language use on the other. Studies have explored national borders within countries (e.g. between Scotland and England), shifting borders between administrative districts, and borders between politically defined nations, as illustrated in the case of Galicia and Portugal below. Overwhelmingly, these studies point, once more, to the constructed nature of place which, while conveniently delineated by political texts and topographers on a map, hides the complexity and variability of perception, identification and performance within. Such studies challenge the objectivity of bounded spaces and point to their practice-based realization. Some of the more pressing research questions have included: how do changing administrative borders within and between nations impact on identity, language perceptions and practice? Do residents on the periphery of a nation experience a heightened sensitivity towards national identity and what is the impact of this on their performativity? What is the role of political/symbolic borders in demarcating group boundaries and how is this realized linguistically and semiotically (such as within the linguistic landscape, e.g. see Kallen 2014)? We consider some of these issues in the context of the UK, drawing on the work of Beal, Llamas and colleagues, and in one other European context – the border between Galicia and Portugal (Beswick 2014).

In a chapter entitled 'Shifting borders and regional identities', Beal (2010) details the ways in which changes to the administration of local governance in the UK, following the Local Government Act of 1972, led in 1974 to the reconfiguration of county borders and the development of new shire and metropolitan counties. Beal argues that this administrative decision had a long-term impact on resident identities and their 'perception and production of local accents and dialects' (p. 219) in many areas. She reports that research in perceptual dialectology reveals that younger people's linguistic identity is not linked to either the traditional or current counties but rather to larger regions and conurbations. For example, younger residents (mainly aged between 18 and 20 years) in the north of England experience great difficulty in associating dialects with the traditional English counties, with the exception of Yorkshire. These perceptual changes are also linked to changes in language use as evidenced in the case of Middlesbrough (Llamas 2001, 2006, 2007) – 'a place between places' as described by *The Sunday Times* (5 March 2000, Llamas 2007: 580) – a town that lies between Yorkshire and the North East of England, and which has experienced repeated boundary changes with accompanying shifts in resident attitude and language use. Llamas (2007: 580) asserts that as its status is neither in one region or another; it 'has meant that the place identity of the urban center is not deep-rooted and firmly felt by either inhabitants or outsiders, as is often the case for localities on the peripheries of regions and nations'. Moreover, the Middlesbrough accent lies somewhere between the Geordie accent of the northern neighbouring district of Newcastle and Tyneside and its southern neighbour, Yorkshire. Middlesbrough is 'transitional … both geographically and dialectally' (p. 585).

Llamas employed a triangulated methodology to elicit data from thirty-two working-class informants differentiated by age (old: 60–80 years, middle: 32–45 years, young: 19–22 years and adolescents: 16–17 years) and gender. Data collection involved deskwork; an Identification Questionnaire (IdQ) designed to garner information on informant attitudes towards their area and language, including 'in-group'/'out-group' orientations; and spoken language data. Linguistic analysis focused on patterns of glottalling and glottalization[8] of the voiceless stops (p, t, k). Glottalization of (p, t, k) in word medial position is a feature of Newcastle upon Tyne and its surrounding areas, Tyneside and Durham, and is identified as a characteristic feature of the north-east. It is not present in the varieties of English spoken in

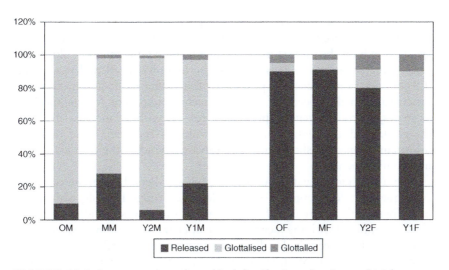

FIGURE 11.1 *Representation of graphical distribution of variants of (p) by age and gender (adapted from Llamas 2007: 590).*

Yorkshire. Llamas (2007) found socially conditioned convergence towards the north-eastern varieties and divergence from Yorkshire pronunciations by the working-class speakers sampled, with subtle patterns of differentiation. In contrast to speakers in Tyneside, for whom glottalling was apparent for (t), Middlesbrough informants articulated [ʔ] for all three variables, with a higher rate of use for (t) recorded across all speakers. (p) glottalization was favoured in both regions (over (t) and (k)) with a greater incidence apparent in Tyneside.

When exploring the sociolinguistic profiles of informants, age and gender reveal significant patterns of difference, as depicted in Figure 11.1. Results show an increasing use of (p) glottalization across apparent time suggesting convergence towards the pronunciation of the north-east. A decrease in the use of [p] suggests a comparable divergence from the standard and Yorkshire pronunciation. (p) glottalization is identified as characteristic of male speech with younger males using it more than older males (over 90 per cent), preferring to align once more with the Tyneside pronunciation. Greater variation across age groups was identified in the female data. Old and middle-aged speakers almost exclusively articulated [p], whereas the younger speakers orient more towards (p) glottalization with greater use among adolescents in comparison to young adults.

Like (p), increased use of [ʔ] for (t) also reveals a change in apparent time with both male and female speakers reaching almost categorical rates (95.8 per cent for males and 90 per cent among adolescent females). Despite this, [t] is still preferred in careful speech demonstrating speaker sensitivity to the indexical value of [ʔ].

In the case of (k), Llamas (p. 591ff) reports variation across age cohorts, although scores are not as high as for the other two variables. Middle-aged speakers exhibit the highest use of (k), while the young favour a glottalized variant. Articulation of [k] is noted to be high across all males, although (k) glottalization reaches its peak with the young adult group, falling in articulation in the speech of the adolescent cohort. For female speakers, as males, there is a general preference for (k) with an increase in use of the glottalized articulation among the younger speakers. Once more, all informants appear to show sensitivity towards avoiding the glottalized form in careful speech.

The use of glottalized features by young speakers, Llamas suggests, is a consequence of 'convergence of MbE [Middlesbrough English] with speech of farther north, where use of the glottalized forms was found to be higher. This is combined with the fact that there appears to be an increase in short-term contact between the localities as a result of improved road and public transport systems' (p. 595). The declining use of released variants is noted to mark divergence away from the speech of Yorkshire people. These findings are further supported by the attitudinal data garnered. Older speakers declared an affiliation to the geographic region of Yorkshire reporting that they spoke with a Yorkshire accent; middle-aged speakers reported an affiliation with the geographic region of 'Teesside'. The young, in contrast, reported that they spoke with a "Middlesbrough" accent. These findings are not coincidental, for older informants spent most of their lives resident in what was termed Middlesbrough, Yorkshire, whereas the middle-age group experienced many changes to the administration of Middlesbrough. The young, in contrast, never lived through a time in which it was administered by or affiliated to Yorkshire. 'This suggests that speakers react to changing political boundaries of the area in which they live, and if such boundaries change, so may the way inhabitants perceive themselves. This may result in changes to the ingroups that speakers perceive, and also to the salience of relevant outgroups to which they compare themselves' (p. 596). Overall, results of the attitude questionnaire revealed significant differences in generational reporting with respect to:

- linguistic orientation in Middlesbrough
- self-image in terms of what accent speakers perceive themselves to have – the locally constructed speech community varies with age and appears to be affected by changes in political divisions. (Llamas 2007: 600)

There was also:

- A lack of overtly positive identification with the dominant center of gravity of the North East, Newcastle.

- The irrelevance of Yorkshire to the identity construction of younger speakers.

- An increase in the perception of Middlesbrough as a place with its own identity. (Llamas 2007: 600)

Llamas's study suitably illustrates the impact of changing political affiliations and spatial boundedness on speaker attitude, performance and identification. Merging a consideration of speakers' place identity with language use supports a motivated explanation for linguistic convergence and divergence from the varieties of others.

In other research – the 'Accents and Identity on the Scottish English Border' (AISEB) project – Llamas (2009, 2010) and Watt and Llamas (2014) – explore the relationship between linguistic variation (and accommodation) and place identity in four regions on the national borders of Scotland and England. Their research highlights the relational and emergent nature of 'doing Scottish' or 'doing English' by inhabitants of four localities on the Scottish/English border: two on the east, Berwick-upon-Tweed (England) and Eyemouth (Scotland) and Carlisle (England) and Gretna (Scotland) to the west. They explore such features as voice onset time and realization of /r/. In one account, Llamas (2010) explores patterns of convergence and divergence studying the (dis)continuity of phonological features across the national borders and the extent to which patterns of use mark ascribed national identities – Scottish, English, British, Scottish-English. Focusing her analysis on rhotic /r/ and attitudinal data related to regional and national identity, she finds geographic differences in perceptions and language performance. Young people in the east appear to be diverging in their language use and attitudes, whereas those on the west are converging. The young people of Eyemouth are noted to use the greatest amount of /r/ in comparison to other older speakers within their locality and in comparison to all four localities. Informants report on a strong national identity and choose to mark their national distinctiveness from people in Berwick through their language use. In the west, she reports that 'inhabitants appear to be non-essentialist in their approach, and not only do younger inhabitants appear to be converging and accepting their shared British identity, but they also report an awareness of the advantages of switching allegiances to enhance a situation (for example, to attract the attention of the opposite sex or to avoid conflict)' (Llamas 2010: 235).

The salience of the border to the inhabitants of the four towns is considered to influence their self- (and other-) ascribed national identities and their language use. Each locality experiences a different relationship with the border for a variety of reasons such as historical events, differences in regional affiliation and amount of cross-border contact as well as differences in 'core-periphery relations' (Llamas 2010: 236). East side patterns of linguistic divergence can be partially explained in relation to the latter, for while Berwick-upon-Tweed and Eyemouth are very close to the border (3 and 6 miles, respectively), Llamas suggests that they harbour different relationships with their national capitals and surrounding regions which means that Berwickers harbour more localized perspectives in contrast to people from Eyemouth. Inhabitants of Berwick-upon-Tweed live further away from their national capital (London) than residents of Eyemouth (Edinburgh); this fact, in conjunction with their negative attitudes towards the major city in their region, Newcastle-upon-Tyne, combines to support ascriptions which are based on local definitions. Berwickers, Llamas (2010:235) asserts, 'define themselves primarily by using a strategy of localism'. Whereas residents of Eyemouth view their space and identities in less local and more national terms, distancing themselves from their English neighbours and considering their Scottish identity as more prestigious.

In considering whether borderland residents experience a heightened sense of national identity, it would appear that results of the AISEB study unearth a complex picture in which national identity is determined as fluid, emergent and relational. On the Scottish-English border, resident's sense of place and linguistic expression certainly plays a role in enacting place identity; however, negotiations across space/places, as noted above (e.g. to strategically avoid conflict between inhabitants of different districts), also uncover the relevance of shared linguistic knowledge and expression and its strategic enactment across borders. Attitudes and behaviour can differ from one group or locality to the next along the same national border and from one moment to the next. Some informants have a more 'fixed' sense of national identity and regional affiliation in comparison to others. However, as noted by Llamas (2010: 236), '[t]his foregrounding of certain aspects of identity in a given moment is something that is available to all speakers, though having the ability to foreground one *national* identity over another while speaking the same language may be a particular fluidity shared by those inhabitants of borderlands who accept and exploit the benefits of their hybrid identity'.

Other studies of politically distinct nations with different national languages similarly reveal how speakers in borderland areas identify with one another through the use of shared phonological patterns and code-switching practices, revealing how identification strategies are employed and motivated in some instances by capital (cultural, economic, social) gain.

Beswick (2014) details the case of the border between Galicia and Portugal taking into consideration the multilingual character of the locality and the sociolinguistic history and relationship between Galician and Castilian Spanish and the Galician's connection to Portuguese, which, was historically, until the Middle Ages, noted to be the same language. Focusing on the towns of Tui (Galicia) and Valença (Portugal), Beswick describes the extent of mutual intelligibility between the dialects spoken in these localities particularly due to phonological levelling. This has facilitated continued contact across the borders. Adopting a socio-psychological approach to identity (drawing on Tajfel's 1978 theory of Social Identity, see Chapters One and Eight), Beswick examines individual linguistic repertoires and their relationship to group boundedness and construction of local identities. The author determines that language use in commercial exchanges influences perceptions of in-/out-group belonging. The study's hypothesis is that in-group identification will motivate the adoption of the same phonological forms in certain contexts of use irrespective of national belonging. Inhabitants of both towns favour their shared variety and accommodate to mark community belonging across borders, particularly for commercial gain, marking themselves out as distinct from groups even within their own nations. The study determines that national identity cannot be determined on linguistic grounds since variation in use exists among those who belong to the same nation (as similarly reported by others, e.g. Joseph 2010; see below) and indeed convergence of use among those who occupy territory in close proximity to one another across borders in different politically defined (national) settings. Further, their situatedness within different nations determines that Portuguese and Galicians experience different senses of national membership(s) to those determined by their 'local' identifications. The Galicians express a Galician national identity (in contrast to Spanish); the Portuguese invoke a Portuguese national identity. The study points once more to the complexity of determination and ascription and the shifting boundaries and configurations of groups, which are contingent on multiple political, historical, social, economic, cultural and contextual factors.

National space

The spatial politics of identity therefore appear in discussions of the nation, where national space is conceived as a politically and geographically delineated territory. The concept of a shared national consciousness and belonging to an 'imagined community' was considered by Anderson to have arisen with the development of the nation-state in the nineteenth century, including the influence of 'print-capitalism, which made it possible for rapidly growing numbers of people to think about themselves, and to relate themselves to others, in profoundly new ways' (Anderson 1991: 36). For Anderson, a common national language was fundamental to the formation of national identity; therefore, creating boundaries around languages was fundamental to the creation of nation-states. However, the relationship between nation and language is more complex than Anderson proposed; rather, each has the potential to construct the other (Joseph 2010). Moreover, the national language is as much a cultural and discursive construction as the 'nation-state myth'[9] and as argued by some sociolinguists and discourse analysts less productive as an object of analysis than the examination of variable speech repertoires by individuals and social groups within (Balibar & Wallerstein 1991; Blommaert & Rampton 2012; Wodak et al. 2009).

One cannot deny, however, that the relationship between national identity and language has been a prominent topic of discussion in sociolinguistics and social-psychology over the last five decades or more, with the relevance of the nation-language link for the purposes of state creation/maintenance identified as foundational to nation-building in some contexts, for example, nation-states where a "one language, one nation" ideology exists[10] such as France (Marek 1998). Similarity and difference, or 'us' versus 'them' dichotomies, are often resonant in accounts and perceptions of 'national identity' (Edwards 2009). However, language is not necessarily foundational to a national myth of belonging in contexts which support more than one language (e.g. Belgium or Switzerland) or in postcolonial settings (Ominiyi 2010[11]). Globally, the nation-language link in the construction of national identity is noted to be rather exceptional with other parameters featuring as core values of nationality, for example, common ancestry or culture (Giddens 1987). Globalization and increased mobility have further complicated matters; some research has identified an increased turn by some citizens towards language as a marker of nationality, others arguing that globalization and mobility have punctured the boundaried nature of the two, with recent sociolinguistic scholarship denaturalizing the notion that there are distinct and whole languages, concentrating rather on the fluidity of speech repertoires at subnational levels (Blommaert & Rampton 2012). Coupland (2014: 151) argues for example in his discussion of Welsh and English in Wales that '[l]anguage and nation rhetoric ... [is] tropic and anachronistic, and at odds with contemporary social realities characterized by mobility and complexity'. Certainly in recent writing, languages are considered as less bounded, or connected to stated or fixed places (/nations); rather, speech repertoires are identified as fluid, sometimes syncretic and mutually constitutive in local contexts of use, thereby complicating the relationship between national language(s) and identity (Heller et al. 2014).

In this section, 'national identity' is conceived as a complex spatial, social and analytic category, marked by practices and processes of language/'languaging' as well as other semiotic forms of representation/symbolism.[12] The discussion focuses on the relational and dynamic social existence of language systems, communities and individuals in contact within and across nations. The discussion highlights the perspectives of researchers who consider language, identity and nation to be socially constructed (Blommaert 2010; Heller 2003; Makoni & Pennycook 2007; Pavlenko & Blackledge 2004). This is not, as Heller et al. (2014: 428) assert to 'assume the decline of "mattering" for most people of purportedly stable and essentialized categories' such as 'national identity' or 'national languages' or in this regard to undermine research that invokes these categories and/or focuses on issues of language choice, attitudes towards national language varieties or indeed work on language planning and policy in various national domains. Indeed for some, there has been a return to the reinforcement of national borders and with it recognition of and a desire for citizens to be competent in national languages.[13] However, instead of viewing nation, language and identity as discrete, bounded or objective entities, we discuss their fluid and dynamic potential in contemporary life. We begin with a discussion of the role of language in creating and negotiating real and imagined borders between international and national (deaf) communities/identities. We then progress to a discussion of the impact of political devolution on national linguistic identity elaborating on Coupland's (2014) account of Wales, before finally discussing the role of language in the promotion and commodification of national/ethnic identity for the purposes of tourism.

As discussed in Chapter Ten, 'D/deaf' geography and history play an important role in theories and discussions of Deaf identity. Changes to the status and empowerment of Deaf communities and the role of sign language in their functioning has meant that in some nations decisions about which sign codes to promote, develop and support (e.g. for education) have had to be made. These decisions have in some instances involved adopting sign languages from more powerful signing communities/nations and this has led to the construction of symbolic borders within and across Deaf communities nationally and internationally. A case in point is the status of American Sign Language (ASL) which has increased in usage and reach over recent decades due to the educational and professional status of its users in the United States, as well as contact by some (influential) Deaf people from nations outside of the United States with American centres of education for the deaf (in particular, Gallaudet University); contact between users of other sign languages with ASL users in international organizations/meetings; in addition to the work of ASL-proficient missionaries working in different countries. In some nations, ASL has been adopted as a language or code by the Deaf community, and for others it is used alongside a national sign language; yet in other nations, ASL features are borrowed into indigenous sign varieties (e.g. British Sign Language), and in others its former influence has waned to the point of rejection such that actions of language purification attempt to strip its influence on indigenous varieties.

Parks (2014) reports on an investigation of eight countries in Latin America and the Caribbean for whom contact with ASL led to a renegotiation of their Deaf community's borders internally and internationally. Most communities she found argued for the importance of ASL for upward mobility and international contact; however, they also expressed fear about its hegemonic power. They perceived it as threatening to the vitality of their national sign languages – codes which they considered fundamental to the expression of their cultural identity. The study found different responses by signing communities and members; for example, some Deaf communities adopted and accepted ASL, others adopted the code but changed its form in order to distinguish themselves from American signers, and yet others rejected the code wholesale.

Parks reports that in Grenada and St. Vincent and the Grenadines, ASL was taken and accepted as a national code because prior to its introduction by educators and missionaries there were no Deaf communities, sign languages or cultures on the islands. Despite its acceptance, inhabitants are still be keen to draw national borders symbolically however. Deaf people in St. Vincent reported that they did not use 'American Sign Language' but a variety called 'ASL' marking a distinction between themselves and signers in the United States. Signers in the Grenadian Deaf community reported on a desire to compile a sign language dictionary which would include local signs for produce (food and plants) and locations on the island.

In contrast, Trinidad and Tobago and Jamaica are reported to have adopted ASL to service the needs of users in only certain domains of use, in particular for education, international contact and contact with hearing and Deaf signers within their countries (including visitors fluent in ASL). Older signers of Trinidad and Tobago Sign Language are noted in particular to press for the increased use of the local language even in schools, in order to preserve their unique Deaf history and culture and support contact between older and younger signers. A bilingual status quo is in operation. In these nations, support is given to sustain the local variety alongside ASL.

Nations such as Ecuador and the Dominican Republic illustrate the former influence of ASL on a sign language community and its now waning influence and rejection in order to establish a unique Deaf national identity. Ecuador in particular is actively working on an Ecuadorian Sign Language dictionary which attempts to replace lexical items borrowed from ASL with items from Ecuadorian Sign Language.

As noted by Parks (2014: 214), 'All three of these responses to the presence of ASL in a country's sign language use show a desire to clarify the boundaries of a national deaf community through the negotiation of the use and perceived use of ASL'. Responses to its presence in different national contexts are varied; however, all demarcate their nation's Deaf communities as distinct from others.

As illustrated in Chapter Ten, Deaf communities are as diverse as hearing communities and in addition to the marking of national borders Parks (2014) demonstrates how perceptions and use of ASL function to construct borders between core and peripheral members as well as hearing and Deaf people within Deaf nations. This pertains to regional claims to national sign language status, sign varieties of Deaf and hearing people and the social status of Deaf people. In Guatemala, for example, two regions (Guatemala City and Quetzaltenango) have vied for their sign variety to be recognized as the national sign language. In constructing their arguments, issues of sign purity are prevalent with influences from ASL seen as intrusions, '[b]oth assert that the other has incorporated great amounts of ASL into its sign variety, while their own variety is more truly respectful of deaf Guatamalan culture' (p. 215). In Jamaica, some Deaf did not want to use Jamaican Sign Language (JSL) with hearing Jamaicans or ASL users from the United States preferring to retain JSL (and code-switching between JSL and ASL) as an in-group code and marker of belonging.

Parks' study demonstrates how Deaf people perceive and perform national identities through language choice and attitudes towards different varieties and speakers. With increased empowerment, defining national borders through the appropriation of distinct sign codes has become particularly salient for Deaf communities/'deafhood'. Defining oneself in relation to hearing members of one's nation is only one facet of a complex process of self and community identification. Definitions and constructions of Deaf national identities are important within the Deaf world and an international sign language such as ASL can be crucial in their negotiation and formation.

The fluid potential afforded from the borrowing of ASL and its selective adoption, adaptation and/or rejection by indigenous communities points to the cultural and creative construction of national languages, boundaries and identities. This too is revealed in spoken languages. Coupland (2014) discusses the nation-language link and the nature of bilingualism in the case of Wales, a country which has undergone political devolution and for whom the Welsh language as a discrete code has become an issue for the promotion of national identity in political and lay discourse. He argues, in light of an examination of various texts including the Welsh national anthem; Language Planning and Policy texts; public notices and a bilingual menu, that 'public debates about language and bilingualism in Wales are limited by an objectivist overdetermination of "what Welsh is" and by under-nuanced understandings of "what bilingualism does"' (p. 139). He illustrates the complexity and syncretic relationship between English and Welsh and highlights how postmodern values and activities have led to the commercialization and commodification of language and national identity. While acknowledging the success of corpus planning measures in supporting Welsh language education and promoting greater use of Welsh, the value of language and its appropriation and adaptation is noted to extend to other symbolic forms and markets. He argues 'that globalising late modernity has already radically reduced the potential of nations to convincingly assert their own bounded priorities ... [w]hatever Wales and the Welsh language are, they will be constructed in the local and evolving and often syncretic practices of speakers' (p. 151). They cannot and should not, in other words, be reduced to essential categories or forms but rather explored and understood in and through their complexity.

The strategic commodification and objectification of national languages and the authentication of their speakers with respect to place is nowhere more evident than in the case of tourism. Foci of academic interest in recent years have included *inter alia* studies of artefacts in museums; mixing and use of local languages in festivals, theatrical performances, service encounters and guided tours; studies of linguistic landscapes; iconography; and 'performative re-mediation and re-contextualisation of location languages in print, broadcast and online travelogues, guidebooks, postcards and other promotional material' (Heller et al. 2014: 431). Through the study of these phenomena, one can see how codes and discourses are used to index place/national identity and authenticity in the presentation of self and in the construction of the 'other', as well as how they are exploited for the purposes of commercialization, for example, the selling of national products as discussed below. Multilingualism, which Heller et al. (2014) define as 'a mélange of intermixed, syncretised, and recontextualised words and expressions' (p. 450), modifies identities such that they become 'emblematic of spatial stratification in the political and economic local-global order' (p. 450). The making and experience of a tourist destination is mediated of course through human contact (Johnstone 2010; Pennycook 2010) as illustrated in the case of 'Francophone Canada', which, as noted by Heller (2008), as a social and political reality following the recognition of the French-speaking Québécois nation in 2006, has experienced the commodification of its language and identity in the penetration of the new globalized economic market. She notes, for example, how French Canadian products sold in French-speaking European contexts (notably France and Belgium) are promoted and also prove attractive to consumers in light of their national origin, for this bears associations with lifestyle and language use in Canada: 'many consumers sought out interactions with the vendors in which they could hear Canadian French and talk about life in Canada before examining the product on sale' (p. 516).

Tourism, travel and greater virtual interconnectivity have created a world of multiple possibilities and interconnections – not least the 'reimagining' of place and self in relation to a global-national-local nexus – offering opportunities too for 'translanguaging' throughout this process. These issues are further explored in the discussion below.

Supranational space

An understanding and thematization of 'place' in sociolinguistics and discourse studies is considered as no less salient than in the examination of its relationship to globalization and the mobility of material, people and symbolic resources above the level of the nation. Once more, this research has challenged a perspective that views place and identity as static, circumscribed, homogeneous and uncontested (Blommaert 2005, 2010; Johnstone 2010). In this section, we briefly explore this issue from three different perspectives: first, we continue with our discussion of tourism by drawing on an account of the sociolinguistic development of a 'global village' for domestic tourists in a residential neighbourhood in rural China (Gao 2012) and illustrate how international resources are invoked in the production of a supranational space; we then discuss the impact of pragmatic and sociolinguistic competence on the construction of global identities in a group of transnational students; and finally, taking a critical discourse perspective, explore the discursive and socio-cognitive transformation of transnational (specifically European) identities as viewed from the perspective of civic citizens. All of these accounts point to a loosening of nation-state structures/frames of reference and an interest, by some, in the exploitation of (symbolic) resources drawn from outside the national space.

In a study of a small, previously agriculturally based neighbourhood, 'West Street' in Yangshuo County, southern China, Gao (2012) reports on the transformation of the area into a tourist-based economy. In contrast to other places where communities have been found to exploit their heritage and cultural distinction for commercial gain (as reported in Chapter Eight; Coupland et al. 2005; Thurlow & Jaworski 2010), this neighbourhood took advantage of 'the symbolic and cultural opportunity brought about the inflow of English-speaking tourists' (p. 337) and the semiotic potential of the English language in constructing a new understanding of place identity for domestic tourism. Gao (2012) explains the motivations for this, which were in part a consequence of language ideology in China in which minority languages are stigmatized, but also a consequence of Chinese tourism and consumer practices. Through an analysis of the discursive practices of Chinese tourists visiting West Street, the author identifies a link between binary discursive stances and the performance of what are termed 'post-' and 'anti-tourist' identities. The former are defined according to the definition of Jamal and Hill (2002: 94) as:

a sophisticated traveller who enjoys ludic experiences … The visitor participates in an illusory, hedonistic consumption of signs, symbols and images where the aesthetic experience rates higher than capturing the 'authentic' original. In this postmodern scenario, accumulating aesthetic and culturally driven experiences becomes a game of achieving status, distinction and 'difference'.

'Anti-tourists' are defined as those who concentrate on 'the expected or perceived shallowness of experience of place within traditional tourism [with] a tendency to condemn superficiality' (McCabe 2005: 91–92).

Drawing on an analysis of travelogues posted to a tourism website, Gao discusses the contrasting stance positions realized. Two examples are provided below from a larger data set, the first by a 'post-tourist' tagged as 'A cloud in the heart':

The bus stopped at the entrance to West Street. Here it is. The legendary West Street, right now in front of us. Yet, I did not feel fully prepared to say to it *'Hello! Nice to meet you'* (A cloud in the heart 2005: para. 6);

….

[Coffee shop name] has comfortable sofas and good coffees. The music is good, too. After we came in many people as xiǎozī[14] as us also had their seats. We just indulged there for the whole afternoon. I guess a real xiǎozī life is just like this. I can't love it more!! (2005: para. 76)

Gao describes how the tourist initially writes about the preparation for her trip in Chinese only switching to English in her account of first seeing West Street. This is noted to index a shift in semiotic space, marking out the new place as foreign and setting up the context for a continued preference to write in English. Her positive stance towards the tourist area is noted to be marked figuratively (through the personification of West Street) and metapragmatically. Moreover, her self-positioning as a middle-class, arguably aspirational, xiǎozī is expressed through the actions she reportedly performs in the setting of the coffee shop (drinking coffee rather than the traditional tea) and also indirectly through her continued cosmopolitan use of English in the extract.

An alternative stance towards xiǎozī identity and all that West Street signifies is expressed in the writing of a *nowherekid*, a writer posting to the travel section of a website entitled 'Sina'. She writes:

We've read many travelogues about West Street. It's said that West Street is not just a place for a tour – it should be lived and enjoyed. So we spent most of our week living there. West Street is actually a place for hedonism, where you can forget everything and just indulge yourself ... From the perspective of a xiǎozī, it's true that Yangshuo is a good place, a habitat for your soul ... But I would not consider myself a xiǎozī, and feel no good about the label ... The heaven for xiǎozī can be a hell for me sometimes ... Things here are overcharged ... the highly commercial atmosphere is disgusting ... As it is, Yangshuo today no longer needs painter Xu Beihong, or National Father Sun Wen.[15] It's just where you can be xiǎozī, lose yourself, and indulge yourself. (*nowherekid* 2010: para. 3–27)

Nowherekid distances herself from what she perceives as the hedonist commercial indulges of the xiǎozī, positioning herself rather in a different sociocultural frame, as an individual seeking the satisfaction of more 'high-brow' intellectual pursuits from the past.

These two accounts show how English is 'mobilised and appropriated as one of the semiotic resources for commodifying a sense of globality for domestic tourists' (p. 351). They also illustrate how differences in stance serve to strategically construct different types of tourist identity in relation to the social meanings inferred and invoked through experiences of consumerism. The construction of the 'global village' is shown therefore to be a contested site 'whose significance corresponds to ideologies of language and culture' (p. 352).

The deterritorialization of languages in performances within and constructions of global contexts and citizenship is often practised by the elite and tied to patterns of contact configured by Western modernity. Behaviour can often be characterized as individualistic and far from grounded in the 'local', for example, in the performance of international business transactions or for the purposes of diplomacy. However, recent accounts point to the construction of a different transnational subject, someone who is sensitive not only to the pragmatic, instrumental value of language but also to its symbolic value in marking solidarity long-term within local contexts/'places'. For example, Kang (2012) details the emergence of the 'Asian global' – South Korean educational migrants living in Singapore, who, through their multiple and changing perceptions and use of three national codes – Mandarin, English and Singlish – construct an identification which marks them out as 'global Asian' distinct from 'the conventional image of high-ranking elites' (p. 165). Focusing on subjects' metapragmatic evaluations about how to effectively and appropriately use varieties in different contexts, the study moves beyond a simple mapping of linguistic features onto social identities to explore how Korean migrants rationalize their linguistic competence and performance. Two language ideologies are identified: 'pragmatism' and 'sociolinguistic competence'. Mandarin and English are recognized as affording their users with actual and 'potential' (in the case of Mandarin) economic and practical capital, whereas Singlish is also recognized as endowing the user with social value in marking solidarity with friends in local contact situations (while at the same time Koreans recognize and wish to be distinguished from local users). This sociolinguistic competence which translates to flexible multilingual performance in diverse social situations marks these individuals out as a different type of transnational, 'one that is more sociocentric and multicultural cosmopolitan but also concerned about locality and solidarity among interlocutors in local contexts' (p. 168).

Kang's account affords a different conceptualization of cosmopolitanism and focuses its analysis on code choice, and attitudes towards code choice, in situated use. Another perspective is afforded by a critical analysis of the discourse of individuals who self-identify as 'transnational' and who actively engage in the promotion of transnational activities. In this regard, there has been much research on the discursive construction of European identities and how these are (re)negotiated and reshaped at local and global levels by institutions and citizens at grass-roots level (Krzyzanowski, 2010; Wodak 2004, 2010; Wodak & Weiss 2005; Zappettini 2015). This perspective is explored in a study of a transnational NGO ('Democratic Change for Europe – DC4E') operating in eight countries whose mission it is to promote civic participation in Europe and new forms of democracy. McEntee-Atalianis and Zappettini (2014) found that members challenged existing representations of Europeanness which were embedded in or drew on reference to 'essential national' referents, instead defining themselves through an interpretative metaphor of networked identities. They argue that 'through this schema members are able to construct and reimagine their belonging along axes that often bypass national identification' (p. 397), supporting a fragmented and deterritorialized perspective of identity evident in 'superdiverse' societies (Vertovec 2007). A spatial dimension is invoked in subject accounts which destabilize a core periphery or bounded perspective revealing author agency and creativity in the imagining of a dynamic and complex process of 'being' within transnational space. Their analysis focused on the metaphorical representation and negotiation of European identity as well as discourses of transnationalism. An example text is provided below, an extract taken from a focus group in which a female Romanian national discusses what the term 'transnational' means to her:

> CA2: ah that ... this thing that I am Romanian. OK so we were doing this exercise yesterday picking a book title for our books in the human library ... and and we were supposed to talk about our identity and I was saying okay I am Romanian but I don't like to think of myself as only Romanian and to limit myself and to put myself in a box, within the boundaries of Romania within the boundaries of Bucharest and I like to consider myself as a world citizen actually not necessarily a European citizen so I guess this is transnationalism [. . .] we don't have to we shouldn't at least from my point of view stick to only one box the Bucharest box or the Romanian box and then we should like distance ourselves and see the world from a more general perspective from the birds eye view perspective'. (p. 407)

Alluding to the CONTAINER metaphor, CA rejects a bounded categorization along social or geopolitical lines seeing herself rather as a citizen of the world. She deconstructs a politics of identity which imposes limits (local/national/European), instead favouring a spatial perspective which is unbounded and distanced from categorization.

The authors found that in deconstructing the boundaried nature of nations and in identifying with Europe and the concept of transnationalism, subjects reconstructed a sense of place identity by invoking the metaphors of JOURNEY and NETWORK to convey their relations and associations, thereby making 'place' a social practice and relational process rather than a bounded state or locality. They conclude that:

> the identification patterns emerging from the discourses of our informants do not reflect clear-cut representations of the interplay between Europeanness and other identities ... nor do members seem to value a hierarchy of pre-ordained core/inner or peripheral/outer order of belonging. Instead ... the processes of identification are realized along polycentric arrangements whereby connections run along multiple lines/

directions linking different nodes and taking multiple shapes ... it is really
the absence of layers or containers that allows multiple identifications to
become salient for European identities described. (p. 409)

Their findings corroborate those of others who have stressed the 'liquid'
and fragmented nature of identities in modern societies (Bauman 2000;
Hall 2012).

Conclusion

This chapter has considered the relationship between place, identity and
language in predominantly sociolinguistic and discourse studies. We have
seen how spaces and places (as identity and language) are not predefined,
stable or uncontested entities but are formed through social practice and
ideology – influenced by changing and unique political, social, cultural
and economic factors. Sociolinguists and discourse analysts have been
able to identify how patterns of linguistic variation and discursive practice
serve to index fluid and emergent identity/ies in relation to personal and
intersubjective circumstances and goals in different scales of space/place –
identifying too how place is constructed through linguistic and other
semiotic means derived from places beyond the local. Place is a facet of
identity that is built via social processes and practice. Current work is
trying to understand how and why place identity is realized and brought
about, sometimes through novel and creative practices and resources, and
the ways in which language users make sense of their engagements as they
determine their place in the world; some of this work points to the salience
of mobility and multiplicity in (inter) subjective realization and contact in
contemporary social life.

CHAPTER TWELVE

Conclusion

Introduction

Throughout this book, we have explored the topic of 'identity' in applied linguistics research from different perspectives and disciplinary bases. The themes chosen for discussion and inclusion are those that remain central to the concerns of the field. As we have seen, the separation of topics into chapters is a heuristic convenience for many concepts, themes, theories, approaches and in some instances, studies overlap; moreover, identities (or identity categories) intersect (see further discussion below). In terms of the choice of material and the studies chosen for discussion and illustration, the aim has been to include seminal work in the field alongside research which may be less well known but which is nonetheless influential and compelling. The intention in writing the book is for the reader to be able to select topics of interest to them and therefore for chapters to 'stand alone' and act as a prompt for further reading. Although it is hoped that researchers working in particular subfields may benefit from reading about research in other areas.

In Chapter One, we reflected on the making of the (post)modern self and the influence of previous philosophies and epistemologies on current research, highlighting continuities and discontinuities in theoretical positions over many centuries and recent decades. We saw how early accounts of a self-determining, unified and consistent subject, guided by universal principles and unencumbered by social influences, contrasted with a postmodern, post-structuralist understanding of identity as socially and discursively constituted – a dynamic outcome of historical, sociocultural and political contexts of lived experience, tied to and emergent within interaction and social practice, and subject to processes of differentiation. The contemporary portrait is thus one of a self-reflexive, performative, albeit (structurally) delimited and engaged subject. Importantly, the contemporary subject is both challenged by and challenging of essentialism. In Western society and applied linguistics studies, the subject is accordingly often referred to as contradictory, complex, fluid, multiple, partial, striving for coherence and meaning and subject to the influences of late-Capitalist society, which not only is constraining but also delivers opportunities for agency and creativity. Throughout most chapters, we saw the influence and dominance of the linguistic and discursive turn towards the study of the social construction of identity in accounts of crises of identity, uncertainty and instability (e.g. as discussed in Chapter Three), and reports of productivity, creativity and liberation even within momentary encounters and in temporary attachments and formations (e.g. as shown in Chapters Two, Five, Seven, Nine and Eleven). However, we also saw the tension between macro- and micro-level discursive theorizations and analyses of identity and reviewed work which did not adopt a discursive approach or methodology. In the following, we reflect on this as we briefly review chapter content and draw out some of the recurrent issues and themes. This overview is followed by further critical reflection and ideas for future research.

Chapter overview

In Chapter Two, we discussed idiosyncratic language production and perception. We explored the concepts of *voice* and *lingual biography* and noted how speaker *style* may not just indirectly index group identities but individual identities too. Drawing on the work of Johnstone and others, we discussed how linguistic expression is socio-cognitively motivated and a matter of strategic choice and individual experience. Subjects may display idiosyncratic styles and vary from one another in their perception of others' identity/ies due to differences in sociolinguistic experience leading to different understandings of linguistic indices. A focus on the individual has enabled applied linguists to investigate the breadth and fluidity of linguistic resources, performances and perceptions within and across individuals and groups. We further noted how linguists are increasingly aware that they must take care to adopt reflexive practices and not 'impose' or 'read off' identities without attending to a number of considerations including the sociocultural and historical context, the views of speakers and listeners themselves as well as critically reflecting on their own personal and sociocultural frames of reference and how these impact on their interpretation of the data.

In Chapter Three, we discussed how a sense of self may be destabilized after the onset of a clinical condition affecting language, such as aphasia or foreign accent syndrome. We noted, for example, how aphasia can magnify the incongruity and dissonance between an individuals' understanding of a past and present self, and also how this may contrast with others' perspectives as subjects come to an understanding of their post-trauma selves through interaction with others. The chapter also explored the important role of *narratives* in maintaining a sense of chronological and temporal continuity and how life stories can be disrupted due to the onset of clinical conditions affecting cognitive processing and language performance. A theme resonating throughout the discussion of clinical cases was the desire by many subjects to maintain and/or renegotiate a consistent, continuous, integrated, albeit multidimensional sense of self. Rehabilitation for many involves not only working on regaining linguistic competence of affected language systems but also re-forming and renegotiating an altered sense of self through language/discourse.

The discussion of forensic linguistic cases in Chapter Four focused on how the subject of identity impacts on the structure, form and process of legal practice and legal language. We explored the approaches, methods and analytic frameworks applied to the identification of speakers and writers by forensic linguists. We noted the importance of studying organic, idiolectal and habitual speaker characteristics for the purposes of profiling, noting in particular the scientific examination of individual anatomy, physiology, social and stylistic characteristics. The chapter also explored the identities *brought about* in the courtroom and throughout the legal process, revealing how judges and lawyers shape and reflect their identities in professional practice, while also constructing the identities of victims, witnesses and defendants for their own aims, by drawing on circulating discourses, interpretative frameworks and multimodal means of communication

We returned to a discussion of *style* in Chapter Five, focusing on the local stylistic practices and social meanings attached to specific linguistic codes/ features by youths in different geographic settings, noting how these inform our understanding of linguistic *creativity* and *agency* in (re)producing and subverting broader social and political ideologies. Stylistic acts enable youths to enact group solidarity and (dis)affiliation and construct personal and social identities. We explored how youths appropriate linguistic variables from within and outside of their communities in order to position and locate themselves within local and global spheres of reference and influence. We saw that linguistic features do not necessarily correlate to pre-specified social categories or locations but can represent a construction of and (dis)alignment from, or to, the traits/qualities/values of others who are positioned in ideological space. The studies reviewed highlight the importance of researching *local* contexts and activities, understanding the play between *agency* and the constraints of *structure* and the importance of exploring members' interpretations of identities and social relationships.

The *contingent* nature of identity construction was further explored in Chapter Six – Workplace and Professional Identities. This chapter considered how identity performance and construction is influenced by political and sociocultural factors and embedded in social practices. We noted how studies have explored the agentive potential of workers while recognizing that subjects are (sometimes unequally) subject to cultural, professional and structural constraints. Recent work has attempted to understand the complexity of identity/ies within contemporary workplaces, revealing them as co-dependent, situated, dynamic, multiple and discursively constituted. Performing professional and worker identity demands learning and using sophisticated and nuanced linguistic, cultural and professional knowledge.

Chapter Seven investigated how identity is discursively and dialogically performed within or for a community of online users of social media (SM). We explored the opportunities and limitations of new technologies, the types and varieties of identities constructed within/via SM (communities) and the potential for the enactment of '(in)*authentic*' identity presentation online. Research findings point to many similarities between offline and online identity construction; for example, issues of *intersectionality*, *hybridity* and *idiosyncrasy* become salient to interpretations of linguistic and sociocultural practice. Moreover, the descriptive and interpretative stability of social categories (e.g. sex, gender) were challenged. As in offline interactions, identities are found to be contingent, multiple and fluid as well as context-dependent and context-creating, motivated and manipulated by the self and the other, including networks of interaction.

Social-psychological and sociolinguistic studies of ethnic and religious identities were reviewed in Chapter Eight. The chapter critiqued the application of Social Identity Theory in the study of the language maintenance of minority groups and discussed the explanatory validity of two sociolinguistic concepts: *ethnolect* and *ethnolinguistic repertoire* in accounts of identity work. We reviewed a range of discourse-related studies in order to discuss how and why ethnic identifications and stances towards them are significant from theoretical and practical perspectives, and as a consequence, some of the themes and issues apparent in other chapters arose. For example, we noted the socio-structural and interactional constraints on self, we discussed how ethnic self-definition and identification involves collaborative negotiation of personal and social category-bound attributes and characteristics and saw how the inability to perform an *authentic* ethnic identity can have negative effects. We also explored the impact of migration and globalization on intergroup relations and (ethnic) identity. The chapter considered ethnicity as both a self-concept and as a process of individual/group performance and experience, and highlighted the importance of studying local conditions (including beliefs/ideologies/ practices) in the investigation of how social meaning is understood and conveyed interactionally, and how language is used to maintain relationships and enact identity/identifications.

A post-structuralist reading of identity was writ large in the discussion of gender and sexual identity in Chapter Nine, particularly in light of the influential work of Judith Butler. The chapter traced significant paradigm shifts in the fields of gender and sexuality research, focusing on a consideration of recent studies about how language both communicates and constructs gender and sexual identities. Three issues impacting on research in gender and sexuality studies were explored: *heteronormativity*, *hegemonic masculinity* and *performativity*. We noted how both fields recognize the importance of studying the influence of power and regulatory structures on subject positioning, and the impact of agency on ideology, linguistic practice and identity construction. Gender and sexual identity were shown as complex, multiple and dynamic. They are constructed in contextually and culturally relevant communities and within local sites of interaction, and therefore arise within intersubjective encounters and are influenced by, and subject to, broader ideologies. Gender and sexual identity were seen to intersect with other identity categories and influences (e.g. ethnicity and social networks). Despite highlighting the recent dominance of the post-structuralist approach, the chapter also discussed the importance of maintaining the temporary use of essentialism (*strategic essentialism*) in order to uncover discrimination against subaltern groups for the protection of individual and group rights.

A Deaf, visual-gestural world view was discussed in Chapter Ten. This chapter reviewed the linguistic and sociocultural manifestations of the Deaf community and Deaf identity – the impact of technology on Deaf people and the multiplicity and fluidity of Deaf identity. We noted how Deaf identity is related to educational, historical, political, sociocultural (including policy) constructions and therefore has changed over time and differs across countries, contexts and individuals. Signed stories have proven crucial to the transmission of Deaf culture and tradition and ICT has afforded Deaf people with burgeoning opportunities for the development of a Deaf space for interaction and performance. We noted how the concept of *Deafhood* has offered an important and rich ontological framework within Deaf studies, and argued for the theoretical and practical application/consideration of a uniquely *visual epistemological perspective* and subaltern experience in identity research.

Finally, Chapter Eleven focused on the relationship between place, identity and language drawing on sociolinguistic and discourse studies. The chapter began by reviewing research on supralocal contexts and ended with the consideration of supranational settings – engaging with analyses at different linguistic levels. The chapter began with an examination of the indexical association between linguistic variables and local identity, for example the use of /r/ in the construction of an 'authentic' place identity for white inhabitants of the Lower East Side of Manhattan, before considering the influence of mobility on dialect levelling and feature reallocation in local contexts. Drawing on contemporary interest in language and borders, the chapter than focused on how language variation is connected to identity in borderland areas and how identity/identification(s) can be influenced and changed by personal, political and social circumstances. The chapter concluded with a discussion of research focusing on national and supranational identity. It became clear that spaces and places, as identity/ ies, are not predefined, stable or indeed uncontested entities but constructed via social practice and ideology. We saw the fluid and emergent nature of 'place' identity and witnessed how place is a facet of identity built via social processes and practice.

Recurring themes and conclusions

A number of recurring themes emerged across chapters from which we can draw some general conclusions. These are distilled in the listing below:

   i.   The fundamental and unquestionable role of language in identity work;

   ii.   continuing debates regarding the dualisms between *agency versus structure* and *essentialism versus social construction*. To what extent and how are subjects constrained by psychological and social structures and what are the limits of their agency? Is there stability even within the socially constructed production of identity?

   iii.   the importance and challenges of appealing to *intersecting biological and social categories, variables* and *attributes* in identity work by individuals, groups and researchers;

   iv.   an appreciation of *idiosyncratic* characteristics and properties of language production and reception. And, connected to the latter, the particularities of personal experience, motivation, history, style and sociocultural connections and influences on identity construction, performance and perception;

   v.   a desire and effort by subjects to maintain and negotiate a *consistent, integrated, 'preferred'/authentic/legitimate sense and presentation of self*, and difficulties experienced when challenges are encountered;

   vi.   the *agentive* and *relational* nature of identity construction, which is at the same time processual, situated, provisional, partial, complex, dynamic and multiple;

   vii.   the importance of understanding the impact of *micro, meso and macro contexts* on individuals and groups – from locally situated practices and sites of interaction, to broader social and political structures and ideologies and systems of power. While also acknowledging differences in researcher perspectives and theoretical/analytical stances with respect to the 'context(s)' of analysis and their use as interpretive resources, (e.g. cf. conversational analysts versus critical discourse analysts; see Chapter One);

   viii.   the value of investigating identity at different and simultaneous *levels of positionality* – from macro-level demographic categories, to local ethnographically defined categories/cultural positions, to interactional and temporary stances and roles;

ix. the importance of investigating identity at different and multiple *linguistic levels of analysis* – from phonetics/phonology to language varieties and everything in between (e.g. identity labels and categorizations, pronouns, mood and modality; pragmatic implicature and presuppositions; figurative language) and appreciating the indirect relationship between linguistic features and identity construction;

x. the role of *narratives* in identity construction and maintenance – in facilitating and supporting chronological and temporal continuity for the individual and group. As well as acting as a pedagogic tool in instructing and socializing neophytes;

xi. the value of adopting diverse *theoretical and methodological approaches* (drawn from linguistics and other disciplines) in the investigation of issues relating to identity. While also appreciating differences and tensions in the way in which 'identity' is theorized and operationalized by researchers.

Unresolved issues

Picking up on the second of the issues (point ii above), two general formulations of identity arose in the accounts reviewed. The first is an *essentialist (social-psychological)* model in which identity is conceived as a stable pre-discursive perceptual object which determines actions by the language user and/or is a predefined category invoked by the researcher. The second is a *social constructionist* model which conceives of identity as a discursive accomplishment embedded in social practices, negotiated and dynamically brought into being through text and talk/sign. We have seen that a social constructionist perspective generally dominates in recent research such that the subject is conceived of as constituted by multiple, contextually dependent and socially constructed personal and social identities. As a consequence, no one identity is considered *a priori* or more important to self-definition than another, since subjects are considered to enact different, sometimes contradictory and multiple selves in response to the social conditions in which they find themselves. The formation of subjectivity is seen as, at least partly, a function of language-mediated processes produced within complex social dynamics. The self is therefore always in process, always an ongoing project, in a state of becoming, and subject to various identification processes including contextual influences (historical, political, sociocultural), processual states (ongoing state of formation and negotiation) and relationality, including comparisons between 'self' and 'other' (Rummins 2003).

Two of the many remaining challenges are, however, how to account for multiplicity and complexity within subjectivity and also how to account for the enduring representations and dynamic psycholinguistic and cognitive operations that prevail within moments of 'becoming'.

In relation to the first problem, if the subject does not have a single stable identity, what is the nature of the relationship between the different identities perceived and performed? How do these cohere, if at all, and what role does language and discourse play in this regard? Sociolinguists and discourse analysts have begun to offer some answers to these questions when looking at identity 'production' and construction. We have seen in the work reviewed great promise in the theorization and application of such concepts as indexicality (Ochs 1992; Silverstein 2003), intersectionality (Levon & Mendes 2016), performativity (Butler 1990), stance (Jaffe 2009) and style (Campbell-Kibler et al. 2006; Eckert 1989, 2000) which have helped to support accounts of the fluidity of subject and group identities, while identifying more stable culturally coded renderings/ readings of identity(/ies) through the study of, for example, stance accretion (Rauniomaa 2003) or the positioning of subjects in between or in reference to (essentialized) identities in momentary encounters (e.g. see accounts of intersectionality in Chapter Nine). Identity (work) arises, or is motivated by complex, intersecting and sometimes contradictory networks of social experiences, practices and relations, not least those discussed in the chapters above, for example, age, class, community (of practice), culture, ethnicity, gender, genre, nationality, medium and context of interaction, place/space, race, sexuality, social networks, stance and style. However, we still need to account for the complexities of these identity categories, practices and subject experiences, and the hierarchies and allegiances of identification which operate at moments of production and comprehension. We also need to account for how categories intersect/conflict with one another in different situations. How do subjects conceptualize, negotiate, separate, move between and/or syncretize multiple subjectivities or identifications? Do categories, for example, function as 'vectors of influence' whereby one category (e.g. gender) influences another (e.g. class) 'in a discrete way', or are categories 'inextricable and interdependent … such that [they] represent an indivisible unit' (Levon 2011: 70)?

A second and related problem is that arguably the turn to a discursive and social constructionist study of identity has placed ever greater emphasis on the 'social' and discourse as a site of identity research, moving the focus away from a consideration of more enduring but also dynamic psycholinguistic and cognitive structures and operations which come into play as individuals enact and perceive identities. We have seen that there is value in attempting to develop or appeal to models which can combine both cognitive and sociocultural and contextual phenomena (e.g. Tracy 2002, see Chapter One, and the work of discursive psychologists, see Chapter Eight). These are able to account for aspects of stability and fluidity. However, such models do not provide detailed psycholinguistic accounts of, for example, the formation and operation of categorization or stereotyping processes as evidenced in discursive accounts, nor do they account for the social conditions and psychological mechanisms which operate as individuals undertake identity work in moments of interaction.

Assuming that linguistic indices of identity/identification and social types/personae (e.g. particular pronunciations, lexical, grammatical features, category labels/terms of reference, metaphorical schemata, stance acts, styles of speaking, etc.) are psychologically as well as socially represented and processed, we need to understand the form that they take, how representations evolve and change as well as how they operate as a resource on a momentary and long-term basis in the passive and active construction of identities. Are there, for example, enduring representations (/mental schemata) of social types/categories and membership/behaviours/discourse scenarios with associated linguistic characteristics emerging from the observation and performance of repeated acts/stylizations? As noted by Johnstone and Kiesling (2008: 29; see Chapter Two) for indexical meaning to be cognitively recognized, there must be 'a correlation available in an individual's environment to which second-order indexical meaning can be attached'. We have also seen how individuals can 'revoice' the productions of others (Mendoza-Denton 1997, 2008; see Chapter Five) for rhetorical effect suggesting enduring cognitive representations linking linguistic behaviour with personae.

Clinical studies of individuals who report having 'lost' a sense of a self once known and recognize the effect of their altered linguistic status (see Chapter Three) demonstrate the importance of exploring the psycholinguistic and cognitive (including memory) operations at play in our identity construction and maintenance. Further, the momentary and longer-term stylistic creativity and fluidity of individuals and language groups across different spaces and times (for example, studies showing how individuals draw on selective linguistic elements from a repertoire of features in their practices of bricolage or crossing, as seen in accounts of youth and ethnic repertoires in Chapters Five and Eight) appeals to a psycholinguistic explanation which can account for the fluid and innovative nature of language processing and performance in real time across different contexts as well as over the life course (e.g. see Benor's 2010 study of intra-speaker variation across the life course in Chapter Eight). It prompts such questions as: how are linguistic/discursive features which constitute repertoires or styles and stances stored, processed and activated or suppressed? How are they recognized and identified by self and others as marking particular personae? Are there, for example, contextual and category-bound attributes and features from which inferences are drawn? How do they intersect with other psychological mechanisms operating at moments of interaction, for example, comparison of self with others, evaluation of context (including interactants) and motivation to enact contextually relevant persona? Further, what is the extent of individual variability in production and comprehension? Studies reporting on linguistic idiosyncrasy have suggested that indexical associations in production and perception may be momentary, fluid and highly individual. We noted in Chapter Two that 'different indexical links between linguistic form and social meaning may become relevant at different moments in interaction or across different discourse genres, and that different people may draw on different, even sometimes idiosyncratic, senses of what choices among variable forms mean, or about whether they mean anything at all' (Johnstone & Kiesling 2008: 12). However, how are these 'senses' cognitively or psychologically represented or operationalized? What impact does social interaction have on their (evolving) representation?

Recently, research on the sociolinguistic perception of social groups/types based on studies of language variation (Campbell-Kibler 2012; Drager 2010; Levon 2007; Squires 2013) has identified the influence of social indices on language comprehension and speaker identification. This work suggests that individuals store and process a perceptual field of indexical relations (Eckert 2008a; see Chapter Five) such that a given meaning is interpreted in a certain way within a particular context of use. It is clear that social, personal and linguistic information does influence linguistic perception and can affect how a speaker is evaluated and perceived; however, the complex nature of the socio-cognitive operations are still to be determined.[1] Answers to the questions posed above need to be investigated jointly by psycholinguists and sociolinguists in order to provide an opportunity to explore the limits and constraints of psychological and social structures and processes, as further discussed below.

Moving towards a dynamic integrated systems approach

As noted above, a focus on the social and discursive construction of identity has arguably underplayed the corresponding role of psychological structures and operations. Indeed, the nature of this dynamic and complex online processual and co-dependent psychosocial (inside-out and outside-in) relationship, as depicted in Figure 12.1, remains undertheorized and underinvestigated but may prove productive in moving the debate about stability within instability and agency versus structure forward, as well as impacting on 'real-world' issues, for example, the remediation of clinical linguistic cases. Recent sociolinguistic work on language perception (as detailed above) has provided an avenue to combine the study of contextualized language use with cognitive considerations. At the very least, we have seen that identities (in all their configurations) are realized/constructed within and via language and influenced by context and relationality. The intersection of social variables, and social action, helps to structure practice and construct matrices within which systems of identification (both enduring and provisional) emerge. However, fluid and provisional enactments of identity in social

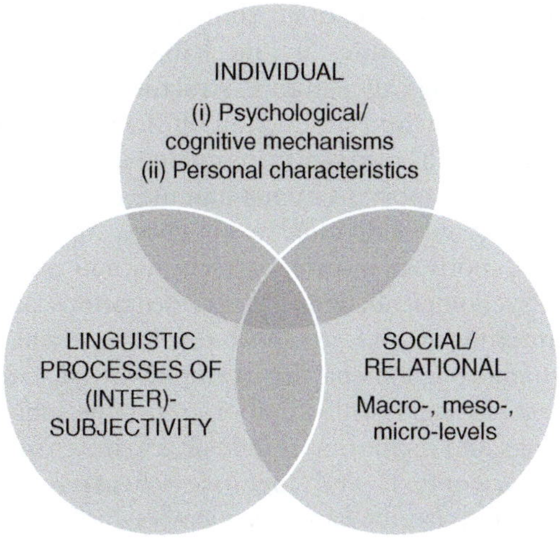

FIGURE 12.1 *Dynamic Integrated Systems Model.*

practice emerge from and undoubtedly impact on dynamic cognitive and psychological representations and operations. Ideally, we need to combine these two perspectives by constructing models which acknowledge the role played by both systems and which can account for their integration and co-dependence. Investigating the nature of this dynamic psychosocial interface may explain how and why speakers adapt their perceptions and productions in response to different contexts of use over time and space (e.g. see Podesva's (2007) study of Heath in Chapters Two and Nine), as well as explain the conditions and operations (psychological and social), which lead to innovation and/or constraints on the perception and performance of individual and group identity/identification. For example, the construction, realization and limits of prototypical and stereotypical representations, as well as socio-pragmatic influences and inferences impacting on real-time processing of linguistic material in contexts in which identity marking becomes salient.

The 'Dynamic Integrated Systems Model'[2] depicted in Figure 12.1 portrays this socio-cognitive interface – the dynamic relationship between psychological, social/relational/interactional and linguistic processes. The three integrated spheres depict the individual (intrapersonal) and social (interpersonal) structures and processes underlying and informing identity work and their mediation via language, as discussed in many studies throughout this book and encapsulated in the general themes emerging from applied linguistics research, as summarized in the section 'Recurring themes and conclusions' (i–ix). These processes are conceived as interacting synchronically in real time, and diachronically, over extended periods of time (including the individual's lifetime) to produce mutable and continuous representations and performances.

Housed within the circle entitled 'Individual' are representations of psychological/cognitive structures and mechanisms, in addition to personal characteristics. Psychological/cognitive structures and mechanisms are involved in the perception and production of identity/ies, and include such mechanisms and features as memory (for as noted in Chapter Three, episodic memory is particularly important in maintaining a sense of continuity/'self' and also in marking out individual experience), affect, attitudes/beliefs/dispositions/values, motivation, category schema and online processing of linguistic data. Psychological/cognitive representations and processes are understood as interlinked and responsible for perceiving and producing enduring and dynamic phenomena. For example, when listening to a speaker, or reading about a particular individual or group, the subject may draw on past understandings and memories of indexical features including linguistic patterns (or styles), contexts and cognitive schemata of social types, in order to recognize and ascribe category membership/identity features (e.g. see Johnstone & Kiesling's (2008) discussion of idiosyncratic perceptions of a Polish radio show host in Chapter Two). It is possible that speakers' sociolinguistic experience impacts on the storage and categorization of individuals/groups which are mediated psycholinguistically via a process of generalization after repeated experience and exposure to the behaviour of social types, including repetitions and recognition of similarities in the performance of varieties/repertoires and styles of speaking. Such experiences may contribute to the construction and ongoing development of cognitive schemata. Moreover, in order to function within diverse environments and to adapt to momentary exigencies, the individual may assess the context, interactional goals, audience, ongoing discussion, etc. and modify their linguistic behaviour accordingly, drawing on a repertoire of linguistic features (e.g. as in the case of Heath, Podesva 2007). The latter presupposes agency in choosing (and suppressing) a combination of variables from a repertoire of available features based on knowledge about language use in social contexts. Further, in constructing personal narratives, the individual draws on past memories and current experiences to develop and negotiate a coherent, continuous and nuanced (depending on audience, goals, etc.) representation of self through the selection (and suppression) of particular material.

The term 'personal characteristics' refers to idiosyncratic features (which can be identified by self and others) including unique anatomical and physiological characteristics, in addition to other identifying characteristics (e.g. accent, style) (see accounts in Chapters Two, Three, Four and Five). It also accounts for the particularities of personal experience, history and sociocultural connections and influences (see the 'Recurring themes and conclusions' section, point iv, above) which impact on language use and perceptions of linguistic variables when produced by others in speaking, signing and writing. We have established that linguistic variables are not interpreted in the same way by all listeners.

The second sphere represents social and relational/interactional influences on individual perception and performance. These extend to macro sociopolitical and sociocultural influences/discourses, ideologies and categories/social types (e.g. class, gender), meso-personae or local cultural positions (e.g. Townie, see Chapter Five) and fluid micro social practices, that is, temporary interactionally specific practices, including role- or style-shifting and stance-taking in conversation. Changes in context, including changes to locality, interlocutors, topic, interactional goals, etc. may impact on individual or group attempts to emphasize adequation or difference, (de)authentication and/or (il)legitimization (e.g. see Bucholtz and Hall's 2005, 'tactics of subjectivity' as described in Chapter One).

Finally, the third circle represents the mediating linguistic and discursive features and resources of identity relations and marking, including linguistic and stylistic features associated with individuals or groups/community practices, for example, pronunciations, category labels and categorizations, transitivity, mood and modality, pronouns, pragmatic presuppositions and implicature in relation to subjective and intersubjective positioning, figurative language, stance-marking, code-choice, etc.

Consideration of the psychosocial interface and its mediation via language, as I suggest here, opens the door to new empirical concerns and questions with regard to the affordances and constraints of psychological and social structures, operations and representations, and the manner in which both systems dynamically interact. For example, how are processes of evaluation, comparison and identification motivated socially and supported (psycho)linguistically? How are identity categories/indices psychologically represented, activated and operationalized in real-time (social) encounters? How do they alter with experience and across contexts?

Mu (2015) has argued that one way to reconcile the differences between social-psychological and post-structuralist accounts, and by extension in dealing with the agency versus structure dualism, is to appeal to Bourdieu's concept of 'habitus' which attempts to account for the historically grounded, socially influenced/constituted attitudes, beliefs and behaviours which make up our various social identities and which predispose us to think and act in relation to self and others, in particular ways. Mu (2015: 250) argues, '[a]s a set of embodied dispositions, habitus is "durable and transposable", rooted in the "structured structures" of cultural history; at the same time, it is not immutable but adaptable, internalising the "structuring structures" of the social world (Bourdieu 1977: 72) ... the notion of habitus [he claims] has the potential to dissolve a plethora of oppositions between social psychological and poststructural schools'. Similarly, Giddens' theory of 'structuration' (see Chapter One) also appeals to a consideration of the processes involved in the mediation between individuals and society. However, while such theories take us so far, accounting, for example, for habitual patterns of use which influence perception, they are rooted in sociological thinking and cannot offer a balanced or detailed account of the dynamic psychosocial interface or the psycholinguistic processes involved in the perception, processing and production of identity discourses, categories, features or linguistic indices (e.g. markers of in- and out-group identification). Nor can they account for the acquisition, alternation, activation or suppression of particular (un) marked linguistic features or discourses within and across different contexts of interaction, depending on such factors as interactional goals, roles and responsibilities, setting, psycholinguistic constraints, etc. More work has yet to be done to explore this complex and dynamic relationship as well as the unique constraints imposed by psychological and social structures and parameters.

Concluding remarks

There have been scholars (Brubaker & Cooper 2000) who have questioned the merit of investigating identity or its use as an analytic category. However, as has been argued throughout this book, the pervasiveness and power of notions of identity mean that it is relevant to our understanding of many areas of social and psychological life. As Taylor (2006: 398) observes, the 'limits' of 'human moral action … are obvious enough. They include our restricted sympathies, our understandable self-preoccupation, and the common human tendency to define one's identity in opposition to some adversary or our group'. Reason enough for the subject of 'identity' to persist as a topic of relevance and importance, not just to philosophers, but also to applied linguists dealing with 'real-world' problems, as illustrated in our accounts of clinical and forensic cases, or studies of minority group language maintenance. Identity continues to be a salient topic of our time, perhaps one of the most salient at the time of writing when world politics is in such a state of flux, forcing ever greater pressure on groups and individuals to (re)define and question who they are and how they behave in response to their ever-changing circumstances. We only have to look at this book's extensive bibliography, which represents just a portion of available studies in applied linguistics, to see that issues of identity are not going away. Identity will continue to fascinate, trouble and occupy the research agenda of applied linguists for many years to come.

However, there is room to caution against an *a priori* reflex to automatically assume the central relevance of identity in the analysis of linguistic data. The danger in such an assumption is summed up by Jenkins (2008: 15): 'if we use "identity" to talk about everything, we are likely to end up talking about very little of any significance'. While the research reviewed has provided strong evidence of links between language and identity, it is clear that language (and discourse) does not always function to signal or define identity. As argued by Alcoff, there is value in assuming 'that identities might be relevant in any context, but … the question of their relevance needs to be asked and evaluated in each context rather than theoretically and methodologically foreclosed' (2010: 158). There is also room to argue, as Alcoff (2010), that it is time to reconsider the tenets of the post-structuralist and postmodern perspectives in considering the nature of identity/ies and their operation and realization. For example, in arguing for the merits of strategic essentialism (see for example, Chapter Nine and discussion above), how does one reconcile essentialism with the socially constructed nature of identities? And how does one reconcile the questions of the researcher with the aims of the political activist? (See, for example, Chapter Ten.) Moreover, the focus of many recent studies has rested on *how* constructions of identity are achieved and their rhetorical function. But have we now become so preoccupied with the 'how' that we are saturated in studies of the 'discursive construction of X' that favour descriptive and anti-theoretical tendencies instead of striving to develop new theoretical trajectories and research questions as suggested above?

Future work in applied linguistics will continue to benefit from recognizing the fluidity and complexity of identity and the need for constant revision of perspectives and approaches. Some of the existing concepts and frameworks are likely to remain useful (e.g. intersectionality, stance, style), but there are others which merit further application, such as the affordances of translanguaging and multimodality for identity work and investigation. Equally, there is a need to be open to a range of data sets, for example, comparisons of large corpora of data with small-scale, contextualized studies of language in use, and to recognize the importance of extending our purview to communities, settings and individuals beyond the predominantly Western and those who move in and out of different political/spatial/social/ cultural networks, contexts and communities.

Finally, as noted previously, applied linguists working on issues of identity must recognize the value and importance of developing ever greater conscious reflexivity, particularly with respect to the assumptions and training that are brought to bear on research design and analysis, as well as their role and 'identities' in data design and gathering. Impartiality is impossible; nevertheless, declaring and appreciating one's own subjectivity (and ideologies) is necessary for interpretations of data. It is also important to reflect on how analysts' research agenda 'fits' with/supports the understanding of, and works towards the alleviation of 'real-world' issues/ problems – further considering the role of research subjects and researchers' responsibility towards them, including investigating topics of importance to them and considering how researchers translate, what are often, very complicated accounts/results in a form that is appealing and understandable to those most affected by, and those effective in, dealing with the issues under scrutiny. In so doing, applied linguists will continue to have a very rich seam to mine and contribute to making real-world improvements in areas demanding their expertise.

NOTES

CHAPTER ONE

1 This review is partial and focuses on Western conceptualizations of identity; however, see Riley (2008: 78ff) for an account of anthropological and ethnographic studies which demonstrate differences in Western and non-Western conceptualizations of the 'self'; also see Harré's (2000) historical discussion of identity in Indian philosophy.

2 The concept of 'identity' is referred to variously, and sometimes interchangeably, using different terms, for example, 'self', 'self-hood', 'subject', 'agent', 'persona', etc. Some terms arise from and can be associated with particular theories or traditions (Benwell & Stokoe 2006). The etymology of 'identity' is from late Latin *identitās*, from *idem* meaning 'the same'. It is thought to have been introduced in the mid-sixteenth century.

3 See Evans (2015: 15–35) for an account of structuralism's support of a Cartesian perspective, in particular Chomsky's (1975) view of Universal Grammar, in which grammatical structures are argued to be part of an innate mental structure within a rational mind.

4 According to Giddens' theory of 'structuration', subject agency is 'something that has to be routinely created and sustained in the reflexive activities of the individual' (1991: 52). He asserts that as individuals we shape and are shaped by social structures; this occurs within locally occasioned social action. See other accounts of social influences on identity construction later in the chapter.

5 Kee (2011) also credits Feuerbach as their influential predecessor.

6 In studies of language and discourse, there are different versions of 'positioning theory'; however, 'positioning' refers to the way in which individuals take on, resist, negotiate or proffer subject positions in talk. See McEntee-Atalianis and Litosseliti (2017) for a description of positioning theory and analysis and its application to narrative analysis, particularly in light of the work of Bamberg (1997, 2011a, b). Positioning analysis provides a performative, relational and action-oriented approach to identities. It focuses on the *process* of positioning through the situated enactment of identity in talk-in-interaction via discursive resources which construct and negotiate temporary and more stable versions of social reality and self.

7 Saussure is credited with being the father of linguistics.

8 Jenkins defines identification as a 'basic cognitive mechanism that humans use to sort out themselves and their fellows, individually and collectively … it is

how we know who's who and what's what … On the other hand [he asserts] identification doesn't determine behaviour, and patterns of identification don't allow us to predict who will do what. This is for a number of reasons: people work with various "maps" or hierarchies of identification, these hierarchies of identification are never clear cut, unambiguous or in consistent agreement with each other, and the relationship between interests and identification is too complex for individual behaviour to be predictable in these terms' (p. 13). Also see Hall's (2012: 16–17) definition of identification.

9　Although Hegel has been credited with the notion that identity is an intersubjective phenomenon and historically and culturally embedded, he also argued that complete self-knowledge is impossible to achieve.

10　Derrida's use of the term 'différance' invokes associations with two French verbs meaning 'differ' and 'defer'. Hall (1990: 229) argues that this term 'challenges fixed binaries which stablise (sic) meaning and representation and show how meaning is never finished or completed … Without relations of difference, no representation could occur. But what is then constituted within representation is always open to being deferred, staggered, serialised'.

11　See du Gay et al. (2012) for readings which challenge the approach to identity as being a subject of discourse/language; also see accounts which argue against a merging of psychoanalytic and genealogical approaches.

12　Benwell and Stokoe (2006: 56, 160) acknowledge that across the social sciences gender identity is conceived as a 'performance'; however, they argue that there is a 'tautology' in operation since the analyst often begins 'knowing the relevant identity of the speakers' – starting with data derived from women and men in order to investigate how gender is constructed – rather than uncovering the identity orientations of the subjects.

13　See Benwell and Stokoe (2006: 34ff) for a more detailed overview of micro and macro approaches to the discursive analysis of identity including: micro – ethnomethodology, conversational analysis, membership categorization analysis and discursive psychology; macro – narrative analysis, positioning theory and critical discourse analysis. Also see accounts below and throughout this book.

14　The concept of 'interpretative repertoires' is defined by Edley (2001: 198) as 'relatively coherent ways of talking about objects and events in the world'. However, the notion of 'interpretative repertoires' was first introduced in the work of Potter and Wetherell (1987) defined more extensively as 'a culturally familiar and habitual line of argument comprised of recognizable themes, common places and tropes (doxa) … [which] comprise members' methods for making sense in [any] context – they are the common sense which organizes accountability and serves as a back-cloth for the realization of locally managed positions in actual interaction (which are always also indexical constructions and invocations) and from which, … accusations and justifications can be launched. The whole argument does not need to be spelt out in detail. Rather, one fragment or phrase … evokes for listeners the relevant context of argumentation – premises, claims and counter-claims' (Wetherell 1998: 400–401).

15　Self-Categorization Theory (Turner 1985, 1991; Turner et al. 1987) further extends the role of categorization as the cognitive foundation of group behaviour.

16 For example, 'Communities of Practice' (Wenger 1998), 'Diaspora' (Hall 1990), 'Hybridity' (Bhabha 1990), 'Speech Accommodation Theory' (Giles et al. 1991), theories of language ideology (Irvine & Gal 2009), 'Audience and Referee Design' (Bell 1984), 'Stylization' (Auer, 2007), 'Crossing' (Rampton 1995/2018), Stance (Jaffe 2009), 'Indexicality' (Silverstein 2003) and 'Enregisterment' (Agha 2003/2006).

17 Baudrillard (1998) argues that we build our identities in and through consumption. See further discussion of post-structuralist accounts of cultural consumption in Chapters Five and Eleven.

18 See Benwell and Stokoe's (2006: 22) account of the differing perspectives.

CHAPTER TWO

1 This is not to say that the approach taken in previous waves has been completely abandoned or superseded: for example, see Hazan (2002).

2 Johnstone (2000: 416) acknowledges the influence of others, for example, Dorian (1994) who also recognized the importance of identifying individual patterns of language variation ('personal pattern variation') in her study of fishing communities in East Sutherland. Dorian observed that despite similarities in social characteristics, speakers varied in their use of some Gaelic features. These differences did not carry social meaning and so were not considered important by community members who accepted and produced variant forms.

3 A process by which linguistic structures become associated with social identities.

4 For example, see account by Stuart-Smith and Timmons (2010) who discuss the influence of the media on individual language practise.

5 'Strategic' does not always imply a conscious act.

6 Studies investigating the relationship between metapragmatic awareness, ideology and identity (Brown 2006) also illustrate how speakers may be aware of the complexity of their linguistic repertoires and how they employ these in order to present particular or different identities, positioning themselves in allegiance with or in opposition to others.

7 See further discussion of these concepts in Chapter Nine.

8 See Agha (2003, 2006).

9 See Johnstone and Kiesling (2008: 8–10) for a comparative reading of Silverstein's schema with Labov's (1972a) 'taxonomy'.

CHAPTER THREE

1 Spasmodic dysphonia (SD) is a rare neurological disorder affecting adults, caused by involuntary spasms in the vocal cords. It can present in different

forms and effects more women than men. The resulting unstable voice quality can make the speaker sound nervous, underconfident, emotional or ill. Sufferers report changes in self-perception alongside changes in emotional and social well-being – these changes in part resulting from negative feedback received from interlocutors who perceive them as lacking in intelligence and/ or socially compromised due to a perceived emotional or physical deficit. For example, see Baylor et al.'s (2005) account of the biopsychosocial effects of SD as reported by suffers in phenomenological interviews.

2   Herpes simplex viral encephalitis (HSVE) is a viral infection of the nervous system. Loss and change of identity is reported by sufferers, along with disorders of mood and anxiety. For example, see Dewar and Gracey (2007).

3   Capgras syndrome is a psychiatric disorder characterized by the delusional misidentification of people or subjects known to the person (family, friends, pets, etc.). Those experiencing the syndrome believe that the person has been replaced by an imposter. It most commonly affects people with paranoid schizophrenia but can also be found in individuals with acquired brain injuries or dementia. For example, see Lucchelli and Spinnler (2007).

4   This description pertains mainly to Germanic and Romance languages but see, for example, Menn and Obler (1985/1989) for cross-linguistic comparisons.

5   Note this is different from 'anomia'(as mentioned above) – the latter denoting word-finding difficulties.

6   See Chapter One for an account of CA. Membership categorization analysis arises from ethnomethodology and Sacks's (1995) lectures on conversation. He developed the concept of the 'membership categorization device' (MCD) in an attempt to explain how certain categories (and members) are understood as associated with another and linked to particular activities ('category-bound activities') and/or characteristics ('natural predicates'). This in turn leads to particular inferences with respect to expectations and ascriptions afforded.

7   This involves a process in which a person is encouraged to detail activities which are connected to their role or membership within a particular category. In the case of the aphasic client, in the context of therapy, this appears to include activities tied to the category of 'communication impaired person with aphasia' (Horton 2007: 295).

8   See Crichton and Koch (2011) who report on a similar activity undertaken for a patient with dementia.

9   Parr (2007) shows how individuals with severe aphasia are socially excluded at 'infra-structural, interpersonal and personal levels' and how severe aphasia is principally constructed through the reactions and behaviour of others in different contexts.

10   Referred to by Bury (1982) as 'biographical disruption'.

11   Where 'self-concept' is defined as 'a dynamic collection of self-representations, which are formed through personal experiences, and interpretations of the environment' (Ellis-Hill & Horn 2000: 280). Note that while 'self-concept' is often used to replace the term 'identity', it is argued by psychologists to form only one part of it – 'self-esteem' and 'behaviour' contributing to the whole (e.g. see discussion in Addis & Tippett 2004: 57).

12 Some aphasics experience great difficulty in constructing narratives of experience; however, see work by Goodwin (2004) and Goodwin et al. (2002) which demonstrates how severe non-fluent aphasics can still be effective conversational partners.

13 See Charmaz (1995: 666) who reports on the non-recognition of illness by others who wish to be recognized as 'ill', due to the lack of a physical manifestation marking illness or disability. Similar accounts are reported by those experiencing mental health issues whose illness is often 'hidden' from view.

14 Alzheimer's disease is the most common cause of dementia with symptoms including difficulties in problem-solving, language, thinking and memory loss.

15 The authors assert that the connection between identity and autobiographical memory may be 'bidirectional, with identity influencing the selection, reconstruction and interpretation of autobiographical memories' (p. 58).

16 Subjects are required to provide twenty responses to the prompt: 'Who am I?'.

17 The Tennessee Self Concept Scale assesses behaviour, identity and satisfaction (i.e. 'self-concept') in five dimensions: 'personal, family, social, moral and physical' (Addis & Tippett 2004: 62).

CHAPTER FOUR

1 For example, see Grant (2017). It must be noted that forensic linguistic work is much broader than authorship analysis.

2 See Coulthard and Johnson (2013) for a flavour of the extensive work in the field.

3 Watt (2010: 80) notes how witnesses' memories of voices may be impaired by the methods employed by police when taking testimony. A phenomenon known as 'verbal overshadowing' may occur when witnesses are asked to describe the voice they heard prior to identifying it in a 'voice parade' or 'voice line-up' (Nolan 2003). This may impede subsequent identification. See Chapter Six by Hollien in Olsson and Luchjenbroers (2014: 101ff) for a description of the various techniques used in earwitness identification.

4 Fundamental frequency is a property of vocal fold vibration and is perceived acoustically as pitch.

5 A formant gives a sound its unique quality and acoustic resonance (vibration). It is measured as a peak in amplitude in spectral analysis. Idiosyncrasies in formant levels and ratios have been identified (Olsen & Luchjenbroers 2014).

6 See Olson and Luchjenbroers 2014, Chapter Six, for a detailed account.

7 Grant (2012) notes that consistency and distinctiveness are a matter of degree.

8 Some of these, such as stylometry, which use statistical methods such as CUSUM (e.g. Chaski 2001; Farringdon 1996) have proven controversial and their linguistic claims have been disputed (Canter 1992; Grant 2008; Robertson et al. 1994). Other techniques include, for example, those that

focus on the analysis of lexemes (e.g. see discussion of Johnson 1997 and Woolls 2003, below) and stylistics (McMenamin 1993, 2002). Grant (2012) acknowledges the value of stylometric measures in distinguishing an individual from any other in a known population (what he terms 'population-level distinctiveness') in contrast to stylistic analyses which facilitate analyses of variation between individuals ('pair-wise distinctiveness'), often using much smaller fragments of texts. Also see Grant's (2013) cognitivist and stylistic theories of 'idiolect' in forensic case work.

9 Prior to the 'Police & Criminal Evidence Act' in the UK in 1984, police were not required to audio or video record interviews with suspects (Coulthard 2007).

10 Particularly noting that similarity in the beginning and endings of the words can be crucial for public recognition of trademarks. Initial and final letters/sounds are easier to remember than medial letters or sounds by the general population (Cutler 1982) – a phenomenon known as the 'bathtub effect' in psycholinguistics.

11 For example, Gerry Spence who acted on behalf of Karen Silkwood's family in the case against the Kerr-McGee nuclear plant. The story famously recreated in the film 'Silkwood'.

12 Use of pronominals is also discussed in Felton Rosulek (2009).

13 My italics.

14 Membership categorization analysis is noted to define an individual's identity as a 'display of, or ascription to, membership in some feature-rich category' (Antaki & Widdicombe 1998: 2).

CHAPTER FIVE

1 'Identification' is used to refer to the constitutive process of association and belonging which helps to define identity. This involves the development and recognition of connections and/or distinctions between ourselves and others, including, for example, similarities or differences in categories of belonging (such as ethnicity, social class, cool versus nerdy groups) and/or behaviour, stances and attitudes.

2 For example, see Cheshire et al. (2008, 2011) and Gardner-Chloros et al. (forthcoming); although contributing enormously to our theorization of language innovation and change, this work also has the potential to contribute to our understanding of identity performance, creation and contestation in multicultural contexts.

3 For example, other studies have focused on contact in neighbourhoods and leisure sites outside of youth clubs.

4 See Gardner-Chloros (2014: 159–160) for a discussion of these different theoretical concepts; also see Holmes and Meyerhoff (1999).

5 This is not to say Eckert was the first or only researcher to do this.

6 The Northern Cities Vowel Shift is a chain shift in the pronunciation of some vowels articulated in the dialects of American English; these include raising and tensing of /æ/, fronting of /ɑ/, lowering of /ɔ/, backing and lowering of /ɛ/ and lowering and backing of /ɪ/ (Labov et al. 2006).

7 Such that 'kite' would sound more like 'koyt'.

8 Space will not permit discussion of student narratives about race; however, see Bucholtz (2011) for an in-depth discussion.

9 'The term *hip-hop* comprises everything from music (especially rap) to clothing choice, attitudes, language, and an approach to culture and cultural artifacts' (Ibrahim 1999: 351). See Alim's (2009) discussion of youth influence on the development of a 'Hip Hop Nation' and hip-hop as a site of identification. He explores how style is not just produced within specific cultural spaces but also across them (sometimes globally via mass media).

10 The parameter of 'cool-ness' was appropriated to distinguish between those who were trendsetters or who engaged in stylistic trends.

11 See Bucholtz (2007) for an in-depth discussion of the social meanings of slang in Californian youth language.

12 Slang terms are found to take on different meanings by members of different social groups, with some African American students objecting to some of the appropriations by white students.

13 Interestingly, Bucholtz (2011: 134) reports that while white boys were not corrected for their use of AAVE, African American pupils were, despite the fact that African American students demonstrated greater sensitivity to situational constraints and had a more sophisticated ability to switch between non-standard and standard forms. African American pupils were therefore subjected to greater scrutiny and monitoring.

14 See Shankar (2011) for a discussion of style, category formation/delineation and migration in two cliques of South Asian American (Desi) teenagers – other ascribed as 'Populars' and 'Fresh off the Boat' – in a high school in Northern California. Shankar illustrates how youth style is not simply a reflection of their neighbourhoods or familial status but is a matter of choice – 'shaped by [the] political economy and local systems of signification.' (p. 666).

15 See also Cheshire et al.'s (2011) account of the development of Multicultural London English among adolescents in inner-city London.

16 Far from suggesting 'fixed boundaries' between CofPs, Moore (2010) also outlines the role of peripheral and marginal members in enacting language change. She points out that one's ability to affect change within a CofP is not just related to one's engagement in practices but also to the quality of that engagement and one's position within it.

17 An 'ethnolect' has been variously defined (as detailed by Jasper 2008: 86–87); however, it is commonly considered as the vernacular variety of a standard 'host' language spoken by members of an ethnic group with deviations in phonological, lexical and morphosyntactic realization. See Chapter Eight for further discussion.

18 Transmigration includes the movement of people, cultural goods and language varieties.

19 Including youths originating from suburban France, North Africa, Pakistan, Poland, Portugal, North and West Africa.

20 As similarly noted to be the case in Eckert and McConnell-Ginet's (1999) account of a Pan-Asian group of students in a school in California.

CHAPTER SIX

1 Where 'professional identity is used to incorporate organisational role and membership ... and expertise and occupation' (Marra & Angouri 2011: 11).

2 See Holmes and Woodhams (2013) for references and an excellent review of research on blue-collar workplaces.

3 See Chapter Five for a definition of 'Community of Practice'.

4 Also see, Chun Nam Mak et al.'s (2012) account of the role of humour in supporting the socialization of new employees in a firm in Hong Kong. Humour is invoked to mark acceptable and/or unacceptable behaviour and is argued therefore to regulate as well as support members within a workplace CofP. Also see Schaefer's (2013) account of the role of humour in co-constructing blue-collar worker identity.

5 Tsui (2007) details the shifting identity and identification of a Chinese EFL learner and teacher through his first six years of teaching. He reports on his struggle to align with enforced institutional practices and reified identity formations and the importance of linguistic and institutional knowledge, membership, participation and legitimacy in identity construction. His stories detail his negotiation of reified meanings and his reclaiming of what it means to be an EFL learner and teacher and as such how he accepts his role and status within the power hierarchy. The study points to the salience of narratives in helping to make sense of his world and the importance of participation in the construction of meaning and identity.

6 See also work on small stories, such as Juzwik and Ives's (2010) account of small stories as resources for the interactional accomplishment of teacher identity, in which they detail how teacher identity is constructed dialogically via pupil and teacher contributions and may accrete over time to form 'solidified roles' (Georgakopoulou 2008) or 'performances of self' (Goffman 1959).

7 Also see Graf (2011) who describes the difficulties experienced by workers whose profession is not yet 'recognized'. Through her analysis of Executive Coaching (EC) sessions, Graf illustrates how ECs meta-discourse about their work in coaching sessions in order to legitimize and execute their work. They topicalize the methods and procedures they will use, as well as provide necessary conceptual background. The way of 'doing' coaching takes precedence in their interaction with clients.

8 For example, see Holmes, Vine and Marra (2009) who examine the leadership styles of two male Māori managers in New Zealand organizations, contexts sensitive to valuing Māori culture. They find that the managers consistently employ and perform Māori values and identities in their work.

9 'Face', defined by Goffman (1967: 5) as 'the positive social value a person effectively claims for himself by the line others assume he has taken during a particular contact', and identity have been conflated by some (e.g. Geyer 2008; Locher 2008, cited in Schnurr & Chan 2011: 190) who define face as a situated or interactional manifestation of self.

10 The negotiation and contestation of leadership identity is further illustrated in a study of a novice team leader who has been newly promoted to a position of authority (Schnurr & Zayts 2011). They discuss how the employee successfully undertakes her role as meeting chair (e.g. managing the floor and agenda), but experiences challenges to her status by other members.

11 In which discourse 'is directed towards the referential object of speech as in ordinary discourse, and toward another's discourse, towards someone else's speech' (Bakhtin 1994: 105 in Baxter 2011: 236).

12 Also see, Wagner and Wodak's (2006) critical discourse analysis of the strategies employed by eight professional women in their reflexive biographical narratives about 'performing success'.

13 In contrast, see Litosseliti's (2006) discussion of the essentialized renderings of men and women tennis players in the media.

14 Campbell and Roberts (2007: 252) citing Scheuer (2001) note differences in the way in which low-paid and more well-paid workers identify themselves in relation to their work. They assert that low-paid workers 'do not use their work to form their identity – and there is, therefore, a wide gulf between the personal discourses they use to talk about themselves, and those they use to speak about the institution. Yet ... organizations increasingly demand such identification'.

CHAPTER SEVEN

1 See http://www.statista.com/statistics/433871/daily-social-media-usage-worldwide/ for current statistics.

2 See Murthy's (2012: 1061) distinction between social media and social network which incorporates a consideration of offline interaction between participants.

3 See Seargeant and Tagg (2014:165ff) for a discussion of 'the affordances of social network sites'.

4 See Murthy's (2012: 1064) discussion of the 'demotic turn' for ordinary users of SM to access media channels in order to self-publicize, break news, etc. He aligns with Turner (2010) by arguing that this turn should not be confused with a greater potential for 'democratainment', that is, media industries still have greater economic and symbolic power.

5 Examples of avatar gender-switching illustrate how and why male and female players may decide to take on different personae. Some men report being helped by their fellow players if they take on a female character, whereas women report that they are taken more seriously and avoid intimidation if they play as men. When adopting different genders, players are forced to adopt stereotypical gendered styles – although not always successfully (Herring & Stoerger 2014).

6 The term 'haafu' is used to refer to individuals who self-ascribe as being of mixed-race heritage with one Japanese and one 'other' parent.

7 According to Bourdieu, 'habitus' is a set of dispositions acquired through involvement in everyday activities within our social milieu. These dispose us to think and act in particular ways. Our habitus is continually reconstituted through ongoing experiences. See further discussion in Chapter Twelve.

8 For an extended discussion of 'Second Language Identities', see Block's (2007) book of the same name which examines three second language learning contexts: migrant contexts, foreign language classrooms and study abroad programmes.

CHAPTER EIGHT

1 See Werbner (2010) for an account of early and contemporary theorizations of religious identity.

2 Although one cannot deny that governments and national institutions/ organizations often construct ethnic labels and boundaries in order to organize populations along the lines of phenotype, ancestry, etc. See account by Wilkinson (2011) below.

3 See Fozdar and Rocha (2017) for a discussion of the evolving concept of 'race' and the continuing dynamic and blurred relationship between race and ethnicity. Also see Eriksen's account of the history of the terms 'ethnic' and 'ethnicity'.

4 Language is not always a salient marker of ethnic identity of course (e.g. Gaelic in Ireland, see Edwards 1988).

5 In a critique of EVT, Ehala (2011: 192) suggests that '[b]ased on the strength of emotional attachment of members to their group, ethnic groups can be categorized into two prototypes: "hot" and "cold"', suggesting that emotional ties to an ethnic group determine "ethnic temperature"'. The concept of ethnic temperature has been applied to studies of ethnic groups for whom religion is a foundational principle of ethnic identity. Nosenko-Stein (2014) discusses the variable and changing ethnic temperature of post-Soviet Jewry for example.

6 Also see Noro (2009: 3) who provides the example 'of a multiethnic person [in Canada, who] might conceive of herself as multiethnic at home but in the company of her Japanese grandmother … may perceive of herself in terms of her Japanese heritage … [as] … the social context has the potential to affect how a multiethnic person views his or her ethnic identity'.

7 See Mu (2015: 240) for a lengthy list of ethnic groups and research studies.

8 Meta-analysis involves advanced statistical modelling via a synthetic analysis of quantitative research studies which focus on the same issue – in this case, studies focusing on a correlation between heritage language use and competence, and ethnic identity.

9 For example, see Sayahi (2005) who reports on the vitality of language and identity among speakers of Spanish in northern Morocco. In this study, the minority group avoids assimilation into the majority culture by not attaining native-like competence in the host country's language. The status of their language, due to the cultural and economic status of their country of origin, supports the maintenance of their group identity and heritage language.

10 Benor (2010: 175) acknowledges that 'while a description of an ethnic group's distinctive repertoire can be pan-regional, the analysis of individuals' language use must be done in relation to regional variables', as linguistic features may carry different meanings in different regions. She cites work by Anderson (2002), Fought (2003) and Wong (2007) as illustrative cases.

11 See Cresswell (2012) for a critique of DP's 'emphasis on in-situ constructions' (p. 553) which do not permit a consideration of historical or extra-situational/ contextual social discourses.

12 See further Merino et al. (2017) for a narrative analysis of Mapuche ethnic identity.

13 See Chapter One for a definition of "interpretative repertoires" by Edley (2001) and Wetherell (1998).

14 The term 'Ingrian' refers to the rural area of 'Ingria' where Finns first emigrated in the seventeenth and early twentieth century. It is situated between St. Petersburg and the Gulf of Finland (Varjonen et al. 2013: 113).

15 See also Cary-Lemon's (2010) account of the provisional and negotiated nature of Irish immigrant identity constructed in oral-history interviews. The author explores this and issues of context-dependency using the Discourse-Historical Approach (Wodak et al. 1999). Also see Van de Mieroop and Clifton's (2012) examination of the negotiation of ethnicity and group membership in talk between an interviewer and a former slave.

CHAPTER NINE

1 The importance of 'identity' in 'language and sexuality' research has been critically explored by Cameron and Kulick (2003) who argue that the complexity of sexual subjectivity needs to be explored beyond the purview of identity to include a consideration of 'desire'. Please see the subsequent response to their work in Bucholtz and Hall (2004) and a further response to Bucholtz and Hall's critique by Cameron and Kulick (2005).

2 A supposition by society/social institutions that heterosexuality is the norm.

3 They note that while significant numbers of babies are born with reproductive or sexual organs that do not conform to standard male or female anatomy, they are subsequently ascribed to one or other category of sex – male or female. They suggest that this illustrates that even sexual categorization originates from social definition not biological presentation/foundations. Bing and Bergvall (2016: 2ff) also point out that there are cultures that recognize more than two sex categories and as such 'this "biological foundationalism" (Bem 1993) is now being challenged'.

4 See Zimman and Hall's (2010) theoretical concept of 'third sex' to denote identities which differ from the binary male/female sex categories. They explore the role of embodied sexual alterity and its relationship to language and identity discussing two illustrative case studies: transsexuals in the United States and Hijras in India.

5 Bing and Bergvall (2016: 7ff) drawing on the writing of Thomas Laqueur document changes in ideology in the eighteenth century, from a one-sex to a two-sex understanding of the body. They assert that until comparatively recently philosophers and physicians considered the female body to be an undeveloped male body – hence assumed the dependency of women and children on men.

6 'Double-bind' has been referred to by a number of scholars who have identified the double constraint that women often experience in public contexts when they adopt particular speech styles. If they adopt a perceptibly masculine style, they can be criticized for being too aggressive or unfeminine; if they adopt a less assertive style, they can be evaluated as weak.

7 LGBTQ is used to designate a group of people whose sexual or gender identities invoke shared social and political concerns.

8 Although as pointed out by Cameron (2005: 483–484), one needs to be cautious, for it is 'not that one approach has been discarded and another has been created to take its place, but the balance between the two has altered. Beginning shortly after 1990, the consensus among language and gender scholars began to shift in favour of ... a "post-modern" view of gender; by the end of the decade this had become the dominant position'. Note too Cameron acknowledges that her use of the terms 'modern' versus 'postmodern' is far from 'unproblematic' (p. 483). Motschenbacher and Stegu (2013) argue that although one can identify similarities between post-structuralist and social constructionist approaches to identity (both seeing it as a performative act), social constructionist work adheres to a (biological) sex versus (social) gender dichotomy that may be fruitful in deconstructing the 'naturalness' of gendered practices but does not address the biological question. Queer linguists question whether it is necessary to consider and contrast female and male categories at all.

9 These studies highlight differences in language use, particularly women favouring more standard forms of pronunciation or grammar; some also point to other explanations for variation within and across groups, for example, social network and class/economic factors.

10 Austin argued that there are utterances that bring about certain social actions or changes to states of affairs, for example, the pronouncement, 'I pronounce

you man and wife' performs the act of marriage and brings about a change of state.

11 Compare to Le Page and Tabouret-Keller's (1985) 'Acts of Identity' in which linguistic marking of identity is considered to exist prior to the act. See Chapter Two.

12 See Kulick's (2000: 256ff) critique of work on gay and lesbian language during and after the 1980s which sought to identify gay and lesbian varieties rather than acknowledging the variety of performances. The author notes how this research has 'failed to come up with structural, morphological or phonological features that are unique to gay men or lesbians … For this reason it is important not to confuse symbolic resources that anyone can appropriate to invoke stereotypical images of homosexuality with the actual language practices, much less the identities of individual gays and lesbians'. See too his argument to 'shift the ground of our inquiry … from identity categories to culturally grounded semiotic practices' (p. 273). Also see account in Podesva et al. (2001: 177).

13 It is important to acknowledge that despite the destabilization of gender/sexual categories in social constructionist and post-structuralist work, if we 'want to examine the ways in which certain types of identities, or forms of sexual desire or behaviour are constructed as queer or not queer … we first have to acknowledge that the identities exist (if only) as social constructs. Obviously this doesn't mean that we should reify or essentialize them, but we do have to refer to them in some way. Clearly, people do self-identify and are labelled by others as male, female, gay, lesbian … etc. These identities "exist" within discourse, shaping the minds, bodies and lives of many people. However queer theory should help us to understand that such identity labels are only "real" for the here and now – they are not set in stone, instead there are many possible configurations' (Baker 2008: 194). Moreover, feminist linguists (Mills 2003) argue that categories of men and women are important to retain in order to challenge the systemic (e.g. state/organizational) and local (family/interactional) discrimination of women.

14 Queer theory is defined as 'a critical inquiry into "heteronormativity", the system which prescribes, enjoins, rewards, and naturalizes a particular kind of heterosexuality – monogamous, reproductive, and based on conventionally complementary gender roles – as the norm on which social arrangements should be based. This concept of heteronormativity has had a significant impact on the study of language and gender' (Cameron 2005: 489), not least because it seeks to disrupt and deconstruct the homo/hetero binary to argue that they are social constructions and therefore also fluid, unstable and multiple. Further, Bucholtz and Hall (2004: 471) note that queer linguistics does not just focus on LGBTQ but researches multiple sexual identities, their practices and ideologies within and across different sociocultural contexts. 'Like feminist theory, queer theory takes different forms; most useful for queer linguistics are those theories that include feminist as well as queer perspectives. Queer linguistics puts at the forefront of linguistic analysis the regulation of sexuality by hegemonic heterosexuality and the ways in which nonnormative sexualities are negotiated in relation to these regulatory structures … it allows

us to talk about sexual ideologies, practices and identities as interconnected issues without losing sight of power relations'. See further discussion of queer linguistic approaches (including discursive approaches) in Motschenbacher (2013) and Motschenbacher and Stegu (2013).

15 Levon and Mendes (2016: 6) argue that researchers such as Cameron and Kulick and Eckert have 'opened up a space for what [they] term an *emergentist* approach to language and sexuality. Rather than taking the construction of sexual identity as an analytical point of departure, work in this framework examines how speakers recruit the meaning potentials of variable forms in order to adopt locally meaningful stances. In certain cases, speakers do this kind of stance-taking as a means of constructing contextually relevant personae'. See discussion of third-wave variationist sociolinguistics in Chapter One.

16 For more extensive reviews of work on language and sexuality, see, for example, Baker (2008); Levon and Mendes (2016); Cameron and Kulick (2003) and Queen (2007, 2014).

17 There is insufficient room here to discuss the extensive debates and differences between different analysts (e.g. conversation analysts, discursive psychologists, critical discourse analysts, etc.) about how gender or sexual identity should be analysed as social categories. For example, conversation analysts argue they should only be a subject of investigation if speakers orient to them, whereas critical discourse analysts argue that identities are frequently shaped by social structures and ideology and as such speakers may not always orient to them. For different positions, see chapters in Coates and Pichler (2011) and Harrington et al. (2008). Also see brief review of discursive approaches in Chapter One.

18 'Signifying relies on the listener's ability to connect the content of an utterance to the context in which it occurs and specifically to sort through the possible meanings and implications of an utterance and realise both the proper meaning and the skill of the speaker in creating multiple potential meanings' (Barrett 2011: 419).

19 Intersectionality is defined as 'the ways in which dynamic systems of social organization mutually constitute one another … a process-centred approach … that views the production of sexuality[/gender] at both the individual and structural levels as inextricably linked to the production of other relevant systems … race/ethnicity, social class and so on and critically interrogating why it is that these categories are linked in this way' (Levon & Mendes 2016: 11–12).

20 Also see for accounts of perception studies.

21 See also Wong (2016) for labelling practices among Hong Kong lesbians.

22 Goffman suggested that speakers can 'animate' different selves within an interaction through the strategic enactment of socially recognizable voices. The layering of multiple voices (lamination) by a speaker reveals the self as multiple (see Chapter One for more details). Bakhtin (1981) also argued that there can be multiple voices (and subject positions) relating to sometimes contradictory social or moral positions. Benwell and Stokoe (2006: 34) argue

that unlike Butler, Goffman's 'sense of "performance" is unproblematically agentive, premised on a rational, intending self able to manage carefully an often idealised, consistent persona, or "front" in order to further his or her interpersonal objectives'.

23 See also other work by Levon (2009, 2012, 2014), for example, how gay men in Israel reconcile their sexuality and religious identities using particular narrative structures; how gay Israeli men use a gay variety *oxtsit* to perform in-group mockery (not to explicitly mark identity).

24 Although this section will focus predominantly on discussion of heteronormativity and hegemonic masculinity, it must be acknowledged that accounts of hegemonic femininity and hegemonic homosexualities also exist (Bordo 1993).

25 Also see how binary representations of men and women and constructions of the 'new man' are exploited for commercial purposes in the media (Litosseliti 2006).

CHAPTER TEN

1 In adherence with convention (Padden & Humphries, 1988; Woodward 1982), 'deaf' with a lower case 'd' is used to denote individuals who have a profound or significant hearing loss but who use spoken language and identify with hearing culture. It is also used to denote the audiological state of being without hearing. 'Deaf' with an upper case 'D' is used to refer to individuals or groups who use sign language as their first or preferred language and who consider themselves to be culturally and socially 'Deaf' – that is, they do not consider their audiological status as pathological, as an impairment or 'lack', but celebrate their visual-gestural means of communication and worldview; enjoying and engaging, for example, in distinct cultural forms such as joketelling, signed narratives, signed poetry and communion with other Deaf people. Some note however (Nakamura 2005) that the distinction between D/deaf is not tenable in some languages.

2 Although some note difficulties in acceptance and integration into the Deaf community for these individuals. See Morris (2008: 16) for a description of the various layers of Deaf community membership, depicted as concentric circles, with 'profoundly Deaf sign language users' at the centre and other members, such as signing family members, interpreters, those working with Deaf people radiating outward from the centre.

3 Alker (in Morris 2008: 14) makes a distinction between 'hard of hearing' which refers to individuals who, with augmented hearing, are able to participate in hearing society; 'profoundly deaf' who are unable to hear, even with hearing aids but who have acquired a spoken language prior to deafness and can speak and think as hearing people; and 'Deaf', individuals who have been deaf from birth or became deaf at a prelingual age.

4 The term 'Deafhood' (Ladd 2003: 3) 'represents a process – the struggle by each Deaf child, Deaf family, and Deaf adult to explain to themselves and each

other their own existence in the world. In sharing their lives with each other as a community, and enacting these explanations ... Deaf people are engaged in a daily praxis, a continuing internal and external dialogue. This dialogue not only acknowledges that existence as a Deaf person is actually a process of *becoming* and maintaining "Deaf", but also reflects different interpretations of Deafhood, of what being a Deaf person in a Deaf community might mean'.

5 This research dialogues with other contemporary studies of subaltern groups, for example, women, LGBT individuals and communities and ethnic minorities.

6 Ladd (2003: 175) argues that they are distinct from disabled groups and other hearing linguistic minorities however. 'To define them simply as disabled is to overlook the linguistic foundation of their cultural life. To define them as a linguistic group is to overlook the very real sensory characteristic of their existence, both positive (a unique visual apprehension of the world out of which sign languages have been constructed) and negative (communication barriers are not simply linguistic, but sonic also).

7 Wilcox et al. (2012: 390) discuss how some nations (e.g. the United States and Germany) have provided official protections for sign languages via the appropriation of disability laws. They critique such acts and question 'Are Deaf people a linguistic minority, or are they people with a disability?' They also describe how Deaf people are framed within international conventions, for example, the UN Convention on the Rights of Persons with Disabilities as 'disabled'. They call for language policies which support sign languages formulated by Deaf people in cooperation with sign linguists and policy specialists who know about sign language studies.

8 See Woll and Ladd (2011) and Wilcox et al. (2012) for a comprehensive discussion of the history of 'social Darwinism' and oralism in Europe and America. They recount the details of scientific 'progress' and shifts in educational (culminating in the fateful 1880 Milan Conference) and social philosophies, including 'Social Darwinist eugenics' (Woll & Ladd 2011: 165) which undermined, at the end of the nineteenth century, attempts to use sign language in the education of the deaf, and the ability of deaf people in thirty states in the United States to marry or procreate. Some would argue that a shift to oralism at this time had long-term negative effects on the Deaf community and reinforced an ideology of disability; others note their crystallizing influence on Deaf communities, leading to the establishment of national associations for the Deaf and an inward turn to self-preservation through community and language. Wilcox et al. (2012) also detail subsequent successful bilingual schemes and note the impact that research on sign language has had on the recognition and importance of sign language in the education of deaf people.

9 Oralist policies continued until the 1980s in the UK. Although since this time, there has been a significant decline in schools for deaf children. Over 90 per cent of deaf children are now mainstreamed and have limited opportunities for signing with their peers or with Deaf role models (Sutton-Spence 2010a).

10 See Sutton-Spence (2010b) for an examination of the use of spatial and orientational metaphor in sign poetry which is used to conceptualize Deaf identity. Signs articulated across different axes – sagittal (front to back),

vertical (up and down) and transverse (left to right) – symbolize different identities. These are noted to index actors (self and others), mark accord and discord/concealment or openness about identities (particularly hearing/Deaf) and the values associated with Deaf identity.

11 Some D/deaf people have complained that they do not enhance hearing and are too noisy and uncomfortable to wear (Leigh 2009).

12 Note how this scale has been criticized by researchers; for example, Foster and Kinuthia (2003: 288) argue that it cannot account for the multiplicity of D/deaf identities and is limited by and even errorful in its assertion that people pass through developmental stages.

13 Also found by Hintermair (2007: 294), however, he argues that 'mental strength' is as important as acculturation in determining 'subjectively satisfying identity patterns ... even under marginal conditions'.

14 See Sutton-Spence and Woll (1999/2003) for studies exploring variant signing and identity performance in relation to gender and sexuality and Black and White signing in the United States.

15 Foster and Kinuthia (2003) explore how Asian, Hispanic and African American college students conceptualize and describe their identities in semi-structured interviews.

CHAPTER ELEVEN

1 In this chapter, 'space' and 'place' are defined respectively as a 'spatial organization and location' and as 'the attachment of meaning to space' (Becker 2009: 636).

2 Not to mention the very practical and contentious role in recent years of dialect/language identification by governments for the purposes of determining refugee status; see, for example, Patrick (2016a, b) and Wilson and Foulkes (2014).

3 Benwell and Stokoe (2006: 211) assert that the 'spatial turn' has its origins 'in post-structuralist and postmodern theory, drawing on Foucault's (1986: 22) observation that we are currently living in an 'epoch of space'. As such both space and identity/ies are mutually constitutive and constraining.

4 The term 'place identity' was first coined by Proshansky and colleagues (Myers 2006: 324).

5 Although Becker (2009: 634) notes that 'places circumscribe a speech community, often offering little more than location for our investigations into social categories and the linguistic practices that correlate with them. As Eckert (2004) notes, descriptions of social variation within class-based, ethnic or gendered categories are often disconnected from the places where they occur.'

6 See debate initiated by Trudgill's (2008) assertion that identity has no bearing on new dialect formation in the journal *Language in Society*, vol. 37.

7 On a different scale, Finnegan (cited in Beal 2010:221) reports on the different perceptions of youths in the north-east and south-west of Sheffield towards

their local identities, perceiving them in more micro-terms in relation to postcode affiliation. These are instantiated in the names appropriated by gangs.

8   'Glottal masking of the oral plosive burst' (Wells 1982: 374, cited in Llamas 2007: 586) or 'a glottal stop is co-articulated with the [p t k] articulation' (Giergerich 1992: 220, cited in Llamas 2007: 586).

9   That is, that nations were 'natural' products. A critique also made by Hobsbawn (1990).

10 This also has implications for citizenship (Piller 2001).

11 Ominiyi (2010: 244) reports that Nigerian English and Nigerian Pidgin are most closely connected to national identity in Nigeria; however, overall ethnic identity is a stronger referent than national identity for many.

12 Billig (1995) argues that the 'banal'/routine production and reproduction of symbols, such as a national flag or national symbols on currency, equally contribute to the ideological locatedness of individuals and the development of national subjectivity. The nation is understood as existing via human action. It is historically, rhetorically and ideologically constituted.

13 For example, at the time of writing this is evidenced in debates about BREXIT in the UK and the need for 'immigrants' to acquire the national language for purposes of 'integration'.

14 Xiǎozī is a term used to refer to a cool, upwardly mobile status.

15 Founder of the Chinese National Party.

CHAPTER TWELVE

1   See also Merono-Fernàndez (2016) who argues in a similar vein for a 'framework for cognitive sociolinguistics'.

2   This is distinct from 'Dynamic Systems Theory' in Mathematics, Developmental Psychology (Thelan 2005) and Second Language Acquisition research (e.g. De Bot et al. 2007). Although the latter two also attempt to account for internal processes (e.g. biological constraints, mental representations) and external influences (experience, external information) and discuss aspects of (in)stability, fluidity and emergence, in addition to the inter-relatedness of system components.

REFERENCES

Abe, H. (2004/2011), 'Lesbian Bar Talk in Shinjuku, Tokyo', in J. Coates and P. Pichler (eds), *Language and Gender: A Reader*, 2nd edn, 375–383, Oxford: Wiley-Blackwell.

Abrams, J., V. Barker and H. Giles (2009), 'An examination of the validity of the Subjective Vitality Questionnaire', *Journal of Multilingual & Multicultural Development*, 30 (1): 59–72.

Action on Hearing Loss, http://www.actiononhearingloss.org.uk/your-hearing/about-deafness-and-hearing-loss/statistics.aspx downloaded 27/8/14.

Addis, D. R. and L. J. Tippett (2004), 'Memory of myself: Autobiographical memory and identity in Alzheimer's disease', *Memory*, 12 (1): 56–74.

Adorno, T. (1981), *Negative Dialectics*, New York: Continuum. Reprint of 1973 translation.

Adorno, T. W. and M. Horkheimer (2002), *Dialectic of Enlightenment*, Stanford, CA: Stanford University Press.

Agha, A. (2003), 'The social life of a cultural value', *Language and Communication*, 23: 231–273.

Agha, A. (2006), *Language and Social Relations*, New York: Cambridge University Press.

Ainsworth, S. and C. Hardy (2007), 'The construction of the older worker: Privilege, paradox and policy', *Discourse & Communication*, 1 (3): 267–285.

Alcoff, L. M. (2010), 'New Epistemologies: Post-Positivist Accounts of Identity', in M. Wetherell and C. T. Moharty (eds), *The Sage Handbook of Identities*, 114–162, London: Sage.

Aldridge, M. (2010), 'Vulnerable Witnesses: Vulnerable Witnesses in the Criminal justice system', in M. Coulthard and A. Johnson (eds), *The Routledge Handbook of Forensic Linguistics*, 296–314, London: Routledge.

Ali, L. and C. C. Sonn (2010), 'Constructing identity as a second generation Cypriot Turkish in Australia: The multi-hyphenated other', *Culture & Psychology*, 16 (3): 416–436.

Alim, H. S. (2009), 'Translocal style communities: Hip hop youth as cultural theorists of style, language, and globalisation', *Pragmatics*, 19 (1): 103–127.

Allard, R. and R. Landry (1994), 'Subjective ethnolinguistic vitality: A comparison of two measures', *International Journal of the Sociology of Language*, 108: 117–144.

Althusser, L. (2004 [1972]), 'Ideology and Ideological State Apparatuses', in J. Rivkin and M. Ryan (eds), *Literary Theory: An Anthology*, 693–702, Oxford: Blackwell.

Althusser, L. (2012), 'Ideology Interpellates Individuals as Subjects', in P. du Gay, J. Evans and P. Redman (eds), *Identity: A Reader*, 31–38, London: Sage.

Anderson, B. (1991), *Imagined Communities: Reflections on the Origin and Spread of Nationalism*, 2nd edn, London and New York: Verso.

Anderson, B. (2002), 'Dialect levelling and /ai/ monophthongization among African American Detroiters', *Journal of Sociolinguistics*, 6: 86–98.

Andersson, M. (2008), 'Constructing young masculinity: A case study of heroic discourse on violence', *Discourse & Society*, 19: 139–161.

Androutsopoulos, J. (2001), *From the Streets to the Screens and Back Again: On the Mediated Diffusion of Ethnolectal Patterns in Contemporary German*, LAUD Linguistic Agency, A522, Essen, Germany: Universitat Essen.

Androutsopoulos, J. (2006a), 'Introduction: Sociolinguistics and computer-mediated communication', *Journal of Sociolinguistics*, 10 (4): 419–438.

Androutsopoulos, J. (2006b), 'Multilingualism, diaspora, and the Internet: Codes and identities on German-based diaspora websites', *Journal of Sociolinguistics*, 10 (4): 520–547.

Androutsopoulos, J. and A. Georgakopoulou, eds (2003), *Discourse Constructions of Youth Identities*, Amsterdam/Philadelphia, PA: John Benjamins.

Ang, I. (2001), *On Not Speaking Chinese: Living between Asia and the West*, London: Routledge.

Angouri, J. and M. Marra (2011a), *Constructing Identities at Work*, Basingstoke: Palgrave MacMillan.

Angouri, J. and M. Marra (2011b), '"OK One Last Thing for Today Then": Constructing Identities in Corporate Meeting Talk', in J. Angouri and M. Marra (eds), *Constructing Identities at Work*, 85–100, Basingstoke: Palgrave MacMillan.

Antaki, C. and S. Widdicombe (1998), *Identities in Talk*, Thousand Oaks, CA: Sage.

Anthias, F. and N. Yuval-Davis (1992), *Racialised Boundaries: Race, Nation, Gender, Colour and Class and the Anti-Racist Struggle*, London: Routledge.

Appel, R. and R. Schoonen (2005), 'Street language. A multilingual youth register in the Netherlands', *Journal of Multilingual and Multicultural Development*, 26 (2): 85–117.

Arminen, I. (2005), *Institutional Interaction: Studies of Talk at Work*, Aldershot: Ashgate.

Armstrong, E., A. Ferguson and L. Mortensen (2011), 'Public and Private Identity: The Co-Construction of Aphasia through Discourse', in C. Candlin and J. Crichton (eds), *Discourses of Deficit*, 215–231, Basingstoke: Palgrave Macmillan.

Armstrong, E. and H. Ulatowsksa (2007), 'Making stories: Evaluative language and the aphasia experience', *Aphasiology*, 21 (6/7/8): 763–774.

Ashcraft, K. L. (2007), 'Appreciating the "work" of discourse: Occupational identity and difference as organizing mechanisms in the case of commercial airline pilots', *Discourse & Communication*, 1 (1): 9–36.

Atanga, L., S. Ellece, L. Litosseliti and J. Sunderland, eds (2012), 'Gender and language in sub-Saharan African contexts: Research agendas' [A Special Issue], *Gender and Language*, 6 (1): 1–20.

Atanga, L., S. Ellece, L. Litosseliti and J. Sunderland (2013), *Gender and Language in African Contexts: Tradition, Struggle and Change*, Amsterdam: Benjamins.

Auer, P., ed (2007), *Style & Social Identities: Alternative Approaches to Linguistic Heterogeneity*, Berlin: Mouton de Gruyter.

Austin, J. L. (1962), *How to Do Things with Words: The William James Lectures Delivered at Harvard University in 1955*, Oxford: Clarendon.

Bailey, B. (2000), 'Language and negotiation of ethnic/racial identity among Dominican Americans', *Language in Society*, 29: 555–582.

Bailey, B. (2001), 'The language of multiple identities among Dominican Americans', *Journal of Linguistic Anthropology*, 10 (2): 190–223.

Baker, C. and D. Cokely (1980), *American Sign Language*, Silver Spring TD: TJ.

Baker, P. (2008), *Sexed Texts: Language, Gender and Sexuality*, London: Equinox.

Baker-Smemoe, W. and B. Jones (2014), 'Religion on the Border: The Effect of Utah English on English and Spanish Use in the Mexican Mormon Colonies', in D. Watt and C. Llamas (eds), *Language, Borders and Identity*, 90–104, Edinburgh: Edinburgh University Press.

Bakhtin, M. (1934), 'Discourse in the novel', *Literary Theory: An Anthology*, 2: 674–685.

Bakhtin, M. (1994), 'Double-Voiced Discourse in Dostoevsky', in P. Morris (ed.), *The Bakhtin Reader: Selected Writings*, 102–111, London: Edward Arnold. (Originally published in 1963.)

Bakhtin, M. M. (1981), *The Dialogic Imagination*, Austin: University of Texas Press.

Balibar, E., and I. M. Wallerstein (1991), *Race, Nation, Class: Ambiguous Identities*, New York: Verso.

Bamberg, M. (1997), 'Positioning between structure and performance', *Journal of Narrative and Life History*, 7 (1–4): 335–342.

Bamberg, M. (2011a), 'Who am I? Narration and its contribution to self and identity', *Theory and Psychology*, 21 (1): 3–24.

Bamberg, M. (2011b), 'Narrative Practice and Identity Navigation', in J. A. Holstein and J. F. Gubrium (eds), *Varieties of Narrative Analysis*, 99–124, London: Sage.

Bamberg, M., A. De Fina and D. Schiffrin, eds (2007), *Selves and Identities in Narrative and Discourse*, Amsterdam: John Benjamins.

Bamberg, M. and A. Georgakopoulou (2008), 'Small Stories as a New Perspective in Narrative and Identity Analysis', in A. De Fina and A. Georgakopoulou (eds), 'Narrative analysis in the shift from text to practices', Special Issue, *Text & Talk*, 28 (3): 377–396.

Bamman, D., J. Eisenstein and T. Schnoebelen (2014), 'Gender identity and lexical variation in social media', *Journal of Sociolinguistics*, 18 (2): 135–160.

Bargiela-Chiappini, F. and S. J. Harris (1997), *Managing Language: The Discourse of Corporate Meetings*, Amsterdam: John Benjamins.

Barker, C. and D. Galasiński (2001), *Cultural Studies and Discourse Analysis: A Dialogue on Language and Identity*, London: Sage.

Barrett, R. (1995/2011), 'Indexing Polyphonous Identity in the Speech of African American Drag Queens', in J. Coates and P. Pichler (eds), *Language and Gender: A Reader*, 2nd edn, 413–429, Oxford: Wiley-Blackwell.

Barrett, R. (1997), 'The Homo-Genius' Speech Community', in A. Livia and K. Hall (eds), *Queerly Phrased*, 181–201, Oxford: Oxford Studies in Sociolinguistics.

Barrett, R. (2002), 'Is Queer Theory Important for Sociolinguistic Theory?', in K. Campbell-Kibler, R. J. Podesva, S. J. Roberts and A. Wong (eds), *Language and Sexuality: Contesting Meaning in Theory and Practice*, 25–43, Stanford, CA: CSLI.

Barrett, M. and M. J. Davidson (2006), *Gender and Communication at Work*, Aldershot: Ashgate.

Barton, D. and C. Lee (2013), *Language Online: Investigating Digital Texts and Practices*, Abingdon: Routledge.

Bat-Chava, Y. (1993), 'Antecedents of self-esteem in deaf people: A meta-analytic review', *Rehabilitation Psychology*, 38 (4): 221–234.

Baudrillard, J. (1998), *The Consumer Society: Myths & Structures*, London: Sage.

Bauman, Z. (2000), *Liquid Modernity*, Cambridge: Polity Press.

Baylor, C. R., K. M. Yorkston and T. L. Eadie (2005), 'The consequences of spasmodic dysphonia on communication-related quality of life: A qualitative study of the insider's experiences', *Journal of Communication Disorders*, 38 (5): 395–419.

Baxter, J. (2003), *Positioning Gender in Discourse: A Feminist Methodology*, Basingstoke: Palgrave Macmillan.

Baxter, J. (2010), *The Language of Female Leadership*, Basingstoke: Palgrave Macmillan.

Baxter. J. (2011), 'Survival or success? A critical exploration of the use of 'double-voiced discourse' by women business leaders in the UK', *Discourse & Communication*, 5 (3): 231–245.

Baxter, J. (2014), '"If you had only listened carefully…': The discursive construction of emerging leadership in a UK all-women management team', *Discourse & Communication*, 8 (1): 23–39.

Baxter, J. and K. Wallace (2009), 'Outside in-group and out-group identities? Constructing male solidarity and female exclusion in UK builders' talk', *Discourse and Society*, 20 (4): 411–429.

Beal, J. (2010), 'Shifting Borders and Shifting Regional Identities', in C. Llamas and D. Watt (eds), *Language and Identities*, 217–226, Edinburgh: Edinburgh University Press.

Beauvoir, S. de (1989 [1949]) *The Second Sex*, trans., H. M. Parshley, New York: Vintage.

Becker, K. (2009), ' /r/ and the construction of place identity on New York City's Lower East Side', *Journal of Sociolinguistics*, 13 (5): 634–658.

Bélanger, E. and M. Verkuyten (2010), 'Hyphenated identities and acculturation: Second-generation Chinese of Canada and the Netherlands', *Identity: An International Journal of Theory and Research*, 10 (3): 141–163.

Bell, A. (1984) 'Language style as audience design', *Language in Society*, 13: 145–204.

Bell, A. (1999), 'Styling the other to define the self: A study in New Zealand identity making', *Journal of Sociolinguistics*, 3: 523–541.

Bem, S. L. (1993), *The Lenses of Gender: Transforming the Debate on Sexual Inequality*, New Haven, CT: Yale University Press.

Benor S. (2001), 'Sounding Learned: The Gendered Use of /t/ in Orthodox Jewish English', in D. E Johnson and T. Sanchez (eds), *Penn Working Papers in Linguistics: Selected Papers from NWAV 29*, 1–16, Philadelphia: University of Pennsylvania.

Benor, S. B. (2010), 'Ethnolinguistic repertoire: Shifting the analytic focus in language and ethnicity', *Journal of Sociolinguistics*, 14 (2): 159–183.

Benwell, B. and E. Stokoe (2006), *Discourse and Identity*, Edinburgh: Edinburgh University Press.

Berger, P. and T. Luckmann (1967), *The Social Construction of Reality*, Harmondsworth: Penguin.

Bergvall, V. L., J. M. Bing and A. Freed, eds (2016), *Rethinking Language and Gender Research: Theory and Practice*, London/New York: Routledge.

Beswick, J. (2014), 'Borders within Borders: Contexts of Language Use and Local Identity Configuration in Southern Galicia', in D. Watt and C. Llamas (eds), *Language, Borders and Identity*, 105–117, Edinburgh: Edinburgh University Press.

Bhabha, H. (1990), 'The Third Space', in J. Rutherford (ed.), *Identity: Community, Culture, Difference*, 207–221, London: Laurence & Wishart.

Bhabha, H. (1994), *The Location of Culture*, London/New York: Routledge.

Billig, M. (1995), *Banal Nationalism*, London: Sage.

Bing, J. M. and V. L. Bergvall (2016), 'The Question of Questions: Beyond Binary Thinking', in V. L. Bergvall, J. M. Bing and A. Freed (eds), *Rethinking Language and Gender Research: Theory and Practice*, 1–30, London/New York: Routledge.

Block, D. (2007), *Second Language Identities*. London: Continuum.

Blommaert, J. (2005), *Discourse: A Critical Introduction*, Cambridge: Cambridge University Press.

Blommaert, J. (2010), *The Sociolinguistics of Globalisation*, Cambridge: Cambridge University Press.

Blommaert, J. and B. Rampton (2012), 'Language and superdiversity', *Diversities*, 13 (2): 1–21. (UNESCO).

Blumer, H. (1969), *Symbolic Interactionism: Perspective and Method*, Englewood Cliffs. NJ: Prentice Hall.

Bodine, A. (1975), 'Androcentrism in prescriptive grammar: Singular "they", sex-indefinite "he", and "he or she"', *Language in Society*, 4 (2): 129–146.

Bolonyai, A. (2005), 'Who was the best? Power, knowledge and rationality in bilingual girls' code choices', *Journal of Sociolinguistics*, 9 (1): 3–27.

Bordo, S. (1993), *Unbearable Weight: Feminism, Western Culture, and the Body*, Berkeley: University of California Press.

Borod, J. C., L. H. Pick, F. Andelman, L. K. Obler, J. Welkowitz and K. D. Rorie (2000), 'Verbal pragmatics following unilateral stroke: Emotional content and valence', *Neuropsychology*, 34 (5): 351–359.

Bourdieu, P. (1977), *Outline of a Theory of Practice*, Cambridge: Cambridge University Press.

Bourhis, R., H. Giles and D. Rosenthal (1981), 'Notes on the construction of "a subjective vitality questionnaire" for ethnolinguistic groups', *Journal of Multilingual and Multicultural Development*, 2 (2): 145–155.

boyd, D. (2014), *It's Complicated: The Social Lives of Networked Teens*, New Haven, CT: Yale University Press.

Bradley, H. (1993), 'Across the Gender Divide: The Entry of Men into "Women's Jobs"', in C. Williams (ed.), *Doing 'Women's Work': Men in Non-Traditional Occupations*, 10–27, London: Sage.

Branson, J., D. Miller, I. J. Marsaja and I. W. Negara (1996), 'Everyone Here Speaks Sign Language, Too: A Deaf Village in Bali, Indonesia', in C. Lucas (ed.), *Multicultural Aspects of Sociolinguistics in Deaf Communities*, 39–57, Washington, DC: Gallaudet University.

Britain, D. (2010), 'Supralocal Regional Dialect Levelling', in C. Llamas and D. Watt (ed.), *Language and Identities*, 193–204, Edinburgh: Edinburgh University Press.

Brown, D. (2006), 'Girls and guys, ghetto and bougie: Metapragmatics, ideology and the management of social identities', *Journal of Sociolinguistics*, 10 (5): 596–610.

Brown, I. and I. Sachdev (2009), 'Bilingual behavior, attitudes, identity and vitality: Some data from Japanese speakers in London, UK', *Journal of Multilingual and Multicultural Development*, 30 (4): 327–343.

Brubaker, R. (2004), *Ethnicity without Groups*, Harvard, MA: Harvard University Press.

Brubaker, R. and F. Cooper (2000), 'Beyond "identity"', *Theory & Society*, 29: 1–47.

Brueggemann, B. J. (2008), 'Think-Between: A Deaf Studies Commonplace Book', in H.-D. Bauman (ed.), *Open Your Eyes: Deaf Studies Talking*, 177–188, Minneapolis: University of Minnesota Press.

Brueggemann, B. J. (2009), *Deaf Subjects: Between Identities and Place*, New York: New York University Press.

Brumfitt, S. (1993), 'Losing your sense of self: What aphasia can do', *Aphasiology*, 7: 569–574.

Bucholtz, M. (1996), 'Geek the Girl: Language, Femininity and Female Nerds', in N. Warner, J. Ahlers, L. Bilmes, M. Oliver, S. Wertheim and M. Chen (eds), *Gender and Belief Systems*, 119–131, Berkeley, CA: Berkeley Women Language Group.

Bucholtz, M. (1999a), 'You da man: Narrating the racial other in the production of white masculinity', *Journal of Sociolinguistics*, 3: 443–460.

Bucholtz, M. (1999b), '"Why be normal?": Language and identity practices in a community of nerd girls', *Language in Society*, 28: 203–223.

Bucholtz, M. (2002), 'Geek Feminism', in S. Benor, M. Rose, D. Sharma, J. Sweetland and Qing Zhang (eds), *Gendered Practices in Language*, 277–307, Stanford CA: Center for the Study of Language and Information.

Bucholtz, M. (2003), 'Sociolinguistic nostalgia and the authentication of identity', *Journal of Sociolinguistics*, 7: 398–416.

Bucholtz, M. (2004), 'Styles and stereotypes: The linguistic negotiation of identity among Laotian American youth', *Pragmatics* 14 (2/3): 127–147.

Bucholtz, M. (2007), 'Word up: Social meanings of slang in California Youth Culture', in L. Monaghan and J. E. Goodman (eds), *A Cultural Approach to Interpersonal Communication. Essential Readings*, 243–267, Oxford: Blackwell.

Bucholtz, M. (2011), *White Kids: Language, Race and Styles of Youth Identity*, Cambridge: Cambridge University Press.

Bucholtz, M. and K. Hall (2004), 'Theorising identity in language and sexuality research', *Language in Society*, 33: 469–515.

Bucholtz, M. and K. Hall (2005), 'Identity and interaction: A sociocultural linguistic approach', *Discourse Studies*, 7 (4–5): 585–614.

Bucholtz, M. and K. Hall (2006), 'Language and Identity', in A. Duranti (ed.), *A Companion to Linguistic Anthropology*, 369–394, Oxford: Blackwell.

Bury, M. (1982), 'Chronic illness as biographical disruption', *Sociology of Health and Illness*, 4: 167–182.

Butler, J. (1990), *Gender Trouble: Feminism and the Subversion of Identity*, New York: Routledge.

Butler, J. (1993), *Bodies That Matter*, New York: Routledge.

Butters, R. R. (2008), 'Trademarks and Other Propriety Terms', in J. Gibbons and M. Turell (eds), *Dimensions of Forensic Linguistics*, 231–247, London: John Benjamins.

Butters, R. R. (2010), 'Trademark Linguistics. Trademarks: Language That One Owns', in M. Coulthard and A. Johnson (eds), *The Routledge Handbook of Forensic Linguistics*, 351–364, London: Routledge.

Cameron, D. (2002), *Good to Talk*, London: Sage.

Cameron, D. (2005), 'Language, gender, and sexuality: Current issues and new directions', *Applied Linguistics*, 26 (4): 482–502.

Cameron, D. (1997/2011), 'Performing Gender Identity: Young Men's Talk and the Construction of Heterosexual Masculinity', in J. Coates and P. Pichler (eds), *Language and Gender: A Reader*, 2nd edn, 250–262, Oxford: Wiley-Blackwell.

Cameron, D. and D. Kulick (2003), *Language and Sexuality*, Cambridge: Cambridge University Press.

Cameron, D. and D. Kulick (2005), 'Identity crisis?', *Language & Communication*, 25: 107–125.

Cameron, D. and J. Coates (1989), 'Some Problems in the Sociolinguistic Explanation of Sex Differences', in J. Coates and D. Cameron (eds), *Women in Their Speech Communities*, 13–26, New York: Longman.

Campbell, S. and C. Roberts (2007), 'Migration, ethnicity and competing discourses in the job interview: Synthesizing the institutional and personal', *Discourse & Society* 18 (3): 243–271.

Campbell-Kibler, K. (2012), 'The implicit association test and sociolinguistic meaning', *Lingua* 122 (7): 753–763.

Campbell-Kibler, K., P. Eckert, N. Mendoza-Denton and E. Moore (2006), 'The elements of style', Poster presented at New Ways of Analysing Variation 35, Columbus.

Candlin, C. N. and S. Sarangi (eds) (2011), *Handbook of Communication in Organisations and Professions*, Vol. 3, Berlin: Walter de Gruyter.

Canter, D. (1992), 'An evaluation of the CUSUM stylistic analysis of confessions', *Expert Evidence*, 1 (2): 93–99.

Cantor, J. B., T. A. Ashman, M. E. Schwartz, W. A. Gordon, M. R. Hibbard, M. Brown, L. Spielman, H. Charatz and Z. Cheng (2005), 'The role of self-discrepancy theory in understanding post-traumatic brain injury affective disorders: A pilot study', *Journal of Head Trauma Rehabilitation*, 20 (6): 527–543.

Carter, P. M. (2013), 'Shared spaces, shared structures: Latino social formation and African American English in the U.S. south', *Journal of Sociolinguistics*, 17 (1): 66–92.

Carty, B. (2006), 'Comments on "w(h)ither the deaf community"', *Sign Language Studies*, 6 (2): 181–189.

Cary-Lemon, J. (2010), '"We're not ethnic, we're Irish!": Oral histories and the discursive construction of immigrant identity', *Discourse & Society*, 21 (1): 5–25.

Castelle, G. (2003), 'Misunderstanding, Wrongful Convictions and Deaf People', in C. Lucas (ed.), *Language and the Law in Deaf Communities*, 168–176, Washington, DC: Gallaudet University Press.

Chaemsaithong, K. (2012), 'Performing self on the witness stand: Stance and relational work in expert witness testimony', *Discourse & Society*, 23 (5): 465–486.

Charmaz, K. (1995), 'The body, identity and self: Adapting to impairment', *The Sociological Quarterly*, 36 (4): 657–680.

Charmaz, K. (2002), 'Stories and silences: Disclosures of self in chronic illness', *Qualitative Inquiry*, 8: 302–328.

Chaski, C. (2001), 'Empirical evaluations of language-based author identification techniques', *Journal of Forensic Linguistics: The International Journal of Speech Language and the Law*, 8 (1):1–65.

Cherny, L. (1994), 'Gender Differences in Text-Based Virtual Reality', in M. Bucholtz, A. C. Liang, L. A. Sutton and C. Hines (eds), *Cultural Performances: Proceedings of the Third Berkeley Women and Language Conference*, 102–115, Berkeley, CA: Berkeley Women and Language Group, University of California.

Chesebro, J. (ed.) (1981), *Gayspeak: Gay Male and Lesbian Communication*, New York: Pilgrim Press.

Cheshire, J. (1978), 'Present Tense Verbs in Reading English', in P. Trudgill (ed.), *Sociolinguistic Patterns in British English*, 52–68, London: Edward Arnold.

Cheshire, J., P. Kerswill and S. Fox (2011), 'Contact, the feature pool and the speech community: The emergence of multicultural London English', *Journal of Sociolinguistics*, 15 (2): 151–196.

Cheshire, J., S. Fox, P. Kerswill and E. Torgersen (2008), 'Ethnicity, friendship network and social practices as the motor of dialect change: Linguistic innovation in London', *Sociolinguistica*, 22: 1–23.

Chiles, T. (2007), 'The construction of an identity as "mentor" in white collar and academic workplaces: A preliminary analysis', *Journal of Pragmatics*, 39: 730–741.

Chomsky, N. (1975), *Reflections on Language*, New York: Pantheon Books.

Chouliaraki, L. and N. Fairclough (1999), *Discourse in Late Modernity: Rethinking Critical Discourse Analysis*, Edinburgh: Edinburgh University Press.

Christensen, A-L. (1997), 'Communication in relation to self-esteem', *Aphasiology*, 11 (7): 727–734.

Christiansen, M. S. (2015), '"*A ondi queras*": *Ranchero* identity construction by U.S. born Mexicans on Facebook', *Journal of Sociolinguistics*, 19 (5): 688–702.

Chun, E. (2009), 'Speaking like Asian immigrants: Intersections of accommodation and mocking at a U.S. high school', *Pragmatics*, 19 (1): 17–38.

Chun Nam Mak, B., Y. Liu and C. C. Deneen (2012), 'Humor in the workplace: A regulating and coping mechanism in socialization', *Discourse & Communication*, 6 (2): 163–179.

Clifford, B., H. Rathbone and R. Bull (1981), 'The effects of delay on voice recognition accuracy', *Law and Human Behaviour*, 5: 201–208.

Clyne, M. (1994), *Inter-Cultural Communication at Work*, Cambridge: Cambridge University Press.

Clyne, M. (2000), 'Lingua franca and ethnolects in Europe and beyond', *Sociolinguistica*, 14: 83–89.

Coates, J. (1993), *Women, Men and Language*, 2nd edn, Harlow: Longman.

Coates, J. (1996), *Women Talk*, Oxford: Blackwell.

Coates, J. (2001/2011), 'Pushing at the Boundaries: The Expression of Alternative Masculinities', in J. Coates and P. Pichler (eds), *Language and Gender: A Reader*, 2nd edn, 263–274, Oxford: Wiley-Blackwell.

Coates, J. (2003), *Women, Men and Language*, 3rd edn, London: Longman.

Coates, J. and P. Pichler (2011), *Language and Gender*, Oxford: Wiley-Blackwell.

Cohen, P. (1999), *New Ethnicities, Old Racisms*, London: Zed Books.

Cokley, K. (2007), 'Critical issues in the measurement of ethnic and racial identity: A referendum on the state of the field', *Journal of Counseling Psychology*, 54 (3): 224–234.

Connell, R. W. (1987), *Gender and Power: Society, the Person and Sexual Politics*, Stanford, CA: Stanford University Press.

Connell, R. W. (1995), *Masculinities*, Cambridge: Polity Press.

Corona , V. (2012), Globalización, identidades y escuela: lo latino en Barcelona, PhD dissertation, Univeristat Autònoma de Barcelona.

Corona, V., L. Nussbaum and V. Unamuno (2013), 'The emergence of new linguistic repertoires among Barcelona's youth of Latin American origin', *International Journal of Bilingual Education and Bilingualism*, 16 (2): 182–194.

Cotterill, J. (2003), *Language and Power in Court: A Linguistic Analysis of the OJ Simpson Trial*, Basingstoke and New York: Palgrave Macmillan.

Coulthard, M. (2002), 'Whose Voice Is It? Invented and Concealed Dialogue in Written Records of Verbal Evidence Produced by the Police', in J. Cotterill (ed.), *Language in the Legal Process*, 19–34, London: Palgrave.

Coulthard, M. (2004), 'Author identification, idiolect, and linguistics uniqueness', *Applied Linguistics*, 25 (4): 431–447.

Coulthard, M. (2007), 'The linguist as expert witness', *Linguistics and the Human Sciences*, 1 (1): 39–58.

Coulthard, M., and A. Johnson (2007), *Introducing Forensic Linguistics*, London: Routledge.

Coulthard, M., A. Johnson, K. Kredens, and D. Woolls (2010), 'Plagiarism: Four Forensic Linguists' Responses to Suspected Plagiarism', in M. Coulthard and A. Johnson (eds), *The Routledge Handbook of Forensic Linguistics*, 523–538, London: Routledge.

Coupland, N. (2007), *Style: Language Variation and Identity*, Cambridge: Cambridge University Press.

Coupland, N. (2014), 'Wales and Welsh: Boundedness and Peripherality', in D. Watt and C. Llamas (eds), *Language, Borders and Identity*, 137–153, Edinburgh: Edinburgh University Press.

Coupland, N., P. Garrett and H. Bishop (2005), 'Wales Underground: Discursive Frames and Authenticities in Welsh Heritage Tourism Events', in A. Jaworski and A. Pritchard (eds), *Discourse, Communication and Tourism*, 199–222, Clevedon: Channel View.

Crandall, J. (2007), 'An Actor Prepares', *CTheory*, 31: 2–7.

Creese, A., A. Bhatt, N. Bhojani and P. Martin (2006), 'Multicultural, heritage and learner identities in complementary schools', *Language and Education*, 20 (1): 23–43.

Creese, A., and A. Blackledge (2010), 'Translanguaging in the bilingual classroom: A pedagogy for learning and teaching?', *The Modern Language Journal*, 94 (1), 103–115.

Cresswell, J. (2012), 'Including social discourses and experience in research on refugees, race, and ethnicity', *Discourse & Society*, 23 (5): 553–575.

Crichton, J., and T. Koch (2011), 'Narrative Identity and Care: Joint Problematisation in a Study of People Living with Dementia', in C. Candlin and J. Crichton (eds), *Discourses of Deficit*, 101–118, Basingstoke: Palgrave Macmillan.

Cross, S., and B. Bagilhole (2002), '"Girls" jobs for the boys? Men, masculinity and non-traditional occupations', *Gender, Work and Organization*, 9 (2), 204–226.

Cutler, A. (1982), 'Guest Editorial: The Reliability of Speech Error Data', in A. Cutler (ed.), *Slips of the Tongue and Language Production*, 561–582, The Hague: Mouton.

Cutler, C. (1999), 'Yorkville Crossing: White teens, hip hop, and African American English', *Journal of Sociolinguistics*, 3 (4): 428–442.

D'Arcy, A. (2010), 'Quoting ethnicity: Constructing dialogue in Aotearoa/New Zealand', *Journal of Sociolinguistics*, 14 (1): 60–88.

Danet, B. (1998), 'Text as a Mask: Gender, Play and Performance on the Internet', in S. Jones (ed.), *Cyberspace 2.0. Revisiting Computer-Mediated Communication and Community*, 129–158, London: Sage.

Dankovičová, J., J. Gurd, J. Marshall, M. MacMahon, J, Stuart-Smith, J. Coleman and A. Slator (2001), 'Aspects of non-native pronunciation in a case of altered accent following stroke (foreign accent syndrome)', *Clinical Linguistics & Phonetics*, 15: 195–218.

Darvin, R. (2016), 'Language and Identity in the Digital Age', in S. Preece (ed.), *The Routledge Handbook of Language and Identity*, 523–541, Oxford: Routledge.

Darvin, R. and B. Norton (2015), 'Identity and a model of investment in applied linguistics', *Annual Review of Applied Linguistics*, 35: 36–56.

Davies, B. and R. Harré (1990), 'Positioning: The discursive production of selves', *Journal for the Theory of Social Behavior*, 20: 43–63.

Davies, C. E. (2007), 'Language and Identity in Discourse in the American South: Sociolinguistic Repertoire as Expressive Resource in the Presentation of Self', in M. Bamberg, A. De Fina and D. Schiffrin (eds), *Selves and Identities in Narrative and Discourse*, 71–88, Amsterdam: John Benjamins.

Davis, L. (2002), *Bending over Backwards: Disability, Dismodernism and Other Difficult Positions*, New York: New York University Press.

Davydova, O. and K. Heikkinen (2004), 'Produced Finnishness in the Context of Remigration', in V. Puuronen, A. Häkkinen, T. Pylkkänen, et al. (eds), *New Challenges for the Welfare Society*, 176–192, Joensuu, Finland: University of Joensuu. Publications of the Karelian Institute.

De Bot, K., L. Wander and M. Verspoor (2007), 'A Dynamic Systems Theory approach to second language acquisition', *Bilingualism: Language and Cognition*, 10 (1): 7–21.

De Clerck, G. (2010), 'Deaf epistemologies as a critique and alternative to practice of science: An anthropological perspective', *American Annals of the Deaf*, 54 (5): 435–446.

De Fina, A. (2003), *Identity in Narrative: A Study of Immigrant Discourse*, Amsterdam: John Benjamins.

De Fina, A. (2007), 'Code-switching and the construction of ethnic identity in a community of practice', *Language in Society*, 36: 371–392.

De Fina, A. (2010), 'Discourse and Identity', in T. Van Dijk (ed.), *Discourse Studies: A Multidisciplinary Introduction*, 263–282, London: Sage.

Deckert, S. (2010), 'Co-animation of and resistance to the construction of witness, victim and perpetrator identities in forensic interviews with children', *Critical Inquiry in Language Studies*, 7 (2–3): 187–206.

DeFrancisco, V. L. (1991), 'The sounds of silence: How men silence women in marital relations', *Discourse & Society*, 2 (4): 413–423.

Delforge, A. M. (2012), '"Nobody wants to sound like a *provinciano*": The recession of unstressed vowel devoicing in the Spanish of Cusco, Perú', *Journal of Sociolinguistics*, 16 (3): 311–335.

Del-Teso-Raviotto, M. (2008), 'Gender and sexual identity authentication in language use: The case of chat rooms', *Discourse Studies*, 10 (2): 251–270.

Derks B. and N. Ellemers (2016), 'Gender and Social Hierarchies: Introduction and Overview', in K. Faniko, F. Lorenzi-Cioldi, O. Sarrasin and E. Mayor (eds), *Gender and Social Hierarchies*, 1–7, Routledge: London.

Derrida, J. (1976), *Of Grammatology*, Baltimore, MD: John Hopkins University Press.

Descartes, R. (1637/1996), *Discourse on Method and Meditations on First philosophy*, Yale: Yale University Press.

Descartes, R. (1644), *Principles of Philosophy*.

Deumert, A. (2014), 'The Performance of a Ludic Self on Social Network(ing) Sites', in P. Seargeant and C. Tagg (eds), *The Language of Social Media: Identity and community on the Internet*, 23–45, Basingstoke: Palgrave MacMillan.

Dewar, B. K., and F. Gracey (2007), '"Am not was": Cognitive behavioral therapy for adjustment and identity change following herpes simplex encephalitis', *Neuropsychological Rehabilitation*, 17 (4–5): 602–620.

Diener, A. C. and J. Hagen (2010), *Borderlines and Borderlands: Political Oddities at the Edge of the Nation-State*, Lanham, MD: Rowman and Littlefield.

Donnan, H. and T. M. Wilson (2010), *Borderlands: Ethnographic Approaches to Security, Power and Identity*, Lanham, MD: University Press of America.

Doran, M. (2004), 'Negotiating between *Bourge* and *Racaille*: Verlan as Youth Identity Practice in suburban Paris', in A. Pavlenko and A. Blackledge (eds), *Negotiation of Identities in Multilingual Contexts*, 93–124, Clevedon: Multilingual Matters Ltd.

Dorian N. (1994), 'Varieties of variation in a very small place: Social homogeneity, prestige norms, and linguistic variation', *Language*, 70: 631–696.

Dovchin, S. (2015), 'Language, multiple authenticities and social media: The online language practices of university students in Mongolia', *Journal of Sociolinguistics*, 19 (4): 437–459.

Drager, K. (2010), 'Sociophonetic variation in speech perception', *Language and Linguistic Compass*, 4 (7): 473–480.

Drew, P. and J. Heritage (eds) (1992), *Talk at Work: Interaction in Institutional Settings*, Cambridge: Cambridge University Press.

Du Gay, P., J. Evans and P. Redman (2012), *Identity: A Reader*, London: Sage.

Dumanig, F. P., M. K. David and C. Dealwis (2011), 'Conversion narratives and construction of identity among Christians in Malaysia', *Multilingua*, 30: 319–331.

Dyer, J. (2010), 'Migration, National Identity and the Reallocation of Forms', in C. Llamas and D. Watt (eds), *Language and Identities*, 205–216, Edinburgh: Edinburgh University Press.

Eades, D. (1994), 'A Case of Communicative Clash: Aboriginal English and the Legal System', in J. Gibbons (ed.), *Language and the Law*, 234–264, London: Longman.

Eades, D. (1996), 'Legal recognition of cultural differences in communication: The case of Robyn Kina', *Language and Communication*, 16 (3): 215–227.

Eades, D. (2005), 'Applied linguistics and language analysis in asylum seeker cases', *Applied Linguistics*, 26 (4): 503–526.

Eades, D. (2007), 'Understanding Aboriginal Silence in Legal Contexts', in H. Kotthoff and H. Spencer-Oatey (eds), *Handbook of Intercultural Communication*, 285–301, Berlin: Mouton de Gruyter.

Eades, D. (2008), 'Language and Disadvantage before the Law', in J. Gibbons and M. Turell (eds), *Dimensions of Forensic Linguistics*, 179–195, London: John Benjamins.

Eades, D. (2010), 'Language Analysis and Asylum Cases', in M. Coulthard and A. Johnson (eds), *The Routledge Handbook of Forensic Linguistics*, 411–422, London: Routledge.

Early, M. and B. Norton (2014), 'Revisiting English as medium of instruction in rural African classrooms', *Journal of Multilingual and Multicultural Development*, 35 (7): 1–18.

Eckert, P. (1989), *Jocks and Burnouts: Social Categories and Identity in the High School*, New York: Teachers College Press.

Eckert, P. (2000), *Linguistic Variation as Social Practice: The Linguistic Construction of Identity at Belten High*, Oxford: Blackwell.

Eckert, P. (2002), 'Constructing meaning in sociolinguistic variation'. Paper presented at the Annual Meeting of the American Anthropological Association, New Orleans, Louisiana [accessible at www.standford.edu/~eckert/AAA02.pdf].

Eckert, P. (2004), 'Variation and Sense of Place', in C. Fought (ed.), *Sociolinguistic Variation: Critical Reflections*, 107–118, Oxford: Oxford University Press.

Eckert, P. (2005), 'Stylistic Practice and the Adolescent Social Order', in A. Williams and C. Thurlow (eds), *Talking Adolescence: Perspectives on Communication in the Teenage Year*, 93–110, New York: Peter Lang.

Eckert, P. (2006), 'Communities of Practice', in K. Brown (ed.), *Encyclopedia of language and linguistics*, 2nd edn, 683–685, Amsterdam: Elsevier.

Eckert, P. (2008a), 'Variation and the indexical field', *Journal of Sociolinguistics*, 12: 453–476.

Eckert, P. (2008b), 'Where do ethnolects stop?', *International Journal of Bilingualism*, 12: 25–42.

Eckert, P. (2012), 'Three waves of variation study: The emergence of meaning in the study of sociolinguistic variation', *Annual Review of Anthropology*, 41: 87–100.

Eckert, P. and S. McConnell-Ginet (1992), 'Think practically and look locally: Language and gender as community-based practice', *Annual Review of Anthropology*, 21: 461–490.

Eckert, P. and S. McConnell-Ginet (1999), 'New generalisations and explanations in language and gender research', *Language in Society*, 28: 185–201.

Eckert, P. and S. McConnell-Ginet (2003), *Language and Gender*, Cambridge: Cambridge University Press.

Eckert, P. and J. R. Rickford (eds) (2001), *Style and Sociolinguistic Variation*, Cambridge: Cambridge University Press.

Eckert, P. and E. Wenger (2005), 'Communities of practice in sociolinguistics', *Journal of Sociolinguistics*, 9 (4): 582–589.

Eco, U. (1990), *Travels in Hyper-reality: Essays*, 1st Harvest/HBJ edn, San Diego, CA: Harcourt Brace Jovanovich.

Edley, N. (2001), 'Analysing Masculinity: Interpretative Repertoires, Ideological Dilemmas and Subject Positions', in M. Wetherell, S. Taylor and S. J. Yates (eds), *Discourse as Data: A Guide to Analysis*, 129–228, London: Sage.

Edley, N. and M. Wetherell (1999), 'Imagined futures: Young men's talk about fatherhood and domestic life', *British Journal of Social Psychology*, 38: 181–194.

Edwards, J. (1988), *Language, Society and Identity*, Oxford: Blackwell.

Edwards, J. (1995), *Multilingualism*, London: Penguin.

Edwards, J. (2009), *Language and Identity*, Cambridge: Cambridge University Press.

Edwards, D. and J. Potter (2001), 'Discursive Psychology', in A. W. McHoul and M. Rapley (eds), *How to Analyse Talk in Institutional Settings: A Casebook of Methods*, 31–48, Cambridge: Cambridge University Press.

Edwards, R., S. Ali, C. Caballero and M. Song (eds) (2012), *International Perspectives on Racial and Ethnic Mixedness and Mixing*, London: Routledge.

Ehala, M. (2011), 'Hot and cold ethnicities: Modes of ethnolinguistic vitality', *Journal of Multilingual and Multicultural Development*, 32 (2): 187–200.

Ehala, M. and K. Niglas (2007), 'Empirical evaluation of a mathematical model of ethnolinguistic vitality: The case of Võro', *Journal of Multilingual and Multicultural Development*, 28 (6): 427–444.

Ehala, M. and A. Zabrodskaja (2011), 'The impact of inter-ethnic discordance on subjective vitality perceptions, *Journal of Multilingual and Multicultural Development*, 32 (2): 121–136.

Ehrlich, S. (2006), 'Trial Discourse and Judicial Decision-Making: Constraining the Boundaries of Gendered Identities', in J. Baxter (ed.), *Speaking Out: The Female Voice in Public Contexts*, 139–158, London: Palgrave.

Ellis, S. (2013), 'The Yorkshire ripper enquiry: Part I', *International Journal of Speech Language and the Law*, 1 (2): 197–206.

Ellis-Hill, C. S. and S. Horn (2000), 'Change in identity and self-concept: A new theoretical approach to recovery following a stroke', *Clinical Rehabilitation*, 14: 279–287.

Ellis-Hill, C. S., S. Payne and C. Ward (2000), 'Self-body split: Issues of identity in physical recovery following a stroke', *Disability and Rehabilitation*, 22 (16): 725–733.

Eriksen, T. H. (2001), 'Ethnic Identity, National Identity and Intergroup Conflict: The Significance of Personal Experiences', in L. A. Jussim (ed.), *Social Identity, Intergroup Conflict and Conflict Reduction*, 42–70, Oxford: Oxford University Press.

Eriksen, T. H. (2010), 'Ethnicity, Race and Nation', in M. Guibernau and J. Rex (eds), *The Ethnicity Reader: Nationalism, Multiculturalism and Migration*, 46–53, Cambridge: Polity Press.

Erikson, E. (1980), *Identity and the Life Cycle*, London: Norton.

Eriksson, A. (2010), 'The Disguised Voice: Imitating Accents or Speech Styles and Impersonating Individuals', in C. Llamas and D. Watt (eds), *Language and Identities*, 86–96, Edinburgh: Edinburgh University Press.

Erting, C. (1978), 'Language policy and Deaf ethnicity in the United States', *Sign Language Studies*, 19, 139–152.

Evans, D. (2015), *Language and Identity*, London: Bloomsbury.

Fairclough, N. (1989/2014), *Language and Power*, Abingdon: Routledge.

Fairclough, N. (1995), *Critical Discourse Analysis: The Critical Study of Language*, Essex: Longman.

Fairclough, N. (2001) 'Critical Discourse Analysis as a Method in Social Scientific Research', in R. Wodak and M. Meyer (eds), *Methods of Critical Discourse Analysis*, 121–138, London: Sage.

Farringdon, J. M. (1996), *Analysing for Authorship: A Guide to the Cusum Technique*, Cardiff: University of Wales Press.

Felton Rosulek, L. (2009), 'The sociolinguistic creation of opposing representations of defendants and victims', *The International Journal of Speech, Language and the Law*, 16 (1): 1–30.

Felton Rosulek, L. (2010), 'Prosecution and Defense Closing Speeches: The Creation of Contrastive Closing Arguments', in M. Coulthard and A. Johnson (eds), *The Routledge Handbook of Forensic Linguistics*, 218–230, London: Routledge.

Figgou, L. and S. Condor (2007), 'Categorising category labels in interview accounts about the "Muslim Minority" in Greece', *Journal of Ethnic and Migration Studies*, 33: 439–359.

Findlay, M., S. Odgers and S. Yeo (2005), *Australian Criminal Justice*, Oxford: Oxford University Press.

Fishman, P. (1980), 'Conversational insecurity', *Language: Social psychological perspectives*, 127–132.

Fishman, P. (1983), 'Interaction: The Work Women Do', in B. Thorne, C. Kramarae and N. Henley (eds), *Language, Gender and Society*, 89–102, Rowley, MA: Newbury House.

Fishman, P. (1990), 'Conversational Insecurity', in D. Cameron (ed.), *The Feminist Critique of Language: A Reader*, 234–250, New York: Routledge.

Foster, D. (2001), *Author Unknown: On the Trail of Anonymous*, London: Macmillan.

Foster, S. and W. Kinuthia (2003), 'Deaf persons of Asian American, Hispanic American, and African American backgrounds: A study of intraindividual diversity and identity', *Journal of Deaf Studies and Deaf Education*, 8 (3): 271–290.

Foucault, M. (1986), 'Of other spaces', *Diacritics* 16, 22–27.

Fought, C. (2003), *Chicano English in Context*, New York: Palgrave Macmillan.

Fought, C. (2006), *Language and Ethnicity*, Cambridge: Cambridge University Press.

Fozdar, F. and Z. Rocha (eds) (2017), *"Mixed Race" in Asia*, London: Routledge.

Fox, S. (2007), *The Demise of Cockneys? Language Change in London's East End*, PhD thesis, University of Essex, UK.

Fox, S. (2010), 'Ethnicity, Religion and Practices: Adolescents in the East End of London', in C. Llamas and D. Watt (eds), *Language and Identities*, 144–156, Edinburgh: Edinburgh University Press.

Francis, B., and C. Skelton (2001), 'Men teachers and the construction of heterosexual masculinity in the classroom', *Sex Education*, 1 (1), 9–21.

Frantzekou, G., S. Gritzalis and S. MacDonell (2004), 'Source code authorship analysis for supporting the cybercrime investigation process', in *Proceedings of the 1st International Conference on E-Business and Telecommunication Networks*, 85–92, Setúbal, Portugal, INSTICC Press.

Fraser, H. (2009), 'The role of "educated native speakers" in providing language analysis for the determination of the origin of asylum seekers', *The International Journal of Speech, Language and the Law*, 16 (1): 113–138.

French, J. P. and P. Harrison (2006), 'Investigative and Evidential Applications of Forensic Speech Science', in A. Heaton-Armstrong, E. Shepherd, G. H. Gudjonsson and D. Wolchover (eds), *Witness Testimony: Psychological Investigative and Evidential Perspectives*, 247–262, Oxford: Oxford University Press.

Freud, S. (1920/2015), *Beyond the Pleasure Principle*, New York Dover.

Freud, S. (1923/2010), *The Ego and the Id*, Seattle, WA: Pacific Publishing Studio.

Fullwood, C., N. Morris and L. Evans (2011), 'Linguistic androgyny on MySpace', *Journal of Language and Social Psychology*, 30 (1): 114–124.

Gao, S. (2012), 'Commodification of place, consumption of identity: The sociolinguistic construction of a "global village" in rural China', *Journal of Sociolinguistics*, 16 (3): 336–357.

García, O. and Li Wei (2014), *Translanguaging: Language, Bilingualism and Education*, Basingstoke: Palgrave Macmillan.

Gardner-Chloros, P. (2014), 'Language, Diversity and Contact', in Li Wei (ed.), *Applied Linguistics*, 151–171, Oxford: Wiley Blackwell.

Gardner-Chloros, P., M. Secova, and F. Atangana (forthcoming), ' "*Il parle normal, il parle comme nous*": Self-Reported Usage and Attitudes in a *banlieue*', in J. Cheshire and P. Gardner-Chloros (eds), *Special Issue, Journal of French Language Studies (JFLS): Language Innovation and Change in Paris*.

Garfinkel, H. (1967), *Studies in Ethnomethodology*, Englewood Cliffs, NJ: Prentice Hall.

Georgakopoulou, A. (2007), *Small stories, interaction and identity*, Amsterdam: John Benjamins.

Georgakopoulou, A. (2008), ' "On MSN with buff boys": Self- and other-identity claims in the context of small stories', *Journal of Sociolinguistics*, 12 (5): 597–626.

Georgakopoulou, A. (2013), 'Small stories research and social media practices: Narrative stancetaking and circulation in a Greek news story', *Sociolinguistica*, 27 (1): 19–36.

Geyer, N. (2008), *Discourse and Politeness: Ambivalent Face in Japanese*, London: Continuum.

Gianettoni, L. and E. Guilley (2016), 'Sexism and the Gendering of Professional Aspirations', in K. Faniko, F. Lorenzi-Cioldi, O. Sarrasin and E. Mayor (eds), *Gender and Social Hierarchies*, 11–25, London: Routledge.

Gibbons, J. (2003), *Forensic Linguistics: An Introduction to Language in the Justice System*, Oxford: Blackwell.

Giddens, A. (1987), *Social Theory and Modern Sociology*, Stanford, CA: Stanford University Press.

Giddens, A. (1991), *Modernity and Self Identity: Self and Society in the Late Modern Age*, Cambridge: Polity Press.

Giergerich, H. (1992) *English Phonology*, Cambridge: Cambridge University Press.

Giles, H. and T. Ogay (2007), 'Communication Accommodation Theory', in B.B. Whaley and W. Samter (eds), *Explaining Communication: Contemporary Theories and Exemplars*, 293–310, Mahwah, NJ: Lawrence Erlbaum.

Giles, H., R. Bourhis and D. Taylor (1977), 'Toward a Theory of Language in Ethnic Group Telations', in H. Giles (ed.), *Language, Ethnicity and Intergroup Relations*, 307–348, New York: Academic Press.

Giles, H., N. Coupland and J. Coupland (1991), 'Accommodation theory: Communication, context and consequence', *Contexts of Accommodation: Developments in Applied Sociolinguistics*, 1–68.

Giles, H., K. Noels, H. Ota, S. Hung Ng, C. Gallois, E. Ryan, A. Williams, L. Tae-Seop, L. Somera, H. Tao and I. Sachdev (2000), 'Age vitality across eleven nations', *Journal of Multilingual and Multicultural Development*, 21 (4): 308–324.

Glickman, N. (1996), 'The Development of Culturally Deaf Identities', in N. Glickman and M. Harvey (eds), *Culturally Affirmative Psychotherapy with Deaf Persons*, 115–153, Abingdon: Routledge.

Goffman, E. (1959), *The Presentation of Self in Everyday Life*, Garden City, NY: Doubleday.

Goffman, E. (1967/2004), 'On Face-Work: An Analysis of Ritual Elements in Social Interaction', reprinted in A. Jaworski and N. Coupland (eds), *The Discourse Reader*, 299–310, London: Routledge.

Goffman, E. (1974), *Frame Analysis*, Boston, MA: Northeastern University Press.

Goffman, E. (1981), *Forms of Talk*, Oxford: Blackwell.

Gogonas, N. (2009), 'Language shift in second generation Albanian immigrants in Greece', *Journal of Multilingual and Multicultural Development*, 30 (2): 95–110.

Goodwin, C. (2004), 'A competent speaker who can't speak: The social life of aphasia', *Journal of Linguistic Anthropology*, 14 (2): 151–170.

Goodwin, C., M. H. Goodwin and D. Olsher (2002), 'Producing Sense with Nonsense Syllables: Turn and Sequence in Conversations with a Man with Severe Aphasia', in C. E. Ford, B. A. Fox and S. A. Thompson (eds), *The Language of Turn and Sequence*, 56–80, Oxford: Oxford University Press.

Gracey, F. and T. Ownsworth (2012), 'The Experience of Self in the World: The Personal and Social Contexts of Identity Change after Brain Injury', in J. J. Haslam and S. A. Haslam (eds), *The Social Cure: Identity, Health and Well-Being*, 273–296, Hove, UK: Psychology Press.

Graf, E-M. (2011), '"Yes Then I Will Tell You Maybe a Little Bit about the Procedure" – Constructing Professional Identity Where There Is Not Yet a Profession: The Case of Executive Coaching', in J. Angouri and M. Marra (eds), *Constructing Identities at Work*, 127–148, Basingstoke: Palgrave MacMillan.

Grant, T. (2008), 'Approaching Questions in Forensic Authorship Analysis', in J. Gibbons and M. Turell (eds), *Dimensions of Forensic Linguistics*, 215–229, London: John Benjamins.

Grant, T. (2012), 'TXT 4N6: Method, consistency, and distinctiveness in the analysis of SMS text messages', *Journal of Law and Policy*, 21: 467–494.

Grant, T. (2013), 'Txt 4n6: Idiolect Free Authorship Analysis?', in M. Coulthard and A. Johnson (eds), *The Routledge Handbook of Forensic Linguistics*, 508–522, London: Routledge.

Grant, T. (2017), 'Duppying yoots in a dog eat dog world, kmt: Determining the senses of slang terms for the Courts', *Semiotica*, 216: 479–495.

Grant, T. and N. Macleod (2016), 'Assuming identities online: Experimental linguistics applied to the policing of online paedophile activity', *Applied Linguistics*, 37 (1): 50–70.

Groce, N. (1985), *Everyone Here Spoke Sign Language*, Cambridge, MA: Harvard University Press.

Grosjean, F. (2010), Bilingualism, biculturalism and deafness, *International Journal of Bilingual Education and Bilingualism*, 13 (2): 133–145.

Gu, M., J. Patkin and A. Kirkpatrick (2014), 'The dynamic identity construction in English as lingua franca intercultural communication: A positioning perspective', *System*, 46: 131–142.

Guiller, J. and A. Durndell (2007), 'Students' linguistic behaviour in online discussion groups: does gender matter?', *Computers in Human Behaviour*, 23 (5): 2240–2255.

Guise, J., A. McKinlay and S. Widdicombe (2010), 'The impact of early stroke on identity: A discourse analytic study', *Health: An Interdisciplinary Journal for the Social Study of Health, Illness and Medicine*, 14 (1): 75–90.

Guise, J., S. Widdicombe and A. McKinlay (2007), '"What's it like to have ME?" The discursive construction of ME in computer-mediated communication and face-to-face interaction', *Health*, 11: 87–108.

Gumperz, J. J. (1982), *Discourse Strategies*, Cambridge: Cambridge University Press.

Günther, S. (2013), 'Communicative Practices among Migrant Youth in Germany: 'Insulting Address Forms' as a Multi-Functional activity', in G. Du Bois and N. Baumgarten (eds), *Multilingual Identities: New Global Perspectives*, 15–34, Oxford: Peter Lang.

Gurd, J., J. Coleman, A. Costello and J. Marshall (2001), 'Organic or functional? A new case of foreign accent syndrome', *Cortex*, 37: 715–718.

Hall, K. (1995), 'Lip Service on the Fantasy Lines', in K. Hall and M. Bucholtz (eds), *Gender Articulated Language and the Socially Constructed Self*, 183–216, London: Routledge.

Hall, K. (2003), 'Exceptional Speakers: Contested and Problemitised Gender Identities', in J. Holmes and M. Meyerhoff (eds), *The Handbook of Language and Gender*, 353–380, Oxford: Blackwell.

Hall, K. (2009/2011), '"Boys" Talk: Hindi, Moustaches and Masculinity in New Delhi," in J. Coates and P. Pichler (eds), *Language and Gender: A Reader*, 2nd edn, 384–400, Oxford: Wiley-Blackwell.

Hall, K. and V. O'Donovan (1996/2016), 'Shifting Gender Positions among Hindi-Speaking Hijras', in V. Bergvall, J. Bing and A. Freed (eds), *Rethinking Language and Gender Research: Theory and Practice*, 228–266, London: Routledge.

Hall, S. (1988), *New Ethnicities*, ICA Document 7, London: ICA.

Hall, S. (1990), 'Cultural Identity & Diaspora', in J. Rutherford (ed.), *Identity: Community, Culture, Difference*, 222–237, London: Laurence & Wishart.

Hall, S. (1996/2012), 'Who Needs "Identity"?', in P. du Gay, J. Evans and P. Redman (eds), *Identity: A Reader*, 15–30, London: Sage.

Handford, M. (2010), *The Language of Business Meetings*, Cambridge: Cambridge University Press.

Hardaker, C. and M. McGlashan (2016), '"Real men don't hate women": Twitter rape threats and group identity', *Journal of Pragmatics*, 91: 80–93.

Harding, T. (2007), 'The construction of men who are nurses as gay', *Journal of Advanced Nursing*, 60: 636–644.

Harré, R. (2000), *One Thousand Years of Philosophy*, Oxford: Blackwell.

Harrington, K., L. Litosseliti, H. Sauntson and J. Sunderland (eds) (2008), *Gender and Language Research Methodologies*, Basingstoke: Palgrave Macmillan.

Hatipoğlu, Ç. (2007), '(Im)politeness, national and professional identities and context: Some evidence from e-mailed "Call for Papers"', *Journal of Pragmatics*, 39: 760–773.

Hatoss, A. (2012), 'Where are you from? Identity construction and experiences of "othering" in the narratives of Sudanese refugee-background Australians', *Discourse & Society*, 23 (1): 47–68.

Hatoss, A. and T. Sheely (2009), 'Language maintenance and identity among Sudanese-Australian refugee-background youth', *Journal of Multilingual and Multicultural Development*, 30 (2): 127–144.

Hazan, K. (2002), 'Identity and language variation in a rural community', *Language*, 78 (2): 240–257.

Hazel, S. (2015), 'Identities at odds: Embedded and implicit language policing in the internationalized workplace', *Language and Intercultural Communication*, 15 (1): 141–160.

Heffer, C. (2005), *The Language of Jury Trial: A Corpus-Aided Analysis of Legal-Lay Discourse*, Basingstoke: Palgrave Macmillan.

Heller, M. (1999), *Linguistic Minorities and Modernity*, London: Longman.

Heller, M. (2003), 'Globalisation, the new economy and the commodification of language and identity', *Journal of Sociolinguistics*, 14: 504–524.

Heller, M. (2008), 'Language and nation-state: Challenges to sociolinguistic theory and practice', *Journal of Sociolinguistics*, 12 (4): 504–524.

Heller, M., A. Jaworski and C. Thurlow (eds) (2014), 'Introduction: Sociolinguistics and tourism – mobilities, markets and multilingualism', *Journal of Sociolinguistics*, 18 (4): 425–458.

Herring, S. C. (1996), 'Two Variants of an Electronic Message Schema', in S. C. Herring (ed.), *Computer-Mediated Communication: Linguistic, Social and Cross-Cultural perspectives*, 81–106, Amsterdam: John Benjamins.

Herring, S. C. (2003), 'Gender and Power in Online Communication', in J. Holmes and M. Meyerhoff (eds), *The Handbook of Language and Gender*, 202–228, Oxford: Blackwell.

Herring, S. C. and J. C. Paolillo (2006), 'Gender and genre variation in weblogs', *Journal of Sociolinguistics*, 10: 439–459.

Herring, S., D. Johnson and T. DiBenedetto (1995), '"This Discussion Is Going Too Far!" Male Resistance to Female Participation on the Internet', in K. Hall and M. Bucholtz (eds), *Gender Articulated: Language and the Socially Constructed Self*, 67–96, New York: Routledge.

Herring, S. C. and S. Stoerger (2014), 'Gender and (A)nonymity in Computer-Mediated Communication', in S. Ehrlich, M. Meyerhoff and J. Holmes (eds), *The Handbook of Language, Gender and Sexuality*, 2nd edn, 567–586, Chichester, UK: Wiley & Sons.

Herring, S. C. and A. Zelenkauskaite (2009), 'Symbolic capital in a virtual heterosexual market', *Written Communication*, 26 (1): 5–31.

Higgins, E. T. (1987), 'Self-discrepancy: A theory relating self and affect', *Psychological Review*, 94(3): 319.

Hill, C. S. (1997), 'Biographical disruption, narrative and identity in stroke: Personal experience in acquired chronic illness', *Auto/Biography*, 5: 131–144.

Hjelmquist, E. (1984), 'Memory for conversations', *Discourse Processes*, 7: 321–336.

Hjelmquist, E. and A. Gidlung (1985), 'Free recall of conversations', *Text*, 3: 169–186.

Ho, V. (2010), 'Constructing identities through request e-mail discourse', *Journal of Pragmatics*, 42: 2253–2261.

Hobbs, P. (2003), 'Is that what we're here about?: A lawyer's use of impression management in a closing argument at trial', *Discourse and Society*, 14 (3): 273–290.

Hobbs, P. (2007), 'Extraterritoriality and extralegality: The United States Supreme Court and Guantanamo Bay', *Text & Talk - An Interdisciplinary Journal of Language, Discourse Communication Studies*, 27 (2): 171–200.

Hobbs, P. (2008), 'It's not what you say but how you say it: The role of personality and identity in trial success', *Critical Discourse Studies*, 5 (3): 231–248.

Hobsbawn, E. (1990), *Nations and Nationalism since 1760*, Cambridge: Cambridge University Press.

Hogg, M., P. d'Agata and D. Abrams (1989), 'Ethnolinguistic betrayal and speaker evaluations among Italian Australians', *Genetic, Social and General Psychology Monographs*, 115: 153–181.

Holland, A. L. and P. M. Beeson (1993), 'Finding a new sense of self: why, who and how?', *Aphasiology*, 7: 581–583.

Hollien, H., G. T. Bennet and M. P. Gelfer (1983), 'Criminal identification comparison: Aural vs. visual identifications resulting from a simulated crime', *Journal of Forensic Science*, 28: 208–221.

Holmes, J. (1986), 'Functions of "you know" in women's and men's speech', *Language in Society*, 15 (1): 1–22.

Holmes, J. (1990), 'Hedges and boosters in women's and men's speech', *Language and Communication*, 10 (3): 185–206.

Holmes, J. (1995), *Women, Men and Politeness*, London: Longman.

Holmes, J. (2006), 'Sharing a laugh: Pragmatic aspects of humor and gender in the workplace', *Journal of Pragmatics*, 38: 26–50.

Holmes, J. (2007/2011), 'Social Constructionism, Postmodernism and Feminist Sociolinguistics', in J. Coates and P. Pichler (eds), *Language and Gender: A Reader*, 2nd edn, 600–610, Oxford: Wiley-Blackwell.

Holmes, J. and M. Marra (2011), 'Harnessing storytelling as a sociopragmatic skill: Applying narrative research to workplace English courses', *TESOL Quarterly*, 45 (3): 510–534.

Holmes, J. and M. Meyerhoff (1999), 'The community of practice: Theories and methodologies in language and gender research', *Language in Society* 28 (2): 173–183.

Holmes, J. and S. Schnurr (2006), 'Doing "femininity" at work: More than just relational practice', *Journal of Sociolinguistics*, 10 (1): 31–51.

Holmes, J., S. Schnurr and M. Marra (2007), 'Leadership and communication: Discursive evidence of a workplace culture change', *Discourse & Communication*, 1 (4): 433–451.

Holmes, J., M. Stubbe and B. Vine (1999), 'Constructing Professional Identity: "Doing Power" in Policy Units', in S. Sarangi and C. Roberts (eds), *Talk, Work and Institutional Order: Discourse in Medical, Mediation and Management Settings*, 351–385, Berlin and New York: Mouton de Gruyter.

Holmes, J., B. Vine and M. Marra (2009), 'Māori men at work: Leadership, discourse and ethnic identity', *Intercultural Pragmatics*, 6 (3): 345–366.

Holmes, J. and J. Woodhams (2013), 'Building interaction: The role of talk in joining a community of practice', *Discourse & Communication*, 7 (3): 275–298.

Hornberger, N. H., and H. Link (2012), 'Translanguaging and transnational literacies in multilingual classrooms: A biliteracy lens', *International Journal of Bilingual Education and Bilingualism*, 15 (3), 261–278.

Horton, S. (2007), 'Topic generation in aphasia language therapy sessions: Issues of identity', *Aphasiology*, 21 (3/4): 283–298.

Horvath, B. (1985), *Variation in Australian English: The Sociolects of Sydney*, Cambridge: Cambridge University Press.

Husband, C. and V. Saifullah Khan (1982), 'The viability of ethnolinguistic vitality: Some creative doubts', *Journal of Multilingual and Multicultural Development*, 3: 193–205.

Hyland, K. (2005), *Metadiscourse*, London: Continuum.

Hyland, K. (2008), 'As can be seen: Lexical bundles and disciplinary variation', *English for Specific Purposes*, 27 (1): 4–21.

Hyland, K. (2010), 'Community and individuality: Performing identity in applied linguistics', *Written Communication*, 27 (2): 159–188.

Ibrahim, A. (1999), 'Becoming black: Rap and hip-hop, race, gender, identity, and the politics of ESL learning', *TESOL Quarterly*, 33 (3): 349–369.

Iedema, R. and H. Scheeres (2003), 'From Doing Work to Talking Work: Renegotiating Knowing, Doing, and Identity', *Applied Linguistics*, 24 (3): 316–337.

Igoudin, A. L. (2013), 'Asian American Girls Who Speak African American English: A Subcultural Language Identity', in G. Du Bois and N. Baumgarten (eds), *Multilingual Identities: New Global Perspectives*, 51–66, Oxford: Peter Lang.

Irvine, J. T. (2001), '"Style" as Distinctiveness: The Culture and Ideology of Linguistic Differentiation', in P. Eckert and J. R. Rickford (eds), *Style and Sociolinguistic Variation*, 21–43, Cambridge: Cambridge University Press.

Irvine, J. T. and S. Gal (2009) 'Language Ideology and Linguistic Differentiation', in A. Duranti (ed.), *Linguistic Anthropology: A Reader*, 402–434, Oxford: Blackwell.

Jacobs-Huey, L. (2006), *From the Kitchen to the Parlor: Language and Becoming in African American Women's Hair Care*, New York: Oxford University Press.

Jacquemet, M. (2009), 'Transcribing refugees: The entextualisation of asylum seekers' hearings in a transidiomatic environment', *Text and Talk*, 29 (5): 525–546.

Jaffe, A. (ed.) (2009a), *Stance: Sociolinguistic Perspectives*, Oxford: Oxford University Press.

Jaffe, A. (2009b), 'Stance in a Corsican School: Institutional and Ideological Orders and the Production of Bilingual Subjects', in A. Jaffe (ed.), *Stance: Sociolinguistic Perspectives*, 119–145, Oxford: Oxford University Press.

Jamal, T. and S. Hill (2002), 'The Home and the World: (Post)touristic Spaces of (In)authenticity?', in G. Dann (ed.), *The Tourist as a Metaphor of the Social World*, 77–108, Wallingford: CABI.

Jaspal, R. and M. Cinirella (2010), 'Coping with potentially incompatible identities: Accounts of religious, ethnic and sexual identities from British Pakistani men who identify as Muslim and gay', *British Journal of Social Psychology*, 49: 1–22.

Jaspers, J. (2008), 'Problematizing ethnolects: Naming linguistics practices in an Antwerp secondary school', *International Journal of Bilingualism*, 12 (1, 2): 85–103.

Jaspers, J. (2011), 'Talking like a "zerolingual": Ambiguous linguistic caricatures at an urban secondary school', *Journal of Pragmatics*, 43: 1264–1278.

Jenkins, R. (2008), *Social Identity*, Abingdon, Oxon: Routledge.

Jespersen, O. (1922), 'The Woman', in D. Cameron (ed.), *The Feminist Critique of Language: A Reader*, 201–220, New York: Routledge.

Jessen, M. (2010), 'The Forensic Phonetician: Forensic Speaker Identification by Experts', in M. Coulthard and A. Johnson (eds), *The Routledge Handbook of Forensic Linguistics*, 378–394, London: Routledge.

Johnson, A. (1997), 'Textual kidnapping – a case of plagiarism among three student texts', *Forensic Linguistics: The International Journal of Speech, Language and the Law*, 4 (2): 210–225.

Johnson, P., H. Giles and R. Bourhis (1983), 'The viability of ethnolinguistic vitality and language attitudes: The Israeli context', *Journal of Multilingual and Multicultural Development*, 4: 225–269.

Johnson, R. E. (1984), 'Sign Language and the Concept of Deafness in a Traditional Yucatec Mayan village', in C. J. Erting, R. E. Johnson, D. L. Smith and B. D. Snider (eds), *The Deaf Way – Perspectives from the International Conference on Deaf Culture 1989*, 102–109, Washington DC: Gallaudet University.

Johnstone, B. (1995), 'Sociolinguistic resources, individual identities and the public speech styles of Texas women', *Journal of Linguistic Anthropology*, 5: 1–20.

Johnstone, B. (1996), *The Linguistic Individual: Self-Expression in Language and Linguistics*, Oxford: Oxford University Press.

Johnstone, B. (1997/2014), 'Southern Speech and Self-Expression in an African-American Woman's Story', in C. Bernstein, T. E. Nunnally and R. Sabino (eds), *Language Variety in the South Revisited*, 87–97. Alabama: University of Alabama Press.

Johnstone, B. (1999), 'Lingual biography and linguistic variation', *Language Sciences*, 21: 313–321.

Johnstone, B. (2000), 'The individual voice in language', *Annual Review of Anthropology*, 29: 405–424.

Johnstone, B. (2004), 'Place, Globalization, and Linguistic Variation', in C. Fought (ed.), *Sociolinguistic Variation: Critical Reflections*, 65–83, Oxford: Oxford University Press.

Johnstone, B. (2009a), 'Pittsburghese shirts: Commodification and the enregisterment of an urban dialect', *American Speech*, 84: 157–175.

Johnstone, B. (2009b), 'Stance, Style and the Linguistic Individual', in A. Jaffe (ed.), *Sociolinguistic Perspectives on Stance*, 29–52, New York: Oxford University Press.

Johnstone, B. (2010), 'Indexing the Local', in N. Coupland (ed.), *The Handbook of Language and Globalisation*, 386–405, Oxford: Wiley-Blackwell.

Johnstone, B. (2011), 'Dialect enregisterment in performance', *Journal of Sociolinguistics*, 15 (5): 657–679.

Johnstone, B. and D. Baumgardt (2004), "Pittsburghese' online: Vernacular norming in conversation', *American Speech*, 79: 115–145.

Johnstone, B. and J. Bean (1997), 'Self-expression and linguistic variation', *Language in Society*, 26: 221–246.

Johnstone, B. and S. Kiesling (2008), 'Indexicality and experience: Exploring the meanings of /aw/-monophthongization in Pittsburgh', *Journal of Sociolinguistics*, 12 (1): 5–13.

Jones, R. H. and C. A. Hafner (2012), *Understanding Digital Literacies: A Practical Introduction*, Abingdon: Routledge.

Joseph, J. E. (2010), *Language and Identity: National, Ethnic, Religious*, Basingstoke: Palgrave Macmillan.

Juzwik, M. and D. Ives (2010), 'Small stories as resources for performing teacher identity: Identity-in-interaction in an urban language arts classroom', *Narrative Inquiry*, 20 (1): 37–61.

Kallen, J. (2014), 'The Political Border and Linguistic Identities in Ireland: What Can the Linguistic Landscape Tell Us?', in D. Watt and C. Llamas (eds), *Language, Borders and Identity*, 154–168, Edinburgh: Edinburgh University Press.

Kamada, L. (2010), *Hybrid Identities and Adolescent Girls*, Bristol: Multilingual Matters.

Kang, Y. (2012), 'Singlish or Globish: Multiple language ideologies and global identities among Korean educational migrants in Singapore', *Journal of Sociolinguistics*, 16 (2): 165–183.

Kaplan, A. and M. Haenlein (2010), 'Users of the world, unite! The challenges and opportunities of social media', *Business Horizons*, 53: 59–68.

Kaplan, J. P., G. M. Green, C. D. Cunningham and J. N. Levi (2013), 'Bringing linguistics into judicial decision making: Semantic analysis submitted to the US Supreme Court', *International Journal of Speech Language and the Law*, 2 (1): 81–98.

Karan, M. (2011) 'Understanding and forecasting ethnolinguistic vitality', *Journal of Multilingual and Multicultural Development*, 32 (2): 137–149.

Kee, A. (2011), *Masters of Suspicion*, London: SCM Press.

Kendall, S. (2008), 'The balancing act: Framing gendered parental identities at dinnertime', *Language in Society*, 37: 539–568.

Kerswill, P. (2013), 'Identity, ethnicity and place: The construction of youth language in London', *Space in Language and Linguistics: Geographical, Interactional, and Cognitive Perspectives (Series: Linguae & Litterae)*, Berlin: de Gruyter.

Kiesling, S. F. (2002/2011), 'Playing the Straight Man: Displaying and Maintaining Male Heterosexuality in Discourse', in J. Coates and P. Pichler (eds), *Language and Gender: A Reader*, 2nd edn, 275–285, Oxford: Wiley-Blackwell.

Kindell, G. and M. P. Lewis (eds) (2000), *Assessing Ethnolinguistic Vitality: Theory and Practice*, Dallas, TX: SIL International.

King, B. (2008), '"Being gay guy, that is the advantage": Queer Korean language learning and identity construction', *Journal of Language, Identity and Education*, 7 (3–4): 230–252.

King, J. F. (2004), 'The Cochlear Implantation of Deaf Children: Unasked and Unanswered Questions', in K. Eldredge, D. Stringha and M. Wilding-Diaz (eds), *Deaf Studies Today: A Kaleidoscope of Knowledge, Learning and Understanding 2004 Conference Proceedings*, 225–232, Utah Valley: Utah Valley State College.

King-O'Riain, R. C., S. Small, M. Mahtani, M. Song and P. Spickard (eds) (2014) *Global Mixed Race*, New York: NYU Press.

Kirkham, S. (2015), 'Intersectionality and the social meanings of variation: Class, ethnicity and social practice', *Language in Society*, 44: 629–652.

Klein, S. and S. Nichols (2012), 'Memory and the sense of personal identity', *Mind*, 121: 677–702.

Koch, S. C., B. Mueller, L. Kruse and J. Zumbach (2005), 'Constructing gender in chat groups', *Sex Roles*, 53 (1/2): 29–41.

Koester, A. (2011), *Investigating Workplace Discourse*, London: Routledge.

Koller, V. (2011), '"Hard-Working, Team-Oriented Individuals": Constructing Professional Identities in Corporate Mission Statements', in J. Angouri and M. Marra (eds), *Constructing Identities at Work*, 103–126, Basingstoke: Palgrave MacMillan.

Komondouros, M. and L. J. McEntee-Atalianis (2007), 'Language attitudes, shift and the ethnolinguistic vitality of the Greek Orthodox community in Istanbul', *Journal of Multilingual and Multicultural Development*, 28 (5): 365–384.

Koven, M. (2002), 'An analysis of speaker role inhabitance in narratives of personal experience', *Journal of Pragmatics*, 34: 167–217.

Kram, K., I. Wasserman and J. Yip (2012), 'Metaphors of identity and professional practice: Learning from the scholar-practitioner', *Journal of Applied Behavioral Science*, 48 (3): 304–341.

Kramsch, C. and S. Thorne (2002), 'Foreign Language Learning as Global Communicative Practice', in D. Block and D. Cameron (eds), *Globalisation and Language Teaching*, 83–100, New York: Routledge.

Krzyzanowski, M. (2010), *The Discursive Construction of European Identities: A Multi-Level Approach to Discourse and Identity in the Transforming European Union*, Frankfurt am Main: Peter Lang.

Kulick, D. (2000), 'Gay and lesbian language', *Annual Review of Anthropology*, 29: 243–285.

Kyle, J., B.Woll, G. Pullen and F. Maddox (1985/1998), *Sign Language: The Study of Deaf People and Their Language*, Cambridge: Cambridge University Press.

Labov, W. (1963), 'The social motivation of a sound change', *Word*, 18: 1–42.

Labov,W. (1972a), *Sociolinguistic Patterns*, Philadelphia, PA: University of Pennsylvania Press.

Labov, W. (1972b), *Language in the Inner City: Studies in the Black English Vernacular*, Philadelphia, PA: University of Pennsylvania Press.

Labov, W. (1989), 'Exact Description of the Speech Community: Short A in Philadelphia', in R. Fasold and D. Schiffrin (eds), *Language Change and Variation*, 1–57, Amsterdam: Benjamins.

Labov, W. (1997), http://linguistlist.org/studentportal/linguists/labov.cfm, date downloaded 26 February 2014.

Labov, W., S. Ash and C. Boberg (2006), *The Atlas of North American English*, Berlin: Mouton-de Gruyter.

Labov, W. and W. Harris (1994), 'Addressing Social Issues Through Linguistic Evidence', in J. Gibbons (ed.), *Language and the Law*, 265–305, London: Longman.

Lacan, J. (1977), *Écrits: A Selection*, New York: W. W. Norton.

Lacan, J. (1989/2012), 'The Mirror Stage', in P. du Gay, J. Evans and P. Redman (eds), *Identity: A Reader*, 44–50, London: Sage.

Ladd, P. (2003), *Understanding Deaf Culture: In Search of Deafhood*, Clevedon: Multilingual Matters.

Ladd, P. (2007), 'Cochlear Implantation, Colonialism, and Deaf Rights', in L. Komesaroff (ed.), *Surgical Consent*, 1–29, Washington, DC: Gallaudet University Press.

Ladefoged, P. and J. Ladefoged (1980), 'The ability of listeners to identify voices', *UCLA Working Papers in Phonetics*, 49: 43–51.

Ladegaard, H. J. (2012), 'Rudeness as a discursive strategy in leadership discourse: Culture, power and gender in a Hong Kong workplace', *Journal of Pragmatics*, 44: 1661–1679.

Lakoff, R. (1973), 'Language and woman's place', *Language in Society*, 2 (1): 45–79.

Lakoff, R. (1975), *Language and Woman's Place*, New York: Harper and Row.

Lam, W. S. E. (2000), 'L2 literacy and the design of the self: A case study of a teenager writing on the Internet', *TESOL Quarterly*, 34 (3): 457–482.

Lam, W. S. E. (2006), Re-envisioning language, literacy and the immigrant subject in new mediascapes, *Pedagogies: An International Journal*, 1 (3): 171–195.

Landry, R., R. Allard and J. Henry (1996), 'French in South Louisiana: Towards language loss', *Journal of Multilingual and Multicultural Development*, 17 (6): 442–468.

Lane, H. (1992), *Medicalization of Cultural Deafness in Historical Perspective*, Sign Media.

Lane, H. (1994), 'The cochlear implant controversy', *WFD News*, 2: 22–28.

Lane, H. (2005), 'Ethnicity, ethics, and the deaf-world', *Journal of Deaf Studies and Deaf Education*, 10: 291–310.

Lappänen, S., S. Kytölä, H. Jousmäki, S. Peuronen and E. Westinen (2014), 'Entextualisation and Resemiotization as Resources for Identification in Social Media', in P. Seargeant and C. Tagg (eds), *The Language of Social Media: Identity and Community on the Internet*, 112–136, Basingstoke: Palgrave MacMillan.

Lave, J. and E. Wenger (1991), *Situated Learning: Legitimate Peripheral Participation*, Cambridge: Cambridge University Press.

Lazar, M. M. (2005), 'Politicizing Gender in Discourse: Feminist Critical Discourse Analysis as Political Perspective and Praxis', in M. M. Lazar (ed.), *Feminist Critical Discourse Analysis*, 1–30, Basingstoke: Palgrave Macmillan.

Leap, W. (1993), *American Indian English*, Salt Lake City, UT: University of Utah Press.

Lee, C. (2014), 'Language Choice and Self-Presentation in Social Media: The Case of University Students in Hong Kong', in P. Seargeant and C. Tagg (eds), *The Language of Social Media*, 91–111, Basingstoke: Palgrave MacMillan.

Lee, J. (2013), '"You know how tough I am?" Discourse analysis of US Midwestern congresswomen's self-presentation', *Discourse & Communication*, 7 (3): 299–317.

Leigh, I. W. (2009), *A Lens on Deaf Identities: Perspectives on Deafness*, New York: Oxford University Press.

LeMaster, B. (2003), 'School Language and Shifts in Irish Deaf Identity', in L. Monaghan, C. Schmaling, K. Nakamura, and G. Turner (eds), *Many Ways to be Deaf: International Variation in Deaf Communities*, 153–172, Washington, DC: Gallaudet University Press.

Le Page, R. and A. Tabouret-Keller (1985), *Acts of Identity: Creole-Based Approaches to Language and Ethnicity*, Cambridge: Cambridge University Press.

Levi, J. N. (1993), 'Evaluating jury comprehension of the Illinois capital sentencing instructions', *American Speech*, 68 (1): 20–49.

Levon, E. (2007), 'Sexuality in context: Variation and the sociolinguistic perception of identity', *Language in Society*, 36: 533–554.

Levon, E. (2009), 'Dimensions of style: Context, politics and motivation in gay Israeli speech', *Journal of Sociolinguistics*, 13 (1): 29–58.

Levon, E. (2011), 'Teasing apart to bring together: Gender and sexuality in variationist research', *American Speech* 86 (1): 69–84.

Levon, E. (2012), 'The voice of others: Identity, alterity and gender normativity among gay men in Israel', *Language in Society*, 41: 187–211.

Levon, E. (2014), 'The "Ideal Gay Man": Narrating Masculinity and National Identity in Israel', in T. M. Milani (ed.), *Language and Masculinities: Performances, Intersections, Dislocations*, 133–155, Routledge: London.

Levon, E. (2016), 'Conflicted Selves: Language, Religion, and Same-Sex Desire in Israel', in E. Levon and R. B. Mendes (eds), *Language, Sexuality, and Power*, 215–239, Oxford: Oxford University Press.

Levon, E. and R. B. Mendes (2016), *Language, Sexuality, and Power*, Oxford: Oxford University Press.

Lewis, C. and B. Fabos (2005), 'Instant messaging, literacies and social identities', *Reading Research Quarterly*, 40 (4): 470–501.

Li Wei (2011), 'Moment analysis and translanguaging space: Discursive construction of identities by multilingual Chinese youth in Britain', *Journal of Pragmatics*, 43 (5): 1222–1235.

Lindgren, S. (2009), 'Representing otherness in youth crime discourse: Youth robberies and racism in the Swedish Press 1998–2002', *Critical Discourse Studies*, 6: 65–77.

Litosseliti, L. (2006), *Gender & Language: Theory and Practice*, London: Hodder Education.

Litosseliti, L., and C. Leadbeater (2013), 'Gendered discourses in speech and language therapy', *Journal of Applied Linguistics and Professional Practice*, 8 (3): 295–314.

Litosseliti, L., R. Gill and L. Favaro (under review), 'Post-feminism as a critical tool for gender and language (study)', *Gender and Language*.

Livia, A. (1995) '"I Ought to Throw a Buick at You": Fictional Representations of Butch/Femme Speech', in K. Hall and M. Bucholtz (eds), *Gender Articulated: Language and the Socially Constructed Self*, New York: Routledge.

Livia, A. (2002), 'The Future of Queer Linguistics', in K. Campbell-Kibler, R. J. Podesva, S. J. Roberts and A. Wong (eds), *Language and Sexuality: Contesting Meaning in Theory and Practice*, 85–97, Stanford, CA: CSLI.

Livia, A. and K. Hall (eds) (1997), *Queerly Phrased: Language, Gender and Sexual Politics*, London: Cassell.

Llamas, C. (2001), *Language Variation and Innovation in Teeside English*, Dissertation, University of Leeds.

Llamas, C. (2006), 'Shifting Identities and Orientations in a Border Town', in T. Omoniyi and G. White (eds), *The Sociolinguistics of Identity*, 92–112, London: Continuum.

Llamas, C. (2007), '"A place between places": Language and identities in a border town', *Language in Society*, 36, 579–604.

Llamas, C. (2010), 'Convergence and Divergence across a National Border', in C. Llamas and D. Watt (eds), *Language and Identities*, 227–236, Edinburgh: Edinburgh University Press.

Llamas, C. and D. Watt (2010), *Language and Identities*, Edinburgh: Edinburgh University Press.

Llamas, C., D. Watt and D. E. Johnson (2009), 'Linguistic accommodation and the salience of national identity markers in a border town', *Journal of Language and Social Psychology*, 28 (4): 381–407.

Lo, A. (1999), 'Codeswitching, speech community membership, and the construction of ethnic identity', *Journal of Sociolinguistics*, 3/4: 461–479.

Locher, M. (2008), 'Relational Work, Politeness and Identity Construction', in G. Antos and E. Ventola in cooperation with T. Weber (eds), *Handbook of interpersonal communication*, 509–540, Berlin: Mouton de Gruyter.

Love, H. (2002), *Attributing Authorship: An Introduction*, Cambridge: Cambridge University Press.

Lucchelli, F. and H. Spinnler (2007), 'The case of lost Wilma: A clinical report of Capgras delusion', *Neurological Sciences*, 28: 188–195.

Luchjenbroers, J. and M. Aldridge (2007), 'Conceptual manipulation with metaphors and frames: Dealing with rape victims in legal discourse', *Text and Talk*, 27 (3): 339–359.

Lunde, A. S. (1956), *The Sociology of the Deaf* (Publisher unknown).

Mackay, R. (2003), '"Tell them who I was": The social construction of aphasia', *Disability and Society*, 18: 811–826.

Makoni, S. and A. Pennycook (2007), 'Disinventing and Reconstituting Languages', in S. Makoni and A. Pennycook (eds), *Disinventing and Reconstituting Languages*, 1–41, Clevedon: Multilingual Matters.

Malhi, R. L., S. D. Boon and T. B. Rogers (2009), '"Being Canadian" and "Being Indian": Subject positions and discourses used in South Asian-Canadian women's talk about ethnic identity', *Culture & Psychology*, 15 (2): 255–283.

Maltz, D. and R. Borker (1998), 'A Cultural Approach to Male-Female Miscommunication', in J. Coates (ed.), *Language and Gender: A Reader*, 417–434, Oxford: Blackwell.

Mannheim, B. and Tedlock, D. (1989) 'Introduction', in D. Tedlock and B. Mannheim (eds), *The Dialogic Emergence of Culture*, 1–31, Urbana and Chicago: University of Illinois Press.

Marek, Y. (1998), 'The Philosophy of the French Language Legislation: Internal and International Aspects', in D. A. Kibbee (ed.), *Language Legislation and Linguistic Rights*, 341–350, Amsterdam and Philadelphia, PA: John Benjamins.

Marra, M. and J. Angouri (2011), 'Investigating the Negotiation of Identity: A View from the Field of Workplace Discourse', in J. Angouri and M. Marra (eds), *Constructing Identities at Work*, 1–14, Basingstoke: Palgrave MacMillan.

Marra, M. and J. Holmes (2008) 'Constructing ethnicity in New Zealand workplace stories', *Text & Talk*, 28: 397–419.

Marwick, A. E. and d. boyd (2011), 'I tweet honestly, I tweet passionately: Twitter users, context collapse, and the imagined audience', *New Media and Society*, 13 (1): 114–133.

Mather, S. and R. Mather (2003), 'Court interpreting for signing jurors: Just transmitting or interpreting?', in C. Lucas (ed.), *Language and the Law in Deaf Communities*, 60–81, Washington DC: Gallaudet University Press.

Matoesian, G. (2008), 'You might win the battle but lose the war. Multimodal, interactive and extralinguistic aspects of witness resistance', *Journal of English Linguistics*, 36 (3): 195–219.

Marx, K. (1859/1971), *A Contribution to the Critique of Political Economy*, London: Lawrence Wishart.

Maxwell-McCaw, D. (2001), *Acculturation and Psychological Well-Being in Deaf and Hard-of-Hearing People*, Unpublished doctoral dissertation, Washington, DC: George Washington University.

Maynard, D. W. (1989), 'On the Ethnography and Analysis of Discourse in Institutional Settings', in J. Holstein and G. Miller (eds.), *Perspectives on social problems. A Research Annual*, 127–146, Greenwich: Jai Press.

McCabe, S. (2005), '"Who is a tourist?": A critical review', *Tourist Studies*, 5: 85–106.

McEntee, L. J. (1993), *Morphosyntactic Aspects of Agrammatism*, Unpublished PhD, University of Newcastle upon Tyne.

McEntee, L. J. and M. Kennedy (1995) 'Profiling agrammatic spoken language: Towards a government and binding framework', *European Journal of Disorders of Communication*, 30 (3): 317–332.

McEntee-Atalianis, L. J. (2011a), 'The value of adopting multiple approaches and methodologies in the investigation of Ethnolinguistic Vitality', *Journal of Multilingual and Multicultural Development*, 32 (2): 151–167.

McEntee-Atalianis, L. J. (2011b), 'The role of metaphor in shaping the identity and agenda of the United Nations: The imagining of an international community and international threat', *Discourse and Communication*, 5 (4): 393–412.

McEntee-Atalianis, L. J. (2013a), 'Language, Identity and Power', in Li Wei (ed.), *Applied Linguistics*, 172–190, Oxford: Wiley Blackwell.

McEntee-Atalianis, L. J. (2013b), 'Stance and metaphor: Mapping changing representations of (organisational) identity', *Discourse and Communication*, 7 (3): 319–340.

McEntee-Atalianis, L. J. and F. Zappettini (2014), 'Networked identities: Changing representations of Europeanness, *Critical Discourse Studies*, 11 (4): 397–415.

McEntee-Atalianis, L. J. and L. Litosseliti (2017), 'Narratives of sex-segregated professional identities', *Narrative Inquiry*, 27 (1): 1–23.

McIlroy, G. and C. Storbeck (2011), 'Development of deaf identity: An ethnographic study', *Journal of Deaf Studies and Deaf Education*, 16 (4): 494–511.

McKee, R. L. (2008), 'The construction of deaf children as marginal bilinguals in the mainstream', *International Journal of Bilingual Education and Bilingualism*, 11 (5): 519–540.

McKinlay, A. and C. McVittae (2011a), *Identities in Context: Individuals and Discourse in Action*, Oxford: Wiley-Blackwell.

McKinlay, A. and C. McVittae (2011b), 'Virtual Identities', in A. McKinlay and C. McVittae (eds), *Identities in Context: Individuals and Discourse in Action*, 176–200, Oxford: Wiley-Blackwell.

McMenamin, G. (2002), *Forensic Linguistics: Advances in Forensic Stylistics*, London: CRC Press.

McMenamin, G. R. (1993), *Forensic Stylistics*, London: Elsevier.

McVittae, C., K. Goodall and S. McFarlane (2009), '"Your cuts are just as important as anyone else's": Individuals' online discussions of self-injury', *Health Psychology Update*, 18: 3–7.

Mead, G. (1934), *Mind, Self and Society*. Chicago, IL: Chicago University Press.

Menard-Warwick, J. (2009), *Gendered Identities and Immigrant Language Learning*, Bristol: Multilingual Matters.

Mendoza-Denton, N. (1997), *Chicana/Mexicana Identity and Linguistic Variation: An Ethnographic and Sociolinguistic Study of Gang Affiliation in an Urban High School*, PhD, Stanford University.

Mendoza-Denton, N. (2008), *Homegirls: Language and Cultural Practice among Latina Youth Gangs*, Malden, MA: Wiley-Blackwell.

Mendoza-Denton, N. (2011), 'Individuals and Communities', in R. Wodak, B. Johnstone and P. Kerswill (eds), *The Sage Handbook of Sociolinguistics*, 181–189, London: Sage.

Mendoza-Denton, N. and D. Osborne (2010), 'Two Languages, Two Identities?', in C. Llamas and D. Watt (eds), *Language and Identities*, 113–122, Edinburgh: Edinburgh University Press.

Menn. L. and L. Obler (1985/1989), *Agrammatic Aphasia: A Cross-Language Narrative Resource Book*, Amsterdam/Philadelphia, PA: John Benjamins.

Merino, M-E. and C. Tileagă (2011), 'The construction of ethnic minority identity: A discursive psychological approach to ethnic self-definition in action', *Discourse & Society*, 22 (1): 86–101.

Merino, M-E., S. Becerra and A. De Fina (2017) 'Narrative discourse in the construction of Mapuche ethnic identity in context of displacement', *Discourse & Society*, 28 (1): 60–80.

Merono-Fernàndez, F. (2016), *A Framework for Cognitive Sociolinguistics*, New York/London: Routledge.

Miller, N. (2010), 'Foreign Accent Syndrome: Between Two Worlds, at Home in Neither', in C. Llamas and D. Watt (eds), *Language and Identities*, 67–75, Edinburgh: Edinburgh University Press.

Miller, N., J. Taylor, C. Howe and J. Read (2011), 'Living with foreign accent syndrome: Insider perspectives', *Aphasiology*, 25 (9): 1053–1068.

Mills, S. (2003), *Gender and Politeness*, Cambridge: Cambridge University Press.

Milroy, L. (1980), *Language and Social Networks*, Oxford: Blackwell.

Modan, G. G. (2007), *Turf Wars: Discourse, Diversity and the Politics of Place*, Malden, MA and Oxford: Blackwell.

Moffatt, L. and B. Norton (2008), 'Reading gender relations and sexuality: Preteens speak out', *Canadian Journal of Education*, 31 (3): 102–123.

Monrad-Krohn, G. H. (1947), 'Dysprosody or altered "melody of language"', *Brain* 70: 405–415

Moody, S. (2014), '"Well, I'm a *Gaijin*": Constructing identity through English and humor in the international workplace', *Journal of Pragmatics*, 60: 75–88.

Moore, E. (2003), *Learning Style and Identity: A Sociolinguistic Analysis of a Bolton High School*, PhD, University of Manchester, UK.

Moore, E. (2004), 'Sociolinguistic style: A multidimensional resource for shared identity creation', *The Canadian Journal of Linguistics/La revue canadienne de linguistique*, 49 (3/4): 375–396.

Moore, E. (2010), 'Communities of Practice and Peripherality', in C. Llamas and D. Watt (eds), *Language and Identities*, 123–133, Edinburgh: Edinburgh University Press.

Moore, E. and R. Podesva (2009), 'Style, indexicality, and the social meaning of tag questions', *Language in Society*, 38: 447–485.

Moores, D. F. (2006), 'Comments on "w(h)ither the deaf community"', *Sign Language Studies*, 6 (2): 202–209.

Morris, W. (2008), *Theology without Words: Theology in the Deaf Community*, Ashgate: University of Chester.

Motschenbacher, H. (2013), '"Now everybody can wear a skirt": Linguistic constructions of non-normativity at Eurovision Song Contest press conferences', *Discourse & Society*, 24 (5): 590–614.

Motschenbacher, H. and M. Stegu (2013), 'Queer linguistic approaches to discourse', *Discourse & Society*, 24 (5): 519–535.

Mu, G. M. (2015), 'A meta-analysis of the correlation between heritage language and ethnic identity', *Journal of Multilingual and Multicultural Development*, 36 (3): 239–254.

Mullany, L. (2006), 'Narrative Constructions of Gender and Professional Identities', in T. Omoniyi and G. White (eds.), *Sociolinguistics of Identity*, 157–172, London: Continuum.

Mullany, L. (2007), *Gendered Discourse in the Professional Workplace*, Basingstoke: Palgrave Macmillan.

Mullany, L. (2010), 'Gendered Identities in the Professional Workplace. Negotiating the Glass Ceiling', in C. Llamas and D. Watts (eds), *Language and Identity*, 179–191, Edinburgh: Edinburgh University Press.

Mullany, L. and L. Litosseliti (2006), 'Gender and Language in the Workplace', in L. Litosseliti (ed.), *Gender and Language: Theory and Practice*, 123–147, London: Hodder Arnold.

Murray, C. D. and B. Harrison (2004), 'The meaning and experience of being a stroke survivor: An interpretative phenomenological analysis', *Disability and Rehabilitation*, 26 (13): 808–816.

Murthy, D. (2012), 'Towards a sociological understanding of social media: Theorizing Twitter', *Sociology*, 46 (6): 1059–1073.

Myers, G. (2006), '"Where are you from?": Identifying place", *Journal of Sociolinguistics*, 10 (3): 320–343.

Nakamura, K. (2005), *Deaf in Japan: Signing and the politics of identity*, Ithaca, NY: Cornell University Press.

Negrón, R. (2014), 'New York City's Latino ethnolinguistic repertoire and the negotiation of latinidad in conversation', *Journal of Sociolinguistics*, 18 (1): 87–118.

Nelson, C. (2009), *Sexual Identities in English Language Education: Classroom Conversations*, New York: Routledge.

Newmark, K., N. Walker and J. Standford (2016), '"The rez accent knows no borders": Native American ethnic identity expressed through English prosody', *Language in Society*, 45: 633–664.

Nicholson, L. (1994), 'Interpreting gender', *Signs: Journal of Women in Culture and Society*, 20 (1): 79–105.

Nikolaraizi, M. and K. Hadjikakou (2006), 'The Role of Educational Experiences in the Development of Deaf Identity', *Journal of Deaf Studies and Deaf Education*, 11 (4): 477–492.

Nochi, M. (1998), '"Loss of self" in the narratives of people with traumatic brain injuries: A qualitative analysis', *Social Science and Medicine*, 46 (7): 869–878.

Nolan, J. F. (1997), *The Phonetic Basis of Speaker Recognition*, Cambridge: Cambridge University Press.

Nolan, J. F. (2003), 'A recent voice parade', *International Journal of Speech, Language and the Law*, 10: 277–91.

Nolan, F. and C. Grigoras (2005), 'A case for formant analysis in forensic speaker identification', *The International Journal of Speech, Language and the Law*, 12 (2): 143–173.

Noro, H. (2009), 'The role of Japanese as a heritage language in constructing ethnic identity among Hapa Japanese Canadian children', *Journal of Multilingual and Multicultural Development*, 30 (1): 1–18.

Norton, B. (1995), 'Social identity, investment, and language learning', *TESOL Quarterly*, 29 (1): 9–31.

Norton, B., S. Jones and D. Ahimbisibwe (2011), 'Learning about HIV/AIDS in Uganda: Digital resources and language learner identities', *Canadian Modern Language Review/La Revue Canadienne des Langues Vivantes*, 67 (4): 568–589.

Norton, B. and A. Pavlenko (eds) (2004), *Gender and English Language Learners*, Alexandria, VA: Teachers of English to Speakers of Other Languages.

Norton, B. and C. J. Williams (2012), 'Digital identities, student investments and eGranary as a placed resource', *Language and Education*, 26 (4): 315–329.

Norton, B. and K. Toohey (2011), 'Identity, language learning, and social change', *Language Teaching*, 44 (4): 412–446.

Nosenko-Stein, E. (2014), 'Still warm but getting colder: Changing ethnic identity of post-Soviet Jewry', *Journal of Multilingual and Multicultural Development*, 35 (1): 27–42.

nowherekid. (2010), 'West Street, Yangshuo: Lose and indulgence'. Last accessed 2 September 2010 at http://travel.sina.com.cn/china/2010--03-18/1042130989. shtml, in S. Gao, 'Commodification of place, consumption of identity: The sociolinguistic construction of a "global village" in rural China', *Journal of Sociolinguistics*, 16 (3): 336–357.

Obasi, C. (2008), 'Seeing the deaf in "deafness"', *Journal of Deaf Studies and Deaf Education*, Advanced Access published April 15.

Obler, L. and K. Gjerlow (2002), *Language and the Brain*. Cambridge: Cambridge University Press.

Ochs, E. (1992), 'Indexing gender', in A. Duranti and C. Goodwin (eds), *Rethinking Context: Language as an Interactive Phenomenon*, 335–358, Cambridge: Cambridge University Press.

Olsson, J. and J. Luchjenbroers (2014), *Forensic Linguistics*, London: Bloomsbury.

Ominiyi, T. (2010), 'Language and Postcolonial Identities: An African Perspective', in C. Llamas and D. Watt (eds), *Language and Identities*, 237–246, Edinburgh: Edinburgh University Press.

Orona, C. J. (1990), 'Temporality and identity loss due to Alzheimer's disease', *Social Science and Medicine*, 30: 1247–1256.

Orona, C. J. (1997), 'Temporality and Identity Loss Due to Alzheimer's Disease', in A. Strauss and J. Corbin (eds), *Grounded Theory in Practice*, 171–196, Thousand Oaks, CA: Sage.

Ostermann, A. C. (2003/2011), 'Communities of Practice at Work: Gender, Facework and the Power of *Habitus* at an All-Female Police Station and a Feminist Crisis Intervention Center in Brazil', in J. Coates and P. Pichler (eds), *Language and Gender: A Reader*, 2nd edn, 332–355, Oxford: Wiley-Blackwell.

Padden, C. and T. Humphries (1988), *Deaf in America – Voices from a Culture*, London: Harvard University Press.

Padden, C. and T. Humphries (2005), *Inside Deaf Culture*, London: Harvard University Press.

Page, R. (2012), 'The linguistics of self-branding and micro-celebrity in Twitter: The role of hashtags', *Discourse & Communication*, 6 (2): 181–201.

Page, R. (2013), *Stories and Social Media: Identities and Interaction*, Oxford: Routledge.

Pahl, K. and J. Rowsell (2010), *Artifactual Literacies: Every Object Tells a Story*, New York: Teachers College Press.

Parks, E. S. (2014), 'Constructing National and International Deaf Identity: Perceived Use of American Sign Language', in D. Watt and C. Llamas (eds), *Language, Borders and Identity*, 206–217, Edinburgh: Edinburgh University Press.

Parr, S. (2007), 'Living with severe aphasia: Tracking social exclusion', *Aphasiology*, 21 (1): 98–123.

Patrick, P. (2016a), 'The Impact of Sociolinguistics on Refugee Status Determination', in R. Lawson and D. Sayers (eds), *Sociolinguistic Research: Application and Impact*, 235–256, London: Routledge.

Patrick, P. (2016b), 'What is the role of expertise in Language Analysis for Determination of Origin (LADO)? A rejoinder to Cambier-Langeveld', *International Journal of Speech, Language and the Law*, 23 (1): 133–139.

Patrick, P. L. (2010), 'Linguistic rights in the asylum context', *Linguistics Matters!*, Cambridge: Cambridge University Press.

Pavlenko, A. and A. Blackledge (2004), *Negotiation of Identities in Multilingual Contexts*, Clevedon/New York: Multilingual Matters.

Peck, J. (2006), 'Women and Promotion: The Influence of Communication Style', in M. Barrett and M. Davidson (eds), *Gender and Communication at Work*, 50–66, Aldershot: Ashgate.

Peirce, B. N. (1995), 'Social identity, investment, and language learning', *TESOL Quarterly*, 29 (1), 9–31.

Pennycook, A. (2010), *Language as a Local Practice*, London: Routledge.

Philips, S. (2003), 'The Power of Gender Ideologies in Discourse', in J. Holmes and M. Meyerhoff (eds), *The Handbook of Language and Gender*, 252–276, Oxford: Oxford University Press.

Phinney, J. S. (1992), 'The Multigroup Ethnic Identity Measure: A Scale for Use with Diverse Groups', *Journal of Adolescent Research*, 7 (2): 156–176.

Phoenix, A. (2010), 'Ethnicities', in M. Wetherell and C. T. Moharty (eds), *The Sage Handbook of Identities*, 297–320, London: Sage.

Pichler, P. (2008/2011), 'Hybrid or In Between Cultures: Traditions of Marriage in a Group of British Bangladeshi Girls', in J. Coates and P. Pichler (eds), *Language and Gender: A Reader*, 2nd edn, 236–249, Oxford: Wiley-Blackwell.

Piller, I. (2001), 'Naturalisation language testing and its basis in ideologies of national identity and citizenship', *International Journal of Bilingualism*, 5 (3), 259–277.

Podesva, R, J. (2007) 'Phonation type as a stylistic variable: The use of falsetto in constructing a persona', *Journal of Sociolinguistics*, 11 (4): 478–504.

Podesva, R. J., S. J. Roberts and K. Campbell-Kibler (2001), 'Sharing Resources and Indexing Meanings in the Production of Gay Styles', in K. Campbell-Kibler, R. J. Podesva, S. J. Roberts and A. Wong (eds), *Language and Sexuality: Contesting Meaning in Theory and Practice*, 175–189, Stanford, CA: CSLI.

Pomerantz, A. (1986), 'Extreme case formulations: A way of legitimising claims', *Human Studies*, 9: 219–229.

Postmes, T and J. Jetten (eds) (2006), *Individuality and the Group: Advances in Social Identity*, London: Sage.

Postmes, T., G. Baray, S. A. Haslam, T. A. Morton and R. I. Swaab (2006), 'The Dynamics of Personal and Social Identity Formation', in T. Postmes and J. Jetten (eds), *Individuality and the Group: Advances in Social Identity*, 215–236, London: Sage.

Potter, J. and M. Wetherell (1987), *Discourse and Social Psychology: Beyond Attitudes and Behaviour*, London and Thousand Oaks, CA: Sage.

Preisler, G., A-L. Tvingstedt and M. Ahlstrom (2005) 'Interviews with deaf children about their experiences using cochlear implants', *American Annals of the Deaf*, 150 (3): 260–267.

Prince, E. (1981), 'Language the law: A case for linguistic pragmatics', *Working Papers in Sociolinguistics*, 112–160, Austin: Southwest Educational Development Laboratory.

Purves, B., H. Logan and S. Marcella (2011), 'Intersections of literal and metaphorical voices in aphasia', *Aphasiology*, 25 (6–7): 688–699.

Queen, R. (2007), 'Sociolinguistic horizons: Language and sexuality', *Language and Linguistics Compass*, 1 (4): 314–330.

Queen, R. (2014), 'Language and sexual identities', in S. Ehrlich, M. Meyerhoff and J. Holmes (eds), *The Handbook of Language, Gender and Sexuality*, 2nd edn, 203–219, Oxford: Blackwell.

Quist, P. (2008), 'Sociolinguistic approaches to multiethnolect: Language variety and stylistic practice', *International Journal of Bilingualism*, 12 (1, 2): 43–61.

Rampton, B. (ed.) (1999), 'Styling the "other": Introduction', *Journal of Sociolinguistics*, 3: 421–427.

Rampton, B. (1995/2014/2018), *Crossing: Language and Ethnicity among Adolescents*, 1st, 2nd, 3rd edn, London and New York: Routledge.

Rauniomaa, M. (2003), 'Stance accretion', Paper presented at the *Language, Interaction and Social Organization Research Focus Group*, University of California, Santa Barbara.

Rees, C. and L. Monrouxe (2010), '"I should be so lucky ha ha ha ha": The construction of power, identity and gender through laughter within medical workplace learning encounters', *Journal of Pragmatics*, 42: 3384–3399.

Reicher, S., R. Spears and S. A. Haslam (2010), 'The Social Identity Approach in Social Psychology', in M. Wetherell and C. T. Moharty (eds), *The Sage Handbook of Identities*, 45–62, London: Sage.

Reisigl, M. (2017), 'The discourse-historical approach', in J. Flowerdew and J. E. Richardson (eds), *The Routledge Handbook of Critical Discourse Studies*, 44-59, London: Routledge.

Remlinger, K. (2009), 'Everyone up here: Enregisterment and identity in Michigan's Keweenaw Peninsula', *American Speech*, 84: 118–137.

Reyes, A. (2007), *Language, Identity, and Stereotype among Southeast Asian American Youth: The Other Asian*, Mahwah, NJ: Lawrence Erlbaum.

Reynolds, J. and M. Wetherell (2003), 'The Discursive Climate of Singleness: The Consequences of Women's Negotiation of a Single Identity', *Feminism and Psychology*, 13: 489–510.

Richards, K. (2011), 'Engaging Identities: Personal Disclosure and Professional Responsibility', in J. Angouri and M. Marra, eds, *Constructing Identities at Work*, 200–222, Basingstoke: Palgrave MacMillan.

Ricoeur, P. (1970), *Freud and Philosophy: An Essay on Interpretation*, New York: Yale University Press.

Riley, P. (2008), *Language, Culture and Identity: An Ethnolinguistic Perspective*, London: Continuum.

Riley, S., K. Rodham and J. Gavin (2009), 'Doing weight: Pro-ana and recovery identities in cyberspace', *Journal of Community and Applied Social Psychology*, 19: 348–359.

Robertson, B., G. A. Vignaux and I. Egerton (1994), 'Stylometric evidence', *Criminal Law Review*, 645–649.

Rogerson-Revell, P. (2011), 'Chairing International Business Meetings: Investigating Humour and Leadership Style in the Workplace', in J. Angouri and M. Marra (eds), *Constructing Identities at Work*, 61–84, Basingstoke: Palgrave MacMillan.

Rosowsky, A. (2012), 'Performance and flow: The religious classical in translocal and transnational linguistic repertoires', *Journal of Sociolinguistics*, 16 (5): 613–637.

Rummins, J. A. (2003), 'Conceptualising identity and diversity: Overlaps, intersections, and processes', *Canadian Ethnic Studies Journal*, 35 (3): 10–25.

Sacks, H. (1995), *Lectures on Conversation*, Vols. 1–2. Edited by G. Jefferson with an introduction by E. A.Schegloff, Oxford: Blackwell-Wiley.

Saisuwan, P. (2016), '*Kathoey* and the Linguistic Construction of Gender Identity in Thailand', in E. Levon and R. B. Mendes (eds), *Language, Sexuality, and Power*, 189–214, Oxford: Oxford University Press.

Sala, E., J. Dandy and M. Rapley (2010), '"Real Italians and Wogs": The discursive construction of Italian identity among first generation Italian immigrants in

Western Australia', *Journal of Community & Applied Social Psychology*, 20 (2): 110–124.

Sandfield, A. and C. Percy (2003), 'Accounting for single status: Heterosexism and ageism in heterosexual women's talk about marriage', *Feminism and Psychology*, 13: 475–488.

Sarangi, S. (2010), 'Reconfiguring Self/Identity/Status/Role: The Case of Professional Role Performance in Healthcare Encounters', in J. Archibald and G. Garzone (eds), *Actors, Identities and Roles in Professional Academic Settings: Discursive Perspectives*, 27–54, Berne: Peter Lang.

Sarangi, S., and C. Roberts (eds) (1999), *Talk, Work and Institutional Order: Discourse in Medical, Mediation and Management Settings*, Vol. 1, Berlin: Walter de Gruyter.

Sari, H. (2005), 'An analysis of the relationship between identity patterns of Turkish for deaf adolescents and the communication modes used in special residential schools for the hearing impaired and the deaf', *Deafness and Education International*, 7: 206–222.

Saussure, F. de. (1916/1983), *Course in General Linguistics*, trans. R. Harris, London: Duckworth.

Sayahi, L. (2005), 'Language and identity among speakers of Spanish in northern Morocco: Between ethnolinguistic vitality and acculturation', *Journal of Sociolinguistics*, 9 (1): 95–107.

Schaefer, Z. (2013), 'Getting dirty with humor: Co-constructing workplace identities through performative scripts', *Humor*, 26 (4): 511–530.

Scheuer, J. (2001), 'Recontextualisation and communicative styles in job interviews', *Discourse Studies*, 3: 223–248.

Schiffrin, D. (1996), 'Narrative as self-portrait: Sociolinguistic constructions of identity', *Language in Society*, 25: 167–203.

Schiller, N. O. and O. Köster (1998), 'The ability of expert witnesses to identify voices: A comparison between trained and untrained listeners', *Forensic Linguistics*, 5 (1): 1–9.

Schilling-Estes, N. (1998), 'Investigating "Self-Conscious" Speech: The Performance of Register in Ocracoke English', *Language in Society*, 27 (1): 53–83.

Schilling-Estes, N. (2002), 'Investigating Stylistic Variation', in J. K. Chambers, P. Trudgill and N. Schilling-Estes (eds), *The Handbook of Language Variation and Change*, 375–401, Malden, MA and Oxford: Blackwell.

Schilling-Estes, N. (2004), 'Constructing ethnicity in interaction', *Journal of Sociolinguistics*, 8: 163–195.

Schnurr, S. and A. Chan (2011), 'When laughter is not enough. Responding to teasing and self-denigrating humour at work', *Journal of Pragmatics*, 43: 20–35.

Schnurr, S. and O. Zayts (2011), 'Be(com)ing a Leader: A Case Study of Co-Constructing Professional Identities at Work', in J. Angouri and M. Marra (eds), *Constructing Identities at Work*, 40–60, Basingstoke: Palgrave MacMillan.

Seargeant, P. and C. Tagg (2014), *The Language of Social Media: Identity and Community on the Internet*, Basingstoke: Palgrave MacMillan.

Sebba, M. and T. Wootton (1998), 'We, They and Identity: Sequential versus Identity-Related Explanation in Code-Switching', in P. Auer (ed.), *Code-Switching in Conversation*, 262–289, London: Routledge.

Selfe, C. L. and P. R. Meyer (1991), 'Testing claims for online conferences', *Written Communication*, 8 (2): 163–192.

Shaddon, B. (2005), 'Aphasia as identity theft: Theory and practice', *Aphasiology*, 19 (3/4/5): 211–223.

Shaddon, B. and J. Agan (2004), 'Renegotiation of identity: The social context of aphasia support groups', *Topics in Language Disorders*, 24 (3): 174–186.

Shaitan, A. and L. J. McEntee-Atalianis (2017), 'Identity Crisis: Half, Hybrid or Culturally Homeless?', in F. Fozdar and Z. Rocha (eds), *"Mixed race" in Asia*, 82–97, London: Routledge.

Shankar, S. (2011), 'Style and language use among youth of the new immigration: Formations of race, ethnicity, gender, and class in everyday practice', *Identities: Global Studies in Culture and Power*, 18 (6): 646–671.

Sharma, B. K. (2012), 'Beyond social networking: Performing global Englishes in Facebook by college youth in Nepal', *Journal of Sociolinguistics*, 16 (4): 483–509.

Sharma, D. (2011), 'Style repertoire and social change in British Asian English', *Journal of Sociolinguistics*, 15 (4): 464–492.

Shaw, S. (2006), "Governed by the Rules?: The Female Voice in Parliamentary Debates', in J. Baxter (ed.), *Speaking Out in Public Contexts*, 81–102, Basingstoke: Palgrave.

Shenk, P. S. (2007), '"I'm Mexican, remember?" Constructing ethnic identities via authenticating discourse', *Journal of Sociolinguistics*, 11 (2): 194–220.

Shuy, R. (1993), *Language Crimes: The Use and Abuse of Language Evidence in the Courtroom*, Cambridge MA: Blackwell.

Shuy, R. (2002), *Linguistic Battles in Trademark Disputes*, New York: Palgrave.

Silverstein, M. (1992), 'The Indeterminacy of Contextualization: When Is Enough Enough?', in P. Auer and A. D. Luzio (eds), *The Contextualization of Language*, 55–76, Amsterdam/Philadelphia, PA: John Benjamins.

Silverstein, M. (1993), 'Metapragmatic Discourse and Metapragmatic Function', in J. A. Lucy (ed.), *Reflexive Language*, 33–58, Cambridge: Cambridge University Press.

Silverstein, M. (2003), 'Indexical order and the dialectics of sociolinguistic life', *Language and Communication*, 23: 193–229.

Simpson, R. (2004), 'Men in non-traditional occupations: Career entry, career orientation and experience of role strain', *Gender Work and Organization*, 12 (4), 363–380.

Sinclair, J. and S. Cunningham (2000), 'Go with the flow: Diasporas and the media', *Television and New Media*, 1: 11–31.

Smiler, K. and R. L. McKee (2007), 'Perceptions of *Māori* deaf identity in New Zealand', *Journal of Deaf studies and Deaf Education*, 12 (1), 93–111.

Soja, E. W. (1989), *Postmodern Geographies: The Reassertion of Space in Critical Social Theory*, London and New York: Verso.

Solan, L. M. and P. M. Tiersma (2005), 'Author identification in American courts', *Applied Linguistics*, 25 (4): 448–465.

Spencer-Oatey, H. (2007), 'Theories of identity and the analysis of face', *Journal of Pragmatics*, 39: 639–656.

Spender, D. (1980), *Man Made language*, London: Routledge and Kegan Paul.

Spivak, G. (1995), 'Subultern Studies: Deconstructing Historiography', in D. Landry and G. MacLean (eds), *The Spivak Reader*, New York: Routledge.

Squires, L. (2013), 'It don't go both ways: Limited bidirectionality in sociolinguistic perception', *Journal of Sociolinguistics*, 17 (2), 200–237.

Stokoe, W. (2005), 'Sign language structure: An outline of the visual communication systems of the American deaf', *Journal of Deaf Studies and Deaf Education*, 10 (1): 3–37.

Stokoe, W. C. (1960), *Sign Language Structure: An Outline of the Visual Communication Systems of the American Deaf*, Buffalo, NY: University of Buffalo.

Stokoe, W. C., D. C. Casterline and C. G. Croneberg (1965), *A Dictionary of American Sign Language on Linguistic Principles*, Washington, DC: Gallaudet College Press.

Stuart-Smith, J., C. Timmons and F. Tweedle (2007), '"Talkin' Jockney"? Variation and change in Glaswegian accent', *Journal of Sociolinguistics*, 11 (2): 221–260.

Stuart-Smith, J. C. and C. Timmons (2010) 'The Role of the Individual in Language Variation and Change', in C. Llamas and D. Watt (eds), *Language and Identities*, 39–54, Edinburgh: Edinburgh University Press.

Sung, C. C. M. (2011), 'Doing gender and leadership: A discourse analysis of media representations in a reality TV show', *English Text Construction*, 4 (1): 85–112.

Sutton-Spence, R. (2010a), 'The role of sign language narratives in developing identity for deaf children', *Journal of Folklore Research* 47 (3): 265–305.

Sutton-Spence, R. (2010b), 'Spatial metaphor and expressions of identity in sign language poetry', *Metaphorik.de*, 19: 1–40.

Sutton-Spence, R. and D. Napoli (2012), 'Deaf jokes and sign language humour', *Humor* 25 (3): 311–337.

Sutton-Spence, R. and B. Woll (1999/2003), *The Linguistics of British Sign Language: An Introduction*, Cambridge: Cambridge University Press.

Svartvik, J. (1968), *The Evans Statements: A Case for Forensic Linguistics*, Gothenburg Studies in English, Gothenburg: University of Gothenburg.

Svennevig, J. (2012), 'Leadership Style in Managers' Feedback in Meetings', in J. Angouri and M. Marra (eds), *Constructing Identities at Work*, 17–39, Basingstoke: Palgrave MacMillan.

Swann, J. (1989/2011), 'Talk Control: An Illustration from the Classroom of Problems in Analysing Male Dominance of Conversation', in J. Coates and P. Pichler (eds), *Language and Gender: A Reader*, 2nd edn, 161–170, Oxford: Wiley-Blackwell.

Szakay, A. (2012), 'Voice quality as a marker of ethnicity in New Zealand: From acoustics to perception', *Journal of Sociolinguistics*, 16 (3): 382–397.

Sznycer, K. (2010), 'Strategies of powerful self-presentations in the discourse of female tennis players', *Discourse & Society*, 21 (4): 458–479.

Tagg, C. (2016), 'Heteroglossia in text-messaging: Performing identity and negotiating relationships in a digital space', *Journal of Sociolinguistics* 20 (1): 59–85.

Tajfel, H. (1982/1986), *Social Identity and Intergroup Relations*, Cambridge: Cambridge University Press.

Tajfel, H. and J. C. Turner (1979), 'An Integrative Theory of Intergroup Conflict', in S. Worchel and W. G. Austin (eds), *The Psychology of Intergroup Relations*, 33–47, Monterey, CA: Brooks-Cole.

Tajfel, H. and J. C.Turner (1986), 'The Social Identity Theory of Intergroup Behavior', in S. Worchel and W. G. Austin (eds), *Psychology of Intergroup Relations*, 2nd edn, 7–24, Chicago, IL: Nelson-Hall.

Tannen, D. (1990), *You Just Don't Understand: Women and Men in Conversation*, New York: William Morrow.

Taylor, C. (1989/2006), *Sources of the Self*, Cambridge: Cambridge University Press.

Tervoort, B. (1953), *Structurele analyse van visueel taalgebruik binnen een groep dove kinderen*, Amsterdam, Noord-Hollandsche Uitg. Mij. (Summary in English).

Thelan, E. (2005), 'Dynamic systems theory and the complexity of change', *Psychoanalytic Dialogues*, 15: 255–283.

Thelwell, M., D. Wilkinson and U. Sukhvinder (2010), 'Data mining emotion in social network communication: Gender differences in MySpace', *Journal of the American Society for Information Science and Technology*, 61 (1): 190–199.

Themistocleous, C. (2015), 'Digital code-switching between Cypriot and Standard Greek: Performance and identity play online', *International Journal of Bilingualism*, 19 (3): 282–297.

Thomas, E. R. and J. Reaser (2004), 'Delimiting perceptual cues used for the ethnic labeling of African American and European American voices', *Journal of Sociolinguistics* 8 (1): 54–87.

Thomas, L. and C. Beauchamp (2011), 'Understanding new teachers' professional identities through metaphor', *Teaching and Teacher Education*, 27: 762–769.

Thurlow, C. and A. Jaworski (2010), *Tourism Discourse: Language and Global Mobility*, Basingstoke: Palgrave Macmillan.

Thurlow, C. and K. Mroczek (eds) (2011), *Digital Discourse: Language in the New Media*, Oxford: Oxford University Press.

Tiersma, P. and L. Solan (2002), 'The linguist on the witness stand: Forensic linguistics in American courts', *Language*, 78 (2): 221–239.

Titus, J. J. (2010), 'Ascribing monstrosity: Judicial categorisation of a juvenile sex offender', *The International Journal of Speech Language and the Law*, 17 (1): 1–23.

Tollefson, J. W. (1991). *Planning Language, Planning Inequality*, London: Longman.

Torgensen, E. and P. Kerswill (2004), 'Internal and external motivation in phonetic change: Dialect levelling outcomes for an English vowel shift', *Journal of Sociolinguistics*, 8: 24–53.

Tossell, C. C., P. Kortum, C. Shepard, L. H. Barg-Walkow, A. Rahmati and L. Zhong (2012), 'A longitudinal study of emoticon use in text messaging from smartphones', *Computers in Human Behaviour*, 28: 659–663.

Tracy, K. (2002), *Everyday Talk: Building and Reflecting Identities*, New York/London: Guildford Press.

Tracy, K. (2009), 'How questioning constructs judge identities: Oral argument about same-sex marriage', *Discourse Studies*, 11 (2): 199–221.

Tracy, K. (2011), 'Identity-Work in Appellate Oral Argument: Ideological Identities within a Professional One', in J. Angouri and M. Marra (eds), *Constructing Identities at Work*, 175–199, Basingstoke: Palgrave MacMillan.

Trudgill, P. (1974), *The Social Differentiation of English in Norwich*, Cambridge: Cambridge University Press.

Trudgill, P. (1978), 'Sex, covert prestige, and linguistic change in the urban British English of Norwich', *Language in Society*, 1: 179–196.

Trudgill, P. (2008), 'Colonial dialect contact in the history of European languages: On the irrelevance of identity to new-dialect formation', *Language in Society*, 37, 241–254.

Tsui, A. (2007), 'Complexity of identity formation: A narrative inquiry of an EFL teacher', *TESOL Quarterly*, 41 (4): 657–680.

Turell, M. T. (2004), 'Textual kidnapping revisited: The case of plagiarism in literary translation', *The International Journal of Speech, Language and the Law*, 11 (1): 1–26.

Turell, M. T. (2008), 'Plagiarism', in J. Gibbons and M. Turell (eds), *Dimensions of Forensic Linguistics*, 265–299, London: John Benjamins.

Turkle, S. (1995), *Life on the Screen*, New York: Simon & Schuster.

Turner, G. (2010), *Ordinary People and the Media: The Demotic Turn*, London: Sage.

Turner, J. C. (1982), 'Towards a cognitive redefinition of the social group', in H. Tajfel (ed.), *Social Identity and Intergroup Relations*, 15–40, Cambridge: Cambridge University Press.

Turner, J. C. (1985), 'Social Categorisation and the Self-Concept: A Social Cognitive Theory of Group Behaviour', in E. Lawler (ed.), *Advances in Group Processes: Theory and Research*, 77–122, Greenwich, CT: JAI.

Turner, J. C. (1991), *Social Influence*, Milton Keynes: Open University Press.

Turner, J. C., M. Hogg, S. Oakes and M. Wetherell (1987), *Rediscovering the Social Group: A Self-Categorisation Theory*, Oxford: Blackwell.

Urry, J. (2003), 'Social networks, travel and talk', *The British Journal of Sociology*, 54 (2): 155–175.

Valentine, G. and T. Skelton (2008), 'Changing spaces: The role of the Internet in shaping deaf geographies', *Social and Cultural Geography*, 9 (5): 469–485.

Van de Mieroop, D. and J. Clifton (2012), 'The interactional negotiation of group membership and ethnicity: The case of an interview with a former slave', *Discourse & Society*, 23 (2): 163–183.

Van Dijk, T. A. (2006), 'Ideology and discourse analysis', *Journal of Political Ideologies*, 11 (2): 115–140.

Van Dijk, T. A. (2010), 'Political Identities in Parliamentary Debates', in C. Ilie (ed.), *European Parliaments under Scrutiny*, 29–56, Amsterdam/ Philadelphia: John Benjamins.

Varjonen, S., L. Arnold and I. Jasinskaja-Lahti (2013), ' "We're Finns here, and Russians there": A longitudinal study on ethnic identity construction in the context of ethnic migration', *Discourse & Society*, 24 (1): 110–134.

Verkuyten, M. (1997), 'Discourses of ethnic minority identity', *British Journal of Social Psychology*, 36: 565–586.

Verkuyten, M. (2005), *The Social Psychology of Ethnic Identity*, London: Psychology Press.

Verkuyten, M. and A. De Wolf (2002), 'Being, feeling, doing: Discourses and ethnic self-definitions among minority group members', *Culture & Psychology*, 8 (4): 371–399.

Vertovec, S. (2007), 'Super-diversity and its implications', *Ethnic and Racial Studies*, 30 (6): 1024–1054.

Wagner, I. and R. Wodak (2006), 'Performing success: Identifying strategies of self-presentation in women's biographical narratives', *Discourse & Society*, 17(3): 385–411.

Wåhrborg, P. (1991), *Assessment and Management of Emotional and Psychosocial Reactions to Brain Damage*, Kibworth: Far Communications.

Walsh, M. (2008), '"Which way?": Difficult options for vulnerable witnesses in Australian aboriginal language claim and native title cases', *Journal of English Linguistics*, 36 (3): 239–265.

Warf, B. and S. Arias (eds) (2009), *The Spatial Turn: Interdisciplinary Perspectives*. Abingdon and New York: Routledge.

Watt, D. (2002), '"I don't speak with a Geordie accent, I speak, like, the Northern accent": Contact-induced levelling in the Tyneside vowel system', *Journal of Sociolinguistics*, 6 (1): 44–63.

Watt, D. (2010), 'The Identification of the Individual through Speech', in C. Llamas and D. Watt (eds), *Language and Identities*, 76–85, Edinburgh: Edinburgh University Press.

Watt, D. and C. Llamas (2014), *Language, Borders and Identity*, Edinburgh: Edinburgh University Press.

Weedon, C. (1987/1997), *Feminist Practice and Poststructuralist Theory*, Oxford: Blackwell.

Wells, J. (1982) *Accents of English* (3 vols.), Cambridge: Cambridge University Press.

Wenger, E. (1998), *Communities of Practice: Learning, Meaning and Identity*, Cambridge: Cambridge University Press.

Werbner, P. (2010), 'Religious Identity', in M. Wetherell and C. T. Moharty (eds), *The Sage Handbook of Identities*, 233–257, London: Sage.

West, C. (1984), 'When the doctor is a "lady": Power, status and gender in physician-patient encounters', *Symbolic Interaction*, 7: 87–106.

West, C. (1998), '"Not just Doctor's Orders": Directive-Response Sequences in Patients' Visits to Women and Men Physicians', in J. Coates (ed.), *Language and Gender: A Reader*, 396–412, Oxford: Blackwell.

West, C. and D. H. Zimmerman (1983), 'Small Insults: A study of Interruptions in Cross-Sex Conversations between Unacquainted Persons', in B. Thorne, C. Kramarae and N. Henley (eds), *Language, Gender and Society*, 102–117, Rowley, MA: Newbury House.

Wetherell, M. (1998), Positioning and interpretative repertoires: Conversation analysis and post-structuralism in dialogue', *Discourse & Society*, 9: 387–412.

Wetherell, M. (ed.) (2009), *Theorising Identities & Social Action*, London: Sage.

Wheeler, A., S. Archbold, S. Gregory and A. Skipp (2007), 'Cochlear implants: The young people's perspective', *Journal of Deaf Studies and Deaf Education*, 12 (3): 303–316.

Wilcox, S., V. Krausneker and D. Armstrong (2012), 'Language Policies and the Deaf Community', in B. Spolsky (ed.), *The Cambridge Handbook of Language Policy*, 374–395, Cambridge: Cambridge University Press.

Wilkinson, S. (2011), 'Constructing ethnicity statistics in talk-in-interaction: Producing the "White European"', *Discourse & Society*, 22 (3): 343–361.

Willemyns, M., J. Pittam and C. Gallois (1993), 'Perceived ethnolinguistic vitality of Vietnamese and English in Australia: A confirmatory factor analysis', *Journal of Multilingual and Multicultural Development*, 14 (6): 481–504.

Williams, G. (1992), *Sociolinguistics: A Sociological Critique*, London: Routledge.

Wilson, J. (2006), 'Developments in Sign Language Poetry', Seminar, Bristol University, Bristol, UK, 24 February.

Wilson, K. and P. Foulkes (2014), 'Borders, Variation and Identity: Language Analysis for the Determination of Origin (LADO)', in D. Watt and C. Llamas (eds), *Language, Borders and Identity*, 218–229, Edinburgh: Edinburgh University Press.

Wilson, T. M. and H. Donnan (eds) (2012), *A Companion to Border Studies*, Hoboken, NJ: Wiley and Sons.

Windle, J. (2008), 'The Racialization of African Youth in Australia', *Social Identities: Journal for the Study of Race, Nation and Culture*, 14: 553–566.

Wodak, R. (2004), 'National and Transnational Identities: European and Other Identities Constructed in Interviews with EU Officials', in R. K. Herrmann, T. Risse and M. B. Brewer (eds), *Transnational Identities: Becoming European in the EU*, 97–128, Oxford: Rowman & Littlefield.

Wodak, R. (2010), '"Communicating Europe": Analyzing, Interpreting, and Understanding Multilingualism and the Discursive Construction of Transnational Identities', in R. Wodak (ed.), *Globalization, Discourse, Media: In a Critical Perspective*, 17–60, Warsaw: Warsaw University Press.

Wodak, R., and G. Weiss (2005), 'Analyzing European Union Discourses: Theories and Applications', in R. Wodak and P. Chilton (eds), *A New Agenda in (Critical) Discourse Analysis: Theory, Methodology and Interdisciplinarity*, 121–133, Amsterdam: J. Benjamins.

Wodak, R., R. de Cillia, M. Reisig and K. Liebhart (2009), *The discursive construction of national identity*, Edinburgh: Edinburgh University Press.

Woll, B. and P. Ladd (2011), 'Deaf Communities', in M. Marschark (ed), *Oxford Handbook of Deaf Studies, Language and Education*, 151–163, Oxford: Oxford University Press.

Wong, A. (2007), 'Two Vernacular Features in the English of Four American-Born Chinese', in T. Cook and K. Evanini (eds), *Penn Working Papers in Linguistics*, 13: 217–230.

Wong, A. D. (2016), 'How Does Oppression Work? Insights from Hong Kong Lesbians' Labeling Practices', in E. Levon and R. B. Mendes (eds), *Language, Sexuality, and Power*, 19–37, Oxford: Oxford University Press.

Wood, C. and W. M. L. Finlay (2008), 'British National Party representations of Muslims in the month after the London bombings: Homogeneity, threat and the conspiracy tradition', *British Journal of Social Psychology*, 47: 707–726.

Woodcock, K. ([1992] 2001), "Cochlear Implants vs. Deaf Culture?" in L. Bragg (ed.), *Deaf World*, 325–332, New York: New York University Press.

Woodhams, J. (2014), '"We're the nurses": Metaphor in the discourse of workplace socialisation', *Language & Communication*, 34: 56–68.

Woodward, J. (ed.) (1982), *How you gonna get to heaven if you can't talk with Jesus: On depathologising deafness*, Silver Spring, MD: T. J. Publishers.

Woolls, D. (2003), 'Better tools for the trade and how to use them', *Forensic Linguistics*, 10 (1): 102–112.

Woolls, D. (2010), 'Computational forensic linguistics: Searching for similarity in large specialised corpora', in M. Coulthard and A. Johnson (eds), *The Routledge Handbook of Forensic Linguistics*, 576–590, London: Routledge.

Yagmur, K. (2009), 'Language use and ethnolinguistic vitality of Turkish compared with the Dutch in the Netherlands', *Journal of Multilingual and Multicultural Development*, 30 (3): 219–233.

Yagmur, K. (2011), 'Does ethnolinguistic vitality theory account for the actual vitality of ethnic groups? A critical evaluation', *Journal of Multilingual and Multicultural Development*, 32 (2): 111–120.

Yagmur, K. and M. Ehala (2011), 'Tradition and innovation in the ethnolinguistic vitality theory', *Journal of Multilingual and Multicultural Development*, 32 (2), 101–110.

Yagmur, K. and S. Kroon (2003), 'Ethnolinguistic vitality perceptions and language revitalization in Bashkortostan', *Journal of Multilingual and Multicultural Development*, 24 (4): 319–336.

Yagmur, K. and S. Kroon (2006), 'Objective and subjective data on Altai and Kazakh ethnolinguistic vitality in the Russian Federation Republic of Altai', *Journal of Multilingual and Multicultural Development*, 27 (3): 241–258.

Zappavigna, M. (2013), 'Enacting identity in microblogging through ambient affiliation', *Discourse and Communication*, 8 (2): 209–228.

Zappettini, F. (2015), The Discursive Construction of Europeanness: A Transnational Perspective. Unpublished PhD, Birkbeck, University of London.

Zhang, Q. (2005), 'A Chinese yuppie in Beijing: Phonological variation and the construction of a new professional identity', *Language in Society*, 34: 431–466.

Zhu Hua and Li Wei (2016), '"Where are you really from?": Nationality and ethnicity talk in everyday interactions', *Applied Linguistics Review*, 7 (4), 449–470.

Zilles, A. and K. King (2005), 'Self-presentation in sociolinguistic interviews: Identities and language variation in Panambi, Brazil', *Journal of Sociolinguistics*, 9 (1): 74–94.

Zimman, L. and K. Hall (2010), 'Language, Embodiment and the "Third Sex"', in C. Llamas and D. Watt (eds), *Language and Identities*, 166–178, Edinburgh: Edinburgh University Press.

INDEX